'Palin reminds me of Samuel Johnson: driven, intellectually formidable, and spurred on by self-reproach and the wholly irrational idea that he's not really getting on with it ... Palin is a seriously good writer. These diaries are full of fine phrases and sharp little sketches of scenes'
Daily Mail

'This is a brisk, pithy, amusing read, teeming with the writer's inner life, crammed with high-quality observations ... and deft ink-pen sketches of his associates' *Spectator*

'Charming and vastly entertaining' *Irish Times*

'His entries are riddled with the astute wit and generosity of spirit that characterise both his performances and his previously published writing'
Time Out (Book of the Week)

'It's clear why Cleese later nominated Palin as his luxury item on *Desert Island Discs* because ... he makes such unfailingly good company ... this is the agreeably written story of how a former Python laid the foundation stone by which he would reinvent himself as a public institution: the People's Palin' *Guardian*

'A fascinating and wry cultural take on the 1980's ... it's also, when added to volume one, proving to be the most beguiling and revealing of ongoing autobiographies' *Sunday Herald*

'This is the Michael Palin with whom the public has fallen in love. A man whose ordinary likeability makes us feel we know him, and that he is incapable of nastiness or an outburst of bad temper' *Sunday Telegraph*

'There are some fabulous and very funny snippets about Alan Bennett and Maggie Smith ... the behind-the-scenes antics of the Pythons and their wider circle make great reading' *Observer*

MICHAEL PALIN is a scriptwriter, comedian, novelist, television presenter, actor and playwright. He established his reputation with *Monty Python's Flying Circus* and *Ripping Yarns*. His work also includes several films with Monty Python, as well as *The Missionary, A Private Function, A Fish Called Wanda, American Friends* and *Fierce Creatures*. His television credits include two films for the BBC's *Great Railway Journeys*, the plays *East of Ipswich* and *Number 27*, and Alan Bleasdale's *GBH*.

In 2006 the first volume of his diaries, *1969–1979: The Python Years*, spent several weeks on the bestseller lists. He has also written books to accompany his seven very successful travel series: *Around the World in 80 Days* (an updated edition of which was published in 2008, twenty years later), *Pole to Pole, Full Circle, Hemingway Adventure, Sahara, Himalaya* and *New Europe*. Most have been No 1 bestsellers and *Himalaya* was No 1 for 11 weeks. He is the author of a number of children's stories, the play *The Weekend* and the novel *Hemingway's Chair*. Visit his website at www.palinstravels.co.uk.

MICHAEL PALIN
DIARIES 1980-1988

Halfway to Hollywood

PHOENIX

A PHOENIX PAPERBACK

First published in Great Britain in 2009
by Weidenfeld & Nicolson
This paperback edition published in 2010
by Phoenix,
an imprint of Orion Books Ltd,
Orion House, 5 Upper St Martin's Lane,
London WC2H 9EA

An Hachette UK company

3 5 7 9 10 8 6 4 2

A CIP catalogue record for this book
is available from the British Library.

ISBN: 978-0-7538-2748-2

Typeset by Input Data Services Ltd,
Bridgwater, Somerset

Printed in Great Britain by Clays Ltd, St Ives plc

The Orion Publishing Group's policy is to use papers that
are natural, renewable and recyclable products and
made from wood grown in sustainable forests. The logging
and manufacturing processes are expected to conform to
the environmental regulations of the country of origin.

www.orionbooks.co.uk

For Angela

Contents

List of illustrations

Dad with children, *Meaning of Life* 1982[9]
Pythons on location, jungle scene, *Meaning of Life* 1982[9]
MP as Jack Lint, *Brazil* 1984[2]
MP, Terry Gilliam and Jonathan Pryce rehearsing *Brazil*, 1984[2]
MP surprised by Jonathan Pryce, *Brazil* 1983[2]
Terry Gilliam with Ray Cooper[2]
MP's mother in New York, January 1984[10]
MP, sister Angela, Nancy Lewis and his mother, New York, January 1984[2]
MP's mother and Angela, *Saturday Night Live* party, January 1984[2]
Tristram Powell and Innes Lloyd, *East of Ipswich* filming, June 1986[2]
End of filming party, *East of Ipswich*[2]
MP, Terry Gilliam, David Robinson, John Cartwright and interpreter, Moscow 1986[2]
MP's mother and neighbour, at Reydon, Southwold, Suffolk[2]
Launching a rebuilt steam engine, Bluebell Railway[2]
'Mash' Patel, newsagent[2]
Sam Jarvis, painter and decorator[2]

Section Three:

Will Palin and Eric Idle, at Eric's cottage in France, 1984[2]
Al Levinson and Norman Rosten, Brooklyn, New York[2]

Filming of *Private Function*, 1984
George H and Denis O'Brien, Executive Producers[3]
Alan Bennett and MP on location in Yorkshire[2]
Maggie Smith and MP on location[11]
Trying to kill the pig. MP, Betty (the pig) and Maggie Smith[11]
Alan Bennett, Maggie Smith, MP with large foot, on location[11]
The two Grannies, Helen and MP, *Private Function* Royal Premiere, November 21st 1984[5]
Denholm Elliott and others in *Private Function* cast, in the gents toilet, Great Western Hotel Paddington[11]
Will, Tom, Rachel and Helen in Majorca, August 1986[2]
MP in cycling publicity shot, March 1986[2]
MP on Joan Rivers show, 1986[12]

A Fish Called Wanda, Summer 1987
MP with Charlie Crichton[2]

MP with stand-in Gerry Paris[2]
MP with Kevin Kline[2]
John Cleese trying to get information from MP[13]
Ken Pile. Fan photo[13]
Jamie Lee Curtis and MP embrace[13]

The family with Granny outside Sunset House, Southwold 1987[2]
MP on location with Joyce Carey, *Number 27*, June 1988[2]

1 Brian Moody
2 Author's Collection
3 HandMade Films Partnership
4 Sam Emerson
5 Pic Photos
6 Trevor Jeal
7 Andy Hanson
8 Chris Richardson
9 David Appleby
10 Mark Mullen
11 David Farrell
12 Erik Heinila
13 David James

While every effort has been made to trace copyright holders, if any have inadvertently been overlooked the publishers will be pleased to acknowledge them in any future editions of this work.

Acknowledgements

As with the first volume, *1969–1979: The Python Years*, I have had to reduce over a million words of diary entries to something nearer a quarter of a million. In this task I have, as before, been sagely advised and supervised by Ion Trewin. Michael Dover at Weidenfeld & Nicolson has been a constant encouragement in the completion and collation of the edit, and Steve Abbott and Paul Bird at my office have been, as ever, hugely supportive.

Once again, I must reserve my most special thanks for Katharine Du Prez for her patience and persistence in the Herculean labour of transcribing the contents of twenty-four close-packed, handwritten notebooks.

Who's Who in the Diaries 1980–1988

FAMILY

Mary Palin, mother, living at Reydon, Southwold, Suffolk. Father died in 1977.
Helen, wife
Children:
Tom born 1968
William born 1970
Rachel born 1975

Angela, sister. Married to **Veryan Herbert** and living at Chilton, Sudbury, Suffolk. Died 1987.
Children:
Jeremy born 1960
Camilla born 1962
Marcus born 1963

Helen's family:
Anne Gibbins, mother
Elder sister, **Mary**, married **Edward Burd** in 1964
Daughter, **Catherine**, born 1966
Younger sister, **Cathy**

FRIENDS, NEIGHBOURS AND COLLEAGUES

Richard and Christine Guedalla, and daughters Louise and Helen, neighbours

Clare Latimer, neighbour

Terry Jones and **Alison**

Terry Gilliam and **Maggie**

John Cleese, formerly married to **Connie Booth**, one daughter, **Cynthia**, born 1971, married **Barbara Trentham** 1981, separated 1987

Graham Chapman, partner **David Sherlock**. **John Tomiczek** (adopted)

Eric Idle, married **Tania Kosevich** 1981

Robert Hewison. Contemporary of MP at Brasenose College, Oxford 1962–5, during which time he persuaded MP to perform and write comedy for first time.

Simon and Phillida Albury. Simon met MP after Oxford in 1965. Television journalist, producer and Gospel music fan.

Ian and Anthea Davidson. Met MP at Oxford. Encouraged him to perform in revue and gave him early work at the BBC. A writer and director and occasional Python performer.

Chris Miller and Bill Stotesbury. Chris looked after Eric's son Carey during *Life of Brian*. Bill is a designer and banjo player.

Neil and Yvonne Innes. Neil, Ex-Bonzo Dog Band. Worked closely with the Pythons especially on their stage appearances. Collaborated with Eric to create the Rutles. Sons: Miles and Luke.

Mel Calman, cartoonist and friend

George Harrison. Musician, ex-Beatle. Married to Olivia Arias, son Dhani born 1978.

Derek and Joan Taylor, Beatles' publicist and wife

Chris Orr, artist and printmaker

Charles McKeown, actor, writer and performer in many MP films and TV shows

Geoffrey Strachan. Editor at Methuen who encouraged Python to go into print. Also published the *Ripping Yarns* books.

Tristram and Virginia Powell. Tristram was director/collaborator on *East of Ipswich*, *Number 27* and worked on development of *American Friends*.

André Jacquemin. Recording engineer, Python recordist, composer (with Dave Howman) of some Python songs. Founder of Redwood Studios.

Trevor Jones/John Du Prez, musician and composer (Python songs and *A Fish Called Wanda*)

Ray Cooper, legendary percussionist who became important go-between and general troubleshooter on all the HandMade films

OFFICE

At Mayday Management/Prominent Features:

Anne James, formerly Henshaw, manager. Married to Jonathan James, a barrister.

Steve Abbott, accountant/management, also film producer (*A Fish Called Wanda*)

Alison Davies

At EuroAtlantic/HandMade:

Denis O'Brien, Chief Executive, Executive Producer (*Time Bandits*, *The Missionary*, *A Private Function*)

Mark Vere Nicoll, legal expert

FILM REGULARS

Richard Loncraine, Director. First wife Judy. Married Felice 1985.

Neville Thompson, Producer

Mark Shivas, Producer

Julian Doyle. Editor, cameraman, who could turn his hand to any part of the film-making process. Indispensable part of both Python and Gilliam films.

John Goldstone, Producer of Monty Python films – *Holy Grail, Life of Brian* and *Meaning of Life*

Sandy Lieberson, Producer and sounding board for many projects, including Terry Gilliam's *Jabberwocky*

Patrick Cassavetti, Producer

IN AMERICA

Al Levinson. After wife Eve's death, married Claudie Calvez in 1979. Gwenola is their daughter.

Nancy Lewis. Publicist for Python in the USA, deserves much credit for getting them on US TV in the first place. Married actor Simon Jones in 1983.

The Films:

MONTY PYTHON LIVE AT THE HOLLYWOOD BOWL

Directors:	Terry Hughes (concert sequences)
	Ian MacNaughton (filmed sequences)
Producers:	Denis O'Brien – Executive Producer
	James Rich Jr – Concert Film Co-producer
	George Harrison – Executive Producer

Cast:	Graham Chapman
	John Cleese
	Terry Gilliam
	Eric Idle
	Terry Jones
	Michael Palin
	Neil Innes
	Carol Cleveland
Writers:	GC, JC, TG, EI, MP, TJ
Additional material:	Tim Brooke-Taylor
	Marty Feldman
	Angus James
	David Lipscomb
Editors:	Julian Doyle (post-production director and editor)
	Jimmy B. Frazier (editor: concert film)

TIME BANDITS

Director:	Terry Gilliam
Producer:	Terry Gilliam
Executive Producers:	George Harrison
	Denis O'Brien
Associate Producer:	Neville C. Thompson
Cast:	John Cleese
	Sean Connery
	Shelley Duvall
	Katherine Helmond
	Ian Holm
	Michael Palin
	Ralph Richardson
	Peter Vaughan
	David Rappaport
	Kenny Baker
	Malcolm Dixon
	Mike Edmonds
	Jack Purvis
	Tiny Ross
	Craig Warnock

Screenplay:	Michael Palin
	Terry Gilliam
Music:	George Harrison
Editor:	Julian Doyle

THE MISSIONARY

Director:	Richard Loncraine
Producers:	Michael Palin
	Neville C. Thompson
Executive Producers:	George Harrison
	Denis O'Brien
Cast:	Michael Palin
	Maggie Smith
	Trevor Howard
	Denholm Elliott
	Michael Hordern
	Phoebe Nicholls
Screenplay:	Michael Palin
Music:	Mike Moran
Editor:	Paul Green

MONTY PYTHON'S THE MEANING OF LIFE

Directors:	Terry Jones
	Terry Gilliam (segment 'The Crimson Permanent Assurance')
Producer:	John Goldstone
Cast:	Graham Chapman
	John Cleese
	Terry Gilliam
	Eric Idle
	Terry Jones
	Michael Palin
	Carol Cleveland
	Simon Jones
	Patricia Quinn
Screenplay:	GC, JC, TG, EI, TJ, MP
Editor:	Julian Doyle

BRAZIL

Director:	Terry Gilliam
Producers:	Patrick Cassavetti (co-producer)
	Arnon Milchan
Cast:	Jonathan Pryce
	Robert De Niro
	Katherine Helmond
	Ian Holm
	Bob Hoskins
	Michael Palin
	Ian Richardson
	Peter Vaughan
Screenplay:	Terry Gilliam
	Tom Stoppard
	Charles McKeown
Editor:	Julian Doyle

A PRIVATE FUNCTION

Director:	Malcolm Mowbray
Producer:	Mark Shivas
Executive Producers:	George Harrison
	Denis O'Brien
Cast:	Michael Palin
	Maggie Smith
	Denholm Elliott
	Richard Griffiths
	Tony Haygarth
	John Normington
	Bill Paterson
	Liz Smith
Screenplay:	Alan Bennett
Original story:	Alan Bennett and Malcolm Mowbray
Music:	John Du Prez
Editor:	Barrie Vince

A FISH CALLED WANDA

Director:	Charles Crichton
Producer:	Michael Shamberg
Executive Producers:	Steve Abbott
	John Cleese
Cast:	John Cleese
	Jamie Lee Curtis
	Kevin Kline
	Michael Palin
	Maria Aitken
	Tom Georgeson
	Patricia Hayes
Screenplay:	John Cleese
Story by:	John Cleese and Charles Crichton
Music:	John Du Prez
Editor:	John Jympson

Timeline

Main work projects during the period January 1980–September 1988

1980:
Writing and acting in *Time Bandits*
Filming 'Confessions of a Trainspotter', one-hour episode for BBC *Great Railway Journeys* series
Acting and filming *Monty Python Live at the Hollywood Bowl.*

1981:
Writing *The Missionary* and *Monty Python's The Meaning of Life*
Time Bandits released
First One-Man Show at Belfast Festival

1982:
Writing and acting in *The Missionary* and *The Meaning of Life*
The Missionary released in USA

1983:
The Missionary released in UK and Australia
The Meaning of Life released in US and UK. Wins Special Jury Prize at Cannes Film Festival
Film *Comic Roots*, one-hour autobiographical documentary for BBC
Second Belfast Festival Show
Begin filming *Brazil*

1984:
Complete *Brazil* filming
Filming *A Private Function*
Shoot short film *The Dress*
A Private Function has Royal Premiere in London and opens in UK

1985:
A Private Function opens in USA

British Film Year
Dr Fegg's Encyclopeadia of <u>All</u> World Knowledge published
Write *East of Ipswich* film screenplay for BBC
Third Belfast Festival Show
Limericks published

1986:
Become Chair of Transport 2000
Brazil released.
East of Ipswich filmed in Southwold, Suffolk
Begin writing 'The Victorian screenplay' (later to become *American Friends*)
The Mirrorstone published
Ripping Yarns premieres on US TV

1987:
East of Ipswich shown on BBC2
Start filming 'Troubles' for LWT (cancelled after one week due to union dispute)
Write *American Friends*, first draft
Write *Number 27* film screenplay for BBC
Filming as Ken Pile in *A Fish Called Wanda*
First discussions for *Around the World in 80 Days*
Fourth Belfast Festival Show
Resign Chair of Transport 2000

1988:
Rewriting, financing and casting trips for *American Friends*
Filming of *Number 27*
A Fish Called Wanda opens in America
Begin London filming on *Around the World in 80 Days*
Leave London to circumnavigate the world

Introduction

These diaries cover a period of my life when, briefly, the prospect of international stardom shimmered on the horizon. As the decade began the Monty Python brand was resurgent. *The Life of Brian* was causing a stir, our stage show was about to be revived at the Hollywood Bowl and there was unprecedented financial interest in any new film we cared to write. By the time these extracts end it was all very different. Python, after many premature obituaries, had, in effect, ceased to be. So, to all intents and purposes, had my chances of a Hollywood career. The last entry records my anxiety, not about films, but about an eighty-day journey around the world.

It wasn't that I hadn't given a film career a try. Between 1980 and 1988 I either wrote, or appeared in, seven movies. In varying degrees, all of them received support and interest from the major studios. Universal picked up *Monty Python's The Meaning of Life* and, together with 20th Century Fox, picked up Terry Gilliam's *Brazil*, Columbia took *The Missionary*, *A Fish Called Wanda* was made for MGM. The doors of Hollywood were open. Nor was I reluctant to look inside. As the diaries show, I was spending more time on the West Coast than the East. I was hobnobbing with studio executives and being flown by Concorde to casting sessions. And yet, in the end, my feet remained firmly on this side of the Atlantic.

I still can't quite work out why all this happened the way it did, and I re-read the diaries with a mixture of curiosity and disbelief. The overall impression is of a kaleidoscope of characters and events, clarity and confusion, of great strides forward and long and rambling cul-de-sacs, from which a pattern emerges, but only briefly, like the moon between clouds on a stormy night. I'm in my late thirties when this volume begins and my mid-forties when it ends, so one might imagine that the course of my life and career would be settling down. But the inescapable conclusion from reading these entries is that this is a man who still doesn't really know what he wants to do, or what he's particularly qualified to do.

If this were a history, or an autobiography written in the future looking back, I feel sure the temptation would be to impose order and reason and logic on this period of my life, to detect themes and trends that led in one direction, in other words to make sense of it all.

But diaries don't allow such luxuries. The events of everyday life are by their nature unpredictable, not at all at ease with the order that we crave as we grow older. Meaning changes, slips, adjusts, evolves. Narrative exists only in its most basic sense.

Which is why I like diaries. The map may be constantly changing, the steering wheel may be spinning all over the place, but diaries are the sound of an engine running, day in and day out.

MICHAEL PALIN
London, April 2009

'I did, I think, nothing'

Evelyn Waugh's diary, *26th June 1924*

1980

As a new decade began I was enmeshed in two new projects. One was collaborating on the screenplay of a children's fantasy dreamt up by Terry Gilliam, and the other a proper serious documentary, on railways, for the BBC. Both of these were off my normal patch, which was exciting in a way but a little less predictable than I'd have liked. The bedrock of the family was being quietly and unsensationally strengthened; Helen and I had been married nearly fourteen years. Tom was eleven and Will was nine and Rachel coming up to five. Which meant a lot more responsibilities than the same time ten years earlier. And I still had no regular job. I was an intuitively stable character living in a state of almost permanent flux. Quite a balancing act.

Keeping a diary had, after tentative beginnings in 1969 and 1970, become an ingrained habit, and a discipline too. Like the running I'd recently taken up, it was something consistent, a necessary complement to the mercurial world of work. Something to keep me grounded.

I continued to write up the diary most mornings, aware as ever how selective I had to be and how little time I ever had for honing and shaping. But I kept the story going. Just about.

Unless otherwise indicated, the entries are written in my house in Oak Village in North London.

Sunday, January 6th

With the social and gastronomic excesses of Christmas and New Year over, life this weekend has returned, after many weeks, to something approaching calm. I find I can easily cope with eight hours' sleep a night. I find I enjoy having time to sort my books out or take the children out or sit in front of the fire. I feel my body and my mind adjusting to a new pace and a new rhythm. I've hardly used the car in the last week. I haven't been into town, or shopping, or having business meetings. And I feel the benefits of this pause, this time to take stock of the present instead of endless worryings over the future or the past.

I've become a little self-sufficient, too. Though Gilliam is a regular visitor – like a mother hen having to keep returning to the nest to make sure the eggs are still all right – I'm responsible for the writing pace at the moment. I know that just over the horizon is the full swirl of a dozen different projects, meetings, responsibilities, considerations and demands, but for now the sea is calm.

Monday, January 7th

Denis [O'Brien] was back from the States today. According to TG he has no backers for the film [*Time Bandits*], but intends to go ahead and do it himself – just to 'spite them all'. I think this leaves me feeling as uncomfortable as it does Terry. But I read him some of the opening scenes, which cheer him up.

Pat Casey[1] rings to know my availability. She has a movie part which was written for Dudley Moore. He's now charging one and a half million dollars a picture and wants to do some serious acting, so Pat is asking me if I would be interested in the part. I have to turn it down as I'm occupied this year.

Wednesday, January 9th

At Redwood [Studios] at four. Eric, moderately well laid-back, occasionally strumming guitar. Trevor Jones[2] bustling. André[3] looking tired, but working faithfully. Graham [Chapman], who is getting £5,000 a month from Python as co-producer of this album [*Monty Python's Contractual Obligation*], sits contentedly, with John [Tomiczek] in attendance. He seems, as usual, not quite in tune with what's going on around him. I record the Headmaster's speech and that's about all.

Up to the Crown at Seven Dials for a drink with Terry Gilliam and Roger Pratt.[4] This is more like the real world for me. I can believe in the three of us and the place and the people around us far more than I can in what's going on at Redwood. Clearly TG feels the same. He's a bit

1 Patricia Casey produced Monty Python's first film *And Now For Something Completely Different* in 1970.
2 Trevor Jones, composer. To avoid confusion with the film composer of the same name he is now known as John Du Prez. Wrote the music for a number of Python songs as well as the film *A Fish Called Wanda* and, with Eric Idle, the musical *Spamalot*.
3 André Jacquemin, long-time Python sound recordist and composer.
4 Roger Pratt, camera operator on *Time Bandits*, later, lighting cameraman on *Brazil* and, more recently, two of the *Harry Potter* films.

confused by Denis's attitude to his film – on the one hand he is supportive and confident in TG – the next he's suggesting stars and names with almost frantic indiscrimination.

Thursday, January 10th

Rachel's first day at Gospel Oak School. It's a rather glum, hard, cold day with weather from the east. I don't see Rachel leave as I'm at the Mornington Foot Clinic. Mr Owen natters and reminisces as he slices at my foot – removing not only the corn but valuable minutes of screenwriting!

Home by ten. Rachel seems to have taken to school without any traumas. In fact Helen seems to have been affected more by the experience.

Unplug the phone and get down to the knotty problems of making an adventure serious and funny. Jim Franklin[1] rings to offer me a part in the Goodies and Pat Casey to try and induce me yet again to take a Dudley Moore cast-off.

Friday, January 11th

Up and running early this morning. The temperature is just on freezing and the grass on top of Parliament Hill is covered with frost. Feel immensely refreshed and thoroughly awoken.

Arrive at T Gilliam's just after 10.30.

Progress is steady but not spectacular, though TG is very amused by the Robin Hood sequence.

To Denis O'B's for a meeting at two. Denis looks weary. He was up working on 'structures' for TG's film until 2.30 yesterday morning. But he seems to be as bright and tenaciously thorough about all my affairs as he ever was.

Home by six. Feel encouraged after our meeting. Denis has talked of an India project – and self-financing of it, rather like TG's film – but basically my encouragement stems from the knowledge that with Denis we are in a different league. For the first time we are being offered the prospect of quite considerable financial rewards. Denis clearly identifies

---

1 Jim Franklin directed four of the *Ripping Yarns*.

money with power – although in our case our 'power', in terms of reputation, was established and created without vast rewards. Now Denis wants the rewards for us and through us for himself.

At the moment he seems to have admirable goals, but I have this nagging feeling that our 'freedom' to do whatever we want may be threatened if Denis is able to build up this juggernaut of Python earning power and influence. A few of the most interesting projects may be rolled flat.

Monday, January 14th

To Anne's [James] for a Python meeting with Denis. JC, fresh returned from Barbados, stands there shivering. Anne, as thoughtful as ever, has provided some lunch. Meeting is basically to discuss Denis's two offers for the next [Monty Python] movie – from Warners and Paramount. Warners want a screenplay before going ahead, Paramount just a treatment. Denis is asking for 6.4 million dollars.

Time is of the essence, as Paramount, who are offering a better financial deal, do require the movie for summer 1981 release. This, I feel, puts pressures on the group which we would rather not have – and thankfully no-one feels any different. But JC suggests that we go along with Paramount at the moment and just see if, after the seven-week March/April writing period, we have enough to give them a treatment – 'In which case we could all go ahead and make a lot of money very quickly.'

Though we all feel the Paramount deal for the next movie is the one to pursue, Denis is proposing to try and place *Grail*, now released from Cinema 5, with Warners, so they can do a *Life of Brian/Holy Grail* re-release in the US next summer. There is no great enthusiasm for selling the Bavaria film as a Python Olympic Special to the US networks in summer of this year. Eric reckons there will be no Olympics anyway. Certainly the Russian invasion of Afghanistan has shaken things up.

TG comes round and we talk over Denis and the movie. But I'm feeling very unsettled about my role in it at the moment. The script is clogged and I've lost a day's writing today. There seems suddenly so much to do and I refuse to give up my railway project [contributing to the BBC's *Great Railway Journeys*], despite reportedly 'generous' financial inducements from Denis to prolong my work on the TG movie.

André arrives very late, bringing a quite beautiful tape of Trevor Jones's arrangement for 'Decomposing Composers'. How the hell I'll sing it, I don't know.

Thursday, January 17th

Go with Tom and Helen to a 'parents' view' at Acland Burghley Comprehensive, one of the three local schools which Tom will have to be selected for, and where he will be well ensconced by this time next year.

A modern school, presenting a forbidding aspect, cloaked as it is in heavy grey concrete. The doors and passageways give the immediate impression of a hard, unpretty, pragmatist mind at work. But the library/reading room, where about 20 of us parents assemble, is warm and bright, the shelves are well-filled. I noticed *Soviet Weekly* alongside *The Economist.*

We were shown into a biology room and given glowing prospects of the future of this school. However I couldn't help noticing a large piece of paper on the front of a cupboard low on the ground near our feet, which bore the simple legend 'Whoever reads this is a cunt'.

Friday, January 18th

The world seems to have started 1980 so badly that I have on occasions this past week questioned the wisdom of working myself to a standstill when all the elements for the start of another global war crowd the newspapers for headline space. Ultimatums are flying around and ultimatums, to me, are synonymous with the outbreak of World War II.

It may in a few years sound rather laughable that Jimmy Carter threatened Russia that he will pull America out of the Olympics if the Russians haven't withdrawn their forces from Afghanistan by mid-February, but combined as this pronouncement is with the volatility of unsettled Iran and the much more threatening stances being taken up in preparation for President Tito's imminent death in Yugoslavia, the potential flashpoints seem sure to light something.

But it all ultimately is unreal and either you panic and sell everything you've got to buy gold, or you just sit down and have breakfast, presuming it won't be the last one. And of course it isn't.

Saturday, January 19th

Denis O'B rings. His proposal for my work on the T Gilliam film is that I be made a partner, along with Terry G, in the production company, so I will be able to share with TG the depreciation on capital which will be worth £60,000 in tax advantages. Don't ask me why, but this is clearly a generous move on the part of George [Harrison] and Denis O'B, who are the providers of the money.

And I can go ahead with the railway documentary – 'If you really want to,' says Denis, unhappily, knowing that there's precious little he can do to squeeze more than £2,400 out of the BBC for what's ostensibly 12 weeks' work!

In the afternoon a two and a half hour visit to Haverstock School. A lived-in, scuffed and battered collection of buildings. Impressed by the straightforwardness of the teachers. Impressed by the lack of waffle about tradition, Latin and prayers and the emphasis on the future and helping all the children of whatever ability equally.

An impossible ideal, some may say, but at least these teachers are confronting the most basic problems of an educational system with great energy and cheeriness. I was encouraged.

Monday, January 21st

The world situation seems to have cooled down, though I see in my *Times* that Paul McCartney is still in jail in Japan after being caught at the airport with naughty substances. How silly. Eric reckons it's a put-up job – part of John Lennon's price, which he's exacting from Paul for being rude to Yoko.

At five I brave the skyscraper-induced blasts of icy wind that whip round the Euston Tower and find myself in Capital Radio, being asked questions on, and reading extracts from, *Decline and Fall*. I find I'm never as lucid when the tape's rolling as I am over a glass of wine at home an hour later and in the course of an hour I get tongue-tied and fail to say even what I meant to say – let alone whether that was worth saying or not. I'm in august company – Denis Norden and Melvyn Bragg are the other two pundits on this particular book. JC has already said his piece about *Twelfth Night* (from which Shakespeare didn't emerge very favourably) and TJ is soon to do *The Spire* by William Golding.

Wednesday, January 23rd

The fine weather's back again. Tito's recovering and the steel strike is still faced with government intransigence. I have either pulled, twisted or bruised some muscle below and to the right of my kneecap, so I rest from running today, despite ideal, dry, cool, bright conditions out there.

Work on with TG script. The end is in sight, but is this writing to order – 6lbs assorted jokes, half a hundredweight of nutty characters and 20 yards of filler dialogue – really going to stand up? I'm encouraged when I think of the general level of movie dialogue – but this movie has to be judged by exceptional, not general level.

Write myself to a standstill by four and drive into the West End to see *Apocalypse Now*. Impressive – there is no other word for it – and the action sequences of the war are rivetingly watchable.

But the last half-hour – the meat, one feels, of Coppola/Milius' message – is a huge con. The action slows, the dialogue and performance become heavy with significance, sluggish with style.

Thursday, January 24th

Stop work at one. A couple of phone calls, then drive down to Neal's Yard for the Grand Unveiling Ceremony of the 14/15 Neal's Yard sign [designed by Terry G]. On one side red lurid lips and teeth bear the legend 'Neal's Yd. Abattoir' (to correct the present unwholesome imbalance in favour of the wholefooders who have proliferated all over the yard) and on the other side 'The British Film Industry Ltd'.

When I arrive it is made clear to me that a few choice words will have to be spoken and yours truly is the man to speak them. So we troop down into the yard and there, on this perfect sunny day, I bewilder all those queuing for non-meat lunches at the bakery by giving a few loud, but brief words, then smashing a champagne bottle against the building. 'God bless her and all who work in her.' It breaks the second time.

Friday, January 25th

To Terry Gilliam's at 10.15 for session on the film. TG likes the Ogre and the Old Ladies scene, but I think feels that the Evil Genius is too much on one level of cod hysteria. I agree, but we still have time to go over the characters again and invest them with a few more quirks.

We go to lunch at the Pizza Express and talk over the more serious problem of the 'content' of the script – the attitude to the characters, to Kevin's adventures – the message which gives the depth to a superficial story of chase and adventure. Really I feel the depth is there anyway, it's a question of how obvious to make it.

Leave for Dr Kieser's[1] surgery, where I have a cut and cover job on one of my front upper teeth – so my dental surgery is in its third decade. At one moment, as he works on the gum and bone, it begins to hurt. 'Is that pressure or pain you're feeling?' asks Kieser urgently. God ... how on earth do I tell?

Friday, February 1st

A rush for the tape. Began reassembling and rewriting the section from the Spider Women to the end at ten. Lunch at the desk.

TG arrives about 7.30 and I stumble to the 'End' by eight. He will get all this mass of stuck-up, crossed-out, type-and-longhand-jumbled sheets to Alison [Davies, at the office] this weekend. All should be returned by Sunday a.m., so I can then read through and learn the awful truth about this amazingly speedy piece of writing.

I go to bed at midnight with the satisfaction of having completed my self-set task of a TG script in the month of January. It would be marvellous if the script were of a high standard, worked and immeasurably increased the confidence of all working on the project. Or was the rush just at the expense of quality, an exercise in the lowest form of writing to a deadline?

I shall see. For now, I'm just very happy with a job (almost) done.

Saturday, February 2nd

In the afternoon the sky clouded and heavy rain set in. Took William, Rachel and the Mini down to the Natural History Museum, whilst Tom P and his friend Tom Owen went 'tracking' on the Heath. Rachel is doing dinosaurs at school and met one or two of her friends there. The central area was very full, but as soon as we ventured into the further recesses of the building there was plenty of space amongst endless glassily-staring models and half-dissected bodies.

---

1 Bernard Kieser, periodontal surgeon extraordinaire, carried on the fight to keep my teeth in my mouth, with increasing success.

Willy went off on his own to, among other things, the human biology section. He is very keen on biology, having just begun talking about it at school. To her great credit, his teacher started straight in with human reproduction, etc, rather than frogs or bees. So Willy now knows all the practical details of procreation, whereas Tom, who affects to know, still calls sexual intercourse 'sexual interchange'.

Sunday, February 3rd

Read papers in the morning. Polls taken in January indicate that more people are expecting World War III to break out now than at any time since Korea. Probably a meaningless statistic, but it makes Python's next film subject gruesomely relevant. Actually the sabre-rattling of the Americans over Afghanistan has died down a little, but they still frighten me more than the Russians.

Terry G brings round the script of the movie, fresh from Alison the typist, and after supper I begin to read. I finish late – it's nearly one. My first reaction is that it's paced wrongly – the individual scenes are in some cases too long themselves, or appear too long when placed next to another, fairly static scene. I missed being gripped by the story, too.

Lay in bed remembering points and scribbling down. Tomorrow I've given a day to Terry G that should be spent on railway research, so that we can talk right through the screenplay.

Monday, February 4th

Up to Terry's. The heavens open and it pours for the rest of the day. Against this gloomy background we slog through. TG liked the script more than I did, I think, and is greatly pleased that Irene Lamb, the casting director, for whom TG has much respect, also likes what she has seen so far and feels there will be little problem in getting good actors interested.

It's clear that there is one more day of writing needed to flesh out the end, especially the hastily-written character of the bureaucratic Supreme Being. So I'll have to restructure the week accordingly. Everything else will have to be squeezed.

Still have no title for the TG epic other than 'The Film That Dares Not Speak Its Name'.

Tuesday, February 5th

Talk over scripts for the new Python film with TJ. We read through and apportion who would be responsible for what.

TJ and I have a game of squash, then a pint of Brakspear's at the Nag's Head in Hampstead. TJ, though bemoaning the fact that he hasn't written anything new for months, is suddenly, and healthily, I think, full of ideas and projects of his own – including the possibility of making a film of *Hitchhiker's Guide to the Galaxy* with Douglas Adams.

Terry goes off to meet Douglas. I drive to a rather swish and un-Pythonlike function at Les Ambassadeurs Club. We are invited here by Warner Brothers Chairman Frank Wells – the man who, TG tells me later, did more than anyone else to try and block the *Life of Brian* deal. He was tall, fit, with those peculiar American spectacles that make a man's face look slightly effeminate; mid-forties, or early fifties, with a firm handshake.

Spread out in the scarlet-panelled, sumptuously-carpeted lower room at the Ambassadeurs was a host of men in grey. An impeccably-manicured host too – hardly a hair out of place on any of them. These were the agents and studio heads and accountants – the businessmen of showbiz.

A cameraman was in attendance, which always indicates that the gathering is a little more than just a thank you from Warners. I was photographed with Eric and with Frank Wells and Jarvis Astaire.[1] I was pleased to see Sandy [Lieberson] and his missus, because Sandy was at least not wearing a grey suit and Birgit was one of the only women there.

Gilliam is wonderfully scruffy, I'm pleased to say.

Leave at 8.15. Avoid getting run over by the sea of chauffeur-driven Rolls Royces and Jags and Mercedes littering Hamilton Place.

Wednesday, February 6th

Work through the last few scenes of the TG film until after lunch, then drive to Denis O'B's. Try to be absolutely clear with him that what I want for Redwood is to keep Bob[2] and André. Denis worries that Bob is 'driving

---

1 Wells was President of Warner Brothers, and later of the Walt Disney Company. He died in a helicopter accident whilst on a heli-skiing trip in 1994.

Jarvis Astaire, businessman and influential sports event promoter. Co-produced the film *Agatha* in 1978.

2 Bob Salmon was André Jacquemin's accountant and helped to set up Redwood Studios.

a wedge' between myself and André. Really he is accusing Bob of all the things that Bob is accusing Denis of doing. Denis will not hear a good word said for Bob – but I've made my decision. I'm not prepared to lose André, and if Bob goes, André goes. So Denis talks business and I talk people and that's that.

Drive back in a rain-sodden rush-hour to Abraxas [sports club in Belsize Park gardens]. Am soundly beaten by Richard [Guedalla, my neighbour] at squash. Makes me very depressed. But recover over a bottle of champagne, which I open to mark my last day on, or delivery of, the TG film script. Read TG the new Supreme Being scenes, which he likes.

Tom arrives back from another disco. Not just 'slow dancing' this time, but girls sitting on boys' laps. Reminds me of Eric's wonderful song for the *Contractual Obligation* album, 'Sit On My Face and Tell Me that You Love Me'.

Monday, February 18th

Springlike weather, with daytime temperatures around 50°F, now into its second week. I cycle up to Terry G's in sunshine. From 9.30 till lunchtime we work through the script – still tentatively, but not very enthusiastically, called 'The Time Bandits'. Fortunately we both agree on the major area for cuts and every little rewrite helps. TG is very unhappy about the vast amounts of money the crew are demanding – inflated by commercials. It doesn't help the 'British' film industry at all.

Down to Redwood Studios, where Eric, TJ and myself record 'Shopping Sketch' and 'All Things Dull and Ugly', plus one or two other snippets for the album.

From Redwood round to Anne J's to take in some more Python scripts from last autumn's writing session to be typed up in preparation for Wednesday's meeting. What is rapidly becoming apparent about *Brian* is that Denis's forecast of earnings from it in 1980 was drastically over-optimistic. The £250,000 figure he mentioned in November now looks likely to be nearer £40,000.

Although the distributor's gross in the US was over nine million dollars, over four million was spent on publicity and advertising – and this was where Warners were weakest. Their posters and their slogans were constantly changed and we never approved any of them – now they present a bill for this fiasco which is equal to the entire production budget of the film. It is a scandal, but there seems to be nothing Denis can do. They won't even supply him with figures.

The upshot is that not only will there be not a penny profit from America from a movie which was one of the top 40 grossers of the year in the US, but the earnings will hardly cover half the production cost. So the chance of making any more money – beyond our £72,000 fee for writing and acting – depends on the rest of the world. Fortunately the UK is looking very strong, Australia is holding up well and France and Germany remain to be seen.

Wednesday, February 20th

Python enters the 80's! Pick up Eric on the way to JC's. Arrive at 10.30. Everyone there and chortling over the latest and looniest batch of selected press cuttings about *Brian*. It's noted that Swansea has banned the film totally. Four hundred people in Watford are petitioning because the local council have recommended the film be an 'X'.

Coffees are poured and we settle round JC's ex-prison table, which now seems to be Python's favourite writing venue. Our ages are checked around the table. I'm still the youngest. No-one wants to spend time on business, we all want to write and make each other laugh, but business has to be done, so it's decided that we will make a clean sweep of it today. So Anne stays with us and Denis is summoned at three.

The disillusion with Hollywood and all things to do with Warners and *Brian* lead us into thinking how nice it would be to do a small-budget film just for the fun of it – keeping our own control and making money in the way *Grail*, with its modest budget, did, and *Brian*, with its Hollywood campaign, didn't. Denis is anxious to set up all sorts of production and syndication deals in the US, and he's talked to CBS about two Python TV specials, for which we would be paid 700,000 dollars each.

No-one wants to do specials for the US, but there is still the German material. Suddenly it all gels. We will use the German material, plus some old sketches, plus anything we wrote in October/November and reshoot as a quick, cheap movie. The mood of the group is unanimous. Fuck Hollywood. Fuck CBS. Let's do something we enjoy in the way we want to do it – and so economically that no-one gets their fingers burned if a Hollywood major *does* turn it down.

DO'B seems unable to respond at our level and talks business jargon for a while. I like Denis, and I think he likes us, but he is only in the early stages of finding out what everyone who's ever dealt with Python has eventually found out – that there is no logic or consistency or even realism behind much of our behaviour. No patterns can be imposed on the group from outside. Or at least they can, but they never stick; they crack up and the internal resolutions of Python are the only ones that last.

From international film business to the waiting room of the Mornington Foot Clinic. Mr Owen uses a 'coagulator' on my corn today. I have to have injections around my little toe, which are rather painful, then a sharp, electrified needle burns up the capillaries. All this counterpointed by Mr Owen's extraordinary views about the evils of the world and socialism in particular. I'm getting worried – I think that he is a character I've invented.

Monday, February 25th

Spent much of the weekend, unsuccessfully, trying to finish *Smiley's People*. Also trying to find time to organise the house, spend time with the children and other worthy hopes doomed to failure!

Rachel pottered around me with her Junior Doctor's Kit, taking my blood, giving me blood, thrusting toy thermometers in my mouth, whilst I tried, hopelessly, to assimilate the mass of opinions, facts, thoughts, figures and ramblings which make up the insidiously attractive substitute for experience that is the Sunday papers.

Collected Eric from Carlton Hill and we drove on to JC's. A talk through material. Eric and John have searched the archives, Terry J has been away, GC doesn't appear to have done much, but I saved my bacon by writing an extension to 'Penis Apology',[1] which produced an outstandingly good reaction. Near hysteria. I think Python is definitely working out all the repressions of childhood – and loving it!

Lunch with the French translator of *Holy Grail* and *Brian* at the Trattoo. A wonderful-looking Frenchman with a very special face which could not belong to any other nation. White hair, eyes droopy with a sort of permanent look of apology, a long, curved nose which never goes far from his face at any point. A lovely, squashed, humorous, used feel to the face like a Gauloise butt in an ashtray.

1 'Penis Apology' was a very long-drawn-out health advisory at the beginning of the film warning the audience that there may be a penis in shot later on. The apology became longer and more complex, including discussions from Bishops for the Church's view etc. It was never used.

Home by six. Have promised TG that I will read the new, shorter version of 'Time Bandits/The Film That Dares Not Speak Its Name', so I spend most of the evening on that. Poor Terry is being given a hard ride by the doubters and the pessimists. On reading I feel that the movie, which is, after all, an act of faith in TG, is, on balance, do-able by May. But only just!

Tuesday, February 26th

The weather has sharpened a little, but most of February has now gone, with no weather that wouldn't have graced an average April. In short, no winter at all here. But I don't feel any benefits. Wake up feeling like a piece of chewed rag. I have a sore throat, a mild coolness of the blood and a general enervation. There are so many loose ends to be tied up. I feel old for a few minutes.

Some work after breakfast, then round to Eric's. That's very cheering – mainly because all of us are happy to be together at the moment and the tapes that André's prepared of the sketches and songs for the LP assembled by Eric, with a certain amount of gentle bullying over the last two months, are a great boost.

To lunch at a nearby French, where Eric chides Graham for not being totally opposed to nuclear power. Eric deals only in certainties. His views, like his lifestyle at any one time, are very positive.

The talk veers to desultory discussion of bizarre sexual exploits. GC caps all, as he puffs at his pipe and declares that he once had an Indian in an aeroplane. JC is quite skittish too and suggests that perhaps the Pythons should set each other a sexual task. I agree to try and seduce the Queen!

I have a brief script chat with T Gilliam (cheering him up, I hope). Then I drive both of us round to a rendezvous with J Cleese, who was given TG's script and wants to, or 'is prepared to', talk to us about it. John is looking after Cynthia at the moment, on his own as far as I can tell, since Connie's in New York for 11 days.

Cynthia answers the door. With her long blonde hair, tastefully ribboned back, and her neat school uniform she looks, at nine years old, like an Estée Lauder model. Very New York, somehow. She chats confidently and behaves quite like a young lady 10 or 15 years older than she is, but she's humorous with it, which keeps her on this side of precociousness.

She comes out to eat with us. No room at the Japanese, so we go on to

Mama San – a clean, smart, soulless Chinese in Holland Park Avenue. Cynthia won't really let John get a word in, but after half an hour she settles to sleep beside an unoccupied table and the three of us talk about the script.

JC speaks with a slight, elder statesman of comedy air, as if he really *does* know how, why and when comedy will work, and we feel a little like naughty boys being told what's good for us. But this is rather unfair to John. I think he went out of the way to try *not* to sound too paternal, and he did give us some sound, unselfish advice, much of which will help in the rewrites. But I couldn't accept his final judgement – that we should postpone the movie on the basis that one day it could be a marvellous film, but if we rush it and go on the present script, it will be just a good-natured mess,

Mind you, JC had a piece of gossip that rather undermined his chances of 'stopping' the movie. He'd heard that Sean Connery was interested and Denis O'B has flown to California to see him!

Friday, February 29th

To Gospel Oak School to see Ron Lendon [the headmaster] about Tom's future.

Ron's report is glowing. Tom, it seems, is regarded very highly indeed. He is in Verbal Reasoning Group 1 – which is the comprehensive system's acknowledgement that abilities have to be tested at some point. There is less chance of him going to William Ellis [school in Highgate Road] if he's Group 1 – the idea is to spread them around the local schools. But Lendon, whose manner is chatty, informal, direct and quite unpatronising, feels that William Ellis is the best place for Tom. His closest friends – Lendon makes much reference to 'peer' groups – will be going there, he's keen on music and Lendon admits that he thinks the academic standards are higher at William E.

An interesting sign of the times is that Tom is one of only three boys amongst 15 in his class who does not come from a broken home.

So we come out greatly heartened and I feel once again the great relief that our children – all of them – will have started out at a school as caring and sympathetic as Gospel Oak.

Work on Python material for a couple of hours, then meet TJ at the Pizza Express in Hampstead. TJ has written something which he cheerfully acknowledges as the ultimate in bad taste – it's all about people throwing up – very childish, but rather well controlled, dare I say – it had me in as prolonged and hysterical a bout of laughter as I can remember.

Saturday, March 1st

Always feel that March is the end of the winter, but this year there has been no winter to speak of and this mild, orderly March morning is only different from much of January and February because the sun isn't shining.

Have to go and talk over script details with TG. The advantage of living within walking distance of your collaborator. Stroll up with my script over the Heath. Up to Terry's mighty attic. Listen to a couple of tracks of the new Elvis Costello.

The good news is that Ian Holm wants to be our Napoleon and loves the script. No further news from Denis who is, much to TG's irritation, still star-searching in Hollywood.

Walk back at 8.15, past South End Green where *Life of Brian* is in '5th Fantastic Week' at the Classic.

Sunday, March 2nd

A most relaxed and happy day. Sun shone – a very springlike Sunday. I cleared my desk prior to beginning the railway script.

Found lots of excuses to talk, drink coffee and generally indulge in what's called a writer's 'negative capability', but eventually was ready to start. Notes assembled, clean sheet of foolscap in the typewriter (I still use a typewriter for the serious stuff!). Then a strange tension gripped me – a tightening of the stomach, a light sweating of the palms just as if I were about to go on stage.

Do all writers, or any writers, suffer this 'typewriter fright', or is it just because I'm a writer/actor and I know that anything I put down now I will have to enact at some future time? Anyway, it's a very difficult task to start the documentary. To actually set this huge and daunting mass of facts and accumulated knowledge in motion.

Monday, March 3rd

Woken by bright sunshine. Rachel unhappy about school. I take her. She tries to be very brave, but bolts back towards the house when we get to the end of Oak Village, and I have to carry her most of the rest of the way. When we arrive at the school, her class are already sitting quietly, waiting for the register.

On the way back up Oak Village, an old lady leans out of her window. She looks distraught. Her gas supply has failed, and she's had no tea or heating. She's asked the gas people to come round, but she's concerned that they're not here. This all takes my mind off Rachel's predicament as I go home, phone up the gas, and Helen goes round to see her and make her tea and fill her hot water bottle.

Set to writing Python stuff. Rachel arrives back from school, a lot happier than when she went, but she *did* cry – 'Only one big tear,' she told me.

Tuesday, March 4th

Another sparkling day. Clear blue skies and a brisk chill giving an edge of freshness to the air. Write more Python material – it's flowing easily and I'm enjoying the chance to write some fairly direct satirical stuff again. Jury vetting was on the list today. And the courts generally.

From two until half past three, TJ and I read. TJ has a good idea for the RAF Pipe-Smokers – extending into wives. I've written huge amounts, as usual, but this time it seems to stand up – and almost nil failure rate over the last two days, which is encouraging. See what the others think on Thursday.

TG has been hearing from Denis O'B in Los Angeles.

Denis, who had sent me a telegram saying the script was 'sensational', is voicing doubts over the quality of writing – especially in the 'Napoleon' and 'Robin Hood' scenes. He even suggested to TG that they could 'get some writers in'. He still hurls out casting suggestions which bear all the hallmarks of a man more desperate about a bank loan than about anything to do with quality of script or trust of the writers – Burt Reynolds for the Evil Genius, Art Carney for the Ogre. All the qualities these actors have are blinded for me by Denis's heavy-handed Hollywood approach. It's killing T Gilliam and may kill the film.

I go to bed trying to put it all out of my mind. But a nagging corner can't be forgotten – I *did* write the script in a month. Denis is right – it *could* be better. Am I just now beginning to get some inklings that I really made a wrong decision to get involved in this project at all? Wrong not because I couldn't do it, but because I couldn't do my best.

I know I'm funnier writing unrestricted Python material. I know I could contribute more as a writer if it had been a 'Ripping Yarn' sort of story. But it wasn't. Will it ever be what everyone wants it to be? Or just a jumble of different ideas and preconceptions? Is it comedy or adventure? Why should it have to be either?

Because that's how Hollywood wants it to be, and Denis wants Hollywood.

Wednesday, March 5th

No brooding today. Up at eight. Buy *The Times* and read of Mugabe's victory in Rhodesia. The Brits have been patting themselves on the back for organising such an orderly election – in best British fashion – so they can hardly grumble at a Marxist getting 62% of the vote. It seems one of the most hopeful transitions from white to black power. But it's taken a guerrilla war to make the point and that must give great heart to guerrilla movements in other countries.

Thursday, March 6th

Rain, most of the day. To Eric's for a Python read-through. Neil [Innes] is staying there. He looks cheery and already his new life in the Suffolk countryside seems to have made him physically different. As though the land has moulded our ex-Lewisham lad. He's rounder. His hair, arranged in a neat coronal around his bald pate, is much fuller and frizzier than I remember before. He looks . . . He looks rather like a Hulme Beaman[1] creation.

Terry J looks tired and harassed and throughout the day there are odd phone calls for him which give one the feeling that his life is a box which is far too full. John C is grumbling about his health again – doing a perfect imitation of the Ogre in *Time Bandits* which he didn't like!

Eric is being very friendly, warm and accommodating. Terry Gilliam isn't there (which provokes some rumblings of discontent from Eric, who, I think, being unaligned to either of the main writing groups, feels that TG's absence deprives him of an ally). GC is as avuncular and benign as ever. And arrives easily last. Eric is trying to get GC to stop smoking his pipe so much. He's the only Python who still smokes.

---

1 S.G. Hulme Beaman created the Toytown stories, some of the earliest children's books and radio programmes I remember.

JC reads out an outrageously funny schoolmaster sex demonstration sketch. Our stuff doesn't go quite as well as expected this morning. Eric has a chilling ending for the film, when the outbreak of nuclear war is announced. He's been reading about the dangers of, and plans in the event of, nuclear war happening.

We talk for a while on this subject, which is so macabre and disturbing because the weapons for our destruction exist – they're pointing at us now – and our response is to build more.

Friday, March 7th

Tried to write a startlingly new and original, brilliantly funny and thought-provoking piece for Python. Did this by staring out of the window, playing with paper clips and shutting my eyes for long periods.

Monday, March 10th

Pressing on. Endless days of writing. They seem to have been going on forever and are stretching on forever. Not that I mind *that* much. I quite enjoy not having to drive across London, not having to go down rain-spattered motorways to locations, not having to make meetings and business lunches, not going out to dinners or buying clothes.

Yes, I'm afraid this monastic existence suits me rather well. I shall keep it up this week, hoping for a breakthrough on Python and a completion of the railway script – then I shall take Concorde to New York at the expense of NBC and 'party' for 24 hours.

Work on Python until it's dark outside, then break and work on the railways until midnight. Impossible. I'm beginning to sink under a mass of names, lines, distances, facts, details, anecdotes, diversions, sidings . . .

Tuesday, March 11th

Denis O'B rings – he's returned from the States and positively glowing with enthusiasm for the TG/MP movie. He has Sean Connery absolutely 'mentally committed' (which means he hasn't enough money for him) and George H, who at first was not at all sure why Denis O'B was putting his money into it, has now re-read the script twice, feels it has great potential and is trying to hustle Jack Nicholson into letting us have his name on the credits!

Paramount have agreed a distribution deal with Denis in the US and are seeing it as a new *Wizard of Oz*! However, they are very keen to get the hottest name in Hollywood – Gilda Radner – onto the credits too. Denis, who knows nothing of Gilda, has promptly turned several circles and is now homing in on Gilda as the Ogre's Wife instead of Ruth Gordon. 'Apparently she does a really good old lady on *Saturday Night Live*.'

I have to puncture Denis's epic enthusiasm here. She may do a great old lady, but Ruth Gordon *is* a great old lady, and would easily be my choice (if we need names) for the part.

Wednesday, March 12th

Schizophrenic weather. Today almost continuous rain – yesterday bright sunshine.

To Eric's for a Python meeting.

Over lunch we discuss the general balance of material, which seems to fall into School, War/Army and North-West Frontier. Lists are made in the p.m. and a putative running order worked out. This is the stage when there is much talk of 'What is the film about?' and how we can relate the various themes – whether we should start conventionally or with an apology for what's to be seen. Quite good progress.

Thursday, March 13th

Revision of the railway script proceeds rather slowly. I think one reason is that I have become so steeped in the material over the last three or four weeks that I've lost a lot of the initial enthusiasm. Also concerned about how funny to make the start. In short, I don't think I've found the right tone yet.

Run off my uncertainties at lunchtime. Back to a phone call from Denis. He has just received a mortal blow to his pride from Edna Jones at BBC Contracts. Denis, international financier and deal-maker extraordinary, cannot get the BBC to budge from a max of £2,400 plus £1,800 once and for all foreign sales on the railway programme. Denis, who believes in the success ethic even more than the work ethic, says he's contemplating throwing himself off his balcony!

Saturday, March 15th: London and New York

A dull morning, but no rain, fog or snow to threaten departure. With only a couple of light bags, a book – *Moviola* by Garson Kanin – and a *Time Bandits* script for Ruth Gordon (Garson Kanin's wife!), drive the Mini to Heathrow and park it, as I'm only away for one night.

Board the 11.15 Concorde, a few minutes late – some problem with the earlier flight. But we're airborne, with thunderous noise, by twelve, and there are no more problems. I'm VIP listed and this means it's impossible to quietly stew in a mixture of champagne, relief and a good book without being hauled out to sign an autograph for the crew and visit the flight deck.

The pilot and co-pilot seem more anxious to ask me about Python than to tell me about Concorde, but I do ascertain that they use five tons of fuel every hour and that the fastest Atlantic crossing so far has been two hours 56 minutes.

Well, they catch up half an hour and I'm at Kennedy and through customs and into bright sunshine and crisp snow cover just after 10.30 NY time.

Arrive at NBC at four. Rehearse the moves cold. See Lorne,[1] the cast, Belushi, who is back to do a special appearance. Of *1941* he says 'I was bad, the film was bad', but he's very pleased with the state of the *Blues Brothers* – his soon to be released picture with Aykroyd.

As usual Belushi's presence does not please everybody. He's very rude about the present state of '*SNL*' – and seems disgruntled that he's come back to do so little. Both points are understandable. The material on this 100th show reflects age rather than quality and Belushi isn't given much funny stuff. He's smarting because he's been cut out of 'Update' to accommodate one of the 'star guests', Ralph Nader.

After an hour of reacquainting myself with everybody and rehearsing in a darkened set, a dull, persistent headache has set in. So I take an hour off before the dress rehearsal, go back to the Berkshire Place and lie down. Don't sleep, but at least I'm not working or talking.

Shower and leave the hotel at seven, US time – which means it's midnight UK time. I have somehow to try and pace myself to perform live in front of the watching millions at what will be, for me, about 5.30 in the morning at the end of a very crowded day.

---

1 Lorne Michaels produced the ground-breaking, talent-spinning NBS *Saturday Night Live* show. And still does.

When 11.30 finally arrived and the signature tune blared out I knew that I would be alright as the adrenaline started working to clear my befuddled system of the combined effects of too much food, alcohol and fatigue.

The sketch went better than ever and I got a gratifying round of recognition applause when the audience saw me for the first time. I also over-acted happily and shamelessly. John Cleese would have been proud of the way I killed the tarantula.

Thursday, March 20th

Spring starts either today or tomorrow, I'm never sure. The rain's stopped, but there was a frost last night. It's cold, clear and clean.

At a quarter to ten Helen, Tom and I drive up in the Mini to William Ellis School for our interview with Mr Perry [the headmaster]. Talk to one of the senior boys – wearing a gown. Will they still keep gowns in the comprehensive era? He was very well-spoken and presentable and surprised me by saying, quite undefensively, that he wanted to become an accountant.

Into Mr Perry's bland but unintimidating study. Tom is asked most of the questions. What he likes about Gospel Oak – Tom, seriously, 'Well, it's very spacious, but quite small.' His hobbies, interests, friends, preferences (Tom declared for science). Tom answered quite unprecociously and at greater length than I expected. Mr Perry said that it was almost an accepted fact that children from Gospel Oak were more articulate than the norm.

Drive over to EuroAtlantic for a meeting with Denis and T Gilliam. Main subject is whether or not we think J Cleese is right for the Evil Genius. Apparently Denis took the bull by the horns and met the disgruntled Cleese, who's not so far forgiven Denis for promising us a quarter of a million pounds each for *Brian*.

Denis has so successfully charmed JC with soft words and capital allowance schemes, that JC can now see the advantage of being in TG's movie after all – as a partner. Denis is keen, but both TG and I are unconvinced. Other names hang in the air. Connery still isn't fixed. Ruth Gordon neither. Denis is disappointed that John cannot be easily fitted in.

Watch the BAFTA awards at 9.30 with a glimmer of hope, but little more than that. The Light Entertainment Award is the first. Bruce Forsyth comes on to present it and does an annoyingly unnecessary and lengthy preamble, whilst Anna Ford, Edward Fox and Princess Anne watch lugubriously.

My first pleasure is to hear the laughter in the hall as they show the shooting scene from 'Roger of the Raj', but I can't believe it when Forsyth announces 'The winner is . . . the winners are: Alan Bell and Jim Franklin for . . . *Ripping Yarns*.' I just leap up and give a few lusty yells. It's like Wednesday scoring twice against Everton in the '66 Cup Final.

The boys come downstairs and stare at me.

Monday, March 24th

TG and I drive down to the King's Road in pouring rain to dine with executives from Paramount and Denis O'B at the Casserole Restaurant.

There were three Paramount people. A young, bright little man, with a combative heckling approach which settled down as one got to know him. He was called Jeffrey Katzenberg, was 29 years old and admitted that he was paid a lot because it was a very high-risk job – the turnover of Hollywood execs is spectacularly fast. His bluffer, less devious, funnier friend was also younger than TG or I and was called David.

They joked heavily as we arrived. Probably to cover their embarrassment at the fact that an hour earlier Paramount HQ had telexed Denis O'B to say that if he stalls on the next Python deal (which he has) then they will stall on the *Time Bandits*. So Paramount in LA are playing Denis's game.

But these two were at pains to deny any close association with their colleagues. These two were interested purely in talent and were keen to know more about the *Time Bandits*. They particularly wanted to be reassured about the dwarves (I mean, just how odd would they look?).

Wednesday, March 26th

At my desk at 9.30 to confront the formidable task of rewriting two scenes for the *Time Bandits* before leaving for the Python promotion in Paris at 3.30. But the muse is helpful and by one I have rewritten the 'Future' and, even more satisfactorily, I hope, the 'Titanic' scene.

Leave for the airport at a quarter past three. Onto an Airbus for Paris. Packed solid – must be two or three hundred people. Read my book on the Greeks by H D F Kitto. Most inspirational. In the air only briefly, but on the plane for over an hour.

Python Sacré Graal is in its 71st week of its third reissue in Paris! So clearly there is a cult here, and it's based on only one movie.

A rather dreadful evening at a Sofitel in the 15th Arrondissement. Up to a bleak room on the 16th floor of this French Holiday Inn, where we ate. No-one knew why we were here, or who all the guests were, but it turned out to be some sort of special viewing for Avis, who are renting us the cars for the three days.

Python spirit was high, despite this debacle, though, and much enjoyment was derived from trying to find how many things on the table we could assemble around John before he noticed. Huge numbers of plates, glasses, bread baskets and even an ornamental bowl of flowers were discreetly manoeuvred in front of him, but he never noticed.

Thursday, March 27th: Paris

Interviews – for *Le Figaro, La Revue de Cinéma* and finally a cartoonist called Gottlib, who has a Gumby fascination and gets me to enunciate clearly and slowly the *exact* words for 'Gumby Flower Arranging' into a small tape recorder. The more seriously I try to oblige, the more ridiculous the situation becomes. Eric doesn't help by constantly cracking up and when I finally make it through to the moment of flower arranging the doors of the room open to reveal an enormous bunch of flowers being carried through. The interviews draw to a close by seven. Terry J and I go off to eat at La Coupole. I have ears and tail – and TJ is most impressed. We talk, for the first time, about the *Time Bandits* script, which TJ has half-read. He wasn't impressed with it until the Greek scene!

Saturday, March 29th: Paris and London

Woken from a very deep sleep in the Hotel Lotti by the soft clinking of a breakfast tray. It's half past seven. Pull myself out of bed and wander across to meet the breakfast, wearing only my underpants, when I'm suddenly aware of the nervous, twitching, apologetic presence of the Very Naughty Valet in my room.

Terry had warned me that there was a man who very lasciviously enquired whether he wanted his shoes cleaned, and here he was, in my room, having caught me with literally everything, apart from my pants, down! He wasn't at all fazed by my appearance, but came on in and started to arrange my chair for breakfast in a most epicene manner.

Finally I fled to the bathroom and made loud and hopefully quite unromantic sounds of ablution until I knew he'd gone. Then I crept out again and got to grips with two fried eggs, coffee out of a swimming pool cup and croissants which were pale imitations of Patisserie Valerie's.

The door I never heard open. But I was aware of the presence of the lustful valet even before he said 'I have something for you, sir ...'. With virgin-like caution I extended my hand to his and he dropped two small bars of soap into it as if they were ripe grapes.

Sunday, March 30th

No work – for the first time in many weeks. The weather back in London is crisp, with high white clouds and breaks of sunshine – and the city looks a lot less grey than Paris.

William and I go for a lunch picnic in St James's Park and walk up the traffic-free Mall. Gentle Sunday strolling in the heart of the city. We eat our lunch on the deckchairs, then improvise a quick game of cricket. Afterwards we drive on to the London Dungeon – William is doing the plague at school, so this *can* be called an educational visit.

This evening Helen – who has bought a £150 dress for the occasion! – and I dine out at Leith's with Denis and Inge [Denis's wife], Terry G, Maggie, George H and Sean Connery – our latest casting coup for *Time Bandits*. Connery is as he seems on screen – big, physically powerful, humorous, relaxed and very attentive to women. He talks with the unaffected ease of a man who is used to having an audience. His main love is clearly golf, but he has some good and sensible suggestions to make on his part as King Agamemnon.

Thursday, April 3rd

Arrive at JC's by ten.

Some progress, but nothing sweeps the gathering off its feet. JC reaches a peak of frustration. 'Nine weeks of writing,' he practically sobs in anguish, 'and we haven't got a *film*.'

But we make lists and from the best elements – mainly 'Kashmir' – I suggest that we play six members of a family – a sort of Python saga, set in the *Ripping Yarns* period of 1900–1930. The idea of telling the story of a family seems to appeal and quite suddenly unblocks the sticky cul-de-sac we appeared to have written ourselves into. It suits me, a *Yarns* film with all the team in it – something I've often been attracted to.

So, quite unexpectedly, the day turns around. At the eleventh hour we have a style, a subject and a framework for the new film.

Ride back with Eric, who becomes very angry when I tell him that John Cleese is doing something in the TG film. He feels this is a plot on Denis's part to make TG's into a new Python film. Eric seems to be able to take *Ripping Yarns* and *Fawlty Towers*, but Gilliam's extra-Python work he has no tolerance for, feeling that it just copies Python and isn't original.

A half-hour phone call with a researcher from the *Dick Cavett Show*, who's doing a pre-interview interview. He says he thought my remark about showbiz being 'a branch of American patriotism' was brilliant, but I can never remember saying it.

Friday, April 4th: Good Friday

The sheer pleasure of having a morning to myself – even though I have to spend it reading the *Time Bandits* latest revised script – is incredibly healing to my creaking system. Clear the desk, write the diary, pull down the blinds against the strong sunlight, brew up strong coffee, and settle down to reading.

To my relief, the *Time Bandits*, as of April 4th, is not in bad shape at all, and most of last week's rapid rewrites, though in many cases the result of writer's cowardice, do seem to improve the shape and pace of the story. So by the time I've completed a thorough read-through I'm feeling very positive.

Up to T Gilliam's to discuss with him. Find him in a house of illness. Amy puffy with mumps, Maggie, newly pregnant, looking very tired, and TG crumpled and dressing-gowned. His temperature returned to 101 last night and he was thrown into a sweating turmoil after a phone call from Denis O'B in Los Angeles. TG thinks he has 'brain fever'.

We talk through for four hours. And by the end I'm exhausted by the effort of keeping concentration and a sense of proportion and not succumbing to Gilliam's periodic moments of eyeball-widening realisation ... 'We only have seven *weeks* ... ' 'I haven't even ... ', etc, etc.

Look forward with glorious anticipation of relief relaxation to my two days off in Southwold this weekend with Rachel.

Sunday, April 6th: Southwold, Easter Sunday

Slept a welcome eight hours. Woken by chirpy Rachel at eight and up and eating croissants on Easter morning by 8.30.

Brian appears to have had some effect on Granny – she confessed that she didn't go to church on Good Friday . . . 'Thinking of you and your film, I just couldn't.' Has it shaken her faith constructively or destructively? She *did* say she couldn't take Pontius Pilate seriously any more!

Tuesday, April 8th

Drive over to Eric's for a Python meeting about the next album, which we have to deliver under the terms of our Arista/Charisma contract.

Eric suggests we call the album 'Monty Python's Legal Obligation Album' and I suggest that we have it introduced by some legal man explaining why we have to deliver it and the penalties if we don't. This replaces the tentative 'Scratch and Sniff' title.

So we are all going back to our notebooks to cull material and have it typed up, and we reassemble on my 37th birthday to record.

Thursday, April 17th

Gilliam has had positive chats with Jonathan Pryce to play the Evil Genius. Pryce is apparently tremendous in *Hamlet* at the Royal Court and if we get him I think it will add to the extraordinarily confusing richness of the cast.

Bike up to Belsize Park then spend an hour sorting out mounds of unanswered fan mail (well, about 40 letters!) to give to the Python office to dispose of. This is quite a milestone as up till now I've always replied myself – even short, scruffy notes – but such is the amount of work behind and before me that I really can't manage the time any more.

Tuesday, April 22nd

A fine drizzle as I cycle round to Mr Owen the Feet at a quarter to nine. Start of Rachel's second term at Gospel Oak today and she doesn't show any sign of nerves.

Mr Owen talks for 40 minutes and cuts away at my corn for five. 'I would have been a professional violinist if it hadn't been for the war . . . '. A cat wanders through the surgery.

Thursday, April 24th

Jonathan Pryce cannot do *Time Bandits* – he's holding out for a part in the new Steven Spielberg – so we discuss alternatives. David Warner top of the list. Denis O'B still wreaking awful havoc with TG's peace of mind. Airily suggesting we try to get [Peter] Sellers to play the Supreme Being. TG sounds tired and heavily pressured.

Friday, April 25th

Train to Manchester. Although I spend most of the journey bent over my books, I can't help overhearing that there has been some sort of US raid on Iran during the night. About one man in the whole restaurant car seems to have heard the early morning news – and says that the Americans launched an Entebbe-style commando attack in Iran which ended with two US aircraft smashing into each other in the dark and killing eight men.

It really does sound like a most perilous affair and makes me aware of that where-I-was-when-I-heard-the-news sort of feeling – here I am speeding towards Manchester on the day the war broke out!

Arrive at twenty to twelve. Met by Roger Laughton, Ken Stephinson's boss at BBC Features.[1] He's a chattery, eloquent, rather macho head of department, who went to Birkdale School, supports Sheffield Wednesday and also went briefly to the same Crusader class[2] as myself! 'Then why weren't we best friends?' he asked, jokingly but quite significantly.

He drives me out of Manchester to Ken's quite extraordinary converted station cottage at Saddleworth. Extraordinary, not just because expresses thunder past not ten feet from his windows, but because the stretch of railway line is magnificent – coming from the south over Saddleworth Viaduct then curving in an impressive long bend to disappear then reappear in the shadow of massive slabs of moorland.

Marjorie cooks us a very tasty, delicate meal, which we eat in the Ladies' Waiting Room, whilst listening solemnly to President Carter's live message to the US people at one o'clock our time, seven o'clock a.m. their

1 Ken Stephinson, BBC Manchester producer who recruited me to present an episode of *Great Railway Journeys*.
2 The Crusaders' Union was an evangelical Bible Class for boys and girls.

time – describing, quite straightforwardly, his own personal responsibility for the immense cock-up.

Monday, April 28th

At Park Square West to meet Ron Devillier,[1] who is on his way back to the US after a TV sales fair in France. Ron is anxious to market the Python TV shows in the US and, in view of his pioneering work in awakening the US to MPFC [*Monty Python's Flying Circus*], we listen to him with interest.

Cleese, who had not met Ron before, clearly warmed to him and at the end of an hour's discussion (Ron emphasising the extraordinary audience ratings which Python still picks up whenever it's shown in the US), John proposed that we should meet in a week's time, when all of us reassemble for the recording of *Python's Contractual Obligation Album*, and we should agree to approach Ron formally and ask him to set out his terms for distributing Python tapes.

Denis is quite actively pursuing a company called Telepictures Inc, who he hopes can be persuaded to handle *all* Python product (in and out of the series).

Again the big business approach of Denis confronts and seems to conflict with the decentralised Python plans, which are born of mistrust of big American companies and trust in individuals whom we like instead. I foresee the Telepictures v Ron Devillier situation becoming a head-on battle between Denis's 'philosophy' and our own.

Tuesday, April 29th

As I drive from Wardour Street up to TG's I'm quite forcibly struck by the inadequacy of the title *Time Bandits*. It just won't create much of a stir on the hoardings, marquees and billboards. My favourite new title is 'Terry Gilliam's Greed'.

---

1 Ron Devillier ran Dallas Public Broadcasting station, the first place in America to show a series of Monty Python uncut and in its entirety, back in 1972.

Saturday, May 3rd

The post brings a very cheering letter from the headmaster of William Ellis to say that Tom has a place at the school from next September. So do most of his best friends, so this is good news indeed, especially as Willy will now automatically be offered a sibling's place.

As a reward I take Tom out for lunch and a trip to the South Ken museums. But the reward turns into quite an effort – for I take Louise and Helen [Guedalla], Rachel and Willy as well as Tom.

Buy the children McDonald's fast food, then drive on down to the Geology Museum. Have to detour as Kensington Gore is cordoned off because of the Iranian Embassy siege at Prince's Gate. Now in its fourth day – and deadlines and threats have passed. There is massive police presence, but a remarkable calm now as the siege becomes a London institution.

Rachel and Helen haul me round the various exhibits and we in fact visit three museums. My mind is a mass of surrealist images from a score of exhibition stands and I am quite exhausted by the time we get home at six.

Wednesday, May 7th

After a poor night's sleep, up in good time and down to Euston by 9.30. Myself and the film crew catch the 9.55 to Manchester. I'm supposed to be an ordinary traveller in an ordinary second-class coach, but will viewers think it entirely coincidental that the only other occupants of the 9.55 today seem to be Orthodox Rabbis?

Monday, May 12th: Grosmont, North Yorkshire

We drive over to Grosmont to interview Kim Mallion about restoring railway engines. It's a strange process trying to appear natural whilst having to do unnatural things like stand in an unusual relationship in order to keep the interviewee's face to camera, having to cut him off in mid-sentence because we have to move casually to another pre-set position and at the same time trying to mentally edit his remarks and your questions, knowing that this whole encounter will probably take up no more than one minute's film. I began to realise why TV interviewers and presenters develop their aggressive pushiness. They're doing their job. Well, I'm glad I'm in comedy.

Tuesday, May 13th: Grosmont

Woke at four to the silence of the countryside.

For a moment or two, lying there in the pre-dawn in the isolation of this tiny North Yorkshire village, I was seized with a crisis of confidence. What I was doing all seemed so unreal. I am not a documentary presenter – I have no special knowledge or authority to talk about railways, or even a special skill in getting people to talk. I have been chosen mainly because of what I have done in the past, which has made me into a reasonably well-known TV figure, but more precisely I've been chosen because Ken senses in my personality something which the viewer will like and identify with.

So there I am, lying, listening to a cuckoo which has just started up in a nearby wood as the grey gives way to the gold creeping light of another hot day, trying to bring into sharp and positive focus this ephemeral 'personality' of mine, which is my chief qualification for this job. How I wish I were dealing in something much more finite – like the skill of an engine driver or a cameraman. Something which you can see, feel, touch, switch on and off. But no, for an hour on national TV I am to be everyone's friend – the traveller that millions are happy to travel with.

Up at a quarter to eight, resolved to treat my predicament in the classic existentialist way – not to worry, just to do. The weather is perfect for our idyllic shots of Egton Station and the Esk Valley Line. I lie in the grass by the track reading Paul Theroux's terrible adventures in La Paz [in *The Old Patagonian Express*] and thinking myself in paradise here, with the hot sun shining from a cloudless sky and wind in the thin line of pines above my head.

Wednesday, May 14th: Teesside

Interviewed a man who knew some details of Stockton-Darlington, the world's first public passenger railway. Only after the interview do I find out that his son had been crushed to death six weeks before owing to the negligence of the nearby factory where he was an apprentice. It would have been his 18th birthday today, the man told me – on the verge of tears. He'd had a lot of personal problems – the break-up of a marriage, etc – and this was the last straw. He apologised for not being able to remember all the details for me, but the doctors had put him on a drug after his nervous breakdown and it left him irritatingly cloudy on memories, he said. He'd half-built a model train. Just an ordinary bloke.

Thursday, May 15th: Newcastle

On to the 125 at Darlington and various shots of The Traveller looking around him. I've long since run out of delightfully informal, spontaneous and casual gestures and am now concentrating on trying not to appear too idiotically interested every time I look out of the window.

My rosy-spectacled view of Newcastle provoked a nice comment from a local. I was raving about the wonderful easiness of the Cumberland pub in the working-class district of the Byker and someone quipped, 'Oh, yes, the Cumberland. They say there's one bar full of locals and one bar full of playgroup leaders.'

Friday, May 16th: Newcastle–Edinburgh

Wake to sunshine and clear skies and the chorus of squeaks, rumbles and soft hissing of diesel exhausts from the station below. Outside a panorama of cars and trains crossing bridges. Tyneside coming to work.

We board an HST for Edinburgh which is half an hour late. I haven't been on a single punctual train this week.

Between Berwick and Edinburgh, as the train staggers home with an out-of-action rear power car (what a bad day for this to happen to British Rail), I sit with three randomly selected 'members of the public' and we're filmed chatting. Maybe the age of television is conditioning us all, but they speak with the easy assurance of people who are interviewed daily.

My last memories of elegant Edinburgh, as serenely unflawed in its beauty as ever, are of a group of very drunken chartered surveyors milling around in the lounge of the North British at midnight, tipping each other in and out of a wheelchair. If they'd been punks they'd have been out in the gutter, but they were Chartered Surveyors of this Fine City and were in dinner jackets and had paid well for their tickets, so no-one stopped them behaving like the worst sort of hooligans. My last image was of them falling on top of each other and knocking back Napoleon brandy from the bottle.

Saturday, May 17th: Kyle of Lochalsh

Up and across the Central Highlands – shot of me reading, etc. On time at Inverness's crabbed and disappointing little station. Inverness full of yobbos, drunks and ladies with twinsets and pearls doing their Saturday shopping. We have time off. I make for the castle, but in front of it are three fairly incapable teenage Scots. One turns and spits long and high into the air. To my astonished horror another runs forward, tries to catch the gob in his own mouth and fails.

The other thing that I notice in Inverness this sunny Saturday afternoon are the number of churches. Severe, pencil-thin towers – the grey pointed fingers of disapproval. Enough to drive you to drink.

So begins the memorable nightmare of the journey to Kyle. The train has an observation car on the end, a special old coach with free-standing armchairs and tables.

Ken's idea is to fill the special coach with travellers whom I casually chat to, plus one or two specially researched guests. One of whom is a Mrs Mackenzie, a 99-year-old who I'm told remembers the railway on the day it opened in 1896. She's a wonderful, bright old lady, but not soft of hearing, and my first question – a tortuously-phrased effort to elicit information as to how old she was – is received with a stony silence. A pleasant smile, but a stony silence. I try it again, then again even louder. The crew and the rest of the compartment must be either splitting their sides or squirming in embarrassment.

For a full ten minutes I persevere, trying everything, but, like a man with an enormous fishing net and six harpoons trying to catch two small fish, I end up with very little for a lot of work. It leaves me exhausted, though still in admiration of old Mrs Mackenzie.

Tuesday, May 20th: Mallaig

At 10.30 I'm filmed boarding the Skye ferry to Kyleakin. The cameras are staying on the mainland to film exteriors from the Kyle train. I'm free until after lunch and, as I have no option but to go on to Skye, I decide on a morning's walking to compensate for much eating and drinking over the last few days.

I stride on out of town, having left my case at the Caledonian MacBrayne [ferry] office. I stop at a hotel which is a country house – red-grey stone and tall pitched roofs – set in very lush gardens with brilliantly deep pink rhododendrons and a settled air of detachment and solid comfort.

But as soon as I step inside my stomach tightens with the identification of a very early feeling of my childhood of a claustrophobia, a fear of being stifled in dark rooms with well-polished doors, in which old ladies move in the shadows.

Mallaig, which we reach in the evening, is even bleaker than Kyle of Lochalsh, a fairly wretched spot to be faced with the prospect of a night in – after a day like today. But I have a room overlooking the Atlantic and the sharp points of Rum and the volcanic spur of Eigg and there is a sunset after all and it looks quite idyllic with a score of fishing boats heading for the harbour.

After the ritual of an evening meal together ('Are the "Melon Cubes" out of a tin?' one of our number enquires ingenuously. 'Oh, *yes . . .*' the waitress assures him quickly), Ken and I go to visit the engine driver whom we will be filming tomorrow, as his wife has called and asked us over.

They're rather a special family – with three children roughly the age of my own, and yet Ronnie McClellan must be over 20 years older then me. He married late to a very bright and articulate district nurse. Their children come down in dressing gowns to meet us (it's 9.45) and shake hands solemnly and politely. They don't have television, but they have dogs, cats and, I think, some animals in the croft. The children kiss their father obediently but warmly. I should imagine he's quite a strict and traditional father.

Back at the empty vastness of the West Highland, the two men who were drinking half and halfs (Scotch and Heavy) at six o'clock are still drinking half and halfs at twelve. Ken beats me three times at pool. Go to bed feeling inadequate.

Nylon sheets and a colour scheme which looks as though an animal's been slaughtered in the room. Read Michael Arlen's *The Green Hat* and enjoy the utter incongruity. It gives me great comfort to know that Cannes and Mallaig exist on the same planet.

Wednesday, May 21st: Mallaig–Glenfinnan

Fresh Mallaig kippers for breakfast. Later I'm told that there's no such thing as a Mallaig kipper as there's a ban on herring fishing. So it was probably a Canadian herring – which may have been kippered in Mallaig. Anyway, I ate two of them.

An especially beautiful journey down along the coast – made more civilised by the presence of a buffet bar and a couple of glasses of wine. I have to be filmed in the said buffet bar with two Danish students and a flavour chemist from Chicago who is over here on a cycling tour of Scotland. He's a great Python fan and he's honestly called Constantine Apostle.

Our hotel here – the Glenfinnan House – is situated in an almost unbeatable Highland surrounding. Pictures of Bonnie Prince Charlie's heroic failures (it was here at Glenfinnan he gathered his forces in the summer of 1745), a set of bagpipes, pieces of igneous rocks on a dark-stained mantelpiece in a passable imitation of a baronial hall.

The house is set beside a lawn surrounded by broadleaved trees and running down to Loch Shiel. Beside a wooden jetty, a couple of rowing boats bob on the water. Walk down to the jetty and look down the length of Loch Shiel, at the sheer magnificence of the spurs of epic mountainside tumbling down to the lakeside.

As we unload, a cool-looking kid of ten or eleven skids up on his bike. 'Do you live here?' I ask ... The boy, in a particularly businesslike way, nods and adds, quite naturally, 'D'you think I'm lucky?'

To bed around midnight. It seems almost a crime to close the curtains against such a view.

Monday, May 26th

A Bank Holiday again. Surfaced mid-morning. Regular phone calls and door bells ringing – mostly for the children, who have the next week off school. There was lots I wanted to do and a big pile of mail. Most of all I wanted to do nothing – to be at no-one's beck and call for a bit.

Terry Gilliam comes round soon after six. The first week of *Time Bandits* is now complete, but the shoot in Morocco was gruelling even by TG's standards. Moroccans less good at organisation than Tunisians, which didn't help, but they managed 97 slates – some in locations only accessible by mule.

After one week in Morocco he'd come back feeling like he did after ten weeks of *Brian*. Rushes on Wednesday will show whether this almighty opening effort will spur everyone on, or be the start of the collapse.

Thursday, May 29th

A heavy day ahead. The sky is grey and lowering, but still no rain. Prepare for the arrival of the BBC unit to film outside and inside the house. Also today we're expecting Al and Claudie[1] to stay, so No. 2 has to be prepared.

As it turns out we have a most successful shoot. We block off Julia Street with a 60-foot hoist to shoot an epic 'leaving home' scene. Helen and the three children all have to do their acting bit and acquit themselves very well on all four takes. Really it's an elaborate reconstruction for the viewing public of what happens every time I leave home for filming away. Rachel, last out, hands me my toothbrush with an easy self-confidence which I hadn't expected at all.

Friday, May 30th

Helen goes out to badminton and Al, Claudie and I make a rambling feast out of quite a simple selection of soup and cold meats, ending with a liqueur tasting – Al determined to try all the bottles he brought over from Brittany. Their Jacques Brel tape played loudly – Al enthusing, as only he can, over each track. 'One of the greatest people of this century' is Al's verdict on Brel.

Claudie comes to life more when the subject turns to France, but her English is now much more confident. But I wish she would eat more and smoke less. Al wants to have a baby – they want a girl and they have a name, 'Chantelle'.

A warm and woozy evening. Much laughter.

Tuesday, June 3rd

Listen to the Python *Contractual Obligation Album*. I'm afraid it does sound rather ordinary. One or two of the songs stand out and there are some conventional sketches of Cleese and Chapman's (man enters shop, etc) which are saved by good performances. Twenty-five percent padding, fifty percent quite acceptable, twenty-five percent good new Python.

---

1 Al Levinson, an American I'd met in the seventies, and some of whose writing I'd published. His second marriage was to Claudie, a young Bretonne.

Saturday, June 7th

Drive up to T Gilliam's for a meeting. Terry is very deflated. He looks and sounds quite pummelled by the pressures of this creature he's brought into life. Filming all week, meetings with actors in the evening, all weekend looking at locations.

Now Amy wants his attention and he wants to give me his attention. So we work on rewrites and additions for next week whilst Amy piles me up with teddy bears and races round the room with a manic energy, shouting, tumbling, grimacing. The only way we can work is by me reading the script corrections as a story to one of Amy's teddies. A bizarre session.

Monday, June 9th

Work and run in the morning. Talk to a fan from Indiana on the telephone at lunchtime – she was visiting England, had seen *Grail* 17 times and *Brian* nine times and loved everything we did.

To Denis's office at two. Meet Peter Cook there. He has a very silly hat, but we have a few laughs, mainly about a pop group Peter had seen in Los Angeles called Bees Attack Victor Mature. Peter rambles on a while, then wanders off – a little concerned as to how he'll find his way out of the EuroAtlantic fortress. Denis has just done a deal for GC's *Yellowbeard* screenplay, provided that the screenplay is rewritten. So Peter Cook, whom Denis was much impressed by at Amnesty, is to rewrite the script with GC – and they have a six-million-dollar production budget. Denis does want to see us all happy.

What Denis doesn't know is that E. Idle has probably slipped the O'Brien net. A very positive letter from him in France – the 'Pirates of Penzance' now looks more likely to happen. Gary Weiss [Eric's director] is a very 'hot' property and he wants to do it. Eric now has a direct phone line in Cotignac, but asks me to promise not to give it to Denis, under threat of setting fire to my stereo.

I leave, having told Denis that the next thing I want to do is a film on my own – probably to shoot next summer.

Watch last hour of the Test Match v West Indies on the box, then Helen and I, suitably tarted up in DJs and long dresses, drive down to Kensington for the reception at the Royal Geographical Society to commemorate their founding 150 years ago.

The Queen and Prince Philip and the Duke of Kent are to be there. We've joked about going and not going, but tell Helen it's my duty as a diarist if nothing else.

Sir John and Lady Hunt are receiving the guests. He's quite frail now and totally white-haired. Lady Hunt seems very bright and on the ball.

I meet the daughter of Lord Curzon, on whose land the RGS HQ was built, and the sparkling wine with strawberries in it is going to my head quite pleasantly when we are asked to move away from the gravel terrace. Quite amiably, but firmly. Around us some people are being lined up as if for some military manoeuvre – not in a long line, but in a number of short ranks, like football teams.

Helen and I are enmeshed with a world authority on gibbons, who also happens to be an enormous *Ripping Yarns* fan and slightly more pissed than we are.

The Duke was, at one point, just beside my right shoulder and sounded to be having quite a jolly time, but entourages always deter chance encounters, so I didn't spring forward. About 10.30 he and Queenie disappeared inside.

Helen and I, quite mellow, but hungry, left about 15 minutes later, but, as we prepared to cross Kensington Gore, there was a shout from a policeman who was standing only 100 yards away from the SAS siege building – 'Stay in the middle!'[1] We froze on the traffic island in the middle of Kensington Gore and realised that the Queen had not yet left.

In fact at this moment her Daimler, with the swollen rear windows for better visibility, was sweeping away from the RGS. The light was on inside so the Queen and the Duke could be seen, and for a moment in time we on our little traffic island and the Head of the British Empire came into eyeball to eyeball contact. Helen waved. The Queen automatically waved back, the Duke grinned and the black limousine curved left and right into Hyde Park and was gone.

Thursday, June 12th: London–Llanwern

To Paddington to catch the 1.15 to Newport. There is a long wait, blamed first on signal failure, then, with what sounded like a stroke of inspiration

---

1 Just over a month earlier the SAS had spectacularly stormed the Iranian Embassy in Prince's Gate, ending a five-day siege by Iranian separatists. Five of the gunmen and one hostage were killed.

from a tired guard, on a bomb scare. But it enables me to complete the 'Robin Hood' rewrites, losing the 'Future' sequence.

Finally arrive at the Gateway Hotel, Llanwern, at about four o'clock. Various members of *Time Bandits* crew are surfacing after the second of their week of night shoots at nearby Raglan Castle. Last night a lady on stilts 'lost her bottle', as Ian Holm put it, but the crew seem to be in good spirits.

TG and I discuss the rewrites. Then I go to my room and watch some of the England v Belgium match – some promising football and one of the great international goals by Wilkins, then fighting on the terraces and the Italian police react fiercely with riot police and tear gas.

TG's fictional recreation of the sack of Castiglione is not unlike the actual scenes I've just witnessed on the terraces in Turin. Both take place in North Italy and in each smoke is drifting everywhere and bodies are falling. But TG's pictures are much more impressive and I'm tantalised by the brief amount I've seen of this strange film that is slowly and painstakingly taking shape in the rain at a nearby castle.

Tuesday, June 24th

Midsummer's Day. And, as it turns out, the first day in the last three weeks when it hasn't rained on the *Time Bandits*.

Out in the mosquito-ridden beauty of the Epping Forest, with the pollarded trees striking wonderfully Gilliamesque poses, with lumps and gnarls and strange growths, Shelley [Duvall who's playing Pansy, one of the star-crossed lovers] and I and the mammoth unit enjoy a dry day. Not 20 miles away, there were fierce storms with hailstones scattering the players at Wimbledon and Lord's.

Wednesday, June 25th

After more shots with the dwarves passing us, Shelley and I get on to the rain sequences. I can't complain. I wrote the dreaded word 'rain', and here it is in all its dispiriting glory, courtesy of the Essex Fire Brigade. Not a terribly good take and the next 40 minutes are spent under a hair-dryer, preparing my wig for a re-take. But then it's lunch and I have to go to the pub with a plastic bag over my head.

Afterwards a fairly horrendous experience in the second rain scene, when Shelley and I are down to our mediaeval underwear. The elements of the developing shot are so various that it takes six takes before we have a satisfactory conclusion. And on each one we have hoses directed on us for about a minute and a half.

Shelley seems much more tolerant of the ordeal than any actress has a right to be. But, as she says in the car on the way home, it's better than having to cry every day for seven months with Kubrick! Nicholson had to take a six-month break after the movie [*The Shining*] was finished to get himself straight again.

Thursday, June 26th

Drive to Pentonville Road, where, on the hill from which the great Victorian painting of St Pancras was made, I find myself in the BUPA medical centre for a screening. No particular reason, I just thought I should have a complete medical check-up and where better than under the personal eye of one of the BUPA centre's leading lights – Alan Bailey.[1]

Alan reassures me on one point: that Parkinson's Disease isn't hereditary. Then he examines me, pokes, prods and fingers my genitals, after which we have a talk about houses, education, the possible break-up of ILEA [Inner London Education Authority], and he offers me a drink from his metal cupboard full of Scotch and other drugs. I have a beer and meet the doctor who is, as Alan cheerfully informs me, 'in charge of the clap clinic here'.

The clap man is neat, less of a character, and we talk about beta-blockers – pills which reduce the heartbeat. He thinks them a quite brilliant advance, and yet could talk only of the dangers of their misuse.

Alan is quite keen to show off the body scanner in the basement and the instant computer details of each patient. So far, all the results of my tests show no danger areas. I'm four pounds lighter than I was when I came seven years ago at eleven stone seven, and I'm five foot eleven inches – which is news to me and means I'm officially taller than I thought I was! Sight and hearing are 100% apart from one frequency of hearing – that of telephone bells and gunshots!

---

1 Alan was one of Graham Chapman's closest friends. They had met as medical students at Bart's Hospital.

Monday, June 30th

I have something of a record in the make-up line today – four layers – my own tightly-cropped hair, a bald bladder on top of that, a wig stuck onto the sides of that and, to top the lot, a toupee. The make-up takes a couple of hours, but Elaine [Carew, my make-up artist] and I now get on so well that I hardly notice the time passing. I can't blame anyone but myself for any inconvenience either, as I wrote it.

Katherine Helmond, of *Soap* fame, who is Ruth Gordon's replacement, is on the set for fittings, etc, together with Peter Vaughan, who plays her Ogre husband. She's delightful, Vaughan strong and quite quiet with his foxy little eyes and mouth easily cracking into a smile.

Shelley and I work all day on an impressive set of the 'Titanic'. Final shot is uncomfortable and involves me losing my toupee and causing a lot of damage. They like it on the third take and we wrap at 7.30.

Tuesday, July 1st

A stormy night as a depression, pushed by cold north winds, crosses over us. The blind flaps and bangs and it's as cold as November. Up at seven and drive through the rain to the studios [at Wembley] by eight.

Into mediaeval outfit this time. A steady morning's work on the coach interiors (Shelley and I sitting in a coach resting on inner tubes of lorry tyres – four men waving trees above our heads).

In the afternoon, as we prepare to shoot the dwarves dropping on Pansy [one of the two star-crossed lovers, played by Shelley] and myself, the director hurtles through the air towards us, strikes Shelley sharply on the left temple and knocks her almost senseless. Gilliam spends the next half-hour comforting a very shaken Shelley. Turns out he was demonstrating to one of the dwarves how safe it was to fall.

I work in my dressing room, waiting for the final call. Rain and wind outside. Quite cosy. Stodgy food and assistant director constantly coming round to ask if there's anything I want. Stardom means eating too much. After eight, Neville Thompson, the associate producer, arrives in my 'suite' to tell me that they will not be getting around to Shelley and myself this evening. The shot has been cancelled, as this was Shelley's last day on the picture.

Wednesday, July 2nd

To Park Square West by ten for a Python meeting. Eric is already there, playing the piano. I've no idea how today's meeting is going to turn out – all I know is that John has told Terry G that he's never felt less like writing Python and yet officially we have this month set aside for just such an enterprise ...

Terry J arrives next, looking mournful – with reason, for he has his arm in a sling. Apparently he threw himself on the ground at a charity cricket match last Sunday and has a hairline fracture of a bone called the humerus.

John arrives – he's growing his Shakespearian beard back again, I think. He claims it went down very well with the ladies and shaving it off (which he did for the *Time Bandits*) only revealed what a tiny mouth he has. I advise John to have his mouth widened. He says he is considering another hair transplant.

We talk briefly about Python's general biz. Denis's call for a business meeting and a meeting to discuss his exciting new proposals for a distribution network of our own are met with almost universal lack of interest. 'Tell him we went off to sleep,' John advises Anne when she is desperately asking what reaction she should relay to DO'B about his proposals.

Then to lunch at Odin's. Cliff Richard at the next table looks permanently off the beach at Barbados. Apart from Eric, the Pythons are white, apart from TJ who's grey. After a long wait, and some white wine, I lead off perhaps provocatively by asking who wants to write the new Python film this month. Then it all comes out.

JC wants a month of leisurely talk and discussion and does not want to face the 'slog' of nine-to-five writing. I suggest that we don't yet have a very clear and positive area or identity for the subject matter of the film and that we should only write when we are really 'hungry' to write. But it's Graham who quite blandly drops the real bombshell – he's working for the next few days on a *Yellowbeard* rewrite and then he hopes to film it in Australia during the winter. This straight pinch from previously discussed Python plans is a real stunner and the well-controlled indignation of Eric and Terry J rises to the surface.

I have the increasing feeling that we are going through a period similar to the post-*Grail* days in '75, '76, when individual Pythons want to stretch their legs. Terry G led the field with *Time Bandits*, I've done the *Yarns* and the 'Railway' documentary. So I'm not too worried about proving myself.

I don't know about Eric, but he was clearly amazed when John suggested we didn't meet together till next Wednesday. At Eric's surprise JC dropped all pretences – he hung his head in his hands and became cross. 'I'm tired ... I've done six weeks of ... ' and so on.

This lunch and the discussions were all part of the painful process of preserving Python. We don't fit into any easy patterns, we ask each other to make enormous compromises, adjustments and U-turns, but we do produce the best comedy in the country.

Not much rest at home, for at 6.30 I'm collected by Graham in his Mercedes and we drive one and a half hours out to Associated Book Publishers in Andover for a sales-force-meet-authors binge. It all seems quite a tiresome waste of time, except that Christopher Isherwood is there, which saves the evening for me. He's 76 and looks fit and neat. His skin is weathered like an elephant's leg, in contrast to the softer, tanned brown of his friend Don Bachardy. Bachardy has bright eyes and looks terribly healthy. He's almost a carbon copy of Isherwood. Isherwood talks to Graham about a supermarket they both share in Brentwood, Los Angeles.

Isherwood talks fluently – like a man used to talking and being listened to (GC tells me his voice has become quite 'stentorian' since doing lecture tours). I would love to spend more time with him and Don – they seem such a bright, lively pair in this drab and colourless sales conference world.

Wednesday, July 9th

To Gospel Oak School for the Infant Concert. Rachel is a sheep. She wears her clean, Persil-white T-shirt and petticoat and a cardboard mask which makes it difficult for her to see, and the sheep bang into each other. Rachel's class less imaginative than the others, but her rather morose teacher did wear black fishnet tights.

Monday, July 14th

Hurry through the rain to 2 Park Square West and a Python meeting. Eric and Denis are already there. I'm wearing a 'Leica' disposable jacket and hood which I acquired [whilst filming] at the Rainhill Trials at the end of May. Eric says I look like a red sperm.

All Pythons present except, of course, Gilliam. Denis has greatly looked forward to this meeting, for this is the first time he has aired his latest proposal to the group as a whole. The proposal is that Python should become involved in the setting-up of an independent UK film distribution company – HandMade Films.

Denis rides all interruptions as he slowly and impressively reveals his plans. But he is not a good judge of people – and of English people especially – and instead of being received with wide-eyed gratitude, his proposals are subjected to a barrage of strong scepticism.

Eric wants to know how much it all will cost us and then queries whether or not we need it, as it will mean yet another source of interminable business meetings. John C queries Denis's assumption that there will be eight 'Python-based' films at least in the next five years. He certainly isn't going to do one, and neither is Eric. Also the assumption that *Time Bandits* and *Yellowbeard* will each make at least £650,000 in the UK is received without conviction.

Denis's worst enemy is his own ingenuous enthusiasm in the face of five very complex, quite sophisticated minds, four at least of which distrust one thing more than anything else – uncritical enthusiasm. So it's left undecided.

Denis rather rapidly runs through the rest of the agenda, but he's lost us. The more he enthuses over terms, deals, percentages, controls, etc, the more John turns his mind to doing anagrams on his agenda (he had a good one for Michael Palin – i.e. Phallic Man).

To lunch at Odin's. Terry suggests the group should spend three days in Cherbourg, writing. John thinks we should do a film about the Iliad. Denis looks bewildered.

Wednesday, July 16th

Children are prepared for school – with the right clothes, shoes, music, forms for teachers, etc. At ten to nine Sam Jarvis arrives to work on painting the outside of the house and settles first of all for his cup of tea. Letters are sorted, diaries written and banks visited on the way to Cleese's for a Python session.

Only John is there at the appointed time. He's thumbing through his address book for someone to take to dinner … 'Come on, Michael, you must know some ravishing creature … ' and so on. He grins happily when I half-jest about the demise of Python. Eric is still unwell, TG's off

... 'I think we should disband this rapidly-crumbling comedy group for at least a year.' John grins ...

At seven leave for Tom's orchestral concert at Gospel Oak. Tom plays a clarinet solo, piano solo and a duet with Holly [Jones] and is one of the two or three stars of the show. I feel very proud, especially as his clarinet piece is quite difficult. Both Helen and I dreadfully nervous in the audience.

Sunday, July 20th

After breakfast and Sunday papers, I retire to workroom (most reluctantly) to prepare for tonight's Save the Whales concert. Various tiresome little props and costume details to sort out, but Anne H is a great help and locates such things as Gumby glasses and the like. I write a new piece – a short monologue about Saving the Plankton.

I complete my plankton piece, gather props and cossies into a big suitcase and, in a state of numbed resignation, set off under grey skies for the Venue in Victoria. I forget Gumby flowers, vase and mallet and have to drive all the way back from Regent's Park.

The Venue is a cabaret-type theatre, with audience at tables eating and drinking, so they don't seem to mind us starting nearly an hour late. From then on I begin to enjoy it. All the lethargy of a Sunday disappears and is replaced by the sharpness of performing adrenaline. 'Plankton' goes especially well and is received all the better for being obviously specially-written material.

Second half the audience are in very good form. 'Save the leopards!' someone shouts as I come on in my leopard-skin coat as the spangly compère of 'Shouting'. I reassure the audience that it *is* artificial, whereupon the rejoinder comes smartly back 'Save the artificial leopards!'

Home with huge feeling of relief and satisfaction – 100% different from the way I felt on leaving seven hours ago. Am I a manic depressive?

Monday, July 21st

Anne rings early to say that Python has been offered four days at the Hollywood Bowl at the end of September. Two weeks in LA in late September, all together, would, I feel, do our writing chances and the group's general commitment to working together so much good that we should decide to go ahead with it as soon as possible.

Wednesday, July 23rd

TJ comes up after lunch. It's actually too hot to work upstairs at No. 4 – sticky, with bright, shining sun unremitting – so we decamp to No. 2, to the leaky double bedroom. TJ rather content here. Says it reminds him of Belsize Park![1] There complete 'Sperm Song'.

In the evening (we work on until 6.30), I ring John C to find him very disappointed with his writing progress. He claims not to have been really well since last Friday and says that he and GC have not written much and he doesn't like the family idea and could we not postpone the entire film for six months?

Thursday, July 24th

Blue skies and high summer again – the fine weather is persisting despite all forecasts. So a fresh buoyancy to my step as I come back from Mansfield Road with the papers – abruptly slowed down by the news that Peter Sellers died last night. Though not as sudden and unexpected as the news seen in a French paper on holiday in 1977 that 'Elvis est Mort!', it affected me in the same way. Sellers and Milligan were to the humour of my pre- and teenage days as Elvis was to the music.

Friday, July 25th

Duly arrive at J Cleese's at ten – bringing Eric. It's a hot day. John is upstairs recovering from taking Cynthia for an early-morning swim. We meet out in John's garden – this prospect of unbroken sunshine is so rare this last month that the sun-worshippers in the group (everyone except TJ) feel unable to ignore it.

JC proposes a moratorium on the film – period unspecified. This rather deflating proposal is perhaps made more acceptable by a general welcoming of the Hollywood Bowl show. This, after brief discussion, is received most constructively. It makes the film postponement seem less like a positive break, more of a long interruption of work in progress. We shall be together for two or three weeks in LA in late September, we will do four nights at the Bowl and it is agreed that it shall be videotaped for sale to US TV.

---

1 When Helen and I married in 1966 we lived in a flat at 82 Belsize Park Gardens.

Our 'break-through' writing of yesterday and the days before is not even read out. John seems happy to let things drift. There's a listless feeling. EI says July is a rotten month to write anything.

No-one has yet really decided how long this 'interruption' should be. Six months is the minimum and any attempt to compromise on this meets very strong objections from John. But six months merely means an almost impossibly short period for the resolution of any alternative plans, so a year is proposed. And reluctantly accepted, as if acknowledging a measure of defeat.

We shall meet again to write the movie in September 1981.

Wednesday, July 30th

Catch the 8.55 Euston–Manchester train to see the first assembly of my 'Great Railway Journey'.

At the BBC we watch the 62-minute first cut on a Steenbeck. My impression is of endless pretty railway trains disappearing behind trees – clichés of this sort of documentary. There is little evidence of my own impact on the journey ... but more disappointingly a very ordinary, flat feeling to the camerawork and strangely the editing as well.

It was a depressing viewing – depressing because I value Ken's friendship and the working relationship between us, depressing because I had hoped that his unconventional choice of presenter indicated his intention of trying some exciting and experimental approach to the programme. Depressing because I had to fight Denis O'B so hard to come up with something so dull. I think Ken is well aware of my feelings, and there is a conspicuous lack of over-enthusiasm.

So when I dash off to catch the Manchester Pullman back to town, I know I have a job of work on – much more than I expected to do at this stage of the programme, but there is hope and I have always in the back of my mind the memory of my first reaction to the initial cut of 'Roger of the Raj'.[1]

---

1 A *Ripping Yarn* which I at first thought hadn't worked at all, but has since become one of my favourites, not least for Richard Vernon and Joan Sanderson's wonderfully played dining room scenes.

Thursday, July 31st

To the foot man at 9.30. He's running very late. I sit in his little surgery in Mornington Road, with a nun and a sad, rather dim, shuffling old Irishman, and write my Python album notes.

Then to EuroAtlantic for what is supposed to be a couple of hours of business and a couple of hours of thought on the content of the stage show. It turns out to be four hours of business and hardly a thought for the content.

Once again Denis pushes us towards the Telepictures video deal and the distribution company. All of us weaken on Telepictures, apart from Eric, who maintains that we should not give video rights for seven years to a company we know nothing about. At one point Eric suggests directly to Denis that he is in some way an interested party on Telepictures' side. Denis denies this. Eric will not be moved, though, and vetoes the agreement until he's thought about it more.

Monday, August 18th

Meet Ken Stephinson for lunch and we have a very productive chat about the documentary. He feels as I do that it's bland and rather dull at the moment, but we hatch plans to revive, restore and enliven it. The only thing that worries me is that I calculate I have a maximum of 12 clear writing days before Hollywood.

Thursday, August 21st: Copenhagen and Malmö

Caught British Airways' 9.25 flight to Copenhagen [for *Life of Brian* publicity] with Terry J and Anne Bennett (of CIC, our distributors) from a marvellously uncrowded Heathrow.

We lost an hour in the air and landed at Copenhagen at 12.05. A Cadillac limousine (looking very out of place) swept us and our Danish hosts through the neat, clean streets of suburban Copenhagen, with row upon row of apartment blocks, but mainly of brick, with pitched roofs and in small units, usually angled to avoid a wilderness of long concrete vistas.

From this neat, clean, modest little capital we took a neat, clean hydrofoil across to Malmö in Sweden.

I hear from TJ (confirmed by Anne Bennett) that Python has not begun too well in Germany. Strong religious anti-reaction in Stuttgart –

elsewhere sluggish. So Brianity is perhaps not to be the new world religion after all.

As we leave Malmö for the University of Lund the wind has freshened. Not much impression of Sweden on the way. An extension of Lincolnshire perhaps.

About a quarter past eight we are introduced and go into a question and answer session. Most of the questions seem to come from Englishmen or Americans. Round about nine TJ is getting rather restless and asks the audience (numbering 300 or so) if he can ask *them* a question. Much eager nodding. 'How many of you want to go to the lavatory?' Our hosts take the hint and wind up the session. For some reason we sing them the 'Lumberjack Song' and that's it. Both of us quite tired by now.

We're driven to the Students' Union and eventually find ourselves in a small, circular room where a table is laid. We each have a glass of rather weak beer – they are not allowed to serve full-strength beer to students – and nothing is happening. Outside the wind is strong and gusting and rain is lashing the panes.

Finally a large plate of Swedish crayfish arrives. They've been marinaded in beer and dill (very popular in Sweden) and are quite tasty. Then bottles of aquavit, which are drunk to the accompaniment of rather hard drinking songs. A lady called Lotta Love, said to be Sweden's foremost groupie, also comes in from somewhere.

Terry J is strongly resisting Anne's and my attempts to get us all onto the last hydrofoil to Copenhagen. I know that we must get back. We have to start early tomorrow and the drinking – already producing a noisy and rather belligerent atmosphere – will only accelerate.

With great difficulty we get TJ up and mutter our apologies. We just manage to get downstairs and into our waiting limousine, which then drives like hell into Malmö. The wind buffets the car on the motorway, causing it to veer dangerously at high speed, but we *do* reach the quay in time and to my intense relief the hydrofoil is still running, despite the storm. We are in Denmark again by one.

Friday, August 22nd: Copenhagen

Terry is terribly thankful that we didn't let him stay in Malmö, and he goes off for a walk whilst I bathe, do my morning exercise and gently test my body and brain for any damage caused by Sweden yesterday.

Outside the life of Copenhagen goes on, very unhurried, like model life in a model village. Even the workmen are clean and I don't believe that they really have the work to do anyway. They must be Play People. Eventually decide that the men engaged in raising and replacing paving stones opposite the hotel are in fact now reduced to cleaning the underneath of the Copenhagen streets.

At about ten o'clock we start interviews in our room, followed by a press conference downstairs, after which we are to give a TV interview. A Danish actor is portraying a Norwegian. The Danes and Swedes both find the Norwegians a Scandinavian joke – slow-witted, thick-headed, humourless fishing folk – and they send them up unmercifully. The fact that Python's *Life of Brian* has been banned in Norway causes our hosts great glee and the Swedes have a poster tagging the film 'So Funny it was Banned in Norway'.

We are then taken to the Tivoli Gardens for lunch and more filming. By now my head is clear, but my stomach is distinctly off-balance. I drink mineral water, eat more ham and eggs, but find to my horror after lunch that we are to be interviewed on the Big Wheel. I'm now feeling very queasy and not at all far from the point of uncontainable nausea.

Here I am, quite likely to be sick even if I just stand still, being loaded onto a big wheel compartment opposite a grinning interviewer, a cameraman and a sound man. The wheel moves up, we hang over Copenhagen then swing down, round, up again, going faster. Only desperate laughter at my plight and Terry's touching concern and huge gulps of cool air as we swing up keep my stomach contents from being vividly reproduced on Danish television.

At last the living hell comes to an end and I'm quite proud to have survived. But the interviewer hasn't finished, he wants more. High over the city we go – I really can't answer any more. Even TJ is going groggy. 'Alright,' is all I can shout. 'I give up! I give up!' At the end of the torture I'm white and wobbling, something's churning away inside. At last I can pause . . . No I can't . . . We're led away to be photographed doing funny things with the Danish comedian.

Then into the limousine, to be driven, with the dubious aid of stomach-lurching power-assisted brakes, to Danish radio. At last our Danish hosts seem to have got the message that I'm unwell, so I'm escorted carefully from the limousine and the first request is a 'toiletten' for Mr Palin.

Monday, August 25th

Work on the 'Railway' programme – looking through the video cassette and running and re-running. I'm very much encouraged, and there is enough in there to give a high-quality look to the programme – now all we need is a cohesive element of typical Palin stuff. I need to inject into the documentary what I can do best – which is not, clearly, being a straight documentary presenter.

Go out for a pizza in Hampstead, full of Bank Holiday revellers. We talk over '*TB*'. Terry is as positive about it as I've heard him since May. Highly excited by the battle scenes at the end.

I feel much encouraged by today – both on '*GRJ*' and '*TB*'. At one time I was feeling that I have fallen between so many stools this year that I can only have done myself harm, but now it looks as though all the hard work and hassle may just have been worth it.

Monday, September 1st

School starts again – Rachel and Willy to Gospel Oak today, Tom to William Ellis tomorrow. Tom has tried on his blazer, matching shirt, dark trousers, dark shoes and hates them. I must say it's a little sad to see him suddenly restricted by a uniform. Some loss of innocence somewhere.

Before I start work I have to go through the unnerving and slightly distasteful business of giving myself an enema – to clear out my bowels in preparation for a visit to the botty doctor this afternoon.

After squeezing the phosphate mixture in, I realise I'm unsure what an enema is quite supposed to do. Should I retain the fluid for a certain time? I'm downstairs looking up 'enema' in the *Shorter Oxford Dictionary* when events overtake me and I just reach the lavatory for ten or fifteen minutes' worth of quite uncomfortable straining, with nothing to read but an article on the state of the economy.

Then to the Medical Centre. Talk with Alan Bailey, then meet Mr Baker, the botty doctor. He takes various particulars, then I'm led to a room next door with various contraptions lying about. My eye flicks over them, wanting – and at the same time, not wanting – to see the sort of thing which will be going up my bum.

The doctor enters, formally, from another doorway. I'm laid down, naked and with my legs up in my chest, and the ordeal begins. His first probings are, after penetration, not too bad, quite bearable, but the higher he gets (and I can feel this tubing peering and turning and twisting and thrusting up into my stomach) the more severe the pain.

I'm told to take deep breaths and I grasp the nurse's hand tightly as he squeezes air and water into my bowels to enlarge them so he can see better. For some moments the pain is acute. I can feel sweat dripping off me. The worst thing is not knowing how long it will last.

Finally the pain eases and he begins to withdraw his instrument. Never have I been so glad to have an examination over. It turns out he's been using a sigmoidoscope and 50 centimetres of thick, black tube. 'Wonderful view,' he says, disarmingly … 'Maybe you ought to do a postcard series,' I suggest, but he doesn't laugh.

Thursday, September 4th

Complete a rough draft of the new 'Railway' commentary by lunchtime. Then run on the Heath – it's almost a year to the day that I began regular running.

I've kept at it, apart from two or three weeks on the 'Railway' documentary and a week in Cyprus. I've run in Central Park and across Fisher's Island and pounded the lanes of Suffolk and the long hills between Abbotsley[1] and Waresley and I've run in rain and snow and 80° sunshine. In darkness and on Christmas Day.

I do always feel better after a run. It's as simple as that. And the physical well-being is very rapidly transformed into a feeling of mental well-being. Running makes me feel relaxed and gives me all the complex satisfaction of a test successfully completed, a feeling of achievement. I hope I shall still be at it in a year's time.

Then I write some extra lines for David Warner in '*TB*'. Manage to get the word 'sigmoidoscope' into the script.

Saturday, September 6th

So full of the joys of spring today that I ring George H and invite myself over for the afternoon.

Have lunch in the garden, scan *The Times*, then leave, taking Tom and Willy and open-roofed Mini. In Henley an hour later. George is mending an electric hedge-cutter which cut through its own flex. As George tinkers

---

1 Abbotsley, a small village near St Neots in Cambridgeshire, is where Helen's mother lives.

in homely fashion with his garden equipment ('I *was* an electrical apprentice,' he assured me. 'For three weeks.') the boys and I swim in the buff in his swimming pool, surrounded by lifelike voyeuristic models of monks and nuns.

Then George took us in a flat-bottomed boat around the lake and at one point into water-filled caves. George told me that Crisp[1] modelled one of the caves on the Blue Grotto on Capri and we went on to talk about Gracie Fields and how King Farouk [of Egypt] had been a great admirer and had come to Capri to live with her, but all his secret servicemen and bodyguards filled the swimming pool all the time and she eventually had to turn him out.

As we stood on the bridge surveying the lakes and the towers and turrets of the extraordinary house, George told me that he really wanted more space. He doesn't want to have people anywhere near him. The other weekend he'd rung up Knight, Frank and Rip-Off,[2] as he calls them in friendly fashion, to enquire about a 1,600-acre farm in Gloucestershire next door to his old friend Steve Winwood. 'Do you want *all* of it ... ?' the man had enquired incredulously.

Thursday, September 11th

Basil Pao[3] comes round for a sort of farewell meal together before he returns to his native Hong Kong for a long stay – perhaps permanent. I like Basil and feel warmth and trust and friendship easily reciprocated. Basil tells how he was known as 'Slits' for five years at his English public school and the reason he was sent to the school was because at the age of twelve he was a heroin runner for the Triads!

He outlines his novel, which is epic and sounds very commercial. Put him into a taxi about 12.45. Sad to see him go, but lots of good intentions to visit.

---

1 Sir Frank Crisp (1843–1919), a successful and eccentric solicitor, created the gardens, when he bought Friar Park in 1895.
2 The estate agents Knight, Frank & Rutley.
3 Basil, a Hong Kong-born designer and photographer, was introduced to me by Eric Idle in 1978, when he brought him in to work on the *Life of Brian* book.

Friday, September 19th: Los Angeles

It's ten minutes to five in the morning. I'm sitting at my desk in my suite at L'Ermitage Hotel on Burton Way in Los Angeles – Beverly Hills to be strictly accurate.

I try to sleep, but my mouth is dry from the air conditioning, so I get up and pour myself water – drink and settle down to sleep again. But my mind refuses to surrender – I notice the refrigerator as it rumbles suddenly into one of its recharging fits. It's huge, much bigger than the one we have at home for our family of five, but only contains four bottles at the moment. And I can't turn it off so I resolve not to worry about that – it's something I must learn to live with, for Suite 411 at L'Ermitage will be home for the next 15 or 16 nights.

I must also learn to live with the air conditioning, which also boosts itself noisily every 45 minutes or so. And I must learn to live with the occasional hiss of water from an invisible tap somewhere near my head, and the metallic clangs and roar of igniting truck engines from the depot outside my window.

It's a desolate time to be awake, the middle of the night. Even in America. I suppose I could watch television, but the thought of yielding to a very bad movie is worse than lying there trying to sleep.

Pour myself a glass of Calistoga mineral water – one of the four bottles in my massive refrigerator department. I tidy the room and try and improve my attitude towards it – to try to get to know it a little better.

The almost obligatory reproduction antique furniture of these hotels gives the place a sort of spray-on 'Europeanism'. It's called a Hotel de Grande Classe (which is an American phrase, not a French one, neatly translated by Neil Innes as 'a hotel of big class') and the place is carefully littered with books of matches and ashtrays. A table before the window has a basket of fruit, courtesy of the management, on it, a bowl of sweets which would set the children's eyes popping, and a rose in a thin vase, which came up with my breakfast yesterday. There are reproductions of European artworks on the wall – I have the 'Night Watch' by Rembrandt behind me as I write.

Saturday morning, September 20th: Los Angeles

At 10.30 we all assembled in the lobby of the hotel and gradually trickled in the direction of our rehearsal room for a first look at the script.

Rehearsal room is a vast hangar of a place, ten minutes' walk from the hotel.

In this bleak great shed, full of Fleetwood Mac equipment in boxes with little wheels, we sit and talk through the show. A couple of short songs from the album are to go in – 'Sit On My Face' at the start of Part II and Terry's 'Never Be Rude to an Arab' (though Terry does very much want to do his Scottish poem about the otter – this doesn't impress over-much, though he auditions it courageously). John and Eric are doing 'Pope and Michelangelo' instead of 'Secret Service' and one of TG's animations – 'History of Flight' – may be cut.

Afternoon spent running words – and making ourselves laugh as we renew acquaintance with the show and material we haven't done together for over four years. In particular 'Salvation Fuzz' – perhaps the most anarchic and unruly and disorderly of all the sketches – gets us going. A very heartening afternoon.

Back to the hotel at five. Sit in the jacuzzi, talk with Neil and Richard Branson of Virgin Records, who is rather pleased with himself having this day sold off Virgin's loss-making US offshoot. Apparently no-one was interested until he doubled the price, then they came right in.

Monday, September 22nd: Los Angeles

To rehearsal at 10.30. André is there, and also Mollie Kirkland – the very efficient stage manager, who worked on the City Center[1] show. Both welcome and reassuring faces. Denis O'B looms in, beaming in such a characteristic Denisian way that we have all started doing it. He gives us all a copy of [Peter Nichols' play] *Privates on Parade*, but is mysterious as to exact reasons why.

Apart from two thoroughly enjoyable run-throughs in our rehearsal cavern, there seems to be little really good news about the shows. Ticket sales are only at 50% so far. The costs are beginning to increase and Roger Hancock is threatening to pull Neil out of the show because of haggling from Denis.

We are all trying to avoid being dragged into all this peripheral activity and are concentrating on tightening, sharpening and adding to the show. And in this we have been successful – our approach and our spirit is much less tense than it was in New York.

---

1 *Monty Python Live at City Center*. New York, 1976.

After the afternoon rehearsal, out to Universal City to see Paul Simon in concert at the Universal Amphitheatre. It's a spotless clean place, staffed not by bouncers, heavies, ex-army PT instructors and the general run of London concert toughs, but by endless numbers of bright-eyed college kids with red blazers.

The concert was clean and crisp too. Under a full moon with the almost unreal shadowy line of the Santa Monica Mountains in the background, Paul did his unspectacular but endearing thing, backed by a superb group of top session musicians playing with a disarming lack of big presentation.

The Jesse Dixon Singers came on and quite dwarfed Simon for a while with their polished, pumping Gospel songs. At one point I thought Paul had been literally swallowed up by one of the massive black ladies with whom he was duetting.

We ate, all of us, afterwards, and at two o'clock TJ swam.

Tuesday, September 23rd: Los Angeles

Wake at eight-ish ... snooze, worry vaguely about voice and the Bowl, then up at nine for a lounge in the jacuzzi under the cloudy morning skies.

I feel time hanging so slowly at the moment.

John said he doubted whether the group could ever agree on anything again and reiterated that he himself no longer enjoyed writing in the group and had never wanted to repeat the 13 weeks of what he considers non-productivity on the script this year. It was history repeating itself. 1972 all over again.

A mood of determined resolution not to be brought down by John's despondency grows. TG, away from so much of the Python meetings this year, is here, and Graham joins us too and we reaffirm a basic aspect of our work together, which JC and Denis O'B and others sometimes tend to cloud, which is that it's fun.

To the Hollywood Bowl. Much standing around here and a photo-session distinguished by marked lack of enthusiasm amongst the Pythons. How old will we have to be to finally stop putting our heads through chairs, eating each other's legs and rolling our eyes? Saw an obviously posed picture of the Three Stooges going through the same ordeal the other day – and they looked about 70.

Wednesday, September 24th: Los Angeles

The air is officially described as 'unhealthful' today.

I lunch with Denis O'B. He's taking all of us away for little chats, but I think it's a sign of the good health of the group that everyone reports back to the others.

He talks of the 'family'. This is his concept of the group. A family in which we all do little creative tasks for each other. I know that he is moving around as he says this, prodding away, waiting for the opening to spring out – yet again – '*Yellowbeard*'! Yes, here it comes. I give a categoric no again. DO'B retreats.

Actually we have a good and open chat over things and he doesn't talk high finance and he restrains his bouts of Denisian 'glee' to a little outburst about all the Warner executives who are coming to the show. 'I tell you, Michael . . . there is so *much* interest . . .'

Drive myself up to the Bowl. Still the rig has not been finished. Neither of the 20-foot-high eidophor screens are up, but otherwise, with drapes now hung, the acting area is beginning to feel and look quite intimate.

We work on until midnight, then back to the hotel for a small party given for us by Martin Scorsese, who has a 'condominium' above us at the hotel. Delightful food, cooked by his chef, Dan; Dom Perignon and Korbel champagne, and Scorsese, who speaks so fast that at a recent film festival he had to have someone to repeat his English to the translator, before the translator even began.

Tells stories of *Raging Bull*, which is the picture he's just done with De Niro – who at one point had to put on 60 lbs.

Friday, September 26th: Los Angeles

Drive down to Musso and Franks for a pre-show meal. TJ declares sensationally that this is the first time he's ever eaten before a show. I remind him of last night. 'Oh . . . yes . . . apart from last night.'

Back at the Bowl, five thousand paying customers. Denis has had to drop the lowest price from ten dollars to seven to try and fill up the extra seats. So there are about five and a half thousand folk out there for opening night.

The show goes well. The audience is reassuringly noisy, familiar, ecstatic as they hear their favourite sketches announced – and it's as if we had never been away. A continuation of the best of our City Center shows. Thanks to the radio mikes my voice holds up.

Afterwards an extraordinary clutch of people in the hospitality room. I'm grabbed, buttonholed, introduced, re-introduced, in a swirl of faces and briefly held handshakes and abruptly-ending conversations. There's: 'I'm Joseph Kendall's nephew . . . ' 'I'm Micky Dolenz's ex-wife . . . ' 'We made the T-shirts you got in 1978 . . . ' 'Do you remember me . . . ?' 'Great show . . . Could you sign this for the guy in the wheelchair?'

Finally we free ourselves of the throng and into the big, black-windowed Batcar, signing as we go, then smoothly speed off to a party, given for us by Steve Martin in Beverly Hills. His house turns out to be an art gallery. Every wall is white, furniture is minimal. The rooms are doorless and quite severe in shape and design. There's a soft pile carpet and it's all quiet and rather lean and hungry. In fact just like its owner.

Martin is very courteous and straight and loves the show. He isn't trying to be funny and we don't have to respond by trying to be funny. But his girlfriend does have a tiny – as Terry J described it – 'sanforized' poodle called Rocco, which pees with both legs in the air.

This is the comedy high spot of the evening.

Sunday, September 28th: Los Angeles

Have booked back four days earlier than I'd expected – on the Tuesday night flight. Back in London on the first day of October – all being well. Helen tells me Rachel cried herself to sleep after talking on the phone to me last Sunday, and asked for a photo of me to put beside her bed!

I don't think I will go to Hugh Hefner's tonight. Graham says it's like getting into Fort Knox, but there's no gold when you get in . . .

GC's book *Autobiography of a Liar* [in fact it was called *A Liar's Autobiography*] has been one of the features of this trip. Coming out at the same time as Roger Wilmut's 'History of Python' – which is straight and competent and almost depressingly like an early obituary – GC's is a sharp, funny, chaotic, wild, touching and extraordinary book. Written in great style, very lively, it's already got TJ very angry about misrepresentation and JC greatly relieved, for some reason, that it doesn't say unpleasant things about him.

Feel very much sharper and better prepared for the show tonight. Probably to do with being less tired. It was a good audience once again.

Afterwards one of the scene boys said how much nicer we were to work for than pop groups! `

Monday, September 29th: Los Angeles

Drive up to Hollywood Boulevard to buy toys, clothes, T-shirts, etc as presents. Everything's there, including the names of stars like Sir Cedric Hardwicke embedded in the sidewalk outside a shop selling erotic lingerie. A sign reads 'It's not expensive to look chic, but it's chic to look expensive'. Another LA motto.

Anne reckons our total BO take over the four nights will be 350,000 dollars – the total possible being 450,000. Not a crashing success, but we'll cover costs. Any revenue will come from the TV sales, which Denis says will only fetch 300,000 dollars. There are, however, the invisible earnings that it's impossible to quantify – record sales, movie re-run attendances, and just keeping the Python name up front there.

Tonight we have a film and a video camera backstage and the audience lights keep going up at strange times. But the audience stay with us and at the end a large section of them won't leave. They wait up to half an hour for an encore we don't have. There'll be outraged letters in *Rolling Stone* about that.

Behind stage, in our small and ill-appointed dressing room beneath the Bowl, we entertain G Harrison, who looks rather shell-shocked after a trip to Montreal to see a Grand Prix, then a drive across the border to New York to avoid a Canadian air-controllers' strike. It's very good to see how he lights up with the satisfaction of seeing us all performing.

Anne has organised bottles for our dressers and drinks behind stage for our rather dour American crew, of whom only a handful have tried to make any contact with us at all – my favourite being a dwarf, who carted huge weights around, generally behaved like a roadie and had an easy, warm, approachable manner.

Eventually I was driven away from the Bowl to a party flung our way by H Nilsson, who lives in a house of modern, airy design, atop a ridge of mountain above Bel Air.

Harry Nilsson, so big, all-embracing, soppily friendly and sporting a complete and refreshing lack of the obligatory LA tan, moves around with his young son on his shoulder. Not drinking, either, as far as I could see. He's terribly happy that George H has surprised him by turning up.

Saturday, October 4th

Today I'm up and out to buy the croissants and the papers. But London disappoints with its shabbiness, with the endless unswept, litter-strewn pavements and the lack of anything new and bright and lively.

A pint and a half of IPA at lunchtime with GC and John Tomiczek at the Freemasons. The remarkable thing about our meeting was that Graham had given up smoking. His most familiar landmark – the pipe with its attendant paraphernalia – proggers, matches, ashtrays and lumps of half-burnt tobacco – have, if he's to be believed, been discarded for ever ...

He says he's not *quite* sure about what he's done, but it was an impulse when he arrived at LA Airport last Wednesday evening and was confronted with some of the worst smog he'd ever seen in the city – so he'd decided not to add to it. So he hasn't used this prop ... that he'd had since the age of 14 ... for almost 72 hours. 'Mind you, I've had to hit the Valium rather hard to make up for it.'

Tuesday, October 7th

Helen and I and parents and all the kids of Gospel Oak packed into All Hallows Church to give thanks for the harvest.

Rachel's class sang a 'Potato' song to Mr Muxworthy's guitar and babies cried as the vicar tried to defy the appalling acoustics of this strange Gothic Revival interior. Talked with Father Coogan afterwards – 'Very Hampsteady food,' he observed, looking down on a font with smoked salmon peeping out from behind Yugoslavian crispbreads.

Have instituted a 'read-a-Shakespeare-play-a-day' regime. More realistically, I've subtitled it 'Read Shakespeare's plays by Christmas and his sonnets by New Year'. Decide to read them through chronologically, as they were written, and completed *Love's Labour's Lost* today. Plenty of laughs and relentless wisecracking. A real Marx Brothers screenplay.

Wednesday, October 8th

Tom is twelve today. He says that 'I only woke up at 5.30 ... that's not bad ...' But he is now a fully-fledged adult as far as air travel goes, as I find out when booking a half-term holiday for us all in Ireland at the end of the month.

A depressing foray to Tottenham Court Road/Oxford Street to buy a new 8 mill film to show at Tom's party. Depressing because of the domination in that corner of London of the awful, blinking, hypnotising spell of video ... There is video equipment everywhere – video films, video games – and it's like a giant amusement arcade providing a sort of temporary electronic alternative to listlessness. Lights flash and disembodied voices bark out of electronic chess games and football games. There doesn't seem to be much joy around here.

Rather staid interview with the BBC at Broadcasting House. TJ does it with me.

The IBA ban on TV or radio advertising of *Monty Python's Contractual Obligation* provides the main gist of the chat.

'Do *you* think it's filth?' she asks us.

'Oh, yes,' we reply hopefully ... and I add 'and worse than that, puerile filth ... '

The nice lady interviewer doesn't know quite what to make of a comedy album called *Monty Python's Contractual Obligation* and neither do we. But all parties try hard.

After the interview TJ and I go to eat at the Gay Hussar in Greek Street. I have quite delicious quenelles of carp and then partridge and lentils. We knock back a couple of bottles of Hungarian wine and admit to each other that neither of us really thinks the album we've just been plugging is much good.

After the meal we walk through Soho to the very hub of its wheel of naughtiness – to Raymond's Revue Bar in Walker's Court. Here there is a small auditorium called the Boulevard Theatre, where a new comedy club called the Comic Strip has just opened. For a long time after the Establishment folded there have been no such clubs in London, but recently the Comedy Store opened and now this. White and Goldstone[1] are involved and this was the second night.

As we wait to collect our guest tickets, a demure voice announces 'The second part of the Festival of Erotica is starting now ... members of the audience may take drinks into the auditorium if they so desire ...' Sober-

---

1 Michael White, a theatre producer, had courageously put money into *Monty Python and the Holy Grail*. It was produced by John Goldstone, who also later produced *Life of Brian* and *The Meaning of Life*.

suited businessmen down drinks and shuffle off to the Festival of Erotica, whilst the rather scruffier, long-Mac brigade troop into the Comic Strip.

In a small, low room with a stage and seating for about 150, only the front two or three rows are full. There are about six or seven acts, including guests. One duo, calling themselves Twentieth Century Coyote, were excellent, with one superb performer. Targets seem to be the new establishment of the left – feminists, alternative society jargon, social workers.

In the intermission buy drinks in the bar and the Comic Strip trendies mingle with the Festival of Erotica straights, whilst two ladies rub and lick each other on a video film projected above the bar. TJ kept wanting to 'just pop in' to the Festival of Erotica, but we stay with the comics and talk to them afterwards. All very young. I wish them well ... but the Twentieth Century Coyotes were the only ones I would really keep my eye on.

Tuesday, October 14th

Into town to see the two and a half hour first assembly of *Time Bandits*.

The effect of the wall sliding back in the room and the first fall into the time hole are stunning, then a series of very funny sequences – Napoleon, Robin Hood, Vincent and Pansy, David Warner and the Court of Eric and the Ogres – lift the film and involve me totally.

It really is the most exciting piece of filming I have seen in ages. I want to be cautious and I want to see all the problems and not be carried away, but the sum total of my impressions leaves me only with heady enthusiasm.

Wednesday, October 15th

Graham Chapman on *Parkinson* (the first Python to be there, I think). Quiet, pipe-less, subdued, but, as an ex-alcoholic homosexual, steals the show.

Thursday, October 23rd

J Goldstone rings to say that the *Life of Brian* appears to be making great progress in Barcelona. Starting slowly, it got good reviews and after two or three days audiences began to pour in. Now didn't I always say I liked the Spaniards?

Write letters and babysit in evening as H goes off to badminton. Watch John C in *Taming of the Shrew*. John gives an excellent performance. Controlled and clear, as you'd expect, and the quiet moments work as well as the screaming. Better, in fact.

He's still not one of those actors who seem to start each new character from scratch, but he did make one listen to every word and as such did a much greater service to Shakespeare – and to J Miller, the director – than most of the other actors.

Friday, October 24th

The weather continues various. Today is bright sunshine, which makes a lunchtime visit to Shepperton all the more agreeable.[1]

First we visit the *Ragtime* lot, which has been built on the triangle of green fields below the reservoir, hired from the Thames Water Board. It's been used sensationally. There are two long New York streets of the 1900's, intersecting halfway. The J P Morgan Library and the brownstones look so solid and substantial and the cobbled streets and paved sidewalks and lampposts so painstakingly reconstructed, that after a few minutes in the middle of all this the only unreality seems to be the Friesian cows munching contentedly in the sunshine behind Madison Avenue.

Then to the newly refurbished canteen and catering block, open now for two weeks. I feel quite elated at what has been achieved after three years of constant nagging, reaching desperation point so often that I almost gave up hope. But today what was so often a running sore on Shepperton's reputation is now bright and gleaming and freshly painted as a set for an ad. The kitchen, through which birds used to fly and, for all I know, nest, is now compact, clean and full of new equipment.

In the bar I meet Iain Johnstone,[2] who is very surprised to hear of my directorship of Shepperton. Iain nodded to the restaurant. 'The *Gandhi* mob are here.' Richard Attenborough is indeed here, for a planning meeting for his forthcoming film on the great man.

---

1 I had been on the board of Shepperton Studios in south-west London since making *Jabberwocky* there in 1976.
2 Journalist, critic and TV producer.

Monday, October 27th: Ballymaloe House, Ireland

It's raining at a quarter to seven when I'm woken by Rachel talking to herself. At eight we go down to breakfast – table with bright blue and white check cloth beside a long window of gracious Georgian proportions. Free-range eggs and bacon like it used to taste before it was sealed and suffocated in cellophane packets, and home-made bread and toast too thick and generously cut to fit in any toaster. This sets us up well for the day and, to improve matters, the rain sputters to a standstill about ten.

We play a word game, trying not to listen to the party nearby talking about operations, diets and how many times they've been on the verge of death (the next morning Helen hears the same woman, pen poised over postcard, asking at the desk how to spell 'anaesthetic').

Thursday, October 30th: Ballymaloe House

On Tuesday afternoon, with the wet weather cleared away and sunlight filling the house, Mel [Calman] idly suggested that he and I collaborate on a children's story. I started work on *Small Harry and the Toothache Pills* that afternoon and completed it and another shorter tale, *Cyril and the Dinner Party*, by Wednesday evening.

I've called them both 'Ballymaloe Stories' and given the scribbled pages (snatched from Rachel's drawing pad) to Mel to think about. Mel says that he isn't the right illustrator for the longer story, but will have a go on Cyril. So that's all rather exciting.

Otherwise I have done very little. I've read a rather fine little book on the history of Ireland by Sean O'Faolain, published in 1943, which makes me stop and think. The English have done some dreadful things to this country in the last four centuries. Greed, adventure, religious conviction or plain bullying have all played a part and even in this quite restrained and tolerant account there is an awful lot to shame England and the English.

I shall hate Irish jokes even more. The lovely thing about the Irish and the way the jokes arise, is their literalness. They seem not to be a guileful people, they're straight, direct, gentle, and yet very good at conversation, at describing beauty and at making strangers feel at their ease.

Our room is full of kids for most of the day, including the ubiquitous Cullin – he of the chunky thighs, who follows Rachel and is rather rough and Irish and makes her alternately excited – 'Can you see what colour my knickers are?' – and prudish – 'Go away, I hate you . . . I *do*.'

Friday, October 31st: Ballymaloe, Cork and London

Last night Mrs Allen chatted to us for a while and said goodbye, as she wouldn't be seeing us this morning. Mel tells me that when working on *The Ballymaloe Cookbook* with her, he found that she kept a little card about guests' vagaries. Some are not welcome again. Against one man she'd written 'Free with his hands in the evening'. Which all makes her sound a rather censorious, stern lady, but she's far from it. She's hardworking, capable, but very tolerant and entertaining. An excellent hostess.

I think we're probably all ready to return to England. My run last night was quite a battle after another lunch, following another solid breakfast, following a fairly unrestrained dinner.

We reach Cork about 9.30, getting lost in the traditional manner. When there are signposts at junctions they invariably have only one arm and one destination (usually where you've come from).

TG rings. Paramount are not interested in *Time Bandits*. Last Monday there was a viewing for Filmways and apparently it went amazingly well. The Filmways head of production was jumping up and down at the end, grabbing TG and calling the film all kinds of success.

The next morning Denis rang TG to say that the Filmways board has rejected it. Too long, too British. TG said he was absolutely stunned at the news after the reaction at the viewing. Denis is now fighting (which he enjoys), but is getting twitchy about his money and the long interest rate on which he's borrowed it.

Sunday, November 2nd

At 3.30 I drive down to BH for appearance with TJ on a chat programme. It's ostensibly about the new *Ripping Yarns* book [*More Ripping Yarns*] and then is to be widened into a whole exploration of the technique, limitations, causes, effects and everything else to do with 'humour'. The sort of thing I dread. A knitting machine operative from Oldham is to be on hand to ask searching questions and a man is on a telephone in Plymouth for further interrogation.

In the event the man in Plymouth never speaks and the poor man from Oldham is tongue-tied with nerves. So Jones and I rattle on and afterwards I have a glass of wine, sign some autographs and meet Kate Adie – a rather dynamic lady who tells me that she was with Princess Anne unveiling something in Darlington. It turned out to be a particularly unprepossessing plaque to 'The Spirit of New Darlington' and, as everyone applauded, Princess Anne leaned over to Kate Adie and muttered a heartfelt 'Fuck me'.

Monday, November 3rd

Attempt to go to Python writing meeting at Anne's on my bike, but the pump decides to treat me badly and sucks air *out* of the tyre. Abandon cycle for the Mini which decides, equally unhelpfully, not to start without much coaxing. So eventually arrive at this first meeting of Pythons Without John for Further Work on the New Film in an unrelaxed rush.

Anne has, I gather on Eric's instigation, kitted out the downstairs room of 2 Park Square West as a Python writing place. We have a table and our own coffee machine and some flowers thoughtfully laid out on top of a filing cabinet.

Tuesday, November 4th

The weather seems to have London in an East European grip.

Still not enough to deter me from cycling to the 'office'. There to find two bits of good news – *Life of Brian*, which, after much censorship to-ing and fro-ing, finally opened in Norway last week and has taken 100,000 dollars in the first three days. And in Australia the album has sold 25,000 copies in a couple of weeks and is now officially a gold album there.

Whether any of these pieces of good news actually strengthen our resolve to persevere with the new movie or not is debatable. But certainly our little room with its fresh flowers, fresh newspapers, fresh coffee and a ping-pong table is the nearest we've come to the Python clubhouse. But I don't remember a great deal of work being done in clubs.

I watch the Carter and Reagan election. It's very obvious that Reagan is going to win. I must confess I've never known why Carter has been so disliked in the US. Also I find it interesting how Reagan, whose initial candidacy was greeted with jeers and sniggers, is already being accepted as a sane and sensible leader of the Western World. No-one on the ITV panel really had the guts to say what they were saying about Reagan before he won. Now it's all smiles.

Tuesday, November 11th

Tonight I go to see *Babylon*, a hard, uncompromising British film set in Brixton.[1] The setting of the film and its subject make me feel very soft as a writer dealing with the Raj and with Robin Hood and railway trains. There is so much energy in the black music – so many good performances from the black actors that their repression should be seen at worst as a scandal – demanding more movies like *Babylon* – and at best a pointless waste of a national asset. For even in their most hysterical moment of frustrated rage against the white neighbours who tell them to shut up and go back to their own country, Trevor Laird yells 'This *is* my fucking country.' They're here. We need them and we need their creative energy far more than we need the energy expended in hate against them.

As I leave there's a black boy with a coloured knitted hat leaving up the stairs with me. Bouncing up with the arrogant, easy stride of the kids in the film. And I wanted to just make contact – say something about what the film had done to me. And I just didn't know how to do or say it. I smiled and that was all.

Sunday, November 16th

To lunch with John and Linda Goldstone. A couple of actors from *Shock Treatment* – the follow-up to the *Rocky Horror* film – are there. One is an actress called Jessica Harper, who is in *Stardust Memories*. When John's next guest – a bubbly, middle-ageing American who talks much about jet-lag – arrives, there occurs the following conversation:
'This is Jessica Harper.'
Man: 'Oh, I *loved* your new movie.'
Man's girlfriend: 'I loved your new movie too.'
Jessica H: 'I'm so glad you loved the movie.'
Man's girlfriend: 'Oh, we really loved the movie.'
Man: 'And you were great.'
Man and friend: 'Oh we *loved* the movie.'

---

1 The story of a young rapper/musician (Brinsley Forde) seeking success in the alienated black community of South London. Directed by Franco Rosso and shot by Chris Menges.

The man was Henry Jaglom, who's got a movie called *Sitting Ducks* at the London Film Festival. He was very funny in a Jewish, improvisatory sort of way. I liked him a lot. His girlfriend, Patrice, was later seen by Helen taking 12 of the largest pills Helen had ever seen. Jessica Harper was a sweet, light, gentle lady who ate no meat and was of such a slight build she looked like a little doll.

And there was an actor called Cliff de Ville (or some such) who had seen us at the Hollywood Bowl and who, sadly for him, spoke and looked just like Jack Nicholson.

Thursday, November 20th

With trepidation to Owen the Feet, having vowed never to return to his shabby little Mornington Foot Clinic, with its fighting dogs in the waiting room and 100-year-old chair.

Today he seems more eccentric than usual and I wonder if he will extract some sort of vengeance upon me for shutting him up rather firmly last time. He injects my toe and gives me the electric needle cauterisation treatment. I was glad to be out of there with the toe still on. He told me that if it was painful in the next week to bear it.

Hobble into the Python meeting at 10.30.

At 12.30 J Cleese arrives to play with the Space Invaders game and watch the 60-minute video of the Hollywood Bowl stage show – which JC has been in charge of editing. All of us feel the sense of occasion is lacking. It is, after all, *Python Live at the Hollywood Bowl* and at the moment it's just Python Live Against Black Drapes. TJ's initial worry that it would look boring is borne out. I'm afraid it doesn't excite any of us.

Should there be a possible 83-minute version for theatrical viewing? TJ and EI feel emphatically no, the rest of us would like to see one assembled. I feel that if the material is well done (and performances at the Bowl weren't bad) and the cartoon film sequences are fresh, we could quite honourably sell it in France, Scandinavia, Australia and possibly Canada at least.

Tuesday, November 25th

To EuroAtlantic.

Denis is in – having just arrived from the West Coast. Without a *Time Bandits* deal. So obviously he's subdued. He asks me what we thought of the video of the Bowl. I said no-one was that elated by it, and there were very strong feelings in the group that we should not even *attempt* to make a movie version.

Travel-crumpled Denis went off to have a haircut (saying he had to look tidy tomorrow because he's going to ask someone to lend him £2 million).

Wednesday, November 26th

Can actually feel the warmth of direct sunlight on my face this morning as I toil over post-synch lines for *Time Bandits*. Rachel sits beside me reading – she's home with a sore throat and suspected flu.

Fortunately I'm in quite good creative flow at the moment and the lines come quite easily. I even find a couple of slogans (which I'm usually rather bad at). '*Time Bandits* – it's all the dreams you've ever had. And not just the bad ones.' (This is changed after I try it out on Tom, who immediately suggests 'not just the good ones'!)

Reading *The Wheels of Chance* by H G Wells, which Jan Francis's husband, a writer called Thomas Ellice, has sent me, hoping that I might be interested in the part of Hoopdriver.

I read the story in about three hours and liked it a lot. H G Wells is a good comic writer – well in the Jerome K Jerome class and even better when he brings in the political angle – the Hampstead women with their New Way of life – and Hoopdriver becomes a full and rounded character, a nonentity who becomes a hero. I love leading characters who are introduced: 'If you had noticed anything about him, it would have been chiefly to notice how little he was noticeable.'

Thursday, November 27th

I visit the eccentric chiropodist, Owen, at 9.30. He launches into a stream of consciousness about prices, his son-in-law, the Jewish mafia who run London Zoo.

He puts on some paste to further kill the beast straddling my toe, assures me it will hurt, tells me not to run for a week and, with a gloomy nod of the head, suggests that there are chiropodists about who wouldn't have touched it at all.

George H rings. He had seen an assembly of '*TB*' and been very worried by some of the 'amateurish' stuff between the boy and the bandits – at the end especially. He felt the film should be a lot shorter and had advised Denis not to hawk it around in its present state. All of which depressed me somewhat.

At nine my episode of the *Great Railway Journeys* is aired. I was relieved how well the programme held together. Most of the potentially embarrassing spots had either been ironed out or well-padded with music and sound effects.

I expect this will not be enough for the critics. But it was enough for me – and Barry Cryer and Angela and my mother – who thought it was the best of the series, 'and not just because I'm your mother'.

Friday, November 28th

Pesky reviews. *Telegraph* generously lukewarm, *Guardian* crustily lukewarm, *Mail* happy. All stop short of personal vilification, all mention the pre-opening credits 'confession' piece as a good sign of comic delights to come and all register various degrees of disappointment that they didn't materialise.

Drive down to Coram's Fields to be present at the launching of a new 'play kit' ('kit' being a radical/progressive word for what used to be called in car showrooms 'literature'). It's being launched by Fair Play for Children, of whom I am a vice-president, to try and help teachers and play leaders with the problems of getting multi-racial kids to play together.

Neil Kinnock MP is there. He's the Labour spokesman on education and carries with him a little notebook, pages scrawled with figures and notes. Gleefully he unearths some figures he'd given to Paul Foot about Heinz beans' current ad campaign – buy Heinz products, collect the labels and you can exchange them for new equipment for your school. For 86,000 labels you can buy a video recorder and camera set. Kinnock did some quick sums, searched in his little book and came up with the triumphant result 'That's £21,000 for a video set-up.'

Glenda Jackson was also there – nice, friendly, open and quite unaffected. There's a small video film made by the organisation, which typifies all their problems. Full of good intentions, but hopelessly over-serious in presentation. Not a smile in it. Just a dose of current sociological jargon. And this is all about play. I said I would be prepared to help their next video presentation. Glenda J agreed too – so they could have quite a cast!

Had to rush away at 12.30 to get to a Python meeting.

A successful read-through. Eric has written a classic – 'The Liberal Family'. GC has made some progress and Terry is very anxious to show Graham his penis. It has some deficiency which he is worried about.

Tuesday, December 2nd

Today we sit and stare at the board on the wall on which cards bearing the names of sketches have been hopefully pinned. Graham muses rather distantly and Terry and I sputter on. But around lunchtime it dies. We only have a working lunch – sandwiches on the table – and afterwards Eric, who has been in one of his silent spells, suddenly galvanises us all into working out a story.

The end of the world, 6,000 AD, the bomber with the Ultimate Weapon, all disappear and we build on the one constant of the month – the working-class family sketch of mine, a fabric of a story about – guess what? – three brothers of the Forbes-Bayter family and the rise to fame, wealth and power of Trevor from obscure working-class origins to become Prime Minister just as the final nuclear war breaks out.

It's all in place by five o'clock, but I feel quite drained of energy as the room empties. I can hardly believe that after all this work and discussion we have come around to a 'Ripping Yarn' which Terry and I could have written in a fortnight on our own.

I find curious solace in talking to a reporter from a Boston, US, radio station. Anne revives me with a scotch and I quite enjoy answering questions from this perky little guy like 'Do you think Britain's really finished?'

Wednesday, December 3rd

I have to say as we meet that I do think the family story we worked out yesterday was a soft option and that the End of the World and the 90-minute countdown remains for me a much more striking idea and a more thoughtful subject altogether. There is no disagreement here and for a while it seems that we have two films. A 'Yarn' and an 'Apocalypse'. Terry J loves the idea of making two films at the same time and showing them at cinemas on alternate nights – Monty Python's two new films.

Friday, December 5th

To EuroAtlantic for the six o'clock Python meeting. Denis O'B has stage-managed the encounter quite carefully. There is an air of calculated informality and there are delicious Indian titbits to disarm us to start with – 'No meat in *any* of them,' Denis assures us, with a significant look at Eric.

Then one by one the various members of the EuroAtlantic team give us a report – which sounds less like a report and more like a justification, at times as blatant as a sales pitch, of their own usefulness. Even though John Cleese isn't present they still sound intimidated and there is an unrelaxed air to the proceedings until Steve Abbott[1] punctures it well.

The atmosphere is very different from the unalloyed enthusiasm of the New Dawn of Python beside the swimming pool at Fisher's Island 14 months ago.

I drive Anne back at the end of the meeting and she is fuming.

I watch *Points of View* which says glowing and wonderful things about the railway programme – 'The finest programme ever' – and flatters me wonderfully. I really seem to have tapped the ageing, middle-class audience.

Saturday, December 6th

I take William over to Upton Park – not more than a 40-minute drive – to watch Sheffield Wednesday versus West Ham. The usual 10–15 minute walk from car to ground, but two tickets are waiting for us – £3.50 comps – left by the Sheffield trainer. And inside it's perfect. A cold, but dry afternoon with a wintry sun lighting up the East Stand opposite us. There's a crowd of 30,000 and an anticipation of good things to come. All the images with which the press have fed us over the last weeks and months of the danger and alienation of the football grounds are absent. I feel quite elated to be there with William and our thermos of hot chocolate and a brass band playing marching stuff over the loudspeakers and an Uncle Mac-type announcer advising the crowd to enjoy themselves judiciously – 'Let's keep the fences away from Upton Park'. And I notice for the first time the absence of the now increasingly common steel barriers to fence in the crowd.

---

1 A bright young Bradford-born accountant, not long down from Cambridge and recently employed by Denis O'Brien's company, EuroAtlantic, in Cadogan Square, Knightsbridge.

Tuesday, December 9th: Southwold

At Gospel Oak Station by a quarter to nine to combine a visit to Southwold with my first opportunity to thoroughly revise the *Time Bandits* script for publication at Easter.

It's a dull and nondescript morning – the shabby, greying clouds have warmed the place up a bit, but that's all. I reach the station in good time. Holly Jones is waiting for her train to school, having just missed the one in front with all her friends on. It's she who tells me that over in New York John Lennon has been shot dead.

A plunge into unreality, or at least into the area of where comprehension slips and the world seems an orderless swirl of disconnected, arbitrary events. How does such a thing happen? How do I, on this grubby station platform in north-west London, begin to comprehend the killing of one of the Beatles? The Rolling Stones were always on the knife-edge of life and death and sudden tragedy was part of their lives, but the Beatles seemed the mortal immortals, the legend that would live and grow old with us. But now, this ordinary December morning, I learn from a schoolgirl that one of my heroes has been shot dead.

My feelings are of indefinable but deeply-felt anger at America. This is, after all, the sort of random slaying of a charismatic, much-loved figure in which America has specialised in the last two decades.

Once I get to Southwold I ring George. And leave a message, because he's not answering.

I work through for a five-hour stretch and we have a drink together by the fire and watch tributes to John Lennon, clumsily put together by newsroom staff who know a good story better than they know good music. And Paul McCartney just says 'It's a drag' and, creditably I think, refuses to emote for the cameras.

What a black day for music. The killer was apparently a fan. The dark side of Beatlemania. The curse that stalks all modern heroes, but is almost unchecked in America – land of the free and the armed and the crazy.

Wednesday, December 10th

Arrive a couple of minutes early at Liverpool Street, enabling me to catch the five to six North London Line. Solemn rush hour travellers, preoccupied in themselves, until a man gets on with a watch which plays a 'digital' version of 'The Yellow Rose of Texas'. This makes many more people than I'd expect start giggling. Which is heartening.

At home pick up car and race out to a meeting with Denis O'B at EuroAtlantic. All routine stuff, until Denis makes me a convoluted offer of 180,000 dollars to go to Sri Lanka (he shows me most alluring pictures) and take Helen and the kids for a while, early next year. I'm a little lost as to why, then suddenly the penny drops. He's trying to get me to rewrite *Yellowbeard* again!

All I commit to Denis is that I shall have a first draft script of my own movie ready by the end of June, 1981. And that's that. Denis does tell me, which I must say I find a bit surprising, that TJ has agreed to the Sri Lanka bait and will be working on *Yellowbeard*. I won't believe this till I see Terry.

Tuesday, December 16th

Watched Ken Loach's *The Gamekeeper* on TV. His lack of sensationalism and his delicate and seemingly effortless portrayal of real life amongst those people generally ignored by the commercial writers and directors is really admirable. He is, I think, the most consistently rewarding director working in Britain. But his marvellously observed celebrations of English working-class life will, it seems, never be as popular as the escapist gloss of *Dallas*. Which is a sad thing. Write 17 letters in reply to some of the 40 or 50 I've had as a result of the 'Railway Journey'. Quite a different audience from the Pythons. Mostly 70 and retired, I think. Is this the Silent Majority?

Wednesday, December 17th

At one I leave for a Shepperton Board Meeting. Fortunately *Ragtime* are about six weeks behind, keeping the studio well-used over Christmas and into January.

One of the few things on offer in early '81 is *Yellowbeard*. I'm not surprised to hear from Charles Gregson [a fellow director of the studio] that he was told that *Yellowbeard* was a Python film and that I was in it.

Thursday, December 18th

My foot is alarmingly red and a little swollen and Helen has looked in her books and is bandying words like 'toxaemia' around. I have two tickets at the Screen on the Hill for the first night of Woody Allen's *Stardust Memories*. I hope that people will mistake me for an aged, but legendary film director as I drag myself, arm round Helen's shoulder, up Haverstock Hill. Actually I feel more like a Lourdes pilgrim fighting off disease and imminent death just to reach the shrine of comedy.

The cinema is full and I like the movie very much indeed. But I can see that my appreciation of some of the scenes depicting horrific excesses of fan worship comes from having experienced this sort of thing and viewed from the other side, this could be seen as Allen kicking people in the teeth.

Though my foot still throbs angrily, I feel the worst is over. I have been cured by a Woody Allen movie!

Saturday, December 20th

The Irish hunger strikers have called off their action within 24 hours of the first expected death. This is the good news for Christmas – though how I abhor the naivety and dangerously ill-informed sensationalism of the *New Standard* billboards in Soho yesterday – 'Total Surrender'. The demise of London evening papers over the last five years is terrible to watch.

1981

Amongst the snippets of information buried away in the Sunday papers under endless travel articles and ads, is one that really made me feel that we live in special times – industrial output in the 1970's in the UK rose by 3%, the only decade when it hasn't reached 10% since 1810. Will this be the decade then that future historians see as the end of the Industrial Revolution?

Tom roller-skates up and down deserted streets outside. It's a chill, dull day. Willy and [his friend] Nathan do experiments – making cork tops fly out under pressure of a murky vinegar and yeast mixture and other Just Williamish pursuits.

Denis O'B calls. Says he's taken a New Year resolution not to mention *Yellowbeard* and probes a little as to my intentions. He can't really operate satisfactorily, I don't think, unless he can have all his clients neatly filed and buttonholed under 'a project'. I am trying – and intending – to be unbuttonholeable for as long as I can.

Wednesday, January 7th

To Owen the Feet at half past nine. Still having difficulty vanquishing the bugger and he re-dresses it, though I expressly forbid any of the acid which nearly burned my foot off just before Christmas. But he's quite gentle and efficient and we get on much better now that our 'political' limits have been drawn up. I learn he was a Mayfair foot man before. He is the society chiropodist I wrote into *The Weekend*.[1]

On to Wardour Street for a viewing of *The Long Good Friday*, which looks like being HandMade Distributors' first product. It's a story about gangland violence and organised crime in London.

Yes, it does glamorise violence, but any violence is glamorous to certain people and you would be irresponsible to only make films about 'nice'

---

1 A play which I'd completed at the end of 1979. It was eventually put on in the West End in 1994 with Richard Wilson in the lead. Michael Medwin played the Foot-Man.

subjects. And Bob Hoskins' portrayal is excellent – and the whole film justifies itself by being a well-written and quite thought-provoking piece. I put it after *Babylon* and *Bloody Kids*[1] in a top ten of recent socially provocative, English-made pictures which all deserve support and a wider audience.

Thursday, January 8th

Jim Beach[2] rings. He wants me to write a 'Biggles' film script. Apparently they have commissioned one which was strong on adventure, but lacking in humour. Just like the 'Biggles' stories, I pointed out. Jim laughed, a little unconvincingly. 'I hear you're unbribable,' he cajoles. Depends what the bribe is, say I. 'Oh, there is a lot of money' – he mentions in rapid succession Robert Stigwood and Disney and director Lewis Gilbert, who was ecstatic when he heard I was being approached. Eric Idle had told Beryl Vertue in Barbados that Michael was *the* world's best 'Biggles' writer.

I weathered all these names and these flatteries and came out with my own individual project intact. Still free. Indeed, strengthened in my determination by these blandishments.

Bought *David O. Selznick's Hollywood*, plus a tin of praline for G Chapman's 40th birthday. We go round to Graham's for a party.

The house reflects the change in GC's living habits. Instead of boxes full of gin and tonic bottles, a rather medically-oriented bookcase. No tobacco wads lying around – the place clean, spotless almost. Graham has a flashing bow tie and is tanned from a sun machine.

Meet Ray Cooper, soft-spoken, rather spare and wispy musician who is Denis's latest client and who will be in charge of the difficult task of coordinating and arranging George H's music for *Time Bandits*. He's a very unassuming, instantly likeable guy, with a bright Greek wife. Has a house in Wapping. In Narrow Street.

As Ray and wife and Helen and I talked on, we realised that most of the heterosexuals had left. Went upstairs to see Kenny Everett, who was sitting in David's room on cushions, with lights low and three or four young lads in attendance.

---

1 *Bloody Kids*, made for TV in 1979, was directed by Stephen Frears, written by Stephen Poliakoff, produced by Barry Hanson and shot, as was *Babylon*, by Chris Menges.
2 Occasional legal adviser-turned-producer. Later became manager of Queen.

Everett was a little drunk. Liked the railways, said he hated television. We had a rather stilted conversation, then he asked me for lunch. I think 1981 could be the year of a thousand lunches.

Friday, January 9th

A year and a fortnight ago it seemed that the world was coming perilously close to a global punch-up when the Russians invaded Afghanistan. But it turned out that it was microphones rather than sabres which were being rattled and everything went off the boil. Looking at *The Times* and *Mirror* headlines this week, I fear we are little further forward, in fact, probably many steps back. Poland, so directly involved in the start of one world war, is, we learn, in danger of being occupied again. Reports resurface in the papers, rather randomly, to the effect that the recent activity of the 'free trade union' movement, Solidarity, is about to goad the Russians into another New Year invasion.

So the pressure is kept on to stand ready to defend ourselves against the still creeping tide of international communism. (This is when our own capitalist alternative is unable to give three million people in this country anything to do.)

This brings me to the heart of the fears which, in my uncharacteristically pessimistic moments, tightened my stomach one morning this week. Dr Kissinger. He's loose again. Talking about the need for more US military involvement in the Middle East and waving away the European peace initiatives. Here is the 'diplomat' of the '70's – the has-been who believes the world must be run by brute force – and it surely cannot be coincidence that his latest iron-fisted threats come only five days before Ronald Reagan becomes President.

Saturday, January 10th

Up at half past eight and taking William down to Hamley's to spend the £7.00 token he's been given by Simon A.[1]

Regent Street is delightfully free of punters. The crescents and stars of the Christmas lights looking naked and forlorn in the sunlight. We wander around, dazzled with choice, in this grubby and overrated toyshop. Willy can't decide what to buy.

---

1 Simon Albury. Old friend and William's godfather.

But I'm less reticent. On an impulse I fork out £59.25 for my first ever electric train set – a Hornby layout with a Coronation Class Pacific. I've waited 28 years for this moment since I used to watch Anthony Jonas in Whitworth Road play with his layout – and occasionally be allowed to put a derailed cattle wagon back on the line.

So begins my 'lost weekend'. Can't wait to get the LMS set home and set it up. In the afternoon the two boys and I make a pilgrimage to Beatties of Holborn and stock up on more track and some rolling stock that's in the sales. Back home again and from then on I resent any interruption.

Monday, January 12th

Decide to make some positive moves on the *Small Harry* story. Go in to see Geoffrey Strachan as a cloudburst of hail hits London. Geoffrey's honesty is something greatly to be valued and I keep forgetting he's the Managing Director of a publisher, so openly does he dispense it.

I left him with the story.

Build a new railway layout.

Tuesday, January 13th

This morning I waited half an hour at the Mornington Foot Clinic for Mr Owen to finish talking to the lady before me. Every word can be heard out in the 'waiting area' and I caught one memorable phrase . . . 'If there's one thing I *don't* like, it's an unshaven man.' Much agreement from the lady patient.

Wednesday, January 21st

A few thousand miles south, the American hostages[1] are flying into Algiers Airport and a few thousand miles west, Reagan is being sworn in as President. Now the enormous humiliation of the hostages is over will Reagan extract some vengeance – just how will he practically live up to his big talk of a Great, Respected America? Watch half in excitement, half in real fear.

1 In November 1979, Iranian militants had taken American Embassy staff in Tehran hostage and held them for 444 days, releasing them only after Jimmy Carter's presidency ended.

Friday, January 23rd

After lunch I drive down to Wapping to see Chris Orr. Wapping High Street is the most unlikely high street left in Britain. Some fine houses remain, but mostly it's corrugated iron and mud and warehouses turned into wine stores.

To Chris's room at New Crane Wharf. I look at his latest etchings. The humour and the style and skill and originality are all there. Now, instead of illustrating prose he's putting words as commentary onto prints.

We walk downstairs and along cobbled streets past warehouses which other artists have moved into, but not greatly changed. Reminds me of Covent Garden just after the fruit market left. To a red-brick building opposite the Prospect of Whitby pub which announces that it was built in 1890 for The London Hydraulic Power Company.

I'm shown around by a young man and an older character, who is quite marvellous and would be a superb TV presenter – a working man's Kenneth Clark. Very articulate, tells a good story, is never lost for words, ideas and references – all presented in a light and original fashion. He tells me about the use of hydraulic power in central London, pumped around a network of ten-inch cast-iron pipes below the ground which would now cost a fortune to lay. When the Hydraulic Power Co finally closed down – only four years ago – it had 3,000 subscribers, controlling the rise and fall of theatre safety curtains, lifts, the vacuum cleaners in the Savoy Hotel and, its star client, Tower Bridge.

Home to hear that *Parkinson* want me to do their show on Wednesday. I've never felt any great loss at not being on Parky – in fact Python as a group refused the dubious honour twice – but the guests with me are to be Sir Peter Parker[1] and Robert de Niro. These two, representing the best of railways and acting, are both men I admire, and out of sheer joie de vivre I accept.

I have to ring Ken Stephinson about something too and I tell him with jovial innocence that he's been scooped by *Parkinson*. There follows a chill of disappointment from the Manchester end of the phone.

I, of course, have completely and clumsily underestimated the office politics of the BBC (not being one who normally experiences such things). I had agreed to go on *Russell Harty* at the end of February and,

1 Popular, accessible Chairman of the British Railways Board from 1976 to 1983, and the only one to have a locomotive named after him. He died in 2002.

from what Ken says, the impact of such an appearance would be lessened if I were to turn up on *Parkinson* less than a month before. The rivalry obviously matters deeply, so I retract and ring the *Parkinson* office and decline to appear.

A rather irritating little episode. All I feel is that, on looking back on it, everyone's reactions will seem ridiculously over-done and quite unnecessary. Including mine. That's enough of that molehill anyway.

Sunday, January 25th

Fine, dry, mild day. Confined to No. 2 for most of the time, varnishing the table for the railway. But the great outdoors beckoned and I felt in such a relaxed and unrushed state that on the spur of the moment, having read the Sundays and discovered what a 'structuralist' was, I decided to take Willy and Rachel into town.

We ended up at the practically deserted Tate Gallery. Both Willy and Rachel excellent company. Willy remarked on how few women artists were represented (a quite amazing disproportion – could only find Gwen John) and, as if by telepathy, just after I had the distinct feeling that the Rothko room reminded me of Stonehenge, Willy said it reminded him of a circle of stones – Stonehenge, he said. Rachel thought all the bums and titties a bit rude, but we all three had a thoroughly enjoyable time – without getting bored or feeling that we were appreciating art out of duty.

Monday, January 26th

Work on the railway again – and try and solve the sidings problem. I find I become so involved in trying to unravel the complexities of it all that it's hard to tolerate any interference. Which tonight comes in the shape of T Gilliam, who brings round some tapes of the sort of music Denis wants George to put into the film. It's average to good George Harrison quavery trillings, with some fine guitar, but seems to be quite at odds with the rather crisp, brittle, neurotic pace of the movie. Well, tomorrow we shall have all this out at a viewing and later chat with George.

I lure TG (quite easily) into playing trains.

Tuesday, January 27th

The days have become so warm, what with this balmy, recycled Florida weather washing over us, that wasps are waking up and flying into my workroom. The garden is coming alive too, eager shoots poking out in trepidation then, sensing it's spring, pushing boldly on. They're probably going to have a terrible time in February.

To Wardour Street for the *Time Bandits* viewing.

I'm very pleased with the way the film looks. The sound effects have revived my enthusiasm, which had waned a little over the last two viewings. Felt today like I did the first time I saw it – that between us we have put together an adventure story full of curiosities.

Still more music to go on, however, and afterwards I go with Terry to Ray Cooper's flat in Wapping to discuss this very matter.

24 Narrow Street, Wapping. Quite an address. We walk across the threshold and into another world. From poverty and desolation to wealth and taste. There is bare brick everywhere – much of it, I gather, the original wall sand-blasted. The brick is of mellow, autumnal gold and very restful and elegant.

Up in the lift two floors and step into a breathtaking open-plan room, with three big windows giving onto a balcony and then the Thames. Wide and impressive at this point, on the base of the U-curve between the Tower of London and the Isle of Dogs.

Everything has its place and the room is carefully and orderly set out, with coffee table books on the coffee table and a round dining table full of salads and delicately set platefuls of taramasalata and things. Crowning the whole a magnum of Château Ducru-Beaucaillou '69.

George arrives (in brand new Porsche), having driven from Cadogan Square in about 15 minutes. He brings Derek Taylor, whom I'm most pleased to see. Derek thrives on chat and good relaxed company and we're never at our best in the artificial world of meetings.

George gives, either coincidentally, but I think actually quite deliberately, the current Denis O'Brien line on *Time Bandits* – that it should be 90 minutes. There's rather a lot George doesn't like about it and I wonder if he really is the best person to be doing the music. But he seems to want to do it, though he does reveal a little petulance over the fact that Denis is constantly asking him to dip in to finance films.

'What the hell, it's only a tax-loss picture,' says George at one point. He laughs. But the laughter must grate on TG.

Wednesday, January 28th

Try to reach Richard Loncraine[1] to explain my decision not to do *Brimstone and Treacle*. Can't reach him.

To Methuen to see Marilyn Malin, the children's editor. I feel on very safe ground with her. She has the Methuen caution. Like Geoffrey. But it transpires that she really does like *Small Harry* and wants to publish it and is happy with Caroline [Holden] as designer.

It all seems to fall into place. I promise to push through the contract with minimum fuss (if terms are reasonable). Methuen undertake to print at least 15,000 copies. So I do feel rather pleased with myself as I walk out and up Holborn to the shops. Thanks to Mel Calman and Ballymaloe!

Home. Reach Loncraine. He's very disappointed, he says kindly. Fox were very interested and both Ken Trodd and Potter himself had been in favour of the casting. But it must be third on my list this year – after my film and my word to Thomas Ellice about 'Wheels of Chance'. To go to the top of my list it would have to have been something that was totally and unequivocally unmissable. And it wasn't that.

Thursday, February 5th

To Charing Cross Station to catch the 10.45 to Hastings to have my portrait painted by John Bratby. I'm looking forward to it, in an intrigued sort of way.

We clatter through the labyrinth of South London. There are no non-stop trains to Hastings, which is perhaps the most indicative clue to the nature of the town itself. A seaside place without the style of Brighton or the industrial and economic usefulness of Southampton or the travelling status of Folkestone or Dover. The train approaches it with an ever-increasing number of stops. As if reluctant to ever get there.

There aren't many getting off this February morning. As I walk down the steps to the booking office and what they nowadays like to call 'the concourse', I catch sight of two figures, peering like co-conspirators in an

---

1 A commercials director and inventor. I'd tried, without success, to get him to direct some of the *Ripping Yarns*. He in turn had asked me if I'd be in his film of Dennis Potter's 1976 TV play *Brimstone and Treacle*, to be produced by Ken Trodd. It was filmed in 1982 with Sting in the starring role.

English 'B' movie of the '50's from behind the window of the refreshment room. They collude, then start to move out.

Bratby is round, small and beaming shyly. He reminds me of Raymond Briggs's Father Christmas. He doesn't say anything or shake hands, but not in an unfriendly way. Dark-haired, dark-skinned wife with good-humoured eyes. She indicates an ordinary, untidy, red station wagon. Of English make, I think. We drive through Hastings, I making my cheerful, mundane observations about the place, their reactions not quite predictable. She doesn't like Hastings.

Their house comes up sooner than I'd expected. A rambling Georgian mansion with a tower on top linked to the house by a glass conservatory in the sky. It's set in quite unpretentious surroundings overlooking the town of Hastings and the sea.

She lets me out then discreetly drives the red car away and John Bratby takes over, showing me the way along a scruffy passage into a studio. Dominating is a big oil painting of Paul McCartney, dated 1967. Paul looks like a sad little waif – and it seems very much at odds with the capable, super-businessman I hear he is. Maybe that's why he left his portrait here.

Bratby, who seems more at ease now he's in his studio, points me to the chair where I must sit. It's like visiting the doctor's. The same relationship between myself, the object, and the professional. On my left side a window, not very clean, on my right a spotlight turned towards me. A big paraffin heater of modern design considerately set for me.

For the first half-hour he doesn't touch the three foot by two foot canvas on a stand in front of him. He compliments me on my healthiness; he is amazed that I'm 37. I find as we talk that he is much concerned with death and ageing. He is also glad to hear that I don't take life too seriously. Only when he reached the age of 50, he said, did he realise that life didn't have to be taken seriously and he wishes he'd discovered this earlier! He is quite ready to laugh and laughs rather well. He amused me too when we both were comparing notes about the fascist tendencies of Kenwood House attendants. Once they accused Bratby of having added a daub of paint to Rembrandt's nose in the self-portrait there.

Patti, his wife, keeps us well filled with coffee. He drinks it in vast mugfuls, as he squeezes more and more tubes of oil paint on to an already thick, full palette. Occasionally he stops talking, which I find disconcerting until I realise that he is concentrating so hard that he has ceased to regard me in the conventional dialogue relationship.

He likes to work in England. He loses his identity when he travels. He works very solidly. He prefers to work in his studio. He is much impressed by people like myself whom he regards as 'the last people' – individuals who stand out from the herd. He's concerned by creeping Bennite egalitarianism, stamping out all quality in life – all the odd ones who by their own great talents stand out ... again this slightly alarming elitist theorising.

After about three and a half hours he asks if I want to see it. And there, amazingly, it is. The canvas is full, with short, thick streaks of oil paint – dozens of colours and shades – and there is me as Bratby sees me. It is done. I have to admire it, because he seems to have achieved so much with such apparent lack of effort. His painting is a complex process, yet he's achieved quite a simple image. He says that while I'm there it's difficult to let the painting speak for itself, but it will, he says, over the next week.

And then the car is ready outside and we're back into the 'B' movie. Patti drives me away to the station and onto the train back to Charing Cross.

Sunday, February 8th: Church Farm, Abbotsley

Wake, most reinvigorated. Breakfast at half past nine. Scan the *Observer*. A really encouraging report that the Minister of Transport, Norman Fowler, is giving his support to a sensible investment plan for the railways – sensible because it plans to inject twice as much government money over six years or so as it does at the moment. Sounds bold. Could all the ads and the publicity skills of P Parker, and even our series of railway documentaries have helped?

On either side of a succulent roast beef lunch I and the boys clear round the pond. Heavy, muddy, but satisfying work. Willy dredges out all sorts of old bits of rubbish – roller skates, tennis balls and bits of old pram – with his usual uncontrollable glee. He falls in eventually.

G. Chapman rings. Obviously pushed by Denis, he rather quickly blurts out that he wants me to be in *Yellowbeard*. Just as quickly I repeat my rejection of the offer. Then he talks about Telepictures. What is my attitude? Against, I say. 'Oh dear,' says the doctor, 'it's going to be a bad week for Denis.'

Monday, February 9th

To Cadogan Square to meet Denis O'B. I tell him that I'm against any
Telepictures deal which involves decimation of the Python shows. This
causes Denis some concern, as he says we have made a deal in good
faith (though Telepictures have been granted the good faith rather than
Python) and he's extremely worried about going back on his word. My
suggestion is that we let Telepictures have Python product on the stipu-
lation it isn't cut at all – and see if they want us badly enough to be able
to accommodate such a demand.

Feeling I've been consistently negative thus far (in D's terms), I agree
in principle to flying to Atlanta in May to speak on the *Time Bandits*
book's behalf at the big publishing sales convention.

As five o'clock and my departure time closes, Denis finally gets around
to *Yellowbeard* again. No, Denis, I'm not budging. It's not worth discussing. 'Wait a minute,' says Denis, 'hear me out.' So he tries to rush
headfirst at the brick wall again – except from a slightly different angle
this time. All he wants is one week of my writing time ... no more ...
just one ... and (as I stand up) ...

'Michael ...'

'I listened to you.'

'... And what's more –' but at that point the Great Salesman is cut
short in mid-pitch by a sharp and silly series of knocks on the door and
George Harrison's head appears, beaming leerily.

George carries a sheaf of company reports and, oblivious to the urgency
of D's business with me, he sits down chattily and shows me one of them –
'Sing Song Ltd' – which has a net loss of £34.

We listen to some of GH's new songs. 'All Those Years Ago' is my
favourite of a number of very good tracks.

Sunday, February 15th

Take the children swimming to the Holiday Inn at Swiss Cottage. We
practically have the pool to ourselves. After I've come back and am
settling down to cold roast pork, the phone rings. It's 9.30 and the *Sun*
newspaper wants to know if there's any truth in the rumour that John
Cleese has been married today in New York. I tell the hackette that
I know nothing, but think it extremely unlikely, what with John being
gay and all that.

She persists in her intrusion, I persist in my fantasy – and she eventually gives up. Silly world.

Monday, February 16th

Eight-fifteen, start to drive down to London Sessions House for two weeks of jury service.

The Sessions House is a solid, impressive, neo-classical building started in 1914. It's been added to and there are now 19 courts within its 'grounds'. Park my car at a meter, then join a mass of some 200 new jurors, who are herded into Court Number 1 – a classic of the TV and film sort, full of wood panelling with a vaguely Baroque flourish. Here we sit and await a preliminary chat. A peculiar feeling – a roomful of 200 people, none of whom knows each other. Early banter tails off, and within five minutes all 200 of us are sitting in a tantalisingly breakable collective silence.

Then we're reduced to groups of 20 as our names are called and the groups are led off to one of the other courts; it's all rather like school.

My fellow jurors seem to be drawn mostly from the working classes, with a sprinkling of woolly-minded liberals like myself. There seems to be a notable absence of anyone looking rich and successful. I suppose you don't have time to do jury service and become rich and successful.

Sit for over an hour in a smoke-filled room. I try to read Sir Walter Scott's *Waverley*, but his convoluted prose and circumlocutory embellishments are not ideal for such a situation. I hear a loud voice beside me . . . 'Yeah, there's a TV personality on one of the juries. Mate of mine saw him this morning . . . Can't remember his name.'

Then, just as the day seems irretrievably lost, our room is called, again, and we are led upstairs. This time I'm called onto the jury. There are no challenges and we actually begin my first 'live' case as a juror. It's not one to enter the annals of Great British Trials, but there are satisfyingly comic complications involved.

The two accused are Indians, two young men with fashionable Western moustaches and pudgy faces, who have six charges against them arising from a fight they are said to have started in a pub in Clapton, E5, on an August Sunday in 1979. (There are very few cases ever heard here that have been waiting less than a year to be called.)

We are now actually belonging to a case – we have a purpose and, for the next two or three days, this judge, the three barristers, the clerks of the court and the two moustachioed Punjabi bandits in the dock will all be locked together in a curiously reassuring intimacy.

Wednesday, February 18th

Drive down to Newington Causeway for more life with the Singhs. Publican and two assistants gave evidence, as did an enormous policeman. Medical evidence was read out as to the seriousness of the eye injury caused by a thrown bottle to an apparently innocent old Indian watching. There is permanent damage to the eye and he has to wear contact lenses. So this is the most serious aspect of the case.

Back at home, Terry Gilliam rings. He has been on the phone to Denis in LA for one and a half hours, discussing *Time Bandits*. After their chat today, in which TG took Denis through the film cut by cut, demolishing nearly all his suggested edits, TG reported Denis to be sounding very unspirited, not to say low, not to say depressed.

I think the process of learning how difficult we all are is more painful than Denis ever in his worst dreams expected.

Thursday, February 19th

At times today as I was locked in an unmoving line of traffic on the approaches to Russell Square, I felt a surge of panic at the thought of keeping His Honour Justice Bruce Campbell QC and his entire court waiting.

But I was there on time and, after a further half-hour of Judge's summing up, our moment of glory arrived, and they had to wait for us whilst we were locked in our windowless little room to try and reach a verdict. Without much dissension we decided to acquit him of the first charge of actual bodily harm, as it was a case of one man's word against his.

The court reassembled, our foreman gave our verdicts, then the antecedents of the accused were read. Both had been in trouble with the police before. Onkar has three children and one about to be born; he's only 23, has not got much of a future either, but has just recently been taken on as a bus driver. Despite the heart-rending pleas of the counsel, our kindly, humorous judge stuck his chin out firmly and became the stern voice of punishment. Onkar Singh was to be jailed for three months, his brother three months, but suspended. And that was that.

Friday, February 20th

Split into a new jury group and assigned to Court 7.

Observed a Jamaican being sent down for eight months for illegally importing and probably dealing in cannabis. I suppose there is a danger that cannabis-dealing leads on to dealing harder drugs – but this was certainly not proven here. The man's girlfriend and mother of his two children had just gone into hospital with a blood clot on the brain, but the judge disregarded all this. Disturbing, especially when I think of the vast number of people – respectable and rich included – who smoke and trade in cannabis freely.

Then a frightened, wide-eyed black kid comes into the dock. He took a knife and threatened a shopkeeper and stole £40.00. He is sent to Borstal, despite this being his first offence and despite strong recommendations in his favour from Lambeth Borough Council, whose representative was present in court.

Monday, February 23rd

I asked at the Bailiff's Office about my chances of avoiding a long case on Thursday (my *Russell Harty* night) and they were most understanding and decided that the safest way was to discharge me from a second week's jury service altogether. This took a moment to sink in, then a great feeling of relief at this unexpected freedom. I had to wait an hour to collect my expenses, so sat in a café opposite the courts and read the paper and mulled over what to do with this free week.

Walked across Waterloo Bridge – something I hardly ever do – stopped and looked in the church of St Mary-Le-Strand, which I never, ever do, being usually far too busy roaring round it in a car. Peace and quiet and Baroque extravagance in the middle of one of London's busiest one-way traffic systems. Noted that the church was built by order of Parliament from money raised by a tax on coal!

Friday, March 6th

This morning – a march against unemployment. Can I come? But despite feeling personally more scornful of Thatcher and her solutions – Surrey Power, as I call it – I still have this aversion to making a lot of noise in a public place in direct support of any political force. Mainly because I don't easily believe in political solutions.

I think you have to work and communicate on a much more basic level than behind banners or tub-thumping on platforms – this is the showbiz side of politics. I personally feel much happier encouraging tolerance and understanding on a man to man level, or through my humour rather than telling people something which I don't believe – i.e. if you follow this leader, or endorse this system, everything will be alright.

Sunday, March 8th

Complete *Waverley* (which works on me like Hardy – demanding much loyalty and dogged persistence to begin with, but finally rewarding perseverance with a good tale and leaving an after-taste of affection towards the worlds he's described and the characters he's filled them with).

This very evening, begin to read Proust's *À La Recherche* ... Feeling limbered up after *Waverley* and *Romola* and spurred on by the purchase, for £50, of a new and much-praised edition by Kilmartin.

Monday, March 9th

Unexpectedly I wake with a hint of tension, usually experienced in more extreme forms when I have to go filming, write a debate speech or appear on *Just a Minute*. But today it's anticipation of my own self-imposed project – the film script, which (in tandem with Proust) I begin today.

Sit at my desk at a quarter past nine, comfortably cocooned against steady, unbroken rain outside, and realise that, despite two months of intended mental refreshment and stimulation, I'm still as riddled with incompatible alternatives for stories as I ever was.

Nothing springs instantly to my pen – no characters so all-consumingly important that I have to write about them. It's a shame really – all those people out there with burning convictions and desperate messages to the world which they can never make anyone listen to and here am I, pen poised to create entertainment for the world and not knowing what I want to say.

Wednesday, March 11th

Go up to William Ellis in the evening to hear about the curriculum, etc. Headmaster clearly pleased with progress so far on the transition from grammar to comprehensive. He does sound as though he loves his work.

Turnout of parents almost all middle-class – others seem to leave the school to get on with it. (Trouble with democracy these days?)

Eric rings later to fix up a Palins/Idles theatre trip next Monday. Tells me that Graham has just been on the phone to ask him to be in *Yellowbeard*. But surely ... ? No, says Eric, *Yellowbeard* is not dead. GC has nine million dollars of Australian money and is planning to film it off the Queensland coast. Eric is worried about how best he can say no yet again.

Thursday, March 12th

Classic writing morning. Up to the desk, clear space and open notebook at about five to ten. Estimate when I should finish. Two-thirty seems reasonable. Yawn. Stretch. Yawn. Look blankly through all I've written this week, trying desperately to summon up any belief in the purpose of these arbitrary scribblings and character snippings. Long for coffee, but it's an hour away.

The hour passes with hardly a line written. It's like insomnia, in reverse. My mind refuses to wake up.

I take the opportunity (rare this week) of a dry spell and run. As I pound up the path to Parliament Hill, a title occurs to me – 'The Missionary Position'.

Maybe, though, that's too whacky, too leading, so I settle for 'The Missionary' and the subject matter of the film swims into clear focus. An idealist, a tortured idealist in the last days of the British Empire – the missionary work would be interpreted as widely as possible, and the title has a nice touch of irony. Come back 45 minutes later muddy but feeling that I've made a breakthrough.

Cook Toulouse sausages with apples for Robert H[ewison].

Over dinner he makes what he calls, with characteristic modesty, a brilliant discovery – that the six Time Bandits are the six Pythons. He's awfully pleased at making this connection and seems quite unmoved by my own denial of any such parallel. For the record, anyway, our casting was: Randall – Cleese, Vermin – Gilliam, Og – Graham, Fidgit – Terry J, Strutter – Eric, Wally – me.

Friday, March 13th

Had a vivid dream this morning. It was set in Halifax. Very positively Halifax.

It was hazy – a mixture of Lowry and Hieronymus Bosch – but on top of the hill the walls were of rich, red stone and I walked through colonnades and arcades built in seventeenth-century classical style and met young students who told me what a wonderful place Halifax was.

At the writing desk by ten. I pursued the idea of *The Missionary*, which began to fall very nicely into place. By lunchtime I had actually sketched out a synopsis – with a beginning, middle and end – which I dared to become quite excited about. In the afternoon I tightened and typed this up. So by four, at the end of the first week's writing, I have a story. I feel, as I say, warily confident. Will see how it survives the weekend.

Tuesday, March 17th

A mighty clap of thunder as a short and violent storm passes overhead as I settle into a piece for the *New York Times* – Howard Goldberg having sent me a telegram asking for a piece on Prince Charles and Lady D. Have completed it by seven.

Ring HG in New York. He's frightfully worried that I will not, as he puts it, 'keep it clean'. 'I'm hired by Calvinists,' he explains. Dictate through to the *Times* later in the evening.

Wednesday, March 18th

Take Tom P (who's been off school today with a cold) up to St Anne's Church, Highgate, for the first night of the William Ellis opera 'Death of Baldur'. This has been the big musical event of the year for the school. It's an English premiere and the composer, David Bedford, is there with short, well-cut grey hair, looking like a natty parent. Tom is in the 'off-stage' choir and is tonight stuffed to the gills with throat sweets, etc, to help his voice.

I cannot understand a word that's being sung throughout the hour, but it's evidently to do with revenge, blindness, the gods and other gloomy Nordic specialities. Not a laugh in it. The orchestra is good, but the church swallows up voices and makes it very difficult to stage.

Very effective integration of pebble-banging – with the 'pebble-choir' ringing the church behind the audience and setting up a wave of staccato sound which had the effect of swirling stereophonic sound.

Home to hear from Howard Goldberg that he had loved my piece for the *NYT* on Prince Charles and was planning to run it on Sunday. He kept going into fits of giggles over the phone whilst checking spellings, etc. Most encouraging.

Thursday, March 19th

Estimated by lunchtime – and ten mornings' work – that I have 20 minutes of good material to start *The Missionary*, and another five or six quite strong.

Friday, March 20th

Driven out to Friar Park in stately fashion in the back of Ray Cooper's elegant and comfortable 26-year-old Bentley – all wooden panelling and a good smell of leather.

On the way Ray tells me that George had a phone call two weeks ago from some anonymous American telling George he had a gun and an air ticket to England. It all sounded like a horrible hoax, but the FBI found that a man in Baltimore had been seen in a bar making just such threats and bragging about his air ticket. George H's place was ringed by police for a week – and he had a bodyguard with him at all times. Considering all this, George met us in very relaxed style. He was up on the slopes of his Matterhorn, with the builders who are busy restoring this fine piece of eccentric garden landscaping.

Saturday, March 28th

Willy and I drive off to go to see Wednesday play at [Leyton] Orient.

It's a warm day, the ground at Brisbane Road is small, neat and feels far more of a local family atmosphere than any others we've been to this season.

It seems that a Wednesday goal has to come, but instead a scuffle at the far end and Orient have scored on one of their rare visits to the Wednesday area.

This stings Wednesday – crowd and players – into some strong retaliatory measures, but within minutes Orient have scored again and it's over – as is probably Wednesday's chance for promotion.

A satisfying incident as we walk to the car. In the long line of cars moving up to the main road are three lads, one of whom leans out of the window and shouts in delight at me ... 'Heh! It's Eric Idle!' I smile, but weakly, I expect, and walk on as they noisily discuss who I'm not.

About 15 yards further on their car approaches and they pass up the road with a chant of 'We know who you are!' This is followed almost immediately by a crunch of colliding metal and a crackle of shattering tail-light as their car thuds into the one in front and pushes that one into the one in front of him.

Monday, March 30th

Drive down to the first of a week's Python meetings at 2 Park Square West.

We appear to be very much in accord over our exasperation, frustration and consternation about Denis's role in our affairs. In Anne's pains-takingly-assembled report on life with EuroAtlantic, she suggested that she and Steve [Abbott] could run our day-to-day affairs from 2 PSW.

A remarkable degree of unanimity within the group that now is the time to sort out this whole question.

To dinner with Clare [Latimer].[1] Excellent food, plenty of drink and jolly company. A vicar from St John's Wood who tells me he took 50 of his most fervent worshippers to see *Life of Brian* last Good Friday – instead of moping about church 'mourning'.

Wednesday, April 1st

A dry, warm day with soft, high cloud. Everyone in a good mood. Eric suggests we all of us make a list of the pros and cons of DO'B. The lists turn out to be remarkably similar. Tax planning and tax structures are commended, but all the pro lists are much shorter than the cons – which include over-secrecy, inability to listen to or understand things he doesn't want to hear, and use of word 'philosophy'.

At lunch – Anne makes us delicious asparagus tart – we get fairly silly. Decide that the Pythons should purchase our own nuclear deterrent. We put a small ad in *The Times* – 'Nuclear Missile wanted, with warhead, London area'.

1 Caterer and next-door neighbour for many years.

Friday, April 3rd

Denis is pleased that we have decided to go ahead with theatrical release of *Hollywood Bowl*. Which we now decide to call, simply, *Monty Python at the Hollywood Bowl*. But try as we can to drill into him that he should go for smaller distributors with more time to listen, the more Denis retreats back to the majors whom he knows.

He claims that the small distributors only handle 'exploitation' pics (violent or sexy or blatantly both, which are so bad that money is only made by a quick, sharp killing in selected theatres). His feeling is that all distributors are idiots, but he will try and find us the most benevolent idiot.

Sunday, April 5th

Denis calls me. He asks me to try and patch up the Gilliam/Harrison relationship. Not that TG has done any more than express reservations about George's music, and the last song in particular, but GH has taken it badly and feels that he no longer cares – and if TG wants to write the music he can write it himself.

I try to defend TG's position by saying that the use of GH's music was rather forced on him. Denis returns to the financial argument (does Terry realise how much money the film is costing?) which is slightly unfair. Anyway, as Denis memorably puts it, 'You just don't treat Beatles this way.'

Monday, April 6th

Collect Rachel from school, then ring George. He isn't angry in the conventional sense – I mean, no shouting or swearing – but he just is sad and a bit fed up. 'I was just a fan,' he puts it, 'who wanted to help you do things because I liked what you all did.'

But after all this comes out, we get down to discussing the end song. I tell him we both like it musically, but we've now got some new lyrics which change only the verses. Let him listen to them and sling them out if he doesn't like them. But of course he does quite like them – and is happy to do them and will send a demo later in the week. I hope all is healed, temporarily at least.

Dash off to the Python meeting.

It's quite obvious that the group as a whole trust Anne more than Denis (JC wanted it to go on record that he mistrusted Denis less than the rest of us) and Eric was the only one who signed the letter to Denis with his surname. 'Denis is the sort of person I want to be on surname terms with,' was the way he put it – and I promised to write that in my diary.

Tuesday, April 7th

To Eric's by car about seven o'clock. He has now assembled enough material for six TV programmes to be made by his company – Rutland Weekend Television – and sold to England, the US, Australia, Canada, etc. They're comedy sketch shows, basically – with music animation special effects and all set in the legendary Rutland Isles, where anything can happen.

Anyway, Eric wants me to come and play one of the three stars, along with himself and possibly Carrie Fisher. Filming would, he thinks, not take more than eight weeks and would be done in the winter on a lovely tropical island.

I'm drawn by the immediacy of doing a TV series on video and by Eric's unportentous, let's-just-get-on-with-it attitude and refusal to treat it as the most important thing ever. But it's a month, at least, accounted for and at that time I may be in pre-production of *The Missionary*.

Saturday, April 11th

Family outing to *Popeye*.[1] We ate excellent hamburgers in Covent Garden and the sun came out and shone on us as we walked through the Garden, past the escapologist, through St Paul's churchyard, where trees have been planted in memory of actors buried there. One rather undernourished little shrub was ironically plaqued 'In memory of Hattie Jacques'.

Home to hear that there was burning and looting going on in Brixton as we had wandered through the quiet bustle of the West End on this sunny Saturday afternoon.

---

1 Film version of the comic-strip. Robin Williams was Popeye and Shelley Duvall Olive Oyl. Robert Altman directed. Jules Feiffer wrote the screenplay and Harry Nilsson the songs.

Monday, April 13th

Help prepare for dinner with Steve Abbott and friend Laurie.

Part of my reason for asking him round is to find out more about his feelings about Denis and Euro. Basically he is concerned about divided loyalties. He cannot carry on working for the Pythons and doing what is best for the Pythons within the EuroAtlantic framework because he feels the decisions taken for the benefit of EuroAtlantic are very often contrary to the benefit of the Pythons.

Both Steve and Laurie are politically to the left, Laurie enough to have changed her bank account from Barclays (naughty South African connections) to the Co-op. Only to find that the Co-op use Barclays as their clearing bank!

Steve is I think a man of good, basic, honest convictions and if for this reason he's leaving EuroAtlantic, it makes me listen very carefully.

Tuesday, April 14th

Dry and cool. Drive down to Crawford Street to have hair cut by Don [Abaka, our family hairdresser for many years]. We talk about the Brixton riot and that Don who is, I should imagine, a very easy-going and law-abiding black – a part of the establishment if you like – still can say, as if a little surprised, 'I've not been in any trouble with the police, but I really feel worried sometimes that if there's trouble in a street they'll pick me out.'

Home to work on *The Missionary*, but for some reason, as the clouds clear and the sun shines from a blue sky, I find myself surrendering to the pleasantness of the day. Sit in the garden seat in the sun and read Bernard Levin's infectious raves about three of his favourite restaurants in Switzerland. Makes my mind drift to thoughts of holidays and sun-soaked balconies in small French towns and poplars motionless above sparkling streams and good wine and company and celebrating.

Watch the space shuttle land most skilfully. Feel, more than I ever did with the moonwalks, that the success of this first reusable spacecraft is the real start of what an American astronaut rather chillingly called 'the exploitation of space'.

Thursday, April 16th

Hardly see Helen, on this our 15th wedding anniversary morning. Am woken by Rachel at a quarter to seven, standing by my bedside, dressed and ready to go. She wakes William by tickling his feet (the only way, he claims, he can be woken up) and the three of us make for the quarter to nine North London Line train to Broad Street.

Uneventful journey to Darsham, though we found ourselves in the breakfast car next to an assured, rich-voiced, late middle-aged Englishman with half-moon glasses, sitting with a fortyish, mousy-blonde lady, with the large, bony, open features of an English upper-class gel.

He began to make notes about some speech he was to make ... 'The recent clashes in Brixton, foreseen by Mr Enoch Powell over fifteen years ago –' His eligible companion interrupts ... '"Clashes"? Do you think "clashes" is a strong enough word?' 'No, no, perhaps you're right ... Battle? ... Mm ...'.

We left them, still composing, at Ipswich. Met by Mother at Darsham. She looked a little wearier than of late and drives a little slower and a little nearer the centre of the road.

Sunday, April 19th: Southwold, Easter Sunday

In the afternoon I read through Robert H's manuscript of the Python censorship book, which he wants me to check before I go to Crete. It's well-researched, thorough, lightly, but not uncritically, biased in our favour. The word I've written in my notes to sum up his endeavour is 'scrupulous'. Unsensational in presentation, but not necessarily in concept – it's really everything I hoped it would be.

Tuesday, April 21st

Over lunch spend a couple of hours with Steve talking about EuroAtlantic, my finances and the possible transfer of our immediate financial affairs to a Steve and Anne-run office.

Steve reveals fresh facets of his straightforward, unassuming but very independent nature. He declines a coffee because it's the Passover and he's eating only Kosher food for a week. He almost apologetically explains that he's not even a born Jew. He just began to take an interest four or five years ago, learnt Hebrew and another Judaic language and set himself certain standards of observation which he readily admits are somewhat inconsistent, but one of them is to eat nothing but Kosher food throughout the Passover period.

Saturday, May 2nd: London to The Chewton Glen Hotel

Drive down to Hampshire for the Python weekend. Collect Gilliam at 7.45, then Eric at eight and, despite some build-up of holiday weekend traffic, we are driving through the New Forest by half past nine and to the hotel, set in a rather nondescript conurbation near New Milton.

The Chewton Glen Hotel is unashamedly expensive – a soft, enveloping atmosphere of thick carpets, armchairs, soft voices, chandeliers. From the BMWs and Jaguars in the car park to the miniature of sherry with the manager's compliments, everything reflects money. Like a padded cell for the very rich. But it suits our purposes – we're here, after all, to concentrate our minds on one of the most important decisions Python has yet made.

There is remarkably little dissension from JC's opening assessment that we should tell Denis that we no longer feel we need a manager. That there should, in the interests of economy and efficiency, be one Python office to administrate the companies, and that future relationships with Denis should be on an ad hoc basis.

Within a couple of hours we've reached a heartening degree of agreement and JC is left to compose a letter. I go to the billiard room with TG for a game on a marvellous full-size table. The balls feel like lead weights after the half-size table at home. Then to lunch. The food is good – delicate and lots of things like lobster and snails and shallots.

Then a game of snooker, a game of squash with Terry J and back for more snooker and dinner. Quite like old times, with Graham leaving early to go to a gay club in Bournemouth (for the second night running, I'm told) – but even better than the old days because GC doesn't get pissed and can drive himself.

Talk, over the champagne and cream of Jerusalem artichoke soup, of Bobby Sands and his hunger strike. Eric and John think it's something you should be able to laugh at – and they do. TJ, and I agree with him, feels that the laughter must come from recognising and sensing a basic truth in what you're laughing at and you can't laugh at something you feel is dishonest – and I think it's dishonest to think of Sands as a worthless villain. And dangerous too.

To bed before midnight. How easily the 'historic' decision has been made. It's not often Python so clearly and unanimously sees the rightness of a decision and it's such a relief that it's happened like that today. It now remains to be seen how DO'B reacts. I hope he will not see it as a stab in the back, but a stab in the front. He should have seen it coming and it shouldn't prove fatal.

Sunday, May 3rd

At eight, feeling good and refreshed and bright, I walk down the drive of the Chewton Glen, taking care not to trip over the floodlighting bar which points up at the pine trees, and, taking the sign for Barton-on-Sea, make for the English Channel cliffs.

I can see the Isle of Wight in the distance. It's a dull morning with the sun only a faint lemon glow in a thickly-padded off-white sky. There are women walking poodles called Pippa and empty seaside hotels and a ravaged and collapsing shoreline which has no drama, excitement or visual splendour. Gardening and Walking the Dog Land 1981.

We assemble about 10.15. There's a re-reading of the letter to Denis and some corrections made. JC is so anxious to emphasise our inconstancy that there's a danger the cold reality of the message may not get through.

Then follows a chat about the next film – and one of the remarkable displays of the collective Python mind doing what it does best, best. Ideas, jokes, themes pour out from everyone round the table so fast that no-one wants to stop and write any of them down for fear of losing this glorious impetus. The court framework for the next movie comes up – the idea of us all being hanged for producing a film that is only a tax-dodge. It's all rich and funny and complex and very satisfying.

Tuesday, May 5th

Starts well, my 38th, with a clear and cloudless morning – the sort of day May ought to be, but hasn't been so far.

Work on the script – slowly but surely. Anne comes round at lunchtime with the letter to Denis to sign. JC has put back some of the wordiness that Eric and I took out, but it seems to be clear and bending over backwards to give us the blame!

I hear Denis will not be back until the weekend and wants a meeting with us next Monday. There's a sort of inexorability about it, like watching someone walk very, very slowly towards a concealed hole you've dug.

Wednesday, May 6th

First thing this morning, am putting out milk bottles when I encounter Peggy from No. 1 Julia Street. She's very sad because a week ago her case against her landlords was dismissed. She's got to move and No. 1 will be sold. Ring Steve and instruct him to try and buy it for me.

My *New Yorker* piece on Cinderella comes back with a rejection. Like A Coren's rejection note from *Punch* some years ago, the worst thing is the profuse apology – almost tangible embarrassment of the contact at the magazine. He's right, of course. He likes the incidental jokes which I like best and feels the whole a little too dull and conventional. A warning sign for all my writing.

Thursday, May 7th

My Bratby portrait has arrived. I hang it, not altogether seriously, but mainly to frighten Helen, above the piano. I don't like his interpretation of me particularly, but his technique of thick oil paint applied with short knife strokes in dozens of colours does make the picture very exciting. It certainly stands out, as an original should, in our houseful of rather restrained repros and prints. Quite ebullient and bright.

Friday, May 8th

Despite many comings and goings in the house (window cleaners to give estimates, recently-robbed neighbours to look at our burglar alarm system), I have the best writing morning of a bad week.

I write a sequence this morning that I know will be funny (the lost butler) and at least breaks a week in the wilderness.

Looking forward to a lazy evening in, when Denis rings. He's back and he has evidently seen the Chewton Glen letter.

He sounded calm, and in a realistic frame of mind. He was not entirely clear about what the letter proposed – could I elucidate? I elucidated as best I could, with kids clamouring for supper and Helen washing up beside me. We wanted DO'B to be an ad hoc, independent figure who we could come to for the major things he'd proved himself good at. Our essential aim was to simplify our business affairs.

DO'B was silent for a moment, but seemed to accept all this.

He talked about his 'upside' and his 'downside' and rather lost me here, but the long and the short of the call was that we should have a meeting as quickly as possible – and it needn't be a long one, he said. I promised I would ring Anne and ask her to set one up for Monday. Throughout Denis's tone was only a little injured and defensive and mainly practical and realistic – and quite friendly.

I talk to Eric later. He sounds unhelpful over the DO'B situation. He doesn't want to meet him and absolutely refuses to give DO'B any sort of preferential option on the next film at this stage. I bit my lip, and nearly my desk as well, at this.

Monday, May 11th

I drove down to BUPA to present Dr Gilkes with a long-running Palin saga – the Great Verruca, or Corn, as it once was.

He examined it and, as it has changed its shape and become less spread out, with more of a peak on it, he reckoned he could cut it out. And without much more ado, this is what he did. Using an instantaneously-acting local anaesthetic, he cut and chopped and sliced – sometimes with such great effort that I could scarcely believe it was my little toe and not some thick oak tree he was working on. Then he cauterised the edges, bandaged it all up and I hobbled out. But at least my verruca, which has been with me for nearly two years, was now in the dustbin.

I'd made Gilkes happy – 'It's been a jolly good day for the knife,' he assured me when we'd agreed on surgery. 'Some days I hardly use it at all,' he added regretfully.

I was to go straight from my verruca operation to a meeting with Denis O'B. It all seemed rather symbolic.

I hobbled in, the last to arrive (apart from Eric, who was just then landing in New York). Anne had thoughtfully provided white wine and some canapes. Denis sat looking a little careworn, but raised a smile. He had a notepad full of appointments and projects which he flipped through – films he was hoping to bring in through HandMade Distributors.

At about 7.20, after we'd been talking for an hour, John had to leave because he was taking someone to the theatre. So it was left to the four of us to decide on the next move with Denis. If we wanted to terminate – as 'I think the letter says' – Denis wanted to do it as quickly as possible.

Was there an alternative to complete and final termination? Terry J asked. Some way in which he could run a financial structure with us and liaise with the office at Park Square West? Denis didn't like this. It was all or nothing. He wanted to be free to concentrate on all the other areas EuroAtlantic could go in. He might, he said, get out of films altogether.

Graham asked if there were any 'offshore structure' which could be kept going. No, again Denis was adamant. Steve could not run a structure such as the one Denis had set up and which he still today talked about with loving pride.

So at about eight o'clock, as a dull evening was drawing to a close outside, we had to take a decision. Should we terminate? It really was the only answer. It was what the letter, signed by us all on May 5th, had said anyway. And so it was agreed and Denis left to begin to take down the structure and prepare for us a list of proposals for the ending of our relationship.

I couldn't believe it. My verruca and manager out, all within four hours.

Wednesday, May 13th

Manage the first full morning's writing this week and feel much better for it. Recently-gouged right toe is preventing me from running, so after lunch go down to Beatties and buy some LNER '30's imported teak rolling stock with the ten quid Ma gave me for my 38th. It crosses my mind that I'm 38 and still sneaking off to toyshops.

Down to Camberwell for dinner with the Joneses and, as it turns out, a rather boozed Richard Boston.[1]

He really doesn't look in good shape, which is a pity as he's such a mine of wondrous information – and knows such gems of political history as the fact that a gorilla once raped a French president's wife in the Elysée Palace, which is, of course, next to the zoo, and for many years afterwards the president was paranoid about gorillas.

And all this on the night the Pope was shot and Tom helped William

---

1 One of the first journalists to 'get' Monty Python, he was also a vigorous campaigner who, with Terry J, started an environmental magazine called the *Vole*. He gave his interests as 'soothsaying, shelling peas and embroidery'.

Ellis swim to a 20 point victory in the schools swimming gala. And another hunger striker died in the Maze.

Saturday, May 16th

Angela and I head for Linton – our great-grandfather's parish from 1865 to 1904. I'm intrigued by Edward Palin – the man of great promise who in his early 30's was senior tutor and bursar of St John's College, Oxford, and who gave up the chance of great things to marry Brita, an Irish orphan girl – herself the subject of a great rags-to-riches story – and settle at this tiny Herefordshire village and raise seven children.

There is the grave in the churchyard where he is buried together with two of his sons who pre-deceased him – one who died at Shrewsbury aged 18, another killed in the trenches of the Somme. Next to his grave and upstaging it is the grave of Caroline Watson, the American who found Brita the orphan and brought her up.

Determined, as a result of this weekend trip, to follow up some leads on the Palins – St John's College being one of them.

Friday, May 22nd

This is the day appointed for the changeover of Python affairs from EuroAtlantic at 26 Cadogan Square back to the more leisurely Nash terraces of Regent's Park. From today Steve and Lena [Granstedt, his assistant] work for Python and not EA.

I remember my embarrassment at having to tell people Python was with EuroAtlantic Ltd – an ugly name really, but I have had very good service from them. I rang Corinna [Soar – EA Company Secretary] – she was very touched by my letter and we had a quite unrecriminatory chat. She says it will be better when the changeover has actually happened. It's the transition process that's painful. I want to say to her how concerned I am about our future – that we don't see our move as a solution, just an inevitable part of the continuing development of Python, but I can't get into all that. I suggest we have lunch. Coward.

Wednesday, May 27th

Drive down to Wardour Street for a *Time Bandits* viewing.

George's single is No. 14 in the US charts and now he's under pressure to release follow-up singles – and we're under pressure to put another George song at the top of *Time Bandits*, as a potential US single. George admits with a smile that 'You grumble at them (the public) like hell when you're *not* in the charts, and then when you are in the charts you grumble at them for putting you there for the wrong reasons' (the aftermath of the Lennon shooting).

I don't like these viewings, especially when I know the room is full of people who have tried desperately to have many sections of the film cut. For the first half-hour everything seems wrong.

The laughs come for the first time on Cleese's 'Robin Hood' scene. From then on the 'audience' loosens up and I relax and George's big, bright arrangement of 'Oh Rye In Aye Ay' caps the film perfectly. At least we can talk to each other at the end. Even George, a harsh critic up to now, thinks the film is almost there, but hates the opening credits.

I must say, after today, I have a chilling feeling that we have fallen between too many stools. Not enough sustained comedy for the Python audience to be satisfied and too much adult content ('Titanic' references, etc) for the children's audience. We could just have created a dodo.

Friday, May 29th

Helen comes up to tell me that a 'For Sale' board is going up on No. 1 Julia Street. Steve A contacts Stickley and Kent, the agents. They are asking £37,500. Steve says he will get the keys.

Look at 1 Julia Street with Steve (financial) and Edward [Burd] (architectural). Damp, crumbling and filthy inside. Steve cannot believe that people were living here only a week ago and can believe even less that anyone should hope to get £37,500 for it. Edward thinks that the external walls, beneath their cracked and powdery rendering, may be stronger than they look. He reckons it would cost £30–£36,000 to renovate, and if we were able to buy the place for £25,000, despite its present state of extreme decay, it would be good value. Ed is going to find out more about the agent's hopes for the house and Steve says he can't wait to start working out how best we can pay for it!

Steve's business sense is as eager as Denis's, but his style utterly different. Denis is real estate and yachts, Steve is going to the March for Jobs rally at the weekend, three-day cricket and Springsteen.

Saturday, May 30th

Watch a clean, efficient, rather soporific goalless draw between Wales and Russia. It does one's perceptions good every now and then to see Russia – the enemy, the nation whose existence justifies enormous expenditure by Estaings, Thatchers, Carters and Reagans on weapons of destruction, the iron threat to Poland and Afghanistan, the home of Philbys and Burgesses, the cruel oppressor of Jewish minorities and cultural dissidents – playing a World Cup game at Wrexham.

Monday, June 1st

Wake to streaming, unequivocal sunshine, which looks set in for the day. Make all sorts of resolutions for the month as I sit down at my desk at a quarter to ten. I am determined to finish the first draft of *The Missionary*.

At half past six the results of my latest foray into consumerism are brought round to the house. A Sony Walkman II – an amazing mini-aturised stereo set, with thin, light headphones and a cassette-sized playing machine. If they can make such sound reproduction quality so small now, what of the next ten years? A button perhaps? A pill you swallow which recreates the 8-track wonders of Beethoven's Ninth from *inside* your body?

Also I'm now the proud owner of a small colour telly with a six-inch screen which fits on the kitchen shelf and will also undoubtedly revolutionise my life, until, in due course, the wonder of these marvellous technological advances wears down into acceptance.

Moral of the tale – do not rest hopes and enjoyments on Sony products. Man cannot live by machinery alone. All technological advances bring built-in dissatisfaction.

Wednesday, June 3rd

A late, light lunch, a few minutes in the sunshine, then back up to the workroom again. But the combination of heaviness from a persistent head cold and some rumbling guts ache knocks me out and, drained of energy, I skip supper and take to my bed about the same time as Rachel.

Just stay awake long enough to catch Terry J's first programme as presenter of *Paperbacks*. Helped on by a sympathetic and very well-mixed selection of guests, Terry came across as Terry at his best – serious, but good fun, mainly sensible, but occasionally enthusiastically carried away, positive but gentle. All in all, I thought, an excellent debut and such a change from the smooth old hands of TV presentation.

And I did take in an awful lot of what was said about the books – it reminded me of how much more I took in of Shakespeare when I watched John Cleese in *Taming of the Shrew*.

And his guest, J L Carr – an ex-schoolmaster who publishes little 35p books from his home in Kettering – was a wonderful find. He is the compiler of such indispensable volumes as *Carr's Dictionary of Extra-ordinary English Cricketers* and *Carr's Dictionary of English Queens, King's Wives, Celebrated Paramours, Handfast Spouses and Royal Changelings*.

Friday, June 5th

A week after first being alerted to Stickley and Kent's board at 1 Julia Street, I ring Stickley's with my £25,000 cash offer. An Irish female most curtly receives the offer and, with hardly any elaboration, tells me crisply that it will not be enough, but she'll take my name. Twenty-five thousand pounds in cash for that dump and she almost puts the phone down on me. Irrational – or perhaps this time rational – anger wells up. Write a letter confirming my offer and refuse to increase it at this stage.

To lunch at Mon Plaisir with TG.

TG and I have a very good, convivial natter and excellent meal. It's as if the major pressures on the *Time Bandits* are now lessening. Our collaboration has perhaps been one of the more successful aspects of the film. There are rumours that Denis is having some success with his '*TB*' viewings in America.

Then I go off to a viewing of the film again.

There is a constant, steady level of appreciation from quite a small audience and at the end I feel so elated, so completely risen from the gloom of the showing nine days ago, that I can hardly run fast enough through sunlit Soho streets back to Neal's Yard.

Terry is upstairs, alone in the big room looking over the yard with an editola in one hand and film in the other, still trimming. 'Sensational' is the only word I can use. At last I feel that *Time Bandits* has lived up to all the work that's gone into it.

Drive up to 2 Park Square West for a Python meeting.

There is a long agenda and yet we spend the first half-hour talking about possible changes to the Hollywood Bowl film. John is quite despairing. He buries his head in his hands and summons up what appear to be his very last resources of patience. 'I crave order,' he groans, looking at the remnants of the agenda, whilst Terry J suggests we put Neil in the film and possibly a bit more animation, and JC moans inwardly that he only wants to do this 'bloody thing' to make some money (I rather agree) and Eric it is who puts the frustrating but incontrovertible arguments for protecting our reputation by putting out only what we think is the best.

Sunday, June 7th

Another eight-hour sleep – too rare these days. The swirling south-westerly winds have died down, but the sky is overcast.

As if to suit the mood of the weather, Angela rings. She says she is in a depression and has been for the last two weeks. She's decided to drop her social worker job and is looking for something 'exciting'. She keeps talking of her low self-esteem. She's not easily consolable either, but puts on a brave and cheerful front. I can offer sympathy but nothing very practical.

I wonder if she finished this Whit Sunday watching, as I did, Cassavetes' *A Woman Under the Influence*. It was about madness and was rivetingly well-played, hard, depressing, uncompromising, but it aired a lot of problems and was ultimately optimistic.

I go to bed sober . . . sobered, anyway.

Monday, June 8th

A day of deck-clearing before an all-out assault on *The Missionary* script's last few scenes, which I hope to complete up in Southwold, with Suffolk countryside for inspiration and no telephones to distract.

Stickley and Kent call to tell me that my offer of £25,000 for No. 1 Julia hasn't been accepted, so I have to work out the next step. I want to make a £30,000 offer to put them on the spot, but after talking to Steve I revise this downward to £28,500 to allow bargaining room up to 30.

Wednesday, June 10th: Southwold

Wake to rich sunshine and birds chattering everywhere. Excellent conditions for a solid morning's writing at the desk presented to my grandfather from 'His grateful patients in Great and Little Ryburgh and Testerton,'[1] fifty years ago this November.

Great strides made in the plot and this writing break has already justified itself completely. No phone calls, no doorbells, no carpet-layers, cleaners, carpenters, painters or television engineers, just my Silvine 'Students' Note Book – Ref 142 – Punched for filing', Grandfather's desk and the soothing, wholesome view – pheasants scurrying through a broad field of new-sown peas and a chaffinch strutting and posing on the telegraph wires outside.

Later, watch Terry J being hypnotised on *Paperbacks*. He says very little and eventually breaks into tears. Rather disturbing, I thought, for the tears don't look like tears of joy but of fear and uncertainty and loss.

Saturday, June 13th

Prepare for our sideshow(s) at the Gospel Oak School Fayre. The Palin contingent (minus H who is at badminton) troop along to the school at 1.15, armed with 'Escalado', blackboard, notices and a bottle of sweets which the nearest number guess can win. Congratulate Ron Lendon, the head, on the MBE he acquired in the honours lists published today.

For three and a half hours solid I take money and start races. 'Escalado' proves to be a compulsive hit. The races are as often as I can physically take the money, pay the winnings and start again. A cluster of a dozen kids keep coming back – addicted. We make 10p per race and by a quarter to six, when I'm hoarse and staggering to start the last race, we've taken about £19.20, which means nearly 200 races.

The whole fete, in warm, dry, sunny, celebratory weather, seems to have done well. Even Willy, who looked very miserable earlier on as he tried to tout custom for his 'guess the sweet' attraction, had taken over £7 by the end and had brightened considerably.

Monday, June 15th

Denis O'B rings from Los Angeles. He doesn't seem to have any ulterior motive than to be reassured that I'm still there and writing a script for

---

1 Edward Watson Palin was a doctor who lived at Fakenham in Norfolk. I still correspond with a retired policeman who remembers Dr Palin taking tonsils out for free in his kitchen after church on Sundays.

him. He doesn't attempt to put pressure on in any direction. He sounds very vulnerable suddenly, as if he genuinely cannot understand how it could possibly be that five majors have already passed on *Time Bandits*.

I feel very sorry for him and if he was deliberately trying to soften me up then he succeeded. Any doubts I may have had about giving him first option on *The Missionary* faded as I put the phone down and left him to Universal.

Tuesday, June 16th

At seven o'clock, despite a last-minute volley of phone calls, I wrote the magic words 'The End' on my film – approximately two and a half working months from that run in mid-March when the title and subject suddenly clarified in my mind.

How good it is I really don't know. A cluster of scenes please me – the rest could go either way. I now have ten days of typing during which I shall tighten it up.

Thursday, June 18th

To Neal's Yard for more '*TB*' publicity – this time an interview for Granada TV's *Clapperboard*. For a simple interview on film there must be about ten people – production secretary, producer, publicity ladies, crew, etc, quite apart from Chris Kelly, who's asking the questions, TG and myself.

Terry has only just embarked on the first serious answer when he dislodges a huge can of film, which crashes to the floor noisily and spectacularly. Granada are very pleased.

Sunday, June 21st

Took Rachel to the zoo. Much activity in the bright sunshine. Baboons copulating, polar bears flat out on their backs with legs immodestly spread, scratching their belly hair slowly – like something out of Tennessee Williams, tigers crapping and penguins looking very dry and unhappy.

This evening we have to decide on how George H's song 'That Which I Have Lost' is accommodated in the opening titles. Neither Ray nor Terry feel satisfied with the song there at all. George, pushed by Denis, has done his best to make a version that works. But it was the wrong song in the first place and no-one has the courage to see that, so tonight we agree on a compromise. Part of the song under the opening names, but keep it clear of the thudding, impressive impact of TG's titles.

Wednesday, June 24th

The only event of any great significance in an otherwise unworkmanlike day is a call from Gilliam halfway through *News at Ten* to tell me that Denis has finally given up hope of selling *Time Bandits* in Hollywood. Disney, who apparently were closest to a deal, finally gave him the thumbs down. Apparently it was a case of the old guard at the top overruling the newer, younger, less conventional execs below.

Perhaps, TG and I feel, it would have been a lot better if Denis had organised a preview – like the *Brian* preview in LA which so impressed Warners. He has only tried to sell it at the top. And failed.

To bed resignedly. I feel sorry for TG. So much now depends on a big success in England. If it does badly here, or even only quite well, there is a real chance of the movie sinking without trace.

Friday, June 26th

Buy *Screen International*. The British film industry does not seem very healthy. Rank have just announced plans to cut 29 cinemas. The head of Fox (*not* an Englishman) in London gives a glib, gloomy, heartless prognosis that sounds like Dr Beeching – cinemas will only survive in about 20 major cities. The British don't go out any more. Video recorder sales are booming. Unfortunately I think he's right. It's going to be hard, if not impossible, to reverse this trend away from theatrical visits.

Wednesday, July 1st

To Gospel Oak Open Day to look at Willy and Rachel's work. Place full of doting, involved Gospel Oak parents. Impressive exhibition in the hall. Willy's dissatisfaction with his teacher this year doesn't seem to be reciprocated – she has given him a very good end of term report. But I can't imagine many circumstances in which Gospel Oak kids would receive bad reports – unless they were mass murderers, possibly. Rachel is as good as gold, I'm told by her nice teacher, Miss Evans.

Work until eleven, when I watch very good (possibly the best) edition of *Paperbacks*. TJ enthusing, as only he can, about Rupert Bear with

Alfred Bestall, 86-year-old chief artist of the stories, there in the studio, complete with loose false teeth.

Monday, July 6th: London–Edinburgh

Helen takes me down to King's Cross to catch the 'Flying Scotsman' to Edinburgh to read the 'Biggles' stories [for BBC AudioBooks]. Full of Americans being roughly treated by a particularly cheeky set of waiters who execute all their tasks with a barely-controlled violence just this side of politeness. What a change from the Liverpool Street lot.

All confirms my feelings that it's the differences between human beings themselves which account for all our economic, social and political injustices and not the other way round. In short, there are plenty of shits in the world and unless we can find some wonder drug to cure them or neutralise them, I think we have to live with the fact that they will always cause trouble.

At Edinburgh by a quarter to three. Meet the team and the adaptor, George Hearten – possibly the complete antithesis of his hero, Captain W E Johns. Ex-Fleet Air Arm, so he knows how to pronounce 'altimeter', he turns out to be a reggae expert and, when we do discuss who we would all like to have been, reckons he's the Glaswegian Albert Camus.

The concentration required on the readings is quite exhausting. We do two stories and Marilyn [Ireland, the producer] sounds pleased.

Then back for story number three. This is harder and towards the end I find myself unable to say 'thousands of splinters flew' and, though we finish it, Marilyn rightly suggests that we stop for the day.

Tuesday, July 7th: Edinburgh

After breakfast walk down to the BBC and, at about eleven, we start one of the most gruelling, physically and mentally demanding day's work I can remember. Again the concentration required is greater than anything I'm prepared for, with preliminary read-throughs of each episode included. I have to speak continuously for two and a half hours, in six or seven different voices. My eyes swim out of focus when I stand up – my brain has rarely been required to work so fast – to process and redigest so much information, all the time knowing that this will be judged as a performance. We plough through five episodes by five o'clock, leaving two for tomorrow.

I feel drained – 'Biggled', I think must be the word, well and truly Biggled – as I lie back in my bath at the North British with a Carlsberg Special as a reward.

Wednesday, July 8th: Edinburgh–London

Up to meet John Gibson of the *Edinburgh Evening News* at breakfast at nine. We talk for almost an hour. He's easy company, and a dutiful journalist – he makes sure he scribbles something down about all my activities. This is primarily a *Time Bandits* piece.

From talking to him I am reinforced in this feeling that's been coming over me lately – that my reputation follows about three or four years behind what I do. Somehow, though none of the individual projects were treated with respect or reverence at the time, the cumulative effect of Python and *Ripping Yarns* and the *Life of Brian* and the 'Great Train Journey' seems to have been to raise my stock to the extent that I am now not only good copy everywhere, but also I sense a sort of respectfulness, as if I'm now an experienced hand and a permanent addition to a gallery of famous British people. It's all very worrying and offers me little comfort, for I know I am still the same bullshitter I always was.

A quick walk through Prince's Gardens – where everyone is lying out in the sun like extras in a documentary about nuclear war. Up the Mound to a restored National Trust house in the Royal Mile. Fascinating, but as soon as I enter it there is quite a stir amongst the nice, middle-class family who run it.

I'm followed from room to room by a breathless young man who finally confronts me in a bedchamber – 'Excuse me, but you are Eric Idle from Monty Python . . . ?'

Friday, July 10th

More rioting on TV tonight.[1] It's replaced sport as the summer's most talked about activity. The scenes are frightening. One can only hope lessons will be learnt fast. Whitelaw and Thatcher go out of their way to support the police, but bad policing and the effects of unemployment vie with each other as the two most oft-quoted reasons for what's happening.

1 One of the most serious in a summer of urban riots took place at Toxteth in Liverpool. A thousand police were injured and many properties destroyed.

Tuesday, July 14th

Settle down to read *The Missionary*, which arrived today from Alison – the first really smart copy. It read far better than I expected. It seems tight, the religious atmosphere is strong, the story and the characters develop well and, all in all, it's just what I had hoped – a strong, convincing, authentic sense of place, mood, period and a dramatic narrative providing a firm base for some very silly comedy.

I finish reading at half past eleven and, though I write these words with great trepidation, I feel the film is over 70% right – maybe even more. Now names of actors, directors, keep coming into my head.

But the chiefest decision of all is how to play Denis. I must show it to him, or I think be prepared for a final breakdown argument with him. The situation is full of uncertainties and dangers. My prestige is such that I could show it to any number of producers and get a sympathetic hearing. But I have told DO'B that I will offer it first to HandMade – so there's the rub.

Wednesday, July 15th

I call Denis in Fisher's Island [his home near New York]. It's half past eight in the morning there and Denis sounds subdued, a little cautious at first, but when he realises it isn't bad news, he begins to wind up and by the end we are both beginning to celebrate.

He asks if I have a director in mind. I mention Richard Loncraine, who I haven't spoken to for a few months, and could still be a long shot. I mention spring of '82 for shooting and he says 'We would have no problem' – 'we' being, I presume, he, EuroAtlantic, Trade Development Bank and George.

Feel relieved that I've taken a positive step forward. It would remove endless complications if Denis accepted the script. Should hear something by the weekend.

To Rachel's end of term concert at Gospel Oak. A rather flat affair. All the children look as though they're acting under orders. Rachel plays a lettuce.

A call from Loncraine. Good news – for me – is that the *Brimstone and Treacle* film has collapsed – Bowie having let them down very much at the last minute. He has two film projects he wants to do, but claims to be very keen to work with me, and wants to see the script as soon as possible.

Thursday, July 16th

Out of the house at a quarter to eight. Stuck in rush-hour traffic, ironically trying to get to Marylebone High Street for Radio London's live programme called *Rush Hour*.

Talk to Jackie Collins, who's also a guest. She's doing the circuits for her new book, *Chances*, which my Radio London interviewer confides to me is 'the filthiest book I've ever read'.

Out in Marylebone High Street by nine o'clock. [*Time Bandits* opened in London yesterday.] Buy all the papers and treat myself to a reviving plate of bacon and eggs and a cup of coffee at a local caff. Read the *Guardian* – 'British, if not best'. Plenty of praise, but all qualified. In the *New Statesman* our friend and *Jabberwocky* fan John Coleman said many things, but concluded that the taste left by the film at the end was not just bad, it was sour. Cheered up by an unequivocal rave in *New Musical Express*. Nothing else.

Drove on down to Terry J's. Terry is on good form. *Paperbacks* has finished and we natter happily over various things. Realise that I'm enjoying writing with an immediate sounding board again. In fact I have rather a good day and add to the 'Catholic Family' sketch rather satisfactorily, whilst Terry deals genially with a mass of phone callers.

Home soon after six. Bad review on Capital. Much praise for the film, but he blatantly calls it the new Monty Python film. If I had more time and energy I'd sue him.

Friday, July 17th

In early evening an important call – the first professional opinion on *The Missionary* – from Richard Loncraine. He liked it up to page ten, then not again until page sixty, from whence he felt it picked up.

But I was hopeful from our short chat for two reasons. One that he doesn't dislike it enough to not want to do it, and the other that all he said about the script and intentions about how to film it I felt very much in agreement with.

Now Denis and Terry J are to report! They're the only others who have copies.

Saturday, July 18th

After lunch a party of ten of us go to see *Time Bandits* at the Plaza.

The audience is responsive, consistent and picks up the jokes, but I find that, at one or two points, we stretch their goodwill by over-extending on a moment that's already been effective. The Giant is on for too long and the trolls don't add much. Heresy I know to agree on this, but the acts *do* hold up Napoleon and *don't* get a positive reaction. And, though I don't object to the parents blowing up at the end, we hold the moments afterwards for too long, as if making a significant statement, and, in doing so, overloading the gloom and killing the black humour.

So I came away feeling a little numbed. Despite three or four people seeking me out to tell me how much they'd enjoyed it, I was disappointed that I'd seen faults in it and that there wasn't a greater sense of excitement amongst the departing audience.

TG rings later. He feels this sense of doom as well.

Sunday, July 19th

Woke to yet another day of concern. I have to learn my 'Plankton' speech for a Save the Whales rally in Hyde Park. Then there's the Sunday papers – how will *Time Bandits* fare today?

A marvellous selection of qualified raves. But somehow the qualifications seem to be significant rather than the raves. I read Alan Brien, who starts wonderfully and then qualifies. Philip French in the *Observer* chunders on at length for a column and a half before one word of doubt. But then it comes in, like a trip wire 20 yards from the tape at the end of a mile race.

As I describe them to Gilliam later – they're the worst set of rave notices I've ever seen.

I feel Alan Brien's observation is the most perceptive thing anyone's said about the film – 'Where it falls below earlier Python movies, or Gilliam's own *Jabberwocky*, is in the sense it gives that once the basic idea was established the makers thought everything else would be easy.'

Still, no time to mope, as I have to take myself and rapidly-learnt script down to Hyde Park to address the Save the Whales rally – which was allowed to go ahead by [Police Commissioner] McNee despite a month-long ban on London marches following the riots, because it was termed 'educational'.

Monday, July 20th

Start of a Python writing fortnight. We tried such a session a year ago and it was not successful. Today, a year later, things feel very different.

Time Bandits is complete, so TG is back with the group. Eric is relaxed and well after France. Terry J has got *Paperbacks* out of the way and is keen to get directing again. Graham, with *Yellowbeard*, and myself, with *The Missionary*, both have projects which look like being completed by summer '82.

We decided, without any bickering or grudging, that we should now work separately until the end of the week. Everyone agreed that this film should not be extended indefinitely and if it was to become a reality it had to be next year.

So, after lunch and an amiable chat, we disperse to our separate writes.

About ten o'clock DO'B rings from Fisher's Island. He's just finished reading *The Missionary*. As I expected, the last thing he wants to do is give any artistic judgement on the script. He talks of it purely from a business point of view. He sounds to have no doubts that it's a commercial reality and he's treating it accordingly.

DO'B reckons it's an eight- or nine-week shoot, 65% studio, and will cost about one and a half million. We are looking at a March, April, early May '82 shoot.

Thursday, July 23rd

Drive over to Richard Loncraine's office in Clarendon Cross. How neat, well-preserved, paved and bollarded this little corner of Notting Hill has become. Charming, I should think is the word. Richard bounds down to answer the door, and is soon showing me his latest gadgets (he runs a toy factory employing 200 people making ridiculous things like eggs with biros in the end), pouring me some wine, raving about *Time Bandits*, which he thought absolutely wonderful, calling *Chariots of Fire* 'Chariots of Bore' and generally bubbling and enthusing like an English version of Gilliam.

Richard is going to do it and will commit to it. He repeats that he wants to work with me and he's doing it largely out of faith in what I can achieve, which is flattering and exciting at the same time, and because, although there is much in the script he thinks doesn't yet work, he thinks there's more that does.

The next step is to bring DO'B and Loncraine together next week. But I think I can say that *The Missionary* became a reality tonight.

Sunday, July 26th

Richard rings to suggest Maggie Smith for Lady Ames, which shows he's been thinking positively about it.

Monday, July 27th

To a Python meeting at 2 Park Square West, giving T Gilliam a lift. A successful day, everyone participating. John tending to chair in a barristerish way, but it's all good Python trough work. We re-read the 'bankers'. They nearly all survive and, by half past three when TJ has to go, we have a solid 50 minutes, with viable links and a sort of coherence.

Ring Terry J to find out if he has read *The Missionary*. He has, and finds it all 'unbelievable'. Not an encouraging reaction. Set off to [Euro-Atlantic in] Cadogan Square. Denis, tall, tanned and looking as confidently turned out as ever, meets me and we walk through the balmy evening to the Chelsea Rendezvous.

I start by telling Denis that all three people who have read *The Missionary* haven't liked it. A little provocative, I suppose, but it's the way I read the reactions. Terry J's, strangely enough, doesn't trouble me as much as I thought. Maybe, as TJ and I just improvised over the phone this evening, it would be better for Welles to be given a mission in England – possibly the saving of fallen women. But talking to Denis I feel, obstinately perhaps, that my instincts are right and that my choice of director is right and that the film can work. Denis is not at all discouraging. Quite the opposite.

Tuesday, July 28th

I wake in the early hours in general discomfort – head and tooth aching and very hot. Just not ready for sleep, so walk about a bit. Then, from three a.m. until half past four I sit and scribble some dialogue for a new scene in *The Missionary* – trying to take the story in a different direction, as I discussed with TJ over the phone.

Drain my cup of tea and look up finally from deep absorption in the work, to see the sky has lightened to a dark, pre-dawn blue. Feel much better. Feel I've defeated the aches and pains! Back to bed.

Later take Granny and the Herberts to *Time Bandits*.

Afterwards we all walk down Regent Street into a Mall thronged with pre-wedding [of Charles to Diana] crowds. A feeling of celebration and slightly noisy camaraderie, as if the revolution had just happened. Of course, quite the opposite; everyone here tonight was celebrating the longevity and resilience of the Establishment.

There was a mass of sleeping bags and plastic all along the edge of the pavement – rarely much class or style, except that under the trees outside the ICA a long table had been set with candles and four men in full dinner jackets and bow ties were sitting down to a meal and wine.

Saturday, August 1st

Time Bandits biz in second week is down, as Denis said, by about 20%, but then so is everyone's except James Bond and *Clash of the Titans*. We move up to No. 3 in London above *Excalibur*, now in its fourth week, and the fading *Cannonball Run*.

Marvellous review by Gavin Millar in the *Listener*. I wonder if TG had time to see it before he went off to France yesterday. The *Ham and High* [the *Hampstead and Highgate Express* – our local paper] and many of the rest of England papers turn in good reviews too, so that all cheers me up. But the bad news is that the figures for week one in Bristol are, by any standards, very disappointing. Cardiff is better, but certainly no signs of it being anything but an average performer outside London.

Sunday, August 2nd: Southwold

An early lunch (cheese and an apple) and drive back through Suffolk villages and down the M11, listening to another tense Test Match. Cloudless sky when I arrive in Oak Village. Australia nearly 100 with only 50 to go and seven wickets standing. But by the time I've unpacked, oiled myself and settled down for a sunbathe on the balcony they have collapsed and within an hour Botham has wiped them out and England have won.

Wednesday, August 5th

I drive into town for lunch with Neville Thompson at Mon Plaisir.

Neville is the third of the main strands of *The Missionary* project. Denis is supplying the money, Loncraine the direction and Neville could be the producer.

Like everyone else he has qualifications about the script, but has faith in the project. I try to give him as many 'outs' as possible, but he clearly feels that there is some rich vein to be tapped wherever Pythons are involved – even if he can't immediately see it in *The Missionary* as it stands. I feel a little like the Missionary myself at the moment, trying to convert the waverers to the joys and virtues of this bloody film.

Loncraine rings. He's back from New York, where he's been to see Sting – of 'Police' – for part in *Brimstone and Treacle*.

Thursday, August 6th

Over to Loncraine's for further talks on *The Missionary*. Richard has read it again and sees certain problem areas. Richard talks from the hip a bit, firing ideas out fast and in a not particularly disciplined way. Tendency to broader jokes, but, on the credit side, we come up with three very good visual additions to the script which I can immediately incorporate in the rewrites. Another heavy storm breaks – starting with an apocalyptic clap of thunder – 'Didn't like that idea, did he?' says Richard, looking out of the window respectfully.

Reagan has dismissed 13,000 of his air traffic controllers for going on an illegal strike, but Sheila [Condit, who was organising our US holiday trip] has checked with LA Airport and international flights are coming in 95% on time.

Friday, August 7th

In the evening Helen goes to badminton. I stay in to watch the news. Whilst Reagan pursues his hard line against the air traffic controllers, European air traffic controllers are quoted as advising against flying to the US. Disturbing stuff – 25 near misses reported in US air space since the strike began, the new military controllers plus non-striking controllers are working longer hours and 'safety is being endangered'. American government says rubbish, and the airlines flying to the States say so too. But not a very comforting way to have to start the holiday. I feel that, if the BA pilots are still prepared to fly with the new controllers then I'm happy – but don't go to bed elated.

We flew to California on August 9th for a family holiday, having rented a
house at Point Dume, near Malibu.

Wednesday, September 2nd

Denis met with Loncraine and got on well and is anxious to sign him up.
Time Bandits is still No. 3 in London. It will not be the blockbuster they
were predicting. They'd been looking for a distributor's gross of a million,
but have revised this downwards to half a million. But he has done a deal
in America. Avco Embassy are to release the *Time Bandits* on November
6th with four million dollars committed to prints and advertising.
Modest, by today's standards, and Avco Embassy are guaranteed against
loss by Denis and George.

Thursday, September 3rd

To my desk to wrestle with the most immediate problems. One of the
first calls on our return, Tuesday, was from a humbled Stickley and Kent
asking if my offer of £28,500 for No. 1 Julia Street still stood. Apparently
they have had some difficulty selling at £37,750. As my offer had been so
summarily dismissed, I told them I would think about it.

Helen is not really keen and sees No. 1 as a lot of hard work, but on the
other hand she does see the advantage of having control over the site.
Edward keen to take on the job and will supervise, so on balance I stick
to my first instinct and renew my interest – at the same time twisting the
knife a little and giving my cash offer as £26,500. We shall see.[1]

On to viewing of *Hollywood Bowl* on screen for first time. Sixty-five
minutes it runs. Sketches well performed and quite well filmed – the rest
a wretched disappointment.

Back at Neal's Yard, those Pythons who saw the film – Terry J, John,
Graham and myself (TG and Eric being in France) – all agree it isn't
right. Main criticisms – links, atmosphere, shapelessness.

I felt very proud of our little group today. In the face of much pressure
to put the '*Bowl*' film out as soon as possible, to recoup our money and
to have done with it, we held out for quality control first.

---

1 We never did buy No. 1, but snapped up No. 3 years later!

Tuesday, September 8th

Drive into town to join the London Library and take out, at last, some books on African missionaries – *Winning over a Primitive People*, etc – to read as background on the film.

Evening of phone calls, latest of which is Denis O'B ringing from New York. I tell him all is well, except that both Richard Loncraine and Neville Thompson think that the budget will be nearer £2 million than £1 million.

Turns out that he has sold *The Missionary* project to George on the basis of a £1.2 million cost.

Thursday, September 10th: Southwold

I watch a programme about the colossal, massive, virtually incredible madness of our world in 1981 – the designing, building and deployment of weapons of self-destruction.

It worries me that we accept now that we have to live with bombs which could kill two million people with one blast. That somewhere in the world there are men designing and manufacturing and loading and aiming and controlling and making serious considerations of policy based on the use of such weapons. Meanwhile we pay for such collective madness with unemployment, a crumbling health service, a polluted planet. It seems we know that we shall destroy ourselves somehow and the multi-megaton bombs are like the cyanide pills which will put us out of our misery instantly.

Wednesday, September 16th

A solid morning's work on *The Missionary*. Few distractions and I fall into a good rhythm.

To the airport to collect Al and Claudie. Wet roads. Repairs close the motorways, London seems empty, ghostly. At the airport soon after ten – find them waiting, the plane was early. Best flight ever, opines the bronzed and ageless poet, pulling eagerly on a cigar as they had sat in non-smoking. Claudie, just a gently convex stomach showing discreetly, looked very well and in good colour.

Friday, September 18th

Up to Burgh House at 6.00 for the Grand Launch [of Al's book of poems, called *Travelogs*]. Robert laid out a display of Signford's[1] wares on the piano of the Music Room and hardly anybody turned up. More and more I had the feel that I was in one of Richmal Crompton's 'William' situations. Involved in one of his 'grate skeems' which never quite work.

But there were enough there for me to rise to my feet and embark on the speech. No sooner had I begun than a dozen latecomers arrived in the next one and a half minutes, so the speech wasn't helped, but the party was. And in the end it was quite difficult to move everyone out.

Then out to Vasco and Piero's [Pavilion Restaurant] with Al, who had been quaffing malts during the afternoon, then much champagne at the party, but was in a big, expansive bear-like mood of delight, Claudie, and Mike Henshaw[2] and his excellent new 'companion' Penny. We all had a wonderful time and Mike paid.

For Mike and me it was a reconciliation. Having been good and close friends for 13 years, accountancy got in the way and we have not spoken or seen each other for two years. We picked up as if nothing had happened.

Wednesday, September 23rd

In mid-afternoon take advantage of dry, still, bright weather for a run across the Heath, then down to Eyre Methuen to discuss with Geoffrey S and Terry J a new edition of Fegg which we agree to call *Dr Fegg's Nasty Book*. We look through the artwork of the old – now seven years past – up in Methuen's boardroom, sipping white wine and looking out over a panorama of city buildings turning reddish-gold in the waning sunlight.

Thursday, September 24th

Work delayed this morning by arrival of TG, fresh from Hollywood, bearing such gems as a market research survey on *Time Bandits* – a wonderfully thorough and conscientious document analysing test

1 Signford was an off-the-shelf name for a small publishing company I had set up, with Robert Hewison's help. Its first book was by the artist Chris Orr.
2 Michael Henshaw, my first accountant, had been married to Anne, who had become my manager, and the Pythons' manager. She had re-married, to Jonathan James, a barrister.

screenings and reactions to all the various elements of the film in that earnest American way which reduces all things to 'product'. They confirm that the film is not for Fresno, but it could well be for bigger, more 'sophisticated' city audiences.

Interesting thing it *did* reveal is that the audience at Sherman Oaks went to the movies on average ten times a month, and in Fresno seven. Which shows the health of movies in the US is still good, whereas here the admissions level is still dropping to all-time lows.

Work on the Fermoy scene, but got involved in helping Tom with his geography homework. Then drive down to the Long Room at the Oval cricket ground for Pavilion Books launching party.

Soon was in the middle of a swirling throng – past the literary editor of the *Express*, Peter Grosvenor, on to a very persistent Scottish lady publisher who wants to have lunch and discuss some project involving Miriam Stoppard, Tom Stoppard and sex, grabbed by Molly Parkin, who's very oncoming – she says I always was her favourite – and meet Max Boyce. 'Oh I love being in a corner with two comedians,' she soothed, as we had photos taken together.

Then Bob Geldof in green lurex jacket, black skin-tight trousers and mediaeval floppy boots approached and we hailed each other like old friends, though I don't know him that well. After a brief exchange of mutual abuse, we talked about school and missionaries and he swore blind that he had been at a missionary school in Ireland where the French master was mainlining quinine, Irish was compulsory and, even if you got seven or eight 'O' Levels, none of them counted if you failed Irish.

Friday, September 25th

Drink in the Nag's Head. Aggressive podgy Cockney looms up.

'Are you Eric Idle?'

'No ...'

'You're Eric Idle.'

'No, I'm not ...'

'Well, it's a very good impression,' he mutters and wanders back to his mates.

Saturday, September 26th

After lunch out with the family to visit Uncle Leon in Hampton Wick, in the tiny, neat, long and narrow cottage which Leon moved into only two weeks before Helen's Aunt Peggy, wife of 38 years, died early this year. He took a long time to recover and said he couldn't bear being alone in the house in the evening. He confessed very touchingly that he's often found himself turning to talk to someone who isn't there.

A big tea with scones and home-made jam, then home under angry skies ranging from slate grey to pitch black, through the well-kept roads of Hampton and Twickenham. Perfect example of Tory middle-class orderliness. No rows of council flats with rubbish flapping around them, or grandiose public works schemes left half undone through lack of funds. This is the tidy, thrifty world of private planning, from which the poor and the underpaid seem absent. But at least personal enterprise is allowed and encouraged to flourish here, when the grey blocks of Camden seem only to have extinguished it.

Back home I watch quite brilliant first film of Bill Douglas trilogy,[1] *My Childhood*.

Tuesday, September 29th

Came near to giving up this morning. For a full hour I sat and stared. Every word I wrote seemed dull and wooden. The last three weeks of fairly solid application (well, two and a half, anyway) seemed to have produced just sludge. And tomorrow was the last day of September, when I had once optimistically estimated I would be finished with the [*Missionary*] rewrites.

But abandoning now would seem so feeble. I had to carry it through. Besides, I'd burnt my boats – turning down every other piece of work. So it was that in the hour and a half before lunch I buckled down and ideas began to flow and in fact I was well into my stride when the door bell rang at 2.30 to herald the arrival of a BBC crew to film me giving testimony in a programme about giving up smoking.

---

1   Made in 1972, it tells the story of a boy born into poverty in Scotland and his relationship with a German POW. Douglas made only four films, all autobiographical; bleak but brilliantly observed.

Sunday, October 4th: Southwold

Woke at 8.30. The boys already downstairs and breakfasted. Outside a steady drizzle, which increased to heavy rain, and the children and I took Mrs Pratt [my mother's neighbour] to morning service at Reydon.

We leave her and drive into Southwold for more secular activities. Despite all my doubts and rational resistance to the dogma of the church, I still feel a powerful guilt at taking the children to the amusement arcade on the end of Southwold Pier on a Sunday morning. You don't notice the presence of the church in London, as you do in Southwold.

Wednesday, October 7th

To the Escargot in Greek Street for meal with Terry and Al. Terry has just returned from his *Fairy Tales* promotion trip to Birmingham (which he hated) and Manchester (which he found well-heeled) and Liverpool (sad tales of the decline of the Adelphi).[1] Give the manager one of my complimentary tickets to Mel Brooks's *History of the World*, which is having a glossy preview at 11.30.

Find myself sitting next to Harold Evans, Editor of the *Times*. He seems to be very anxious to please – asking me what I'm doing, as if he knows me. Make some jokes about the SDP, then he admits that he does think they are a very sensible lot. This, together with a propensity to do the right thing by clapping whenever Mel Brooks appears on screen, makes me suspect him. Surely *Times* editors should be made of harder stuff?

The film is dreadful. Having dispensed early on with any claim to historical accuracy or authenticity and any exceptional attention to visual detail, the whole thing depends on the quality of the gags. And the quality is poor. It's like a huge, expensive, grotesquely-inflated stand-up act. A night club act with elephantiasis.

Thursday, October 8th

Tom becomes a teenager. Just writing those words makes me abruptly aware of time passing. He has lots of books about aircraft and Helen

---

1 A once-glamorous hotel for transatlantic liner passengers. Helen is convinced our daughter Rachel was conceived there on the night of my friend Sean Duncan's wedding in 1974.

and I are to buy him a new clarinet. He goes off to school very happy.

I take him and three friends out to Century City in Mayfair – a new hamburger place, all silver-sprayed 'hi-tech' décor. Only open three weeks, but looking decidedly run down. Still, the food was good and we all sat inside a dome painted silver. At one point Alex Robertson declares, almost proudly, 'Gosh, my mum and dad wouldn't have been able to afford *this*.' Echoes from all round the table.

Saturday, October 10th

Buy presents for the evening's celebrations to mark EuroAtlantic's tenth anniversary. The celebration is to be held, somehow appropriately, aboard a boat called the *Silver Barracuda*.

Mark Vere Nicoll [EuroAtlantic's legal wiz] makes a speech and presents Denis with a leather-covered photo album which is also a music box. Denis gives a long speech in reply. Quite fluent and informal. But he does at one point pay tribute to Peter Sellers – adding, somewhat unnecessarily, 'Who can't be with us tonight.' George, ever in touch with the other world, shouts back, 'Don't be so sure, Denis.'

Wednesday, October 14th

Helen is 39. But looks a lot younger.

Mary, Edward and Catherine Gib arrive at 8.00 and I take them all out for what turns out to be a very successful Mystery Evening. First to the Gay Hussar – good food and efficient, old-fashioned service. Then on to Ronnie Scott's to see Panama Francis and the Savoy Sultans – a Harlem Thirties jazz and swing band. Beautiful to listen to, presented stylishly and with the added poignancy that they are a dying breed. In ten years many of them won't be left. But the two hours we spent there in their soothing, infectious company were rare magic.

Thursday, October 22nd

Just after five o'clock I suddenly found myself at the end of *The Missionary* rewrites.

I've spent about five and a half solid working weeks on the rewrite and there are only about a dozen pages left intact from the 121-page first version. So I have virtually written a second film in about half the time it took to write the first.

But for the moment, at the end of this crisp and invigorating day, the feeling is just one of an onrush of freedom – of time to spare – the emergence from isolation.

Monday, October 26th: Ballymaloe House, Ireland

We landed at Cork at ten o'clock, our VW minibus was waiting and we drove without incident to Ballymaloe. The bright sunshine of London was replaced by rain in Ireland. By early evening it's clear enough for me to go for a run – up past barking dogs and along a narrow road which grows more and more wild and directionless – giving rise in the dark corners of my mind to California-like fears of sudden mindless violence. (I was not to know that about one hour before, in the London we had just left, a bomb had exploded in a Wimpy bar in Oxford Street[1] – the IRA claimed credit.)

Thursday, October 29th: Ballymaloe

Woke about 8.00 to hear Rachel colouring industriously across the other side of the room. Then to breakfast – which now stretches from nine till ten. I love our little tableful and it's a joy and complete relaxation to sit, after children have gone, with a dependably tasty cup of coffee and gaze out of the long Georgian windows at the damp autumn countryside.

We have a packed lunch today and, on advice from an Irishman staying here, drive to Cobh and Fota Island.

Cobh, an old fishing town and fadedly elegant resort, is approached across a causeway, past an old blockhouse or pill-box on which are daubed the words 'Cobh supports the hunger strikers'. Then there are a number of small black flags on short makeshift flagpoles nailed up to telegraph poles.

Unlike anywhere else we've been in Southern Ireland, this year or last, there is a definite frisson of hostility in Cobh. It's clearly official municipal policy to support the IRA – although these initials are never mentioned. It's always 'our boys' or 'our countrymen'. Beside the station, now a fish-unloading yard, posters are stuck on the wall – clenched fists surmounted

---

1 Killing the man who was trying to defuse it.

with the words 'Stand Up To Britain' and an incongruous picture of Maggie Thatcher with the words beneath 'Wanted. For The Torture Of Irish Prisoners'.

The memorial to those who died in the *Lusitania* has been turned into an IRA memorial, with placards hung round the necks of the 1915 sailors giving the names of the hunger strikers. Like so much in Ireland it is a rough and ready gesture – there's no style or care particularly taken. It's functional, rather ugly and very depressing.

Mary [Burd] gets fish lobbed in her direction by the unloaders and there's some laughing and sending-up. My final image of this potentially rather attractive Georgian town is of a grimy 40-foot trailer being driven at violent, shaking speed along crowded streets, blood pouring out of the back and onto the road.

Wednesday, November 4th: New York

The car horns start to blare and I know I'm in Manhattan [for the opening of *Time Bandits*]. A fine 27th storey view out over Central Park. The trees in full autumn colours, mustards, russets, yellows. Very fine, a stretch of calm on this restless island.

General atmosphere of cautious excitement improved by continuing news of fresh enthusiastic reviews. Jack Lyons [Avco-Embassy's publicity man] says he has nearly all the majors covered, but so far his spies in the *NY Times* have not been any help with leaks about the Canby review.[1] Canby's review will be out on Friday, but, if all else fails, Jack says he'll get a leak from one of the compositors on Thursday afternoon!

In the evening we have a Gala Premiere and I drink an awful lot of champagne. Jack has arranged for me to escort Eleanor Mondale, a rather classically good-looking 21-year-old blonde, who resembles, especially, with her hair-do and use of knickerbockers, a chunky Princess Diana.[2] She is quite used to the bright lights and walks with a serene sort of Scandinavian poise through all the ballyhoo. And there *is* ballyhoo.

We are driven to the theatre in limousines and disgorged before a small waiting crowd gathered good-humouredly rather than ecstatically behind

---

1 Chief film critic of the *New York Times*. He died in 2000.
2 Walter Mondale was Jimmy Carter's Vice-President from 1976 to 1981. Eleanor, a radio presenter, was diagnosed with a brain tumour in 2005, but seems to have successfully fought it.

wooden barriers. Then we go inside and meet the good people who have been invited along. Meet Frank Capra Jnr, the new head of Avco-Embassy, whom I quite like. James Taylor, looking like the earnest maths master in a prep school, comes up and re-introduces himself.

After the movie begins, Terry G, Nancy, Eleanor Mondale and I take off to a ceilinged, fashionable but un-chic restaurant down on 18th called Joanne's. Shelley [Duvall] joins us later with news of a complete fiasco at the Gala Premiere. It was held in a twin cinema complex and apparently the sound was very bad in the first one for ten minutes, and in the second the picture came on upside down after the first couple of reels.

Thursday, November 5th: New York

Driven by a talkative chauffeur – they don't call them chauffeurs over here, I notice, but 'drivers'. This one goes into a monologue about 'celebrities'. 'I do like celebrities. They're very nice people.' He tells me how, as a cabbie, he gave a ride to Frank Sinatra and then rushed home and rang his mother at three in the morning to tell her the news. He also has taken Gilda Radner to the dentist and tells me all sorts of intimate details about her bridge work.

I notice that the driver is totally grey – cap, trousers, jacket, shoes, hair and face. Amazing. To the mid-West Side in sight of the big liner bays, for the *Dick Cavett Show*.

The programme progresses in uneasy fencing between comedy and seriousness. Cavett doesn't want to look like the dullard, so he indulges my subversive silliness instead of bringing it under a tight rein. The result is that some comedy works and there is nothing to fall back on when it doesn't.

The limousine takes us on to NBC and the *Robert Klein Hour*. This is a radio show I have come to enjoy greatly. Klein is relaxed, sharp, funny and good at guiding a disparate guest list – which includes Meat Loaf and Loudon Wainwright III – who remembers straight away that we met last in a massage parlour.

End up eating at Elaine's. Shelley is along with us for a while. Good Italian food, nice busy atmosphere.

TG gets his first sight of the Vincent Canby review. I'll never forget his face as he studies it, at the table beside Woody Allen and Mia Farrow, with the waiters pushing by. 'Studies' is far too mild a word for the extraordinary intensity of Terry's expression. His eyes stare fearfully like some Walter Crane drawing of an Arthurian knight confronting the face of Evil. Two years of solid commitment can be rendered quite spare in one review. At the end he lays the paper down ... 'Yes ... it's good ...'

Monday, November 9th

'*The Missionary* Mark II' arrives from the typist's, and I fall on it and read it through eagerly. It reads very well and I'm happy with the last-minute cuts and readjustments. And I laughed more, much more, than at Mk I.

Send the script round by cabs to Neville and Richard L. Watch some television. Can't keep my mind on writing. I'm half hoping the phone will ring before I go to bed and bring some breathless enthusiasm from one or other of them for the new script. This is what I need now.

At 11.30 the phone does ring. It's Rita from Los Angeles. Though it's only lunchtime Monday in LA, she tells me (in strictest confidence, she says) that *Time Bandits* took 6.2 million dollars over three days of its first weekend. This is bigger than any film ever handled by Avco (including *The Graduate*).

I'd still rather have had a phone call about *The Missionary*.

Tuesday, November 10th

Halfway through the morning Neville Thompson rings. My heart sinks utterly as he tells me that he wants to see the original script, because he feels I've lost a lot in the rewrites. I'm sure he doesn't realise what a dashing blow this is after two months' rewriting. Anything but wild enthusiasm is a dashing blow!

Denis calls in the afternoon and brightens me up with the news that *Time Bandits* has taken (officially) 6.5 million dollars in its first three days in the US. He estimates it will overtake *Life of Brian*'s total US take in two and a half weeks. Incredible news, almost as incredible as Neville not liking the new script.

Wednesday, November 11th: Belfast

Still no word from Richard L. Off to Heathrow at 11.00 to take the 12.30 shuttle to Belfast. Bag searched very thoroughly and wrapped in a cellophane cover before loading. Flight half full. Land at Aldergrove at a quarter to two.[1]

Belfast is not unlike Manchester or Liverpool. A once proud and thriving city centre suffering from the scars of industrial decline. Fine, red-brick warehouses empty. New office blocks – featureless and undistinguished. The university and its surrounding streets quite elegant; Georgian and early Victorian Gothic.

The Europa Hotel is screened at the front by a ten-foot-high mesh wire and everyone has to enter through a small hut, where my bag was searched again and my name checked on the hotel list. Then into the hotel, with its thick carpets and Madison Suites. No-one seems to find it remarkable any more that such a smart façade should be upstaged by a makeshift hut and barbed wire. Will they make the hut permanent one day? Will it be landscaped – or would that spell victory for the forces of disorder?

I have a pleasant two-room suite with an 8th floor view. Michael Barnes, tall, with long hair and sweeping beard, is very charming. 'I know we'll get on,' he said, 'because you write such good letters.' And vice-versa, I should have said, for it was something about his first approach to me by letter that brought me here.

Michael B told me that I was the second Festival attraction to sell out – two days after Yehudi Menuhin and two days ahead of Max Boyce! Anyway it was quite restorative for my ego to see a long queue of people waiting to get into the Arts Theatre.

Up tatty stairs to a small dressing room with light bulbs missing. Sort out my false noses, moustaches and at a quarter to eight I go on. The first part of the programme is what I've written and cobbled together since returning from New York. It goes well, but, after what seems an interminable and gruelling length of time, I glance at my watch between changes and, to my astonishment and despair, it's still only eight o'clock.

In fact it's just after 8.30 when I finish 'Fish in Comedy' – and I'm very hot and sweaty. For a moment the question and answer session seems doomed. Then all of a sudden it begins to happen. A steady stream of well-phrased, fairly sensible enquiries give me ample scope to talk about and enact scenes from all the favourite Python topics – censorship, the Muggeridge/Southwark interviews, etc.

---

1 I had been asked by Michael Barnes, director of the Belfast Festival, to go over and give a performance. It was my first one-man show. I was to do more, but only ever at Belfast. The Troubles were at their height.

There are some very enterprising audience suggestions – 'Did you know, Mr Palin, that it is a tradition for solo performers who visit the Arts Theatre, Belfast, to run round the auditorium from one side of the theatre to the other? The record is held by Groucho Marx at 45 seconds.' So I peeled off my jacket, paced out the course and went off like a rocket. 38 seconds. Whoever he was, I should have thanked him.

So I rambled on until ten to ten, just over two hours on the stage. Thoroughly enjoyable. Michael Barnes very pleased backstage.

Friday, November 13th

Gemma, a helper at the Festival and English girl, says that the worst thing about living in Northern Ireland is the way people have become used to the violence. They hardly turn a hair when a bomb goes off. Her father, who has worked here for years, will return to England when he retires. Resignation and survival rather than hope or rebuilding seem to be the watchwords.

I leave on the 10.30 shuttle. We take 55 minutes, with the help of a north-westerly tailwind, to reach Heathrow, where it's dry and sunny.

At half past two Neville Thompson arrived to talk about *The Missionary*. His doubts, which had worried me so much earlier in the week, seemed less substantial as we talked and I think I was able to persuade him that there were very funny things in the script. He in turn gave me a thought about Fortescue's character which clarified something very constructively – that Fortescue should enjoy sex. A simple, but clear observation, which gives greater point, irony and tension throughout.

Saturday, November 14th

This is one of those mornings when it's worth buying *Variety*. 'Bandits Abscond With 69G in St Lou', 'Boston's Ambitious Bandits Bag 269G', 'Bandits' Larcenous 45G in KC', 'Bandits Looting LA. Hot 368G'. Lovely breakfast reading.

Sunday, November 15th

Work in the afternoon, watch Miles Kington's 'Great Railway Journey', which makes me want to start travelling again. But the best news of the week is that Loncraine rings with a very positive reaction to the new script. He thinks it's an easier read and much funnier. Eight out of ten, he thinks, rather than six for the first one.

Monday, November 16th

I had to bestir myself and turn out, on an evening I dreadfully wanted to be in, to run the auction for Westfield College in Hampstead. Predictably chaotic student organisation, but on the whole very nice people. They gave me a list of nearly 100 items to be individually auctioned.

The slave auction at the end *was* fun. Boys offering their services to do anything for 24 hours. Girls offering massage. I won that myself – with a bid of £23.00. Finally I had to auction my own face, on to which anyone could push a custard pie. Not once, but five times. Collected nearly 30 quid for this alone. All the pies were delivered by girls, and the last two gave me kisses through the foam!

Thursday, November 19th

At six o'clock take Willy and Tom to the Circus World Championships on a common in Parsons Green. This is a Simon Albury trip – his present to Willy on his 11th birthday.

It's mainly a TV event with cameras all over the place and a wonderful BBC floor manager squashed into a very tight-fitting evening dress with white socks on and an arse so prominent it looks like a caricature of Max Wall. Simon has secured us seats right by the ring – so we can see the sweaty armpits, the toupees and the torn tights that the viewers at home will miss.

The things I like least about circuses are animals and clowns and there are neither tonight. Instead about a dozen different varieties of balancing act. Russians holding ladies doing headstands on top of a 20-foot pole balanced on their forehead, petite Chinese ladies who throw (and catch) coffee tables from one to another with their feet. A Bulgarian boy who jumps backwards off a springboard and lands on the shoulders of a man, who is in turn on the shoulders of three other men.

The virtuosity on display is dazzling. One Polish woman can do a double backward somersault off a pole and land on the pole again. Dangerous area for punning.

In the middle of it all Willy has the evening made for him by being called out by the ringmaster as a birthday boy. There in the middle of the ring in the middle of the Circus World Championships, Willy publicly declares his support for Sheffield Wednesday! We don't get back until 11.00. Boys tired and happy and I hungry.

Saturday, November 21st

Time Bandits is No. 1 grossing film in the US almost exactly two years after *Brian* held the top spot. I still can't get over a sense of awed surprise. US new releases are falling like nine-pins. The brightest successes, apart from *Time Bandits*, are *Chariots of Fire*, still only on limited release, and *The French Lieutenant's Woman*, which is going well, but not spectacularly. Three English movies setting the pace.

George rings. He's got my *Missionary* script – but said he'd do the film just from the letter I sent with it! What *did* I say? He does express a worry as to whether *The Missionary* will interfere with the Python film and says he doesn't want to be the cause of any split in Python. As I told TG later, this didn't sound like a spontaneous George H concern. I mustn't get paranoid, but it suggested to me that someone somewhere was trying to shut down *The Missionary* for unspecified reasons.

Monday, November 23rd

Richard Loncraine rings early. He just wants to talk and make sure we are still happy. I give my usual reassurances, though I must admit I haven't had time to read the script for a week! RL's main concern seems to be making a movie that will be noticed – especially in the States. I tell him that, with *Time Bandits*, *Chariots of Fire* and *The French Lieutenant's Woman* doing good business over there, they are just ready for a beautifully photographed, sensitive portrayal of Edwardian period life, full of belters.

I hope he's convinced. I know it will be better when people are signed and the movie is an established fact, but at the moment I feel the strain of dealing with bigger egos than I became used to at the BBC – where people were just falling over themselves to get near a 'Ripping Yarn'!

Wednesday, November 25th

To Park Square West for Python writing. Very cold today. The house in which Python has been through so much now has a beleaguered air. As

Anne and family have moved out to Dulwich it's now just an office, and a temporary one at that. But we are well looked after. Jackie [Parker] scurries about making us coffee, setting out biscuits and nuts and putting Tabs for Graham and Perrier for the rest of us in the fridge. The result is that we ingest steadily. Anne even ensures that a plate of sweets – Glacier mints, chewing gum and Polos – is on the table after our quiche and salad lunch.

Usual desultory chat – about *Brideshead*[1] on TV again – generally agreed it's overblown. TJ wants to talk about sex or get angry about the way Thorn-EMI have put *Brian* onto video, cropping it for TV. John will suddenly call me over: 'Mickey. Tell me what books you've read in the last four months.' Today I give him Al Levinson's *Travelogs* to read. It sends him quite apoplectic. He cannot understand how people can write modern poetry. 'It makes me quite Fawltyish,' he cries.

We proceed well on a general pattern and order of sketches. But at one point the Oxford/Cambridge split, avoided most successfully for the rest of this week, suddenly gapes. The point on which we argue is not a major one, but John rationalises his obstinacy as being the result of his grasp of 'the structure'. It's hard work, but in the end he wins his point.

I find myself telling TJ that I shall be mightily relieved when this next Python film is done and out of the way and we don't have to write together for another four years.

Monday, November 30th

Full of Monday hope and optimism, I launch into Python writing. Feel much less rushed, muddled and negative than on Friday.

To Covent Garden for a special tenth anniversary meal given by Geoffrey and Eyre Methuen for the Pythons.

All of us are there, as well as wives, except Alison Jones (who is out planning a campaign of action against school cuts). Anne and Jonathan, Nancy Lewis [our Python manager in America] and several Eyre Methuen types. A beautiful Gumby cake and indoor fireworks adorn the table in our own dining room.

Eric is in a suit, and myself too – otherwise all the Pythons look exactly

---

1 An 11-part adaptation of Evelyn Waugh's book had begun on Granada Television in October, and proved hugely popular. Jeremy Irons was Charles, Anthony Andrews Sebastian and Diana Quick Julia. Charles Sturridge directed.

the same as they always did. Graham [Sherlock] is there with David, and I sit next to John's new wife, Barbara. She says she desperately wants to take him back to LA for a few months, but he won't go as it gives him the creeps.

Tuesday, December 1st

Into Python meeting at 10.30. I read the large chunk that TJ and I have put together right from the start to beyond 'Middle of the Film' and into the 'randy' sequence – which goes exceptionally well. The whole lot is very well received and even applauded.

JC and GC have written some first-class stuff about an Ayatollah, but then one or two of their later scenes – especially a torture sequence – drags on and becomes a bore. Eric has written a couple of nice things and plays us a song he's recorded – 'Christmas in Heaven'.

We discuss which of the Pythons has talked the most in group activities since we began 13 years ago. John will have it that I'm the outright winner, but I think he greatly underestimates himself and, of course, Terry J. Graham happily accepts the Trappist sixth position, and when JC wants to know whether he or TJ talk most I have to say it's absolutely equal, because whatever statement one of them makes is almost automatically contradicted by the other.

Then much talk of where we go to write in January. GC wants to go to Rio for naughty reasons. I suggest a mountain chalet in cool, clear Alpine air. But swimming and associated aquatic releases are considered important. No conclusion. Except that we don't go to Rio.

Watch *Brideshead*. Halfway through, when Charles is just about to crack Julia, the doorbell rings and we're brought down to mundane earth with the news that the sun-roof on the Mini has been slashed open and the cassette/tuner has been ripped out. The police seem wholly unconcerned with the possibility of apprehending anyone. 'Be round in the next couple of days,' is their reaction.

Wednesday, December 2nd

TJ arrives at 1.30. Unfortunately only a small part of the section I'm rather proud of makes TJ laugh, so we ditch most of it and, in the two and a half hours remaining, cobble together a possible penultimate sequence, starting with the Ayatollah breaking into the sex lecture and the firing squad of menstruating women. It's mainly TJ's work.

Neville rings with the best news so far on *The Missionary*. Irene Lamb, the casting director who was so good on *Time Bandits*, has read the script and likes it 'immensely'. Clearly she's had a most positive effect on Neville. Tonight he says 'You know, Michael, I think that *very* little needs changing.' John Gielgud is available, and Irene has already made the best suggestion so far on the knotty problem of Lady Ames – Anne Bancroft.

Saturday, December 5th

Buy *Variety*, *Screen International* and croissants. All are nice. *Time Bandits* still No. 1 in the US after three weeks, with *Raiders of the Lost Ark* chasing behind.

I drive over to Notting Hill for meeting on *Missionary*.

Some very good ideas come from our session and I find RL's suggestions – especially for setting each scene somewhere interesting, trains, etc – very encouraging and exciting.

At half past five Denis O'B arrives, and we have our first meeting together – DO'B, RL, Neville and myself. I've brought a bottle of champagne with which we christen the film.

Then some thoughts on casting. RL floats Laurence Olivier, with whose wife he's working at the moment. Denis throws up his eyebrows in horror. 'He's a sick man!' This rattles RL a bit and nothing is solved.

I drive Hollywood's currently most successful executive producer back to Hyde Park Corner, in my Mini with the slashed roof lining hanging down above his head.

Sunday, December 6th

Time for quick breakfast. Drive rapidly, for it's a Sunday morning, over to Clarendon Cross.

Richard is already in his office with his business partner Peter Broxton. They're looking at Loncraine-Broxton toy ideas for 1982. Boiled sweets in a box which is a moulded resin mock-up of a boiled sweet wrapper.

We begin, or rather continue, our work on the *Missionary* script at half past nine and work, very thoroughly, without interruption, until midday. Careful concentration and analysis. This is the least funny, but very necessary stage of the script. Does it convince? Do the characters fulfil a function? Is there a moral? Is the story clearly told? And so on.

Monday, December 7th

Write a grovelling letter to Sir Alec Guinness, accompanying a script, then to meeting with Denis O'B. I'm there for nearly three hours. I try to keep our thoughts on *The Missionary*, to impress upon Denis that I think he has been over-optimistic in only allowing £1.6 million budget. He in turn tells me that it is the most expensive of the three films HandMade Productions are planning for 1982. Mai Zetterling's *Scrubbers* is £525,000 and *Privates on Parade* (with J Cleese) is £1.2 million. But he won't give me final cut in the contract – says only Python get that and Gilliam didn't on *Time Bandits*.

The dynamic and shifty-eyed duo of Jeff Katzenberg and Don Simpson[1] are back in town. But this time, over a drink and inexhaustible servings of nuts amongst the green fronds of the Inn on the Park lobby, they pitch to all of us, bar John Cleese.

Basically they don't want to lose out again as they did on *Brian* and *Time Bandits*. They want us badly and sugar this with rather unjustifiable statements of the 'You're better now than you ever were' variety. Unfortunately I have to leave at 8.30 before the 'nitty-gritty' is discussed, but I can feel the incorrigibly plausible double act beginning to soften the Pythons' notorious antipathy to Hollywood majors.

Tuesday, December 8th

All quiet. Everywhere. Even at eight o'clock. Helen the first to notice the snow. Everywhere. Not a sprinkling fast turning to slush, but a 14-carat four-inch-thick blanket of snow, which is still being quietly augmented from a low, heavy, colourless sky. Lovely to see Rachel at the window of the sitting room in her long nightie, unable to take her eyes off the wonder of it all.

Wednesday, December 9th

To a viewing theatre to see *Elephant Man*. A private showing, organised by Neville so we could see the most recent performance of Anne Bancroft.

---

1 In 1982, Simpson was superseded as head of production at Paramount by Katzenberg. He nevertheless went on to co-produce successes like *Beverly Hills Cop* and *Top Gun*. He lived hard and died of a drug overdose in 1996.

A very fine film. Admirable in its unsensational, underplaying treatment of the man. Some weird and wonderful images of London mark David Lynch out as a most original director. Almost unbearably moving for an hour, then somehow the attitudes became so clean – liberals versus working-class louts and drunks – that I lost some of the intensity of involvement which I had when [John] Hurt was a piteous, grunting creature being treated kindly for the first time.

I think Anne Bancroft could be too old and maybe too strongly dramatic. Lady A must have a skittishness ... a light, naughty side, of which, I think, youth may be a not inconsiderable part.

Friday, December 11th: Southwold

A cold grey morning. Helen rings to warn us of more heavy snowfalls in London, at least double what came down on Tuesday and it's still falling. Four people have been killed in a train accident in thick snow in Buckinghamshire and Ipswich Station has closed. So I decide to stay put.

Denis rings. He has given Loncraine the fee and percentage he asked for, but wants to defer L's last £5,000 until he's brought the picture in on budget. Loncraine refuses and won't even meet Denis until the deferment is sorted out. DO'B wants to be tough – walk away and let RL come running back to him – but fears that this will have a deleterious effect on relationships. I agree with this. I also think the money being fought over is so paltry in view of Loncraine's value to the project. So Denis reluctantly backs down.

All this over a crackly line from London, whilst next door, in my little writing room overlooking the snowswept fields, with the tiny two-bar electric fire, is my script and my scribbles, on which nearly £2 million-worth of expenditure depends.

Sunday, December 13th

As I write (7 p.m.), wind is flicking snow against my writing room windows, there are reports that blizzards have hit the South-West and the electricity has failed there too. A bomb has gone off in a car in Connaught Square, killing two, and there is a news blanket over the army take-over in Poland.

An almost apocalyptically gloomy day. The sort of day to make one question the point of writing comedy – or writing anything. Actually it also makes me feel, so far, comfortable, cosy and rather anxious to get on with work. But then I have money to afford light and heat and food and drink in abundance, and I have four other bright, lively, busy people in the house with me. I *am* one of the fortunate ones, this bleak, snowswept, wind-howling evening.

Monday, December 14th

Disappointment on the faces of the children as the snow has been whittled down to brown slushy piles. I have a clear work day at home. Neville rings – says he has budgeted *Missionary*, and it comes out at £2.5 million overall – £1.3 million beyond Denis's first figure and 0.5 million beyond the Loncraine estimate. But Neville very level-headed about it, says there are trims that can be made, but this is what he will present Denis with.

Wednesday, December 16th

Below freezing again – making this Day Nine of the very cold wintry spell. But clear skies. Work well on script in the morning.

To bed at 12.30. George H rang earlier in the evening. He was anxious that I would have to give up some of my *Time Bandits* money as a result of possible renegotiations and he didn't think I ought to. He was very flattering about my role in keeping the thing together. Very touched.

Monday, December 21st

The forecasted thaw in nearly two weeks of freezing weather did not materialise and we wake to thick, swirling snow, two to three inches deep, which has once again caught everyone by surprise.

Go to see *Chariots of Fire*, as I'm dining with Puttnam tomorrow. A very fine and noble film – like a sophisticated advert for the British Way of Life. Some marvellous, memorable sequences and a riveting performance by Ben Cross as Harold Abrahams. I came out feeling as I used to when we saw films like *Dambusters* 25 years ago.

Found disturbingly similar sequences in *Chariots* and *The Missionary*, and also began to get colly-wobbles about *Missionary* casting. Ian Holm and John Gielgud merely will emphasise how similar we are to other British films. But then we haven't got Ian Holm or Gielgud yet.

Tuesday, December 22nd

Very cold and gloomy with swirls of snow. Ice in Julia Street for a fortnight now.

Have lunch appointment with David Puttnam. Just about to brave the elements when Neville rings with the news that Gielgud has turned down the Lord Ames part. What stings me more is that there was no particular reason given – he just didn't want to do it.

I gave up the attempt to drive to Odin's and slithered down traffic-packed side streets. Puttnam about 20 minutes late. He's immediately friendly, open, and he does seem to know everybody, especially amongst the 'establishment' of TV and films – Alasdair Milne, Huw Wheldon. He meets them on all his committees. Nice story that Huw Wheldon was to have been in *Chariots of Fire*, but couldn't do it and was deputised at the last minute by Lindsay Anderson.

Puttnam talks at a clipped, brisk pace, as if there's so much to say and so little time to say it. I think he's proud of his success and his work rate – a revealing cliché about being 'just a boy from a grammar school . . .' He's complimentary about *Ripping Yarns* – thinks the toast scene in 'Roger of the Raj' one of the funniest things he's ever seen.

He's keen, almost over-keen, to talk business, and writes down the names of a couple of books I mention to him as filmable (*Good Man in Africa* and *Silver City*). He says Goldcrest Productions have a lot of money and promises to get one of the bosses to ring me re the financing of the next Python movie. He also sounds quite positive about *Greystoke*, with its £1 million forest set, coming to Shepperton.

Friday, December 25th: Christmas Day

And it is a White Christmas. The snow is not fresh, deep, crisp and even, but it's only a couple of days old and soon the clouds clear and give it a sparkling brightness – of the sort that is always depicted but never happens.

Tom opens his stocking at 2.30 and goes to sleep again, but we don't get jumped on until eight o'clock. A bedful of all the Palins (except Granny) as Helen and I undo our stockings.

Tuesday, December 29th

At one I have to drive into town for lunch with Ray Cooper to discuss his doing the part of the Bishop. Ray has laid on a lunch at Duke's Hotel, in a Dickensian side street off St James's and opposite 'The house from which Frédéric Chopin left to make his last public appearance at the Guildhall'.

Small, expensive, immaculately tasteful little dining room – rather in the Denis class of spending, though. A bottle of Corton Charlemagne, oeuf en gelée (rather tasteless) and some very delicious fegato alla Veneziana. We talk about casting of *The Missionary*. Ray's choices for Lady A would be Helen Mirren or Faye Dunaway – both strong on projecting sexuality. And he knows Dunaway.

Wonderful table-talk from the only other occupied table – 'I have a little Bulgarian.' 'There's quite a lot of jewellery Brenda doesn't wear all the time.' And things like this.

Up into Soho to meet Eric for a drink at the French Pub. The French is full of weird people, who seem already drunk when they come in. One man is kneeling on the bar trying to pull up the barmaid's skirt. It's all rather like being in a Chris Orr print.

Eric and I, in quite playful mood after the champagne, drive over to Claridge's where we are to meet Sherry Lansing, the studio head of Twentieth Century Fox, and the most powerful woman in American movies.

What Sherry Lansing offers us in Claridge's is much more straightforward and uncluttered by looks, whispers and double-talk than what Paramount offered us at the Inn on the Park. Twentieth Century Fox want the next Python movie and they are prepared to finance it and distribute it however and wherever we want. The board would give us complete control over its production unless they thought the script totally worthless. Tim Hampton would be Fox's representative and could be used as little or as much as we wanted. It was as clear and as positive as that. We told her she was making a big mistake and she laughed. I liked her very much. We said we didn't like *History of the World Part One* and she didn't seem to mind.

At 8.00, with a kiss on both cheeks, she left us and I took Eric back in my grubby little Mini and we decided that we should get drunk together more often.

Thursday, December 31st

Rather a miserable day on which to end the year. I feel quite a few degrees below good health. Nothing very dramatic, just aches and lethargy. This deterioration could not have come at a worse time, as I have Neville chasing me and Richard Loncraine returning from Wales, doubtless vital and restored by Christmas, to read with great anticipation the new script that I have put together. The final, very important twists and turns must be written today and tomorrow.

I set to, but lose quite a bit of time talking with Denis (from Switzerland) and Neville (about casting – he's suddenly strong on Ann-Margret).

I think I'm probably cleaning my teeth when 1982 begins. Helen and I see the New Year in without fuss – on fruit juice and Disprins, not champagne, for me. I hope the way I feel is not an augury for 1982, when, if all goes to plan, I shall need every scrap of energy.

1982

Sunday, January 3rd

Up at ten feeling fully restored and unbearably bouncy for a while. I take Rachel up to the playground on Parliament Hill. The sun's shining and it's very warm for early January. Lots of the attractions in the playground are empty or broken. It's a sadly declined place. This gentle, unambitious meandering walk up to the swings is something I haven't done much in the last three or four years, and it used to be de rigueur every weekend we spent in London, when the children were small. I forget that Rachel still is small.

We have a lovely time together, pottering, nattering, playing at trains in the Adventure Playground. It makes me sad and nostalgic – and this makes me cross, because I know I'm regretting being older – or getting older, anyway.

Monday, January 4th

To see Phoebe Nicholls, who was Cordelia in *Brideshead*, and who I'm recommended as a Deborah. Meet her in Langan's Brasserie. She's much slighter than I'd expected, with ringlets of curly dark hair, and big dark eyes, in a narrow little oval face.

I embark on a laborious explanation of the story and she watches in politely rapt attention. 'Oh, but it's lovely,' she says, as though it's a living thing. A baby or a new puppy. I instinctively feel that she will be interesting. She has a certain delicateness about her which I think will help convince the audience that she really *can* think Fallen Women are women who've hurt their knees.

Tuesday, January 5th

To EuroAtlantic Towers at 10.00 for a casting meeting re *Missionary*. Gielgud's rejection has left us with two less adequate possibilities of replacement – Donald Pleasance and Trevor Howard.

Perhaps our strongest advance in this morning's session was to eliminate any spectacular, but possibly dumb, beauties in favour of Maggie Smith – attractive, striking, skilful actress. Parts too, we hope, for Ronnie Barker and Ian Holm.

Friday, January 8th

Ominously quiet outside as we wake. Another heavy snowfall – the third already this winter and the papers are full of articles about The New Ice Age and the Frozen Eighties. It's thin powdery stuff blown all over the place by a bitter north-east wind. It's coming through the cracks in my study window and has covered Tom's homework books with a thin layer of snow.

We struggle up to William Ellis School at midday with William, for his interview with the headmaster. Have to sit in the corridor for 15 to 20 minutes with boys thundering by between lessons. Quite liked the atmosphere there. Am in my worst old jeans, sneakers and a windcheater – my father would never have entered the headmaster's study in less than a suit and spit-and-polished shoes.

Saturday, January 9th

Drive car out through snowdrifts and slither down into an agreeably empty London for a viewing of the *Hollywood Bowl* film – the first since Julian [Doyle] spent weeks trying to lick it into shape in LA. And it is greatly improved – linked far more smoothly and the sense of live occasion much stronger now there are better-chosen cut-backs to audience, etc. In short, a film which we now feel we will not be ashamed of. Performances very strong, particularly Eric.

Home by two o'clock. It really is so cold that all my systems seem to seize up. An hour in a catatonic trance before the sitting room fire improves things and I then set to with all the last-minute *Missionary* calls – to Richard and Denis (who has rung John Calley[1] in the US to ask whether he thinks Maggie Smith or Anne Bancroft would be the bigger box-office name. Calley told him neither meant a thing!) He says, as he puts it, I can have my head over Maggie Smith and he won't stand in my way.

---

1 Calley, a friend of Denis's, is one of the most successful producers in the film industry. He headed Warners and was later CEO of Sony Pictures, owners of Columbia.

Call George in Henley at nine o'clock. After a few rather terse exchanges he says 'You're obviously not a *Dallas* fan, then' and I realise I've interrupted a favourite viewing.

It had been decided that, as with The Life of Brian *and Barbados, we needed somewhere exotic to finalise the new film script; Jamaica had been chosen.*

Sunday, January 10th: Jamaica

Touch down in Montego Bay about 8.30. Soft, stifling blanket of hot, humid air takes me by surprise.

A large black limousine is backed up outside and Brian, our driver (why is there always a Brian wherever Python goes?), squeezes us all and luggage in.

About an hour's cramped and uncomfortable drive through the night along the north coast of the island. We turn into the drive of a long, low, unadorned rectangular mansion, called 'Unity', some time after ten o'clock. A youngish black man, Winford, and a middle-aged, beaming black lady, Beryl, come out to settle us in.

Our main problem is the selection of bedrooms. Four of the rooms, all off a long passageway/landing on the first floor, are splendid – spacious and well-furnished and one has a full tester four-poster. But there are three other rather small rooms, less well-furnished and clearly intended as children's rooms, annexed on to the main bedrooms.

So we sit in the grand downstairs sitting room, with a fine selection of polished wooden cabinets and Persian carpets, and wing-backed armchairs and some attractive maritime oil paintings, and draw our bedrooms out of the hat. J Cleese has been very crafty and claims there is only one bed which he, being so tall, can fit in, and that so happens to be in one of the 'master' bedrooms, so he isn't included.

Terry G and I pick the two sub-bedrooms. At least they all look across the lawn to the sea (about 100 yards away) and mine has a bathroom. A heavily stained bathroom with rotting lino and no hot water, but a bathroom all the same – though I share it with Mr Cleese, who has the big double bedroom of which mine is the 'attachment'.

Winford advises us not to swim tonight as there are barracuda which come in from behind the reef at night-time. This puts a stop to any midnight high-jinks, though Terry J goes and sits in the sea. But it's a lovely night with a big full moon and, apart from the inequality of rooms, I think Unity will serve us well.

GC is quietly puffing away as we sit outside. He looks like any trustworthy GP. But his pipe is well-stocked with Brian's ganja.

Monday, January 11th: Unity, Runaway Bay, Jamaica

I sleep very little. Possibly three and a half to four hours. Doze and listen to the sea. I sit up, turn on the light and read our script at 5 a.m. It's light just before seven and I walk outside, having unlocked my room door and the heavy iron doors at the top of the stairs and then the iron and wood double doors out to the garden. Clearly this property is a target.

The house is right beside the sea, only a lawn and a few trees between us and the Caribbean – and the trees are healthy-looking and have leaves of many and rich colours. The house is kept spotless, and already the leaf-scratcher is removing the six or seven leaves that have fallen on the patio overnight. The house is not so grand as Heron Bay [the villa in Barbados where we worked on *Life of Brian*] – there are no soaring Palladian columns. Its simple shape and plain limestone construction dates, they say, two or three hundred years back, when it was the chief house on the Runaway Bay plantation. The mountains rise up behind the house and across to the west.

I sit at the table and read my script. There are one or two young black boys hanging around the beach. One of them comes over and sits down and introduces himself as Junior and offers me ganja and a trip to see Bob Marley's grave. He says he's 19 and he grows his own pot up in the mountains.

Run up the beach as far as the Runaway Bay Hotel and back. Nearly a mile. Then a swim in the limpid, lukewarm waters of the Caribbean.

Breakfast is good coffee, fresh grapefruit and eggs and bacon and toast from very boring sliced bread.

Everyone's reactions to the script are then discussed. All of us, to some extent, feel disappointed. I think the material is still very static. It could still be a radio show. The rain seems set in for the day as we sit around for a long afternoon discussion session.

It's agreed that we should proceed from the material we have and create a strong story or framework to contain it. Some silly moments in this free and fairly relaxed session – including a title from TG, 'Jesus's Revenge'. But though everyone occasionally flashes and sparkles nothing ignites.

Supper is early – about 6.30. We've bought in some wine from the supermarket across the road and we have a delicious starter of fish mixed with akee fruit – a little black, olive-like fruit off one of the garden trees.

Then a group of us go up to the Club Caribbean next door. A black lady pinches Graham's bottom and GC altruistically turns her over to TJ. It turns out she is a hooker. She looks a nice, open, smiley lady, and keeps dropping her price in a determined effort to interest any of us. As TJ finally leaves, empty-handed, she asks him for two dollars.

Wednesday, January 13th: Jamaica

An early breakfast, and splitting into groups by 9.30. Terry J and Terry G, Eric and JC, myself and Graham.

GC and I, however, soon find ourselves in one of the most bizarre and distracted writing sessions of all time. Beryl, the cook, was under the impression that someone would take her up to the market, eight miles away, for all the provisions she will need for the Jamaican food we've asked her to produce. So GC and I decide to take her and work on the way.

It starts quite well as we drive up winding mountain roads for a half-hour and emerge into a busy little township with a stout stone Anglican church set in the middle of it. GC and I make a quick shopping sortie for shoes and swimming trunks then back to the car. Vegetables in the back, but no Beryl.

Still talking over our idea for a John Buchan-type story framework, we have a Red Stripe beer in a small bar. Beryl comes back and deposits fish, but then has to sally back into the market for yams.

Halfway down the perfectly named Orange Valley, beside stone walls and almost classic English parkland, is an akee-seller. We skid to a halt. When we proceed again we not only have akees, but also two black boys who want a lift. Stop at the supermarket for bully beef, and our writing session finally turns into the gates of Unity two and a half hours after we set out.

I ring Rachel and wish her a happy seventh birthday in still-frozen London.

After lunch we sit and present our ideas. I present GC's and mine. A breathtaking, marvellously choreographed musical overture all about fish – with us in spectacular fishy costumes. Then into an exciting Buchan mystery tale, involving strange disappearances, unexplained deaths, all pointing to Kashmir. The hero would have to unravel the story by various clues, which bring in our existing sketches.

John and Eric have taken the view that the film is primarily about sex and they've reinstated the Janine/girls' paradise idea that I'd gone off a year ago. Even less response to this idea.

TG and TJ have gone back to first Python principles to link it – a rag-bag of non-sequiturs and complex connections. It's full and frantic and, when TJ's finished describing it, there is silence. It's as if no-one can really cope with any more 'solutions'. As if this is the moment that this material – the best of three years' writing – finally defeated us.

I take Eric's advice and we walk up to the Runaway Bay Hotel and sit on the terrace there and have three very strong rum punches and get very silly and laugh a lot and devise the idea of a Yorkshire Heaven, in which Yorkshiremen are revealed to have been the chosen people.

Thursday, January 14th: Jamaica

Wake to sunshine and a feeling that today is make-or-break for the film. We certainly cannot continue stumbling into the darkness as we did yesterday.

TJ says that, from the timings of the sketches we all like alone, we have over 100 minutes of material. This seems to spur people into another effort. TJ suggests a trilogy. The idea of a rather pretentious Three Ages of Man comes up and a title 'Monty Python's Meaning of Life', to which Eric adds the sub-head 'See it now! Before it's out of date'.

We decide to group the material together into phoney pseudo-scientific headings – 'Birth', 'Fighting Each Other' and 'Death'. Suddenly ideas come spilling out and within an hour there seems to be a remarkable change in the film's fortunes.

Friday, January 15th: Jamaica

Writing has definitely taken a turn for the better. Eric, TJ and I in the big room make some encouraging progress on linking the 'War'/'Fighting Each Other' section. TG stands on a sea-urchin just before lunch. He's in some agony for a bit and has about nine or ten black quills in his heel. Doc Chapman ministers to him. Neville T rings from London to say the

[*Missionary*] script is probably two hours long. When I tell the Pythons that Sir Laurence Olivier has never heard of us, he is heaped with abuse.

Out to dinner with Jonathan and Shelagh Routh.[1] This involves a convoy into Ocho Rios and beyond.

Rather characterful house, very different from the mansion of Unity. It's a collection of wood-framed cottages, set on the edge of a low cliff down to the sea. Foliage everywhere. About 20 people amongst the foliage. An Australian diplomat – who, at 25, seems to run their High Commission – his Texan wife, who seems bored with Australian diplomacy. There's an English artist called Graham, tall and rather aristocratic, a French/Australian who writes novels and tells me that Jamaica is a very restless society and not what it seems on the surface. Much resentment of whites.

On my way from the Rouths' a man in khaki tries to hitch a lift, but I speed on. Only later do I realise I've driven straight through an army roadblock.

Saturday, January 16th: Jamaica

Snooze a little, watch Eric doing Tai Chi on the lawn, then breakfast at 9.00, and set to with Eric and TJ to put the last section of *The Meaning of Life* into shape. Not very inspired work and we get rather bogged down on the 'Christmas in Heaven' song.

At 4.30 everyone returns from various postcard-writing, T-shirt-buying trips to read through work assembled over the last three days. JC and GC and TG have come up with a tremendously good, strong opening set in a hospital during the birth of a child, and there is only one section of the film about which people have doubts.

The *Meaning of Life* theme and structure does seem to have saved the film and justified our being here. There are now tightenings and improvements to be done and songs to be written and these will occupy us for our four remaining writing days. Tomorrow we have off.

A beautiful 'zebra' butterfly flutters around us as we read. A good omen, perhaps.

---

1 Jonathan Routh introduced and presented the enormously popular *Candid Camera* TV series in the 1960's. He died in 2008.

Monday, January 18th: Jamaica

GC announces at breakfast, after one of his regular and interminable phone calls to London, that he is going to sue Denis O'B. This causes a few dropped jaws over the toast and marmalade. Apparently GC, having enlisted the help of Oscar Beuselinck[1] to try and buy back the *Yellowbeard* rights from Denis, who keeps increasing his demands and conditions, has just heard that Beuselinck has found enough ground for negligence in Denis, and Anne, to proceed with a lawsuit. As GC says, the shit has hit the fan in London.

All of us are concerned that Anne should not be hauled over the coals – especially as she has been doing everything to try and improve GC's financial position over the last few months by getting the rest of us to withhold payments, etc. But GC lights his pipe in determined fashion and sounds terse and unmoving.

Late lunch, and at 4.30 Jonathan and Shelagh Routh arrive to collect and lead us to a place called Round Hill, where a friend of theirs is laying on a beach party for us.

Pleasant, countrified drive, avoiding mongooses which are apt to suddenly scuttle across the road. When JC returned from his trip to Kingston and said he'd passed four dead dogs and a calf, GC speculated that journey distances in Jamaica could be categorised quite usefully as a 'two dead dog journey' or a 'three dog, one pig journey'.

Round Hill turns out to be an estate of luxurious holiday homes set on a headland with very beautiful views. We are taken to a little house higher up the hill, set amongst the trees, for a party given by 'a prominent Washington horsewoman'. She welcomes us with a bright, quick, sympathetic smile and sincere handshake. Her long blonde hair is swept up on top of her head most dramatically, but giving the physical impression that her face has somehow been swept up as well and is pinned painfully somewhere in the scalp. She wears a long white dress. I am in running shorts – thinking only that we were coming to a beach party.

JC lies flat on his back on the grass at one point, worrying the hostess who thinks he's passed out drunk. He is in a wicked mood and clearly hates these sorts of people.

---

1 Prominent and flamboyant entertainment lawyer, whom Python had consulted after Bernard Delfont and EMI had pulled out of *Life of Brian* at the last minute.

Tuesday, January 19th: Jamaica

In the afternoon we read what has been done so far. JC and GC's 'Death' sequence is not in the same class as their marvellous 'Birth' opener of last week, so everyone becomes disconsolate again. It's too late in the afternoon to whip up much enthusiasm, so a rather important day peters out.

The two Terries and I accept Winford's invitation to go to a local birthday party celebration.

We walk about half a mile up to Bent's Bar. It's 8.30 and a four-piece Jamaican band – rhumba box (home-made and very effective), a thumping banjo, a guitar and a high-pitched, effective little singer. He looks well-stoned by 8.30 and, as the evening goes on, he becomes progressively more incoherent until he ends up clearing the tables whilst some imitator takes his place in front of the band.

The birthday is of Mr Bent, a large, paternal-looking black with greying frizzy hair, who introduces himself to Terry with a broad smile, a firm handshake, and the words 'Hello, I'm Bent'. He, like most others we've met, either has been to England or has relations there. I note that not even the most courteous Jamaicans have said anything about their relatives enjoying England.

Wednesday, January 20th: Jamaica

There isn't a lot to do but type up. It's decided to meet in London for three days in mid-February and then to take a final decision on whether to go ahead.

No-one, I think, feels we have a *Brian* on our hands, but there is a hope that we have something which we all feel we could film in the summer.

And so to bed, for the last time, in my 'servant's' quarters.

Sunday, January 24th

Late afternoon settle to read *The Missionary*. It is indeed a hefty script – 149 pages, and closely written, too. Glad to find that my own notes for cuts correspond by and large with Neville's and those suggestions of Penny Eyles[1] who timed the script. Neville rings, anxious to know when I can produce the 30-minute shorter version.

1 One of the most sought-after script supervisors in the UK. She'd worked with me on Stephen Frears' *Three Men in a Boat* and on *Monty Python and The Holy Grail*.

Tuesday, January 26th

There has been good news this morning – Maggie Smith likes the script and wants to meet. Apparently her comment was 'The fellers get the best lines, so I want the best frocks.'

Opening of Eric's *Pass the Butler* at the Globe. Crowd of celebrities and celebrity-spotters throng the cramped foyer as this is first night. Meet Lauren Hutton, model, actress and, as it turns out, world traveller. 'Ask me about any island,' she challenges. I catch her out with the Maldives. But she does seem to have been everywhere and is going to give us some information on Sierra Leone [which we'd chosen for a family winter break]. She advises us to have every possible injection there is.

Wednesday, January 27th

Down to the Cavendish early for the rest of my inoculations. Young male doctor this time, with vaguely jokey patter. He arranged in a line all the various syringes, then went to work. Tetanus followed typhoid and cholera into my upper left arm, then he stuck gamma globulin in my left buttock and waggled it about (the buttock, not the gamma globulin).

Back home for another two hours' work on the script, then down to the London Library. There is a two-day rail strike on as train drivers battle against BR Management's latest 'modernisation' plans. Park in St James's Square, and select some books on East African missionaries amongst the labyrinthine passageways and dark back rooms of this eccentric library. I get lost in the Topography section and can't find Uganda.

Come away at half past five armed with such gems as *In the Heart of Savagedom.*

I'm outside the Berkeley Hotel, where we're to meet Maggie Smith, a quarter of an hour early.

I realise that this meeting with Maggie Smith is one of the most crucial on *The Missionary* so far. She is the first 'name' we seem to have a chance of securing, and her part is the most crucial in the film apart from my own. She knows nothing about me, yet is expected to help create with me the complex relationship that is at the heart of the story.

She arrives about ten minutes late. Reminds me of Angela somehow – with her neat, almost elfin features. She is dressed expensively and with

a hint of flamboyance and her red hair looks as though it's just been done.
Which leads me to wonder, just for a moment, if she had taken all this
trouble for the meeting.

I congratulate her on her *Evening Standard* Actress of the Year Award
[for *Virginia*], which she won last night. She looks rather weary but she
has an instantly likeable naturalness and there is no difficulty in feeling
that one's known her for ages.

She was very cross that the 'fellers get the lines, I want the frocks' line
had been quoted to us, and claims she never said that. She was a mite
worried about Olivier as Lord Ames – and in a polite but unambiguous
way made it clear she regards him as having a 'very odd' sense of humour
(i.e. none).

Richard arrived, bubbling like an excited schoolboy. His keenness
seemed like over-enthusiasm at times, especially contrasted with Maggie
Smith's languor. She drank vodka and tonic and we drank Löwenbräus.
I settled into the sofa, also affected by her calm. She had no problems,
she said, about the script, and when we left, after an hour together, she
kissed me warmly and her face lit up again and she congratulated me
once more on the script and was gone.

Thursday, January 28th

Take an hour and a half for a run. The Heath chilly, muddy and grey.
Then down to Broadcasting House, to which I have been invited to
celebrate forty years of *Desert Island Discs*.

I arrive in the Council Chamber, a semi-circular room above the main
entrance, just as a group photo is being taken. About 20 cameramen, and
television video cameras photographing little dapper Roy Plomley, who
sold the series to the BBC the year before I was born.

Clustering around him I can see the Beverley Sisters – all dressed alike –
Michael Parkinson, not a hair out of place, Frankie Howerd, Lord Hill.[1]
It's like being at Madame Tussaud's. I'm hustled into the far corner of the
crowd, next to the tall, slightly shambling figure of Roald Dahl. 'Let's just
hope they've got wide-angle lenses,' he observes unenthusiastically.

I have to go and sign a book to be presented to Mr Plomley. I see Roald
Dahl sitting quite happily on his own, so I go and introduce myself and

1 Best known as the BBC's Radio Doctor during the Second World War, he became
Chairman of the BBC, retiring in 1972. He died in 1989.

bother him with praise. He confides that a good 'standard' popular kids' book is the way to make money. A successful children's author will do a lot better in the long run than Graham Greene. We talk about children being over-protected by authors, and he tells me that he has received many letters of complaint about his books from teachers, and *Danny* [*Champion of the World*] is banned in Denmark because it 'teaches children to cheat'.

We're having a jolly conversation and have only been photographed once, when Dr Jonathan Miller looms up, being frightfully energetic and effervescent and solicitously enquiring after my future plans because he does want to get Pythons back on stage – not doing Python, but Shakespeare or whatever. (Interesting that J Cleese had come up with the idea in Jamaica of the Pythons doing a Shakespeare play together.)

Friday, January 29th

Drive up to Bishop's Stortford to talk to the school sixth form.

Questions routine and orderly until one boy rose and asked 'How difficult is it to get into the BBC if you're not gay?' I couldn't quite meet this with cool equanimity, but I got my best laugh of the afternoon by telling the boy that I was sure he'd have no problem getting in. 'That naughty boy Robertson,' as I heard him referred to quite endearingly in the staff room afterwards.

Neville rang to tell me Olivier has asked for a million dollars to play Lord Ames. Which makes a decision very easy. Not Olivier.

Thursday, February 11th

Down to the London Library to procure books on prostitutes. They are all filed under 'S' for 'Sex' and I can't for the life of me find the 'Sex' section. End up abjectly having to ask a girl attendant. 'I'm looking for Sex,' is all I can say.

In the evening Helen plays badminton. I go out to see *Arthur*. Dudley very funny – manages to make all his jokes and gags have that attractive quality of spontaneous asides. That rare thing – a comedy with laughs all the way through *and* a happy ending. Sets me to thinking about the *Missionary* ending.

Friday, February 12th

Drive down to Methuen to look over Caroline Holden's artwork for *Small Harry*. It's bright and full of life and though on occasion her attention to detail lapses and she loses a face or an expression, I'm really very pleased. Take her for a drink at the Printer's Devil in Fetter Lane. She finished the book up at her parents' house – Mum and Dad helping out. Caroline still poor and having to work in a pub to make ends meet. I do hope the book does well for her sake.

Monday, February 15th

Drive over to Clarendon Cross, arriving there at ten. Spend the day with Richard and Irene seeing 24 young ladies at 15-minute intervals to select from amongst them our Fallen Women. By 6.00 we've talked, laughed and explained ourselves almost to a standstill.

Home. Talk to Denis, who rings to find out how we got on with the prostitutes. (George H terribly keen to be there during auditions.) Terry G rings spluttering with uncontrollable laughter. He had just finished reading 'Mr Creosote' and had to tell someone how near to jelly it had reduced him.

Wednesday, February 17th

We see about 20 more actresses. A half-dozen are good enough for speaking parts – and the results of Monday's work and today's are very encouraging. But other clouds on the horizon – mainly financial. Richard thinks that the Art Department budget is impracticably small and both Richard and Neville told me yesterday that there is no way the present script can be shot in nine weeks. It'll need ten at the minimum.

All those things to think of as I drive to Anne's for an afternoon Python session. A strange feeling to sit at the table listening to other people's offerings without having had time to provide anything myself. JC/GC have put together a quite funny Grim Reaper piece. Eric has written a new opening song and a very short but effective visual before the 'Penis Apology'. Terry J has also been prolific.

At the very end of the meeting, just as I'm off to see Denis O'B, Anne tells us that Graham would like us to meet Oscar Beuselinck, the lawyer, tomorrow. Why Graham couldn't tell us I don't know. It's another bombshell from Chapman – who evidently is still going to sue Denis and wants us all to meet Oscar tomorrow and hear the whys and wherefores. All more than a little irritating.

Thursday, February 18th

Decide I shouldn't go to Graham's meeting with Oscar Beuselinck. Lawyers on the warpath are a dangerous breed and I am concerned that attending a meeting called specifically to point out all the bad points of Denis O'B may not be the best thing to do when I'm currently trying to get an extra £500,000 out of him. And Oscar would be only too keen to say he'd 'met with the Pythons'.

I have an hour or so of the afternoon left for writing before TJ arrives. We compare notes, then he goes off to the GC meeting, whilst I carry on extending the 'Hotel Sketch'.

A meeting with Denis. DO'B clearly won't accept Neville's latest budget figure of £2.5 million, but on the other hand he is not asking us to reduce, nor even stick at £2 million. He's now talking of £2.2 million. Our whole discussion is helped by the fact that Trevor Howard has accepted the part of Lord Ames. (Neville said he was especially keen to do it when he heard *I* was in it!)

Round to Clarendon Cross and then on to Julie's [Restaurant] for supper. We go through the script – take out the dockside sequence, which has some jokes but is very expensive, and also one or two short exteriors, and we find that we can still make cuts without irreparably damaging the film. Indeed, we have one very positive new idea, which is to open on a school honours board with the name being painted out.

Tuesday, March 2nd

Best news of last week is that Michael Hordern, who was reported to have turned down the part of Slatterthwaite, has now had second thoughts, likes the script, finds it 'immensely funny' and has been signed up. So Moretonhampstead, with Maggie Smith, Trevor Howard and Michael Hordern, is looking like a quality household.

Wednesday, March 3rd

Assailed with information (Irene), opinions (Richard) and warnings (Neville) on all sides as we attempt to cast the medium and small parts. Any featured (i.e. speaking) actor has, under a new Equity agreement, to be 'bought out' – i.e. given enough pay to make up for the actor relinquishing rights on future TV, video and other sales. It boils down to a minimum of about £157.00 per day for a 'cast' actor. So the morning is one of continuous small compromises to cut down the use of such actors – a process which surely wouldn't please Equity if they saw it.

There are still some major roles unfilled. Graham Crowden has had a hip operation and may not be well enough to play the Bishop.[1] Richard suggests Denholm Elliott, other front-runners are Nigel Hawthorne and Ian Richardson. Elliott will be twice as expensive.

Ray Cooper comes over at lunch and meets Richard for the first time. They got on well, as I knew they would. Both are artists, and indeed Ray C endears himself to Richard by remembering him as a sculptor. Ray is to be Music Co-ordinator for *The Missionary*, which fills me with great confidence.

Bombshell of lunchtime, as far as Richard is concerned, anyway, is that Freddie Jones, for whom Richard was prepared to move heaven and earth to accommodate in the picture, now says he doesn't want to do it anyway. This has plunged Richard into a bad mood performance and he rails on about faithless actors and how shitty the entire thespian profession is. I blame his diet.

Friday, March 5th

Through exceptionally slow-moving traffic to Holland Park, to talk with Ken Lintott, who made my *Brian* beard and who is head of make-up on *The Missionary*. I've lost a lot of weight, he says. He wants me to try growing a moustache again.

---

1 In the end he took the part of the Reverend Fitzbanks, Fortescue's prospective father-in-law.

Wednesday, March 10th

Neville says we've no more money left. Everything is accounted for. There's no spare. But the cast we're assembling is most encouraging. Even Celia Johnson may be on again. She likes the script, but wants the name of her character changed, as one of her greatest friends is Lady Fermoy! Denholm Elliott, Graham Crowden and Peter Vaughan look certain. Fulton Mackay less so, as he has been offered five weeks by Puttnam on a new Bill Forsyth picture.

Richard rings. Denis will not agree to the test viewing clauses RL wants in his director's contract. In America it is standard in Screen Directors' Guild contracts that, should the producer want to alter the director's delivered cut, the director has the right to insist on there being two test screenings before audiences of not less than 500 people. Anyway Denis now says that this is out of the question. It's not really my problem, but I assure RL that I'll support him. He talks of leaving the picture, which I don't think is all that likely.

Thursday, March 11th

Work and run in the morning, then to Bermans to meet Trevor Howard. Find the great man in a first-floor dressing room, standing in stockinged feet half in and half out of a hound's-tooth tweed hunting outfit, surrounded by dressers and costume designers. To my surprise Howard strikes me as a diminutive figure. His full head of fine, carroty red hair stands out.

He gives me a rich, warm smile and shakes my hand as if he's really been wanting to meet me for ages. He talks sleepily and when after the fitting we suggest taking him out for a drink he brightens visibly. Though his breath already smells of alcohol, he says emphatically, 'Yes, why not! I've been on the wagon for three weeks and I feel *so* tired.' We take him down to Odin's. He has a gin and tonic, RL and I a bottle of Muscadet.

He keeps repeating how much he's looking forward to doing the part, though curiously, in the midst of all this enthusiasm, he expresses great concern over the brief little bedroom scene between Ames and the butler. He's very unhappy about any hint of homosexuality. We agree to talk about this later, and he leaves to collect his passport for a trip to China he's making for a British film week there.

Back to Bermans at 4.30 to meet Michael Hordern. He looks older and his face redder and veinier than I'd expected. He has a straggly beard – better advanced than my moustache – which he's growing for the BBC's *King Lear*. Quite eccentric in his delivery, and sentences tend to end abruptly and be completed with a sort of distinctive hand gesture. He says he can understand about Trevor Howard – worried about a 'machismo image' as Hordern puts it. The two of them worked together on *Heart of the Matter*, but Hordern is characteristically vague about the details.

Whilst at Bermans, Neville rings and asks to meet me as urgently as possible, as a problem has arisen over the credits. It transpires that Denholm Elliott wants star billing alongside Maggie S and Trevor H. I have no objection – I always tend to think that the problems start when people read the script and *don't* want a credit. But Denis won't have it.

Neville, who is in charge of negotiations with the artists, wants me to intercede with DO'B, who is skiing in Colorado at the moment.

Home for delayed supper at eleven o'clock, followed by three-quarters of an hour on the phone to DO'B in Colorado. The process of trying to change Denis's mind is like opening doors with a battering ram. Eventually they'll give, but one has to be prepared to patiently, insistently, repeatedly run at them from exactly the same direction each time.

Saturday, March 13th

It's a very bright, clear, sunny morning. Work in the garden, then take the children down to the London Dungeon. All three love it there – the frisson of fear is very cleverly maintained throughout, yet the place is not insidious or unpleasant. The victims of the rack and the murdered Thomas à Becket and the plague rats (live) all co-exist in a rather friendly, reassuring way.

Certainly all these dreadful horrors put all the children in a very good humour and we drive back across London Bridge to see the Barbican Centre, opened last week. It's a 'culture complex' within the Barbican estate. Approach, across a piazza, as they describe cold, windswept open spaces these days, to buildings that house the theatre, cinema, library and conference hall. In front of them is another 'piazza', with fountains and lots of captive water, which looks very green and stagnant and has napkins which have blown from the outdoor restaurant soggily drifting in it.

The place is full of lost people, and men with walkie-talkies looking anxious. The children love running up and down the stairs with mirrored ceilings or sitting in the comfortable new cinema. But at the moment it feels like a giant Ideal Home Exhibit, new and half-unwrapped and not at all integrated with the rest of the Barbican estate – on which one sees nobody. But then those who can afford flats in the Barbican can probably also afford second homes for the weekend.

To the BBC by 6.30 [for an appearance on *Parkinson*]. In a hospitality suite I talk to Parky and he runs through the questions. Researcher Alex accompanies me everywhere – even to the toilets. At 7.30 the recording begins. Jimmy Savile is on first, then there's a brief chat from Andrew Lloyd Webber and a song from Marti Webb, then I stand listening to my introduction on the filthy piece of backstage carpet which leads – cue applause – to the spotless piece of carpet the viewers see and a seat next to Parky.

Parky is much easier to talk to than Russell Harty – he's more relaxed and seems content to find out rather than turn fine phrases. I feel comfortable and am able to be natural – hence probably my best performance on a chat show yet.

Donald Sinden comes on third and when, in his rich, plummy RADA voice, he refers, with some pride, to meeting Lord Alfred Douglas, Jimmy Savile says "oo?". Sinden doesn't seem to mind being interrupted that much, but Parkinson affects mock-headmasterly gravity and banishes Savile and me to 'sit with the girls' [the backing singers for the band]. Probably to his surprise, and certainly to the surprise of most of the cameras and the floor manager, we do just that. We so upstage Sinden's interview that he is asked back on again next Wednesday.

Afterwards I chat to Andrew Lloyd Webber, who gives me his phone number as he lives right beside Highclere House, where we're filming the Fermoy scenes. He also asks if I write lyrics! Savile drops the information that he is paid more to do his ads for the railways than Sir Peter Parker is for running them.

Sunday, March 14th

Up to Abbotsley for Granny G's 69th birthday. I take Granny a life-size cardboard replica of Margaret Thatcher (whom she hates), some flowers and a bottle of Vosne Romanee '64.

Grand football match on the back lawn by the barn. Rachel, Auntie Catherine and me v the two boys. We lose on penalties. Rachel quite fearless in the tackle. Leave for home at 6.00.

Monday, March 15th

To BUPA House to have a pile injected. A not very painful, but strangely uncomfortable sensation. As I lay curled up, proffering my bum, I remembered that this was the first day of the *Romans in Britain* High Court trial.[1] How suitable.

Wednesday, March 17th

Donald Sinden appears for the second time on the *Parkinson* show, armed with blunderbuss and whip. Parky seeks to make light of Saturday's 'incidents' and Sinden says that his children thought Saturday's programme very funny – and a 'classic Parkinson'. The whole episode has achieved some notoriety, as if Jimmy Savile and I had broken some unwritten rule, that no-one should enjoy themselves on *Parkinson* when someone else is plugging their latest product.

Friday, March 19th

To Dorney Reach near Maidenhead, to look at the rectory.

Much readjusting of thoughts, but, again, after a prolonged, concentrated and wearing debate, we settle on the exact shots. Neville dictates rather tersely into his pocket recorder as RL orders lighting towers and mock walls, etc. I admire RL for his endless enthusiasm for filling frames and his refusal to scale down *his* vision of the film. Neville hints darkly that Monday, when the heads of departments put their bills in, could be a day of reckoning.

Back from Dorney to buildings around St Pancras and King's Cross. A rooftop on some condemned flats will be the Mission roof.[2] Wonderful period panoramas of Industrial Revolution Britain, but not too easy to enjoy them as steady drizzle comes down, putting a fine twist of unpleasantness on an already cold and prematurely dark evening. After recceing brothels and walking shots, we pack up about a quarter to seven.

---

1 Howard Brenton's play, produced by the National Theatre in 1980, contained scenes of simulated anal rape. Mary Whitehouse, the morality campaigner, brought a private prosecution against the production. She later withdrew from the case.
2 Culross Buildings stood defiantly until the summer of 2008, when they were destroyed for the King's Cross redevelopment.

Monday, March 22nd

A long Python film meeting.

The apportionment of parts, which took us a couple of very good-humoured hours after lunch, is such an important moment in the creation of the film; we've been writing for three and a half years, and yet the impact of the movie for audiences is probably far more affected by what happened in the 75 minutes at Park Square West this afternoon.

I don't think there are any rank sores or festering injustices, though TJ thinks Eric may have wanted to do the end song, which has gone to Graham – doing a Tony Bennett impersonation!

Universal have few qualms about giving us the money – three million dollars up front, assuring us each of over £150,000 by the end of the year, well before the movie goes out. Python has never had better terms.

Tuesday, March 23rd

Parkinson programme calls up to ask if I will present an engraved shovel to Parky at a special surprise party to mark the end of his last BBC series next Wednesday. [He's a great fan of the shovel-owning Eric Olthwaite from *Ripping Yarns*.] I must have been rehabilitated!

Wednesday, March 24th

To Upper Wimpole Street to see a specialist about the ache in my ear. He rather throws me by asking if I've come about my nose. I feel myself falling into a Python sketch ...

'My nose ... No.'

'It's just bent to the right, that's all ...'

'Really?'

'Oh yes, but nothing serious. Let's talk about the ear ...'

(Pause)

'You don't have any trouble with the nose ...?'

'No.'

'Well, I should leave it then.'

With Laurel and Hardy in the garden. I bought them off a market stall on Canal Street, New York. Hardy's neck broke in the plane's luggage locker.

'Take Rachel on a mystery tour. By lucky chance there is a raising of the bridge as we are there. Watch from an abandoned little jetty upstream from the Tower' October 27 1984

Tom with Denis the cat.

The eternal dream. By a pool, with a book, somewhere hot. Kenyan holiday, January 1983

'I've got to have fruit!' Tied to a tree with Shelley Duvall, as Vincent and Pansy in *Time Bandits*, 1981

Shooting the *Time Bandits*' Giant on the roof of Wembley Studios. Among those looking bored, Maggie Gilliam and Julian Doyle on camera.

Pythons in Hollywood. MP, Terry J, Eric I, Graham C, Terry G and John C. Behind us, the Bowl. September 1980

On the set of *Time Bandits*. (left to right) Neville C Thompson, Associate Producer, John Cleese (Robin Hood), George Harrison and Denis O'Brien, Executive Producers. Summer 1980

Monty Python Live at The Hollywood Bowl, September 1980

John rehearses his Silly Walk.

Dead Parrot sketch always went down well. Never more so than with the performers.

Disrobing after the judge's summing up.

The Missionary, 1982

Fortescue and his women. Caught between fiancée Deborah Fitzbanks (Phoebe Nicholls, left) and Lady Ames, benefactress, (Maggie Smith, right)

Nepotism at work. Rachel Palin, (centre), on the set at Finsbury Circus, April 24 1982

'No people, no sun-oil, no deck-chairs, no poolside bars selling over-priced drinks'. Bathing in the waterfall at Shava Lodge after the Kenya shoot, June 13 1982

'As I wait for the clouds to clear the sun, I see our two Executive Producers emerging from the orchard'. Richard Loncraine, director, George H and Denis O'Brien on location, May 1 1982

John Kelleher of HandMade (centre) and I collect our most cherished, and only, award, from the French town of Chamrousse. 'I check in the atlas. It does exist' March 26 1985

Charles Fortescue, man with a Mission.

Missionary publicity. Judging, and participating in, a custard pie throwing contest at the Southern Methodist University, Dallas, Texas, October 7 1982

Playing a TV Presenter for *Comic Roots*. Behind me, on the left, the house in which I was born and brought up. Sheffield, July 1983

Thursday, March 25th

Only the continuing gorgeous weather keeps me going. After yet another all too brief night's sleep, I'm up to grab some breakfast and leave for a recce to Longleat[1] at eight o'clock. Somewhere on the way to look in the car I collect a large evil lump of sticky, smelly dogshit on my shoes, and I've transferred it all over the house. I resign myself with ill grace to missing breakfast and set to to clean it up, but can find no disinfectant.

At this point I crack and fly into a helpless state of rage, banging the dressing table in the bedroom so hard that Helen wakes up thinking World War III's started, tearing my shoe off and generally behaving quite hysterically. It's a combination of the pressure of work – burning the candle at both ends – and the lack of time I've had to talk to Helen about everything that's happening. But it passes, I'm collected by Brian, H forgives me before I go and I feel a storm centre has passed.

Richard drives me on to Longleat and we work and talk on the way. Arrive at midday. Take the guided tour, then meet with Christopher Thynne, the second son, who runs the house. Knows me from one of Eric Idle's parties, he says.

He came with Georgie Fame who broke a table.

He shows us wonderful passages. Bedrooms that are workable but a little small (all country house bedrooms it seems are a lot smaller than one would think). He shows us into Lord Weymouth's part of the house where garish paintings of all sorts of sexual endeavour cover the walls. He shows us the first printed book in England, a collection of Adolf Hitler's signed watercolours, plus a paper which has Adolf's signed approval of one of three designs for the Swastika symbol.

Sunday, March 28th

Leave for Abbotsley around 11.00. Sun shining in London, but mist is still thick as we drive up into Hertfordshire. Arrive at Church Farm at 12.30 – and I go for a last run for many weeks.

As I pound up the hill beside silent ploughed fields with the mist clinging around me like a cool refreshing blanket, I feel ready for *The Missionary* and ready for Python. I know in a sense that I'm entering a

1 Longleat House, an Elizabethan stately home which has been in the same family, the Thynnes, for over four hundred years. The head of the family is the Marquess of Bath.

tunnel from which I shall not emerge until October, at least.

I hit out at the air with my fists like a boxer, feeling ready.

Back to Abbotsley for lunch. The sun comes out. The boys play football. I teach Rachel to ride her bike, on the same stretch of road up to Pitsdean Hill on which I taught Willy, in the teeth of a storm, a few years ago.

Today in the still sunshine, Rachel's little triumph seemed to have greater significance. I sensed one of those special moments between us. We both felt so proud.

Monday, March 29th

Brian [Brookner] drives me in his red Mercedes to the National Liberal Club off Whitehall. First glimpse of the reality of *The Missionary* is a string of Lee Electric trucks parked in this quiet street. On the other side of the road Richard's Winnebago. Cables run across the pavement into the wide lobby of this once grand, marble-floored Victorian club.

The first time I appear as Charles Fortescue is in this lobby and, by almost eerie coincidence, the character is born beside a huge contemporary oil painting of Gladstone's first Cabinet, in the centre of which sits one C. Fortescue – a youngish man, not at all unlike the missionary I'm playing.

The conversion of the National Liberal Club's billiard room into a gymnasium has been stunningly successful. Opening shot is ready by ten, but the generator goes on the blink and we don't complete my entrance to the club until eleven.

As the slow pattern of waiting established itself, I nodded off twice. My cold continues to tumble out, but didn't seem to affect my mood or performance. Now that filming has begun I know I shall survive, but now it's a question of keeping standards high – and producing something better than anything I've done before (apart from the Fish Slapping Dance, of course).

Tuesday, March 30th

Lunch is a meeting with Geoffrey S, Richard, the stills photographer and myself, to discuss the book [of *The Missionary*]. Eat up in one of the vast, dusty galleries at the top of the building.

RL clearly feels GS is too cautious and GS does not react well to RL's expensive ideas for the book. I find having to conciliate the most tiring work of the day. It means no relaxation at lunch either and I have to rush down to do close-ups in the first real dialogue scene with Denholm.

Feel a surge of nerves as I wait to go on. I look round at this huge room, filled, just for me, with 30 period gymnasts. I look round at the 40 or so faces of the crew, all watching, waiting to see what I do. As if this isn't enough, I catch sight of Angela, Jeremy and Veryan up in the balcony, looking down.

I start to wobble. I have to go into this scene clutching briefcase, hat and full cup of tea. I'm convinced the tea-cup will rattle so much that I'll be asked to do it again – and that'll make it worse – and what am I doing here anyway? We do the shot, and I control the cup and the moment of blind panic passes, and I feel settled and refreshed and the rest of the day seems light and easy.

Up to Lee Studios to look at the first rushes. They look marvellous. [Peter] Hannan's lighting is of the very best – I've hardly ever seen my stuff looking so good. The various textures of the wood and tiles come across strongly and clearly. It looks interesting and gives everything in the frame a particular quality and to the whole an atmosphere you can almost smell and touch.

As to the performance – although Denholm does not do the Bishop as Graham Crowden would have done, he nevertheless comes over strongly on screen, and manages the mixture of comedy and seriousness very effectively.

I leave Lee's in great euphoria and raring to get on with the film.

Wednesday, March 31st

Picked up at the relatively civilised hour of 7.45. To Culross Buildings behind King's Cross and St Pancras. Marvellous location for trainspotters. The sky is grey and it's cold, but we start shooting without much ado amidst the flapping washing. First scenes with our prostitutes.

I have a small and rather tatty caravan, with a basin, but no running water, and a seat which shatters immediately I sit down. Denholm a little more together on his words today than yesterday at the club, but, like any actor, is bucked up tremendously by praise of any kind – and it helps him that I can enthuse so much over the rushes.

All goes ahead well until after lunch when the sun comes out, which makes the roof of the tenement buildings a much more agreeable place to be, but impossible to work on because of the light change. Go down to my caravan and sleep for an hour. After a two- or three-hour wait, RL decides to abandon shooting for the rest of the day on account of the sunshine. Denholm and I run tomorrow's scenes through.

Then off to rushes at Lee's and home for an hour before taking a taxi down to the Main Squeeze Club in King's Road, where M Parkinson's 'surprise' end of series party is to take place. I've rehearsed a little speech as Eric Olthwaite.

Arrive to find small, rather empty basement club. No-one I know. Parky arrives and is cheered, moderately, and at about 11.15 I'm asked to make the presentation. I'm shown onto a small stage, on which I'm blocked to view for half the people there. Then the microphone feeds back – whines and whistles – and I find myself having to make ad-libs with the likes of Kenny Lynch, Jimmy Tarbuck, Spike and Billy Connolly only feet away.

I survive, just, and there are laughs at the right places. Present the shovel to Michael Parkinson as 'The Second Most Boring Man in Yorkshire'.

Stay on at the club for about an hour. Talked to Michael Caine – about Maggie S mostly. 'She's brilliant,' he said, 'but watch her.' Told me I'd have to work hard to keep in the scene with her.

Then a hatchet-faced 'adviser' signalled discreetly to Caine that he should be moving on. I left soon too.

To bed about a quarter to one. Duty done. Slept like a log.

Thursday, April 1st

This morning it's raining. So for a couple of hours I sit in my caravan in Battle Bridge Road and catch up on work – e.g. reading page-proofs of *Small Harry and the Toothache Pills*.

At eleven it clears and we work steadily through the scene, finishing by six. Denholm takes a long while on his close-ups; his daughter's come to watch him. 'Amazing how difficult it is to act with one's family around,' Denholm confides, and, for a man who has made 73 films, he certainly doesn't seem to have the secret of instant relaxation.

After filming, which ends at 7.30 with a beautiful street shot with a background of the St Pancras gasholders silhouetted against a rosy dusk sky, and Peter H personally wetting the cobblestones to catch the evening light, I go with Irene in the Winnebago to talk over casting as we drive to rushes. The Winnebago has been dreadfully ill-fated this week, breaking down everywhere. And tonight is no exception. Richard curses modern technology roundly as we lumber up the Marylebone Road with the handbrake stuck on.

To rushes at Rank's executive viewing theatre in Hill Street, Mayfair. First glimpse of my relationship with the girls. It looks relaxed and unforced. Fingers crossed we've seen nothing bad so far.

Denis claims to have finalised a deal with Columbia for *The Missionary* and the latest news is that they are preparing a 1,000 print release in the US for late October. This is exhilarating, rather terrifying news.

Friday, April 2nd

Leave home at 7.30. We are filming at the Royal Mint in Tower Hill. Abandoned ten years ago, it has a fine classical main building (used in *Elephant Man*) and workshop outbuildings. A very satisfactory set up for my scene with McEvoy (Peter Vaughan) as we can use three levels and drive a Chapman Hoist into the interior courtyard and follow the actors down. It is our Healed Leper shot, really, one long developing shot.[1] Only here it is more satisfying and better used, as the various elements of the bottling factory are introduced as we walk. It ends with us passing a fully practical steam engine – driving three belt-drive machines, and a loading bay with period vehicle, as well as a horse and cart glimpsed out in the yard.

Peter and I walk through the scene at 8.15, but the first take is not until 3.50 in the afternoon.

It is very hard work for an actor to come in for one day and shine as expected, under great pressure of time. But Peter's performance is always word perfect and, though a little tighter and tenser than I'd hoped, he's still excellent and solid. After seven takes all sides are satisfied and we finish work at seven.

To the West End for dinner with Maggie Smith. Maggie is funny, much less made-up and more attractive than when I last saw her, and quite obviously looking forward to the thing immensely. She brushes aside any apologetic concerns RL and I have for the shooting schedule – which involves her first of all appearing at 5.45 a.m. on Monday up to her knees in mud on Wapping Flats.

---

1 Most of the 'Healed Leper' scene in *Life of Brian* was played in one shot, with camera operator John Stanier, a Steadi-Cam strapped to his body, walking backwards through 'the streets of Jerusalem' for some three minutes.

We go off, arms linked, past crowds clustering round a police-raided night club, the best of chums.

Saturday, April 3rd

I'm losing a sense of time already. I wake to my alarm and obediently swing my legs off the bed and make for the bathroom, like a battery hen. Shave, clean teeth, go downstairs to do exercises, dress up in the bedroom.

Brian [Brookner] arrives today at 7.50, and carts me away. Must, however awful I may feel, arrive in a jolly mood at the location – co-producer, actor and writer can't be seen to weaken. Actually, once up and about I feel fine and the only frustration of today is the length of time filming takes.

I'm at Ada's brothel, situated in the old Fish Office on the Railway Lands. From the brothel window, as I stand ready to be Charles Fortescue, I can see the trains slipping in and out of St Pancras.

A long wait whilst Peter H lights Ada's room. It has no outside light source, so he has to create this impression from scratch. Listen to the Grand National, in which a horse called Monty Python keeps up courageously before refusing at Becher's the second time around. Much more sensible than falling, I think.

At tea Angela, Veryan and Jeremy arrive. Tea in RL's Winnebago. Richard is one of the few directors who, after six consecutive, very full days of filming, can still bother to make tea for his star's family.

Sunday, April 4th

Breakfast in the garden and read, with a certain disbelief, the news that we are virtually at war with Argentina over the Falkland Islands. It seems a situation better suited to the days of *The Missionary* than 1982. It may feel unreal, but papers like the *News of the World* are howling for vengeance and Ardiles was booed every time he touched the ball for Tottenham yesterday.

Took Rachel and Louise to the swimming pool at Swiss Cottage and was just sitting down to evening 'Sunday lunch' of roast lamb and a bottle of Château Bellac, when the door bell rang and TG appeared, breathless for information on the first week of *The Missionary*. He wanted to know what had gone wrong and how far we were behind! Children behaved abominably (with the exception of Tom) at the meal as TG rabbited on.

Later Willy explained that he had founded a Get Rid of Guests Club.

TG is waiting for Stoppard to finish his involvements with Solidarity before beginning work on *Brazil*, for which TG has now signed a deal with an Israeli super-financier.

Monday, April 5th

Arrive at location in Wapping at 5.15.

God is very definitely with us this morning. The sun rises into an almost clear sky – with just a hint of cloud, to add contrast and perspective. There is a little wind and the Thames has a strip of still, reflecting water across it, ruffled into the softest ripples on either side. It is a perfect dawn and, as the sun and the river rise, we film hard for three hours and a half – from 6.15 until nearly ten, when our last reaction shot of the little boy – 'Will it be a mission?' – is shot with water lapping around the camera legs.

This was Maggie Smith's first day. She uncomplainingly began work on *The Missionary* standing in a foot of muddy Thames water, pulling a ship's wheel out of the slime, and managed to smile winningly and help us push the barrow over wet and slippery rocks in take after take.

Then on to the Mission – in Lant Street, Southwark, and another tremendous boost for morale. The set – of the girls' dormitory – was quite superb. When I first walked into it, I was quite moved. Something about the pathos of the simple beds with their few possessions beside them, grafted on to a bleak industrial interior.

Lunch with Maggie S and Richard in the Winnebago. All amicable and quite easy, though I still find Maggie S and the long experience of acting she represents quite a daunting prospect.

Tuesday, April 6th

Down to the Mission in pouring rain. If our dawn shot had been today it would have been disastrous. As it is we are inside all the time, completing the scene in which Maggie leaves the Mission. I find it hard work to start with. Maggie is smooth, efficient and professional – consummately skilled at timing and delivery. Keeping up to her standard, particularly when we don't yet know each other that well, and when the fatigue of eight days' hard filming in the last nine takes the edge off one's energies, is not easy. But I survive.

I fluff a line on a take, which annoys me, as I'm usually pretty efficient at lines myself. Then Maggie mistimes a move on a later take, which makes me feel much better. Eventually the complicated master shot is in the can and I feel much relief.

Terry G comes down to watch the shooting. He's impressed by the Mission set and says of Maggie, in some surprise, 'She's really funny . . .'

A journalist called Chris Auty – jeans, leather jacket and matching tape recorder – is here from *City Limits*. I waffle between takes. Must try and work out in my own mind what this film is about – instead of relying on visiting journalists to make up my mind for me.

Thursday, April 8th

I have a more luxurious caravan today. Richard approves. Maggie S is still in one of the poky little ones. 'You could hang meat in it,' she drawls elegantly, referring to the spectacular lack of heating.

Maggie and I work on the scene where she finds me in bed with the girls – Maggie being released about five. RL thinks something was lacking in her performance today.

Then to look at rushes. Helen comes along – her first glimpse of anything to do with the film. She hasn't even read the script!

Much relieved and pleased that the first major scene between Maggie and myself makes people laugh. It looks fine and beautiful – *every*thing looks fine and beautiful, but it's good to hear naked, unadorned laughter and especially as these are the last rushes before Denis returns.

Friday, April 9th: Good Friday

Feel good and virtuous and only a little cross at having to speak to a Danish journalist on the phone from Copenhagen about my 'Railway Journey', which goes out there next week. Had to explain trainspotting to him. He told me *Time Bandits* was a great success in his country, where it isn't shown to under-15s because of 'the violence'. It's also called, quite shamelessly, 'Monty Python's Time Bandits'.

Sunday, April 11th: Southwold, Easter Sunday

Strongish north wind throwing showery rain against the house. Take Ma to Southwold Church for the Easter service.

Before the service, conducted by the same vicar with the same permanent grin of redemption that he wore when Dad was put in the ground almost five years ago, we go to see the grave. It's in a small plot with several other crematees. As Mum happens upon it, she raises her voice in horror, 'They're all *dead!*'

She means the flowers.

I don't feel I can take communion with her – I just don't believe securely enough. So after the main service of rousing Easter hymns, I walk along to the front, in the teeth of a wrinkling north wind, past some of the old haunts, counting the years Southwold has been part of my life – about 25.

Home, for Granny's stew, then venture out in a still-inhospitable afternoon, though there is no rain. We walk along the beach, throw stones, push each other about, chase and generally have a very happy time.

Tuesday, April 13th

The news which dampens all our spirits is that Denis O'B, back from the States, has seen the assembly thus far and word, via Neville and Ray, is that he found the sound very difficult to hear and the pictures too dark. I suppose, because we were all so euphoric about the results, we took this news much more heavily than perhaps it was intended. But his reaction undoubtedly casts a pall over the proceedings.

Thursday, April 15th

Our first day at the Ezra Street location, where controversial amounts of the construction budget have been spent to improve the look of this East End neighbourhood. Something like £100,000, I think. Ezra Street itself has been resurrected, with a 50-yard frontage of mock houses, so well made that an old lady pointed one out as the house where she was born and another asked the council if she could be moved into it.

There are practical steam engines, piles of cobble-stones, and huge letters have transformed the local school into a Missions to Seamen Home. There are four complete streets we can use – over a quarter of a mile in all. It's the most impressive build I've seen on a film since the 'Ribat' [at Monastir for the *Life of Brian*] – and I think tops even that.

Friday, April 16th

Our day is plagued by the presence of a *Nationwide* film crew, who trap me in my caravan and suggest that I play all the locals when they interview them. I quickly abort that idea and send them off to talk to the *real* locals ... 'Oh, yes, that's quite an idea.'

A *Daily Express* lady, quite unfazed, sticks stolidly to her questions as I change in my caravan. I'm in and out of costume and make-up changes all morning, which leaves me with few reserves of patience and, when at last lunch comes and my poached trout is being borne to my caravan, the very last thing I need is an interview with *Nationwide*. But that's the moment they've chosen. The result is a very bad interview and considerable irritation. 'Oh, you were in the *Life of Brian*, were you?' asks the interviewer at one point.

In the afternoon Maggie S hides in her caravan to avoid having to talk to *Nationwide*, the *Daily Express* lady quietly and doggedly continues with her questions and I concentrate on trying to preserve sanity and remember what the hell I'm doing in Whitechapel, dressed as a clergyman.

Saturday, April 17th

Lunch with Denis to discuss my personal stuff – contracts and the like. I still do not have a signed contract, nor have I accepted any payment for *Missionary*. We walk from Cadogan Square to a pleasant, almost empty Chinese restaurant in a basement off Knightsbridge.

Denis tells me more about the Columbia deal, which, as far as I'm concerned, is the most unbelievable part of the *Missionary* saga. That we should have completed three weeks of shooting, only 13 months after the first word was written, is fantastic enough, but that we should be going out with the finished product in a thousand theatres across the US after 19 months is almost terrifying. But our little film is, give or take settlement of details, Columbia's big film for October/November.

Denis was in conciliatory mood – anxious to talk about the good things in the film. He's pleased with Richard, he was very impressed by Ezra Street and he thinks my performance has 'captured all the nuances'.

Back home I was just nodding off after lunchtime wine when TJ dropped in, having walked across the Heath. We sat in the sun and drank coffee. He had seen the assembly yesterday – chiefly to look at Peter

Hannan's work with a view to using him on *Meaning of Life*. It was enormously encouraging to hear that he had liked it so much he'd kept forgetting to look at the camerawork. Not only looks was he complimentary about, but also the humour.

Thursday, April 22nd

Work out at Dorney in the morning and then nearby to a beautiful avenue of trees down by the river for a shot to out-Tess *Tess*. This is the first longish dialogue scene between myself and Phoebe. Phoebe a little apprehensive. I've written her one of my 'jargon' parts – a lot of detail about filing systems which she has to learn parrot-fashion.

I keep correcting her when she says 'Pacific sub-sections' instead of 'specific sub-sections', but it turns out she's virtually dyslexic on this particular word. A huge shire horse drawing a plough clatters past at the start of each take.

The waving green wheatfields shine in the late evening sun. Phoebe looks slim and delicate in her wasp-waisted long dress, and the jets from Heathrow bank steeply to left and right above us.

Saturday, April 24th

Up at seven. I take Rachel with me this morning, to be part of the crowd in a 'busy London street' shot, which we're shooting in Finsbury Circus. Ninety extras and a dozen vehicles, including two horse-drawn buses. Signs of our own making cover up banks and travel agencies. A big scene.

Lunch in Richard's Winnebago with a journalist lady and Maggie S. Maggie very solicitous of Rachel, who sits with unusually well-behaved taciturnity, nibbling a cheese sandwich. We chat to the journalist. Maggie S clearly not enamoured of the press and resists attempts to be photographed by the *Sunday Mirror*.

Home, collecting a McDonald's for Rachel on the way, about a quarter to eight. Ring George H, who is just back from Los Angeles. He's jet-lagged and watching the Eurovision Song Contest. I just want to communicate to him some of the end-of-the-week elation I'm feeling. He promises to come and see us next week.

Monday, April 26th

Picked up by Brian at seven. Graham Crowden in car as well. Very genial and avuncular. As we drive into Oxfordshire, on a disappointingly grey, though still dry morning, he describes how he was shot by his own Sergeant-Major during arms drill in Scotland in 1943. He said that when the rifle went off there was none of the usual histrionics that actors and writers usually put into such tragedies, just a dawning realisation and a desire to be as polite as possible about it. 'I think you've shot me, Sergeant,' was all he could say – and the Sergeant's reply was 'What is it *now*, Crowden?'

Thursday, April 29th

This ridiculous confrontation with Argentina looks more and more like sliding from bluster and bluff into killing. But the government's popularity has risen 10% overnight since the re-taking of South Georgia and Murdoch's *Sun* is writing about 'blasting the Argies out of the sky'. This episode shows the true face of the nasties. Crimson, angry, twisted, bitter faces.

Saturday, May 1st

Not used during the morning as a series of sharp and hostile showers passed over. Some hail. Whilst they filmed Deborah and the photography scene I remained in the caravan, completing various tasks like thank you letters to the actors, and writing a new introductory narration for *Jabberwocky*, which I heard from TG yesterday is to be re-released in the US during the summer. He's very excited by the improvements made by Julian in re-editing.

Give lunch in my caravan to the 'Repertory Company' – Graham, Phoebe, Tim [Spall], Anne-Marie [Marriott]. Open champagne to celebrate good work done and, sadly, our last day all together. Quite a smutty lunch with RL's description of Long Don Silver, a man with a huge dong and varicose veins, who used to be featured in a club on Sunset Strip – hung upside down.

In one of the afternoon's sunny spells we grab a shot of myself in a horse and trap arriving home. As I wait for the clouds to clear the sun I see our two executive producers emerging from the orchard. George looks like Denis's son. His hair has reverted to Hamburg style, swept backwards off the forehead. He hands me a magnum of Dom Perignon with a pink ribbon tied round the neck. I embrace him warmly, then the cue comes through and I'm swept away round the corner.

They stay around for the next shot – a small, hot bedroom scene between Deborah and myself. George squashes himself into a corner of the room behind the lights, but only a yard or so from Phoebe. She's quite clearly made nervous by his presence and her face and neck flush and we do three very unrelaxed takes. Then George gets uncomfortable and moves off and we finish the scene.

Sunday, May 2nd

J Cleese rings to hear how things are going – having read his *Sunday Times* and been reminded it's my birthday on Wednesday. He starts *Privates on Parade*[1] a week Monday. Says he can't remember what he's been doing for the past few weeks, but his pet project at the moment is the book with his psychiatrist. We wish each other well and he offers his services as a critic at the first fine cut stage of *The Missionary* in June.

T Gilliam arrives before lunch and we actually find ourselves writing together again – on the intro to *Jabberwocky*. He points out that I could be 'starring' in three separate movies in the US this summer: '*Bowl*' opens in late June, *Jabberwocky* in July and *Missionary* in October.

After he's gone, Tom beats me at snooker, I drink a beer I didn't really want and am suddenly faced with a lot of learning for the Fermoy scene and a 'surprise' party ahead of my pre-39th birthday tonight. I am at my worst – grumpy, resentful and unhelpful.

About half past eight Terry G and Maggie and the Joneses arrive and I cheer up with some champagne. Nancy [Lewis] and Ron [Devillier] are a surprise, as are Ian and Anthea [Davidson] – who I haven't seen for ages. Also the Walmsleys,[2] Ray Cooper – who brings me lead

1 Peter Nichols' stage play about a British Army theatrical troupe in Malaysia in 1947 would be Denis O'Brien's next HandMade production, directed by Michael Blakemore and starring John Cleese.
2 Nigel and Jane Walmsley. Nigel Walmsley was at Oxford with Terry Jones and myself. He went on to run, among other things, Capital Radio, Carlton TV and the television ratings organisation BARB. Jane was a journalist and TV presenter.

soldiers and a bottle of Roederer Cristal champagne. Robert H and Jackie – six months pregnant. Chris Miller and Bill are there and the Alburys. Twenty people in all. The Inneses are the only ones who couldn't make it.

It's a lovely party and I don't deserve it after being so surly in the p.m.

I drift – no, I plummet to sleep, thinking how nice it is to have a birthday party and wake up the next day, the same age.

Monday, May 3rd

To the Odeon Leicester Square for showing of rough assembly of *Missionary* – mainly for George H and Denis.

The projectionists are very slovenly with the focussing and as each cut comes up there is a long wait until it's sharpened up – only to go again on the next cut. But the laughter comes – especially from Denis – and the gymnasium scene (which had worried RL and myself) goes extremely well. At the end George turns and shakes my hand. Denis has been oohing and aahing at the beauty of shots and is quite genuinely and spontaneously pleased by it all.

This is just the boost we needed before starting on the last lap of the film – in Longleat and Scotland. But it pleases me most that George likes it, for it's his enthusiasm and love of the *Yarns* and the work I've done in Python that really made it all possible.

He tells me that there may soon be a settlement in the Apple business. 'Twenty years and we're just starting to get royalties for *Please, Please Me*.' As we go down in the lift he assures me that there will be no problem financing this film ... 'Denis wants to keep everything tight ... but ... the money's there, you know ... if you want it.'

Tuesday, May 4th

Leave home at 6.20 and drive, with Brian and Rosamund Greenwood, up the M4 to Highclere in Hampshire. The crisp, clean beauty of the countryside making the news that we have torpedoed an Argentinian battleship off the Falkland Islands seem even more unreal.

Arrive at Highclere just before eight o'clock. Already in the car I've been reassured and relieved to hear Rosamund Greenwood read the scene, with a gentle touch, but drawing every bit of comedy from it. When we 'line-up' at half past eight, I'm doubly happy to hear Roland Culver, who at 82 has an excellent combination of good acting and sparkle in the eyes. His sole line, 'Hello', brings the library down.

It's a very gruelling day, learning and retaining these long speeches, but we work on until eight o'clock, leaving three close-ups still to be done and a forbidding amount of work for tomorrow. Brian drives me to the salubrious Ladbroke Mercury Motor Inn at Aldermaston Roundabout.

A message from Terry J to ring him. As I do so, at 9.30, he's watching the news, which has just come in, of the sinking of a British destroyer in the 'non-war'. The first British casualties. How crazy. Talk about TJ's rewrites on 'Every Sperm is Sacred'. He's elaborated on the sequence quite considerably.

Wednesday, May 5th: Highclere House

In the papers, 'HMS Sheffield Sunk' on the front page. It's been a cold night. Light frost on the cars outside the Mercury Motor Inn.

Drive up with Neville to the location, arrive at Highclere at eight. Quickly into close-ups of the death scene, which we complete by mid-morning. Everyone who came down on the coach this morning knows it's my birthday – they announced it on the radio!

Lord Carnarvon potters amongst us with good-humoured nods and bits of chat to the ladies. He looks like every American's idea of a belted earl – down to his velvet carpet slippers with the interlinked 'C' monogram embroidered on them.

With hard and concentrated work we finish at eight o'clock in the great hall at Highclere. It's goodbye to Phoebe, Graham Crowden (a lovely man, but a terrible worrier about his acting. As Ray C says, Crowden raises worry to an art form) and Rosamund Greenwood.

One of our unit drivers has left the picture without telling anyone, so I find myself driving in Richard's Winnebago in a pelting rainstorm past Stonehenge at half past ten. It's a stormy pitch-black night. We stop at a lay-by and RL makes toasted sandwiches for my birthday dinner.

Sunday, May 9th: Longleat House

On location by 7.45.

After a day and a half languishing unhappily at her hotel, Maggie is here, but looking rather frail. After an early shot in the hall, Michael [Hordern] is allowed off for a day's fishing, and Maggie, RL and myself rehearse lines and moves, alone, in the Chinese bedroom. The scene plays very neatly and both Maggie and I find it very funny to do. Feel quite pleased with myself – as a writer this time.

A long lighting set-up.

Maggie and I make a start on the scene, but it's late in the afternoon and jolly tiring to act on the peak of form then. The very funny run-through in the morning, before the cameras were in, now seems utterly remote. We wrap at six o'clock and Neville, in the midst of his gloom, has to laugh when he tells me the news that Trevor Howard has arrived, but passed out in the lounge of the hotel, which he thought was his bedroom.

We talk for 45 minutes – Neville, Richard and myself – while the rest of the unit stream up the road to the birthday party I'm giving for them at the Bath Arms. Neville estimates a budget overage of nearly £200,000 if we go two days over at Longleat. It's the confrontation with EuroAtlantic which he is trying desperately to avoid for he knows that once they start interfering his job will quickly become impossible.

Monday, May 10th

Quite cloudless sky today, as we drive through leafy lanes up to Longleat. I discuss with Neville my thoughts early this morning – for cuts and reschedulings to help us through the week.

In mid-morning word goes round the unit that 'Trevor is on his way'. Trevor duly arrives and is guided to his caravan. When I go to see him he grins glazedly, but welcomingly, like a great bear just hit by a tranquillising dart. We eat lunch together, then I give him script changes and he is loaded back into his car and driven off to the hotel.

Back up in the Chinese room, Maggie and I finally get into bed. The scene seems to play well and when we wrap at seven we only have two shots left to do. A showing of assembled material for all the crew has to be cancelled as we all sit expectantly in the library and the projector fails.

Tuesday, May 11th

All wait with rather bated breath, but Trevor is fine. Fortunately he's seated at a desk, writing to *The Times*, so he can virtually read his lines, which he does, writing them out carefully, with shaky hand, on the paper in front of him.

Meanwhile I wait around, unused to the inactivity. Every now and then a shout from Michael Hordern as he bangs his head yet again on some projecting part of his caravan. His head is now covered in wounds.

Wednesday, May 12th

Outside the weather is gorgeous, inside it's hot, difficult work as I do one of my few dialogue pieces with Trevor. He is sitting there trying to survive. We collect the lines on the most basic level – if he can put the words in the right order, that's a good take. I find it a strain and cannot act with any ease or comfort. Richard feels impatient and the crew have to break the brisk momentum they're into whilst lines are rehearsed.

Maggie's cool and competent delivery picks up the pace again in the afternoon and we remain on schedule when we wrap at seven.

Thursday, May 13th

Met at the location today by news from Bobby Wright, second assistant – known affectionately by Maggie as Bobby Wrong. 'Bad news, Michael. There's a neg. scratch across the bedroom scene.' Maggie and I had joked about this on Tuesday when we'd completed the scene in a fast, efficient, very hard day. But then I hear from Richard it's only on two easy shots.

Finish the sitting room scene. Trevor much better today.

At lunch we're invaded again. RL's bank manager, two children, two secretaries, as well as the 'NatWest House Magazine' photographer *and* Richard's mother and her two friends descend. There is no real relaxing over lunch today. 'When you're acting,' asks one of the secretaries of me, 'how do you know when to do all those expressions?'

Friday, May 14th

RL is shooting the entire dining room sequence on a master – dwelling longer on Maggie and myself and Hordern than on Trevor, who sits in splendid isolation at the far end of the table, a good ten yards from Maggie and myself.

About three o'clock we enter the hot, airless dining room and start to work on the scene, which has a soup-pouring slapstick joke in the middle of it, which requires quite a bit of working out. We do seven takes. RL enthusiastic about the last two. We manage close-ups on all three of us, though one long speech (six lines) defeats Trevor utterly and we have to abandon it, in close-up, anyway.

General elation at completing dead on seven o'clock. Drinks with Lord Christopher and wife, who have been very kind and accommodating, and at eight Neville, Brian Brookner and myself are in the car heading east to London.

Suddenly we are within two weeks of completion.

Sunday, May 16th

TJ rings. He says he reckons doing *Meaning of Life* will be a doddle. I gather Peter Hannan has been sent a script and is first choice for cameraman.

Open house for the rest of the day – variety of children and friends in and out. The boys, much more independent now, up to the Lido with friends. Helen and Rachel together playing some all-embracing, mysterious game. How could I want to leave all this? I do value it so much and sometimes wish I had a freeze-frame mechanism which could seal me in this present sense of contentment. But it is a fragment and soon the time comes for me to move on, collecting other fragments.

Monday, May 17th: London–Aviemore, Scotland

Wake in a Simenon novel – three in the morning, train stationary in a sodium-lamplit marshalling yard. We must be somewhere near Glasgow, where the train splits, half for Fort William, half for Inverness. To sleep again, lulled Lethe-wards by the friendly clatter of wheel on steel. Arrive at Aviemore a few minutes late at twenty past seven. We drive the 45 minutes to Ardverikie House.

Work progresses slowly as it always does with a new location and new people. We have period vehicles, including an 1899 Daimler, which prove temperamental, and the weather alternates unhelpfully between sun and cloud.

I have a room in the house, which is far less preferable to a caravan. It's like being entombed in this cold, grey temple to deer slaughter. I start the day with rowing shots and wet feet as I clamber from Loch Laggan and run towards the house. Smoke guns in the birch groves on the opposite bank complicate (but improve) the shot, and Neville is already twitchy enough by lunchtime to confer with Richard and myself about the Scottish schedule. Richard is bristly and will not compromise on rowing shots. Uneasy peace.

We are staying 45 minutes' drive away from the location in the ghetto of the Aviemore Centre. A bleak and inhospitable attempt to create a 'leisure complex' of the late '60's style, which proves once again that the more impressive the surrounding landscape, the less impressive are the powers of human design and imagination. I have a suite, but it overlooks the car park.

Go to bed feeling a bit surly, after ordering trout and champagne on room service, which arrives quite efficiently, with a flurry of autograph books.

Tuesday, May 18th: Aviemore

Drive to Ardverikie – on the way pick up a hitch-hiker with a dog, who turns out to be one of our extras, who's missed the bus. A young man with a weather-beaten face, he's a casual labourer with a wife and child. They sound like gentle people, ingenuous and idealistic. The £15 a day they are getting to do our 'Chariots of Fire' joke has, he says, 'made all the difference'.

I know Richard is uneasy about this whole section. He says he's not sure how to direct it. Both of us know it's on the thin red line between us and 'Two Ronnies'/'Carry-On'-style mannerism.

'You're glum,' says Maggie to me, in some surprise. 'You never look glum.'

After lunch we set up for a grand shot of the procession leaving the house. Two cameras, a crane, lovely sunshine between the clouds, but both the old cars refuse to function properly and we have to abandon the shot. I climb in through a window, and that's that for the day.

Back at the hotel, I eat with Maggie. Salmon is good and we sit and talk on until the place is long-empty. She does worry and things do get her down. She reminds me of Angela, bright, but brittle.

Wednesday, May 19th: Aviemore

Looming clouds after much rain in the night. Lighting and planning the interiors takes time and I feel weary and unenergetic. Still can't set my mind to anything else. Have hardly read a book since The Missionary began.

We work on the extra hour, until eight. Like yesterday I am only needed in the last shot – to be squashed behind a door. For various reasons the scene between Corbett [David Suchet] and Lady A does not play right, and Maggie is uncomfortable. We wrap at 8.15, but, though the scene was satisfactory, neither Richard nor I felt it was exceptional, which is why we employ Maggie.

Back at the hotel after shooting, ring home, ring Ma, and settle down to watch a Ken Loach film set in Sheffield. Have ordered a halibut and champagne from room service. But Neville comes to see me, and another crisis has to be faced. The need to re-shoot the scene with Maggie and D Suchet tonight has really only confirmed Neville's fears that we will not collect the Scottish stuff in eight days.

I have looked as clearly and constructively as I can at script and cuts, but I think back to the *Ripping Yarns* and how we always left the 'adventure' finales to the end of shooting and almost inevitably compromised. So we must get this one right.

Halfway through our gloomy discussion, the halibut arrives, ushered in by the maître d'hotel himself and two flunkeys, like some life-support machine. It's already been delivered to Maggie Smith by mistake.

Thursday, May 20th: Aviemore

Not called early today, but cannot sleep very soundly after noisy departure of unit vehicles at seven. Feel very low for various reasons. Lack of central involvement with what's going on is primary. Ring home and talk to Rachel and Helen, who says TG rang and raved about the look of what he'd seen of *Missionary*. Somewhat cheered, set out at nine for the first day on the moors location.

After parking car am driven up a steep and rutted track, along which two bridges have been built by P Verard and the construction team. On the side of a broad slope our caravans are perched, and a motley collection of minibuses, Land and Range Rovers, Weasels, Sno-Cats and other vehicles. This is base camp.

Half a mile away the picnic scene is being set up in a very picturesque bend of a stream. The champagne and the strawberries and the cut-glass set out on a table perched on a cart (a good idea of Richard's) look wonderful.

Richard maintains he doesn't ever want to direct sequences like this again. He wants to work on films of the scale of *The Last Detail* – with small locations and small casts.

George Perry of the *Sunday Times* is in attendance. He's rather well-read and has wide terms of reference and I feel very dull and boring as I talk to him about *The Missionary* in my caravan.

Afterwards we wander down to the picnic location and it's quite pleasantly warm and sunny as the unit lounges on the grass. I'm used for one shot about five o'clock, then come back to my caravan with George.

I gather that further down the track there have been ructions with Maggie as she does the last shot of the day. Can't find out what's gone on, but as she walks back to base camp she looks grim.

Friday, May 21st: Aviemore

At base camp by eleven. Most of the actors wandering around in an unused state. Apparently no shots have been done yet as the Sno-Cat, go-anywhere, do-anything Arctic exploration vehicle has stuck halfway to the location, and toppled most of the camera equipment out.

Very slowly the unit straggles across the mountainside to the butts. Maggie in full Edwardian costume and wig looks very bizarre in the creeping caterpillar vehicles. I talk to her about yesterday. 'How *is* Richard?' she asks drily. She cannot understand his rapid changes from gloom to manic enthusiasm. It was this that threw her, she claims.

By midday our little army has been moved to the location, even as rumours are confirmed that we have landed again on the Falkland Islands. I note that the 'conflict', as they are still calling the Falkland confrontation, has been running almost exactly as long as our filming. Both seem to be reaching crisis point at about the same time!

After a Perrier and pork chop lunch, I walk over the hill to the location, accompanied by Bobby Wright, who occasionally screams into his walkie-talkie. 'They want to know how many blacks Richard wants in the crowd at Liverpool? ... No, *blacks* ... Five percent? ... Chinese? ... Alright, no blacks, but five percent Chinese ... ' And so on ... It all drifts away into the silent vastness of the Scottish hills.

Sunday, May 23rd: Aviemore

The Scottish *Daily Mail* has hysterical headlines about our 5,000 heroes – the men who yesterday went ashore in the first official re-invasion of the Falkland Islands. Even the *Times* is full of diagrams with graphic explosions and heroically-sweeping arrows. It's real war out there now and the implication in all the reports is that it will escalate and many lives will be lost before anyone can stop it.

Drive Maggie to Ardverikie House, where we are invited to late lunch with Richard in the Winnebago. RL, with his restless energy, wants us to go and eat on the island in the middle of the loch. Maggie, with her equally strong determination not to be impressed by such mad suggestions, demurs. In the end we compromise and RL takes us out onto the loch in his little dinghy. It pours with rain – a prolonged, cold shower – we've nowhere to shelter and the only wine he's brought is a rich Sauternes.

Arrive back drenched and Richard gives us a complete change of clothes. Maggie looks lost in a huge pair of his trousers. But it's jollied us along. Peter Hannan arrives and helps barbecue the steaks – with oregano and tarragon. Very nice. The showers pass and there's a period of beautiful early evening sunshine.

Tuesday, May 25th: Aviemore

We have an important scene to play this morning – Maggie's 'dying words' in the cart. Our first scene of real, unadorned affection for each other.

The wind blows as violently as yesterday, but it's warmer and our real problem today is too much sunshine. We have to play the scene whenever a cloud comes over, and it takes two or three hours. But it plays easily and naturally, without great dramatics, which I'm sure is the right way. Maggie happier today, which helps. I fool around a bit and try to keep morale up. But the relentless battering from the wind eventually gets through to me, as we push ourselves into a series of wide shots as the sun goes down and the wind takes on a bitter, unfriendly edge. But at least the rain holds off and we finish all we need on the grouse moor.

Back to the hotel. Glorious hot bath. Then have to summon up shred of strength from somewhere to attend a unit party downstairs in the Post House. Second wind and end up dancing and talking until four o'clock. Need to let off steam.

Friday, May 28th

Wake quite early and doze. Rachel comes into our bed about 7.15 to cuddle up with me. Bright sunshine and the papers full of the Pope's first visit to Britain. Brief, illusory feeling that we have finished. Buy the paper for the first time in weeks, eat breakfast at my own table – other delusions of freedom.

Down to Tite Street in Chelsea with Brian. London looking marvellous in perfect May sunshine. We are shooting in a wonderfully cluttered old studio – a marvellous, characterful, eccentric house in a street full of marvellous, characterful, eccentric houses, mostly studios dating from the 1890s and decorated in early Art Nouveau style.

When we *do* shoot, Trevor takes a long time and has to have his words on an idiot board. Maggie says she should have seen the warning lights this morning when Trevor arrived in Tite Street with a broad smile at a quarter past ten, looked at his watch and said 'Open in a quarter of an hour.'

Tuesday, June 1st: London–Aviemore, Scotland

Awake most of the night – not troubled, just very hot and sticky and aware that I have only till 5.35 to sleep. Brian calls for me at 6.15. We pick up RL and catch the 7.40 Inverness flight from Heathrow, with the 39 others in our reduced unit.

Drive to Ardverikie House. 'Decathlon acting' this afternoon – riding horses, leaping and running onto carts and finally endless rowing shots back and forth across Loch Laggan.

Even after the sun had sunk behind Creag Meagoidh there was a soft pink glow in the sky over the loch, whilst the sharp outlines of the mountains behind us were slowly concealed by a soft mist. The water was still, the mosquitoes frequent, and it was very, very beautiful. I was still out there – a madly rowing vicar – at 9.30.

Wednesday, June 2nd: Aviemore

Work in the afternoon – running up stairs and along corridors.

RL has organised a party after shooting – there are two lambs roasted on the spit, a bonfire, candles in the trees, sangria and beers to drink.

A 'band' arrives, comprising two rather sullen young Scotsmen, who sit, slumped, on the side of the specially erected stage beside the shore, with drooping cigarettes, murdering popular ballads, and being saved only by a bagpiper and Ken Lintott and Ramon singing 'Sit On My Face'.

Towards ten o'clock RL prepared for his illuminated spoon-playing performance. As part of his 'light show', he ignited explosive on his hat, which shot a blast into the sky and made a much appreciated smoke ring eddy over the gathering before anyone realised that Richard had quite severely burnt his hand. He was taken off to a local doctor.

Thursday, June 3rd: Aviemore

For an hour or so this morning the bedroom scene, in which I try to dissuade Maggie from killing Lord A, became rather heavy work. First it lay rather flat, then RL wanted me to be more assertive, which led to me being louder and stronger, but making the lines sound suddenly melodramatic.

The scene clicked when we played it softly, listening to what each other was saying and responding accordingly – which sounds obvious, but is actually a difficult effect to achieve in a film, with marks, tight, precise movements and a clutter of camera, mikes and semi-slumbering members of the crew all around.

Saturday, June 5th: Aviemore

Another clear, still, sunny morning. Yesterday was the hottest of the year in Scotland and today seems set to cap it. Am soon put to work on ride-through shots up in the woods beside the loch. Shafts of sunlight through the trees and hordes of midges.

Rest of the day doing interiors – running up twisting staircases à la *Jabberwocky* and hanging off battlements. All in my hat and long black coat, which is very uncomfortable today.

In the garden a man plays with his children. It's all hot, still, unmoving and vaguely unreal. Reminds me of the *Grande Meaulnes* or *Picnic at Hanging Rock*. A feeling of melancholy in the back of my mind as I look out. Regret and some sadness.

Of course, it's the last day of main shooting. These people who've helped me and been a daily part of my life for the last ten weeks will be strangers again tomorrow.

About 6.30 I do my last shot up in the turret room. There's a smattering of applause. Maggie dashes off because she can't bear goodbyes. I leave the crew filming a stunt man on the battlements and head back to Aviemore. On the way I stop at Maggie's hotel to drop something off for Ramon. Meet Maggie on the way out. Her eyes start to fill with tears. Find a lovely note from her back at the Post House.

Bathe, collect some champagne and sandwiches and catch the 9.34 sleeper to Euston. A party in my compartment with the camera crew, Chuck Finch and Ken Lintott. No chance for further melancholy.

A much-reduced unit then moved out to Africa, to shoot Fortescue's days as a missionary.

Wednesday, June 9th: Samburu Lodge, Kenya

A good night's sleep, but woken by the accumulating cacophony of birdsongs and screeches and baboon roars. At breakfast hornbills and yellow weaver birds fly to the table-side and a vervet monkey makes a sudden lightning dash and removes Peter Hannan's toast. A moment or two later a vervet disappears up the tree with a sugar bowl. The waiters throw rocks after the monkeys in desultory fashion, but I should think deep down they rather enjoy the guests being made a monkey of.

About eight we set out to see the mud-walled Mission hut which Peter Verard and Norman Garwood have been here for a week constructing. It looks marvellous. Beside it is my tent – with portable writing table – and three mud huts made by Samburu ladies.

At the local school we are treated as VIPs as we arrive to listen to 'Greenland's Icy Mountains' sung in English by the Samburu kids. Proudly their teacher, Leonard, conducts them, and solemnly the children sing. A little flat in parts, but the words ring out clearly from a score of serious little black faces – 'The heathen in his wisdom bows down to wood and stone.'

Thursday, June 10th: Kenya

My first day of *Missionary* work in Africa. Alarm goes at half past five. Shave and dress and it's still dark outside. Assemble, cups of coffee and tea, and out to the location, nearby in the park, ready to cycle at first light. Pass an angry bull elephant, impala, gerenuk (the deer that never drinks) and the little black drongo bird.

At 6.30 punctually the sun comes up – so fast that there is little time for red skies and orange light – it's almost straight into a soft yellowy-green. On 'Action!' I set our vintage cycle in motion, but the pedal snaps.

Later, I'm walking past some camels with my umbrella up, when the sound camera breaks down. Lunchtime crisis. The camera, with all its sophisticated technological bowels spread open, lies on the bulrush benches in the little mud chapel. It's pronounced dead and all sorts of gloom descends. Urgent messages to London, but the nearest telephone contact is 40 miles away in Nanyuki.

We carry on with a mute Arriflex.

Friday, June 11th: Kenya

We are ready to start filming in front of the Mission hut at six o'clock. Me writing a letter home beside a roaring fire. There's a brisk wind and sometimes the flames threaten to engulf my writing desk.

We take a two-and-a-half-hour break in the middle of the day. Walk with RL (who never stops) amongst the trees and scrub, looking for insects. He finds mainly dung and scarab beetles and puts them in his jar.

Just after lunch the village kills a cow. It's a ritual slaughter carried out by the morani. The women of the village are not allowed to be a party to it, so the ceremony takes place beyond the thorn branches which mark the limits of the manyatta.

After being cruelly manhandled out of the truck, the cow is killed with a warrior's spear driven quickly and neatly into the back of the head to sever the spinal cord. I remember now the repeated dull crack of metal on bone as the spear was driven home. Then the twitching cow is laid on its side and a cup is carefully made from the loose skin on the throat. This is filled with blood, and the elders of the tribe are the first ones to stoop and drink the blood.

As I watch from the discreet shade of a thorn tree, the chief calls to me, 'Hey, Padre!' and beckons to the makeshift cup of blood. I mutter something apologetically about having to get back to acting and hurry off to the manyatta.

The other unlikely event of the afternoon was the arrival of Neville Thompson with a new synch sound camera. The message had reached him at 5.30 on Thursday evening and, with commendably quick thinking, N was in Nairobi with new equipment at nine Friday morning. Neville, white and rather haggard, appeared briefly in amongst the huts as I was trying to put together an ad-libbed argument with an aged Samburu. Then he was gone.

Saturday, June 12th: Kenya

This is the morning when we do Fortescue walking past wild animal shots.

When we sighted elephants after 30 minutes of driving, engines were cut and I walked out and past the beasts whilst Bagaboi – a Samburu ranger – covered me with a loaded rifle from behind a hedge. They all thought I was very brave. 'Hasn't he ever seen anyone trampled to death by an elephant?' Bagaboi asked, and of course that was absolutely the point. I hadn't. What appeared to them as courage was just massive ignorance.

Unsuccessfully tried to get near giraffe and crested cranes. I was told to walk slowly and deliberately through the grass 'because of the snakes'.

We shot the choir in the Mission hut in the afternoon. They had managed to learn three more verses of Bishop Heber's convoluted prose in the last two days and we were very pleased and applauded them.

Sunday, June 13th: Kenya

Today the reward of safari with no filming. Derek Barnes [our Kenya location manager] is taking myself, RL, Shuna [Harwood, costume designer], Gary White [first assistant director] and Peter Hannan to Shava Park, near to the Samburu but, he says, much quieter. So we assemble once again around the bougainvillea-clad entrance to the lodge, just as the sun is rising. Baboons scurry after the trailer taking rubbish to the tip, like dealers at a jumble sale.

After two and a half hours we drive up to Shava Lodge. The sun shines in shafts of light through the foliage and gives the whole place a Garden of Eden-like quality. And they are well-equipped too. A full English breakfast – bacon, sausage, the lot – is cooked for us on a barbecue and served with thick-cut marmalade and toast. On an impulse I suggest Buck's Fizz and, extraordinarily enough, they have a bottle of champagne chilled.

Oohs and aahs of quiet pleasure, added to by the gentle hurrying of streams which flow from a diverted river down through the lodge gardens to the river.

Derek, armed with a panga, cuts a route down to the base of the waterfall and Hannan, Gary and myself strip off and walk beneath the waterfall itself. The hard, cooling water thuds down on us. Afterwards we sunbathe naked on a rock by the river. It's quite perfect and I could easily stay there until the end of the day – no people, no sun-oil, no deck-chairs, no pool-side bars selling over-priced drinks – just sun and water and solitude.

Out to the airport. At ten to twelve, with RL supine on a customs counter, the camera crew, Norman Garwood and myself partook of our last Tusker beers at the airport bar.

A rather crumbling, tired little group we were – with the results of our three days' intensive filming in brown boxes in an airport trolley. As someone said, this really was the end of picture party.

Thursday, June 17th

Drive up to Lee's for a viewing of the latest rough assembly of *Missionary*. Present are a half-dozen besuited young executives from Huttons [HandMade's advertising agency].

Denis is there, looking very cheery, because even *Scrubbers* seems to be going the right way now.

We see about one and a half hours of the film. Start is sticky as usual, but once it gets going, largely helped by DO'B's infectious laughter, it works well and smoothly. No standing ovation at the end, but people clearly impressed.

Interesting reaction from Huttons was that it took them by surprise. It was nothing they had expected from either the synopsis or from previous work of mine. They all talked very positively about it – shook my hand and congratulated me.

Have to leave early to go to a Python wig-fitting.

Monday, June 21st

Halfway through one of the most hectic years of my life. That in itself is encouraging. I'm still alive and healthy. A few grey hairs showing since *The Missionary*, but I feel quite trim (11.1) and just about on top of things.

Take Rachel to school. Apparently her teacher says she has been much better this last week. I think she needs her dad and I feel very relieved that my five weeks' absence on *The Missionary* is over (longer, I suppose, if one counts the weekends and the early starts and late finishes we worked even when we were in London).

A showing of the film so far at four.

There is much good laughter and the Slatterthwaite sequence goes so well that it's impossible to follow in terms of audience reaction.

The Scottish sequence is disappointing to me in terms of performance. The last 15 minutes become very serious and very quiet and I don't enjoy them at all in the present company. I know they're wishing Michael Hordern would come on again (says he paranoically).

RL is very anxious for me to work with him on the next two weeks' editing – for we have to present a fine cut at the end of that time.

He wants me to cancel my trip to Columbia in LA. I feel it's essential to meet these faceless people before I go into Python confinement, so we compromise. I will go to the States for two days instead of three, returning Friday lunchtime and working with Richard right through the weekend.

Tuesday, June 22nd

At 9.20 a car collects me and takes me down to the US Embassy to collect my passport. There is a tube strike so the roads are packed. It's raining heavily. Into the dreadful world of visa applications – rows of faces looking anxiously to a row of faceless clerks behind desks. No-one wants to be there. I collect my passport – have to sign that I'm not a communist or a Nazi, and several pieces of paper for fans who work in the Passport Office.

Then out to Heathrow, where I arrive at eleven. The delights of travelling First Class then take over. I have only hand baggage so check quickly through and into the BA Executive Lounge for some coffee and another long call to RL. I feel we should not show Columbia the end of *The Missionary* until it's right, but Denis has a video with everything we saw yesterday on it – so we'll have to do a re-editing job, and erase some of the tape. Get Rose Mary Woods[1] in as adviser!

The flight leaves a half-hour late. DO'B travelled Club Class with his two daughters. I visited them occasionally – taking them smoked salmon and other First Class delights. Denis's daughters sat, very well-behaved, and read and coloured books whilst DO'B immersed himself in columns of figures. Most of his deals, he says proudly, were worked out at 35,000 feet.

---

1 At the Watergate hearings in 1973 the hapless Rose Mary Woods, President Nixon's secretary, claimed she'd 'pressed the wrong button' on her tape recorder, accidentally erasing four and a half minutes of what could have been incriminating testimony.

Wednesday, June 23rd: Beverly Wilshire Hotel, Los Angeles

Denis calls about nine o'clock to tell me that their reactions to the three video segments of the movie which they've already seen have been excellent. Everyone from Antonowsky (he's the President of Marketing) downwards filled with enthusiasm. That's a good start.

Am picked up by Denis and Inge at ten. He rents a brand new Mercedes, and we drive out to his office at Burbank. There meet Dan Polier – a thin, slowly-precise talking, late-middle-aged man with neat silver-grey hair – and David Knopf his chunky junior partner. They are Denis's sidekicks on film distribution.

'Just been working with a fan of yours,' says Polier. 'Steven Spielberg.' That doesn't spoil the morning either. Apparently they are working on *ET*, which looks set to be the biggest box-office picture ever.

At midday we walk over to Columbia Pics.

Long, low, modern office. Softly and thickly carpeted. Tall, gaunt figure of Marvin Antonowsky looming over them all. He stands like a great bird, eyes flicking around, his lean frame held back almost apologetically. He welcomes me into his office with some kind words about what he's seen, then a group of about eight or nine Columbia hacks are brought in. All seem very quiet and respectable and deferential. Young – mostly my age or less. Ken Blancato, the creative publicity head, is neat and trim and looks like a hairdresser. They don't immediately strike me as an intimidatingly forceful team. Very well-behaved in the presence of their president, behind whose desk is a shelf full of maybe 40 screenplays. I notice *Scrubbers* is there, alongside *The Missionary*.

Antonowsky and Blancato are very confident that they have some wonderful campaign ideas and, without much ado, an artist reveals six of the most crass and dreadful drawings I've seen in my life. If I had set down on paper my worst fears of what they might produce, these would be they. A grinning, Animal House-like caricature of myself with girls dressed in 1960's Playboy Bunny-style outfits, with tits and thighs emphasised at the expense of period, beauty, truth, honesty and everything else. I have to say I find them a little obvious. 'Oh, yeah, well that's why we have another version ...'

Ah, the subtle one. The subtle one consists of me kneeling at a long bed, with a dozen 1950's beauties lined up on either side of me in a parody of the Last Supper. I sit there, with all these expectant faces looking towards me, and I wish the floor would open and swallow me up – or swallow them up, anyway. If ever there was a moment when I wanted a Los Angeles earthquake, this was it.

But the moment passed and they proved to be not at all unadaptable. It was not a terribly easy session, though. They revealed, with a sparkling air of revelation, their slogan: 'He gave his body to save their souls.' Denis sat there remarkably unmoved and I couldn't leap up and down with excitement.

Thursday, June 24th: Los Angeles

Some more writing of blurb for ads, then Denis collects me at ten. Drive to his office at Warners and I show him, Knopf and Polier my suggested ad lines and synopses. They are instantly typed up, to be presented to Columbia at our 11.30 meeting.

Also sketch out an idea for a trailer – very quick, short one-liners showing Fortescue becoming progressively more trapped. DO'B loves this and, when we file into the even more gaunt and haggard Antonowsky's office, DO'B cheerfully announces that I've solved everything – we have radio, TV and trailer advertising all sewn up. His faith in me is embarrassing, as I fumble with pieces of paper to try and bear out this hyperbolic introduction.

I read them some of the ad lines – quite a few chuckles. Outline the trailer idea, which is also met with approval. 'He had a lover, a fiancée and 28 fallen women. And he said yes to all of them' sounds the favourite, though they still cling to their 'He gave his body to save their souls' line. But Antonowsky reacts well, directs them to work on the lines I've proposed and, unless he is just flannelling me, I feel that we have progressed by leaps and bounds since yesterday – and hopefully my work yesterday evening and this morning has given me the initiative.

Taken to Hamptons – a big, noisy hamburger restaurant just beside Warners' Burbank studio – by Polier, Knopf and Denis O'B. Then a return visit to Columbia, in which I am wheeled into a conference room where about 15 PR people sit round a table. Ed Roginski, a rather calm, soft-spoken and intelligent head of publicity, chairs the meeting and all those around the table introduce themselves to me – name and position.

They ask me things like whether I have any special needs I would like catered for when I go on promotion. They are (thankfully) against a three-week cross-country whistle-stop tour (which TG underwent for *Time Bandits*). They suggest instead a week and a weekend in New York –

including a 'Junket Day', when they bring key out-of-town press and radio into the city, all expenses paid, and throw me and, they hope, Maggie to them.

Polier and Knopf feel that the sooner exhibitors can see *The Missionary* the better for choice of cinemas, etc. Columbia is going through a bad time with *Annie*[1] – despite enormous amounts of publicity effort it has not brought the house down on its nationwide launch – and there really isn't any picture they can get excited about (apart from *Python Live at the Hollywood Bowl*, which opens tomorrow) until *Missionary* comes along.

A limousine picks me up at 4.30 and I'm driven back to the airport. Onto the 6.30 flight.

Sleep through *On Golden Pond* for the second time in three weeks.

Monday, June 28th

The start of Python rehearsals and writing for *Meaning of Life* coincides with the first national rail strike for 27 years and a London tube and partial bus stoppage. I drive quite easily to Regent's Park, and by great good fortune, find a parking space right outside the new office, and arrive only just after JC. He, too, is sporting a moustache. He grins delightedly at me and says I look *quite* different. Not sure how to take this.

Python Live at the Hollywood Bowl opened at 60–70 cinemas in NYC and Philadelphia to overwhelming apathy. Various reasons put forward – first weekend of excellent weather in NYC; very strong opposition from Spielberg, *Star Wars* and *Rocky*; opening too wide with too little publicity. EI very strongly blames *Secret Policeman's Ball*, which GC advertised on American TV evidently.

After a half-hour discussion it's clear that no-one has an answer. The movie collected good reviews in both the big NYC papers.

Eric wins 'The Meaning of Life' song with no declared supporters for TJ's version apart from myself and TG, and neither of us felt Eric's version deserving of any stick. But on 'Every Sperm is Sacred', on which TJ has done – *had* to do – so much work, there is quite a strong split. Eric takes up the position that his version is much better, musically and in every other way, than TJ's. GC bears him out quite vehemently. TJ says that his version is better, musically and in every other way, than Eric's.

1 A big-budget movie based on the cartoon strip Little Orphan Annie, starring Albert Finney and Carol Burnett and directed by John Huston.

Once we start discussion it's clearly crucial that JC comes down firmly in favour of TJ's version.

Tuesday, June 29th

Sandwiches at lunch and talk over the ending. Eric feels that we have cheated the audience by not having come to grips with our title. I see our title as being a statement in itself. There is no way we can tell anyone the meaning of life – it's a cliché and we are using it ironically to show how irrelevant we can be when faced with such a pretentious subject. John sees fish as the answer to our problem.

Eventually I ad-lib, with Eric's help, a very short and dismissive lady presenter winding up the film and reading the meaning of life from an envelope – this fed on from a nice idea of a Hollywood awards-type ceremony where we asked a glittery compere to come on and reveal the meaning of life. He opens a gold envelope and reads . . . 'And the meaning of life is . . . Colin Welland!' I think this was the best laugh of the day.[1]

We broke up about 3.30. I had a cab driver who at one point came out with the line 'Do you know how long I spent in the shower last night . . . ? One and a half hours . . . Mind you, I felt better at the end of it.'

Saturday, July 3rd

Bowl returns even worse than Denis had led me to believe at the beginning of the week – we were 'gasping' in Philadelphia to a gross less than that of a *Bambi* reissue the week before and in NYC only managed 125,000 dollars at 58 sites! Dreadful.

If the cliché 'you've seen one, you've seen them all' applies to any sphere of human activity, it must be school fairs – or 'fayres' as they're wont to call them. As with the Gospel Oak Fayre two weeks ago, the William Ellis version was the usual collection of bric-a-brac, shabby clothes and grubby books for sale. A few gallant sideshows run by the boys. Two tombolas run with steely-eyed efficiency by the sort of parents who like running things. Some rather wet chicken tikka out in the car park, and not much else.

Helen had put together a hamper and she sat for nearly three hours

---

1 At the 1982 Academy Awards Welland had famously brandished the Oscar for *Chariots of Fire* and shouted 'The British Are Coming!'

beside it for about £17.00. Tom played in the wind band in the main hall at four, which was a very pleasant addition to the usual format. Took the girls back via a toyshop and bookshop in Kentish Town (I bought Mary Kingsley's *Travels in West Africa*), then home.

Am I getting more like my father in old age? I've noticed definite signs of easily roused impatience and intolerance since *The Missionary*. I put it down to the fact that co-producing, writing and acting was a giant public relations job in which I had to be all things to all men every day for eleven weeks, and the thing I need the rest from most is not acting or writing, but people.

Saturday, July 4th

Take the children for a swim. Re-read W L Warren's book about my favourite English king – John. Discover Angevins had violent tempers. Also that the twelfth century was the best-documented in English mediaeval history.

Monday, July 5th

To Python rehearsal, to find that Neil Simon had been on the phone and wants to meet me – he has some film project.

After a costume fitting I drive up to Britannia Row Studios in Islington to record 'Every Sperm' track. Ring Neil Simon. He professes himself to be a fan, says he is halfway through 'one of the best things I've written' and there's a part in it for me. Arrange to meet him on Wednesday.

The recording session is delayed while they find a piano tuner, so I sit in the big and comfortable games room and watch England start their vital match with Spain. They must win and by two goals to be certain of going into the semi-finals. Our defence is unshakeable, mid-field quite fast and controlling most of the game, but we can't score. 0–0 at half-time.

In between play I've been singing 'Sperm Song' to Trevor Jones's rather solid beat. Eventually we find a combination of takes we're comfortable with and I drive home to watch the second half. England fail to score and slide out of the World Cup. It's a hot evening.

Tuesday, July 6th

Third day of another rail strike. NUR gave in rather pathetically last week. Now it's ASLEF's turn [ASLEF was the train-drivers' union]. Reprehensible Thatcher statements likening ASLEF to the Argentinians we defeated 'so gloriously' in the Falklands.

Drive in at ten and we rehearse three or four sketches, on sofas doubling as First World War trenches, with our scripts in hand. Fizzles out about one. Costume fitting for me as a schoolboy.

Home for a run, do some work, then I have to change, bathe and go down to meet Marvin Antonowsky at Odin's. I've arranged the meal at his instigation, and he says he's very pleased that it's only the two of us, as he would just like us to get to know each other a little better.

He seems to be rather ill at ease with the food and the ordering, but talks quite fluently about his early days in advertising, his admiration for Frank Price – the President of Columbia – his stint as head of programmes at NBC, during which he claimed credit for starting *Saturday Night Live*; his move to ABC and eventual elevation to marketing head at Columbia.

He compliments me, with a sort of little head on one side smile, 'You're a good little actor ... you come over well on screen.' He clearly wants to work together again and assures me that Columbia would like to do the next thing I come up with. When I tell him I'm meeting Neil Simon to discuss a part he gets very excited. Like all Californians he uses hyperbole quite undiscriminatingly, starting with 'wonderful' for people whose guts he probably hates and working up through 'amazing' and 'marvellous' to 'absolutely incredible' human beings. Neil is 'absolutely incredible' and 'a great friend'.

Wednesday, July 7th

Over to Inn on the Park to meet Neil Simon. A man of about my height with a warm, friendly manner answers the door. He apologises for walking with a lean, but five days ago he slipped a disc, after watching Wimbledon (at Wimbledon – he's a tennis freak). Apparently he went into spasm one morning as room service called and he retold, with comedy writer's relish, how he pulled himself across the room and collapsed at the open door as he let in his breakfast. He couldn't be moved from the doorway for two hours – body half out in the passage as curious guests walked by.

After some talk and some morale-boosting admiration of my 'natural and likeable' acting persona, he told me of his project – a half-written play with a part just right for me. Apologising for being unable to précis the idea, he asked if I had time enough to read the 60 pages of his typed first draft. I agreed readily. He gave me the script, then went discreetly into his bedroom with the two *Ripping Yarns* books I'd brought as a present for him.

I recall the play was called 'Heaven and Hell' and began, with a disconcerting resemblance to *Arthur*, on a scene between an elderly butler and a very rich young man who is a miser. He's bashed on the head in a carefully organised collision in his car and taken by a gang to a warehouse which has been got up as heaven.

It looks so like the heaven that this character has come to know from the 1940's movies he always watches, that he believes in it, and when they tell him he has three days to go back to earth and raise enough money to avoid them sending him to hell, he falls for it. Some very funny lines, but a disappointingly one-dimensional character.

I find my attention wandering as I read to what I'm going to say to this most famous of all American comedy writers when I've finished. Fortunately he makes it very easy for me and we talk about the character and I can express some of my feelings about him being real and understandable and Simon agrees and says he will put in more at the beginning explaining the young man's miserliness. I have to say that I can't make up my mind, that I'm very flattered, etc, etc, but being a writer myself I will probably want to write something of my own after *Missionary*.

Truth be told, I found the play lightweight in the two areas I enjoy so much – character and detail. I'm very tickled to see he has a rather insignificant character in his play called 'Antonowsky'.

Thursday, July 8th

To Claridge's to meet Ken Blancato – Columbia's VP of publicity [to organise a shoot for their poster]. Am not allowed into the cocktail lounge, as I have no tie or jacket. 'Rather silly in this weather, I know, sir ...' agrees the porter in thick overcoat who escorts us out.

Sit in the lobby and have a couple of beers. Blancato is a New Yorker and worked in Madison Avenue. He's also a frustrated writer. When I reiterate my reservations about the roof-top shots with the girls, etc, he grins rather wearily. I feel I'm just making a nuisance of myself.

I go on from Claridge's to Neal's Yard, to try another recording of

'Every Sperm', as Monday's didn't sound entirely satisfactory. André and Trevor have rather different views of how to approach my vocal, and it's not a particularly successful session, as I'm in a rush anyway.

On to Mon Plaisir for a meal with TG. He says he'd rather like to be a monk. We talk some business. We've seen figures that show 17 million dollars returned to [Avco] Embassy [from *Time Bandits*] and none of that is owed to either of us.

Friday, July 9th

Car picks me up at 8.30 and drives me down to the Great Northern Hotel. King's Cross and St Pancras silent and deserted at the end of the first week of the rail strike.

Onto the rooftop – another hot, slightly hazy morning. Richard is there with son Joe, a bit subdued. Also he doesn't like what David Alexander [the photographer] and Camille – the bored, drawling, world-weary Columbia lady who is Blancato's number two – are doing. He's very quiet as Alexander sets up the shot and fires off reels of film like there's no tomorrow.

At lunchtime we're finished and down the contraceptive-scattered stairwells into cars and on to Lant Street, where Norman Garwood and co have rebuilt my Mission bedroom.

I have to work rather hard leaping up and down and presenting endless expressions to seemingly endless rolls of film, whilst the photographer urges me on with shouts ranging from '*Won*derful,' which means very ordinary, to 'Just the best!' when I'm trying a bit.

At one point Camille, who looks dreadfully out of place in her Beverly Hills straw hat and white strides, steps in to change a shot in which three Mission girls are in bed, and I'm below. We're not allowed to show any rude bit, or suggestion of a rude bit, so I've made sure that the girls are well-wrapped in sheets (quite unlike the way they appear in the film). But this is not enough for Camille, who fears that the very suggestion that the girls might be nude *under* the sheets could result in the ad running into trouble in the Deep South.

At this my fatigue – that intolerable fatigue of working hard on a job in which you have no confidence – causes me to crack and we have a heated exchange on the subject of *The Missionary* and the Deep South. 'It's not me . . .' she keeps pleading, which makes it worse, because I want to know who it is who wants to do this to our film. That there are more than averagely narrow-minded people in the Deep South I don't doubt, but what are we all doing here today, working our asses off to try and reach down to their level?

Monday, July 12th

Slept unsatisfactorily – woke at intervals from four o'clock onwards. The adrenaline is beginning to flow – the surge of nervous energy that I will need in the next ten weeks has to come from somewhere and the last two weeks since *Missionary* 'finished' have not really been enough to get right away from one film and into the other.

To the Royal Masonic School in Bushey, a largely red-brick amalgam of all the old public school architectural clichés. A few flying buttresses here, a clock tower and some cloisters there.

JC asks me about ASLEF and the implications of and background to their strike. I think he might be sending me up, but he's quite serious. I was quoted, somewhat misleadingly, in the *Mirror* on Saturday as saying I supported ASLEF. It's just that I can't stand to hear this self-righteous government trying to pretend it's more of a friend to the railways than the proud, independent, much-maligned and bullied train drivers' union. If the government really had the good of the railways at heart this present action would never have happened.

We're starting with a scene involving Cleese and myself and an entire chapelful of boys and masters. I play a chaplain and the similarities to March 29th continue as I don a dog collar and have my hair swept back. I even keep my *Missionary* moustache.

Thursday, July 15th

To the Masonic School again. Feeling of despondency as Brian drives me into the gates. I feel no emotional attachment to this location, as I did to those on *The Missionary*. It's a place of work. The weather doesn't help – it's overcast and looks like rain. Caravans are a good walk away from the location – so nowhere really to rest during the day.

EI cheers me up. He's in good form and we sit and make each other laugh whilst waiting for lighting set-ups in the classroom. I've brought him Signford's two Chris Orr books, which he wants for David Bowie, who has much admired Eric's Orr collection.

Keep in touch with *Missionary*, where Maggie S is patiently waiting for me to come in and post-synch with her. But have to keep giving them increasingly pessimistic estimates and in the end the session is abandoned and I find myself still being a schoolboy in Bushey at seven o'clock.

Sunday, July 18th

Leave at eight and drive out to Twickenham. I enjoy the sunshine and the emptiness of the roads and the little courtyard at Twickenham Studios, with flower tubs everywhere, is convivial and friendly. Richard has arrived on his bike, which he describes disarmingly, as 'Probably the best that money can buy' – and then proceeds to tell stories about how he fell off it and rode into parked cars.

Post-synch the entire 'Bottling Factory'[1] scene and we finish at one o'clock.

As I arrive back at Julia Street I find a group of kids around a cat lying in the gutter – obviously barely alive after being hit by a car. I ring the local RSPCA and they ask if I could bring the cat in. Am just loading it into the hamper I won about 30 years ago in a Fry's Chocolate competition when the Browns – the Irish family on the corner opposite – return from their Sunday lunchtime trip to the pub. Mrs Brown becomes very tearful when she identifies the cat I'm bundling rather unceremoniously into my hamper as once belonging to her granddaughter Deborah, who died tragically of appendicitis after a doctor's mix-up.

I drive to Seven Sisters Road. RSPCA man thinks there's a fair chance of its survival, which I wouldn't have expected. Cats' broken pelvises do heal quite successfully usually.

Home to the Browns to bear them this welcome news. Mr Brown, who calls me 'Palin' or 'Young Palin', insists that I stay and have a drink. A Scotch is all that's on offer – served in what looks like an Austrian wine glass. But it's very pleasant – like walking into the snug bar of a very convivial pub. No introductions or all the delicate, defensive small talk which the middle classes are plagued with – the Scotch warms me physically and mentally and I have a lovely half-hour. Mr Brown very Irish, with lilting voice, soft and very articulate, and always a quiet smile in

---

1 This scene, in which Fortescue goes to ask for money for his Mission, was shot, rather grandly, at the old Royal Mint on Tower Hill. Sadly, it held up the story and never made the final cut.

everything he says. They couldn't be more different from the sobbing group I left half an hour before. They celebrate their happiness just as enthusiastically and openly as their grief.

Friday, July 23rd

My twelfth early start, and twelfth working day on the trot. At least this morning I am spurred on by the sight of light at the end of the tunnel – by the prospect of not only a weekend off, but then seven filming days in which I'm not involved.

But today is no easy downhill slope. For a start Eric and I have a long dialogue scene [in the hotel sequence] – four and a half minutes or so. TG has a wonderfully complex and grotesque make-up as the Arab Porter. Then there is much re-lighting and building of rostrums after TJ decides to shoot the whole scene in one. So Eric and I walk through at 8.30, then wait, in make-up and costume, until a quarter to one before they are ready.

We do two or three takes at about 1.30, and in two of them I forget my lines and have to stop – which is unusual enough for me to make me rather cross and depressed when lunchtime comes. I really feel the accumulated fatigue of an eleven-week shoot and then these last twelve working days. Fortunately after lunch with EI and the strangely attired Gilliam, I feel better and, although I have to push myself physically hard, I find that I'm actually enjoying the piece.

TG, with his blind eye (as used in *Holy Grail*), nose too big for him and the wheel on his false hand broken, has created for himself his own peculiar nightmare, and he will be trapped in it again on Monday.

Sunday, July 25th

A party at Barry Cryer's in Hatch End. Roomful of comedians. R Barker, R Corbett, Eric Morecambe, Frankie Howerd, Peter Cook prominent.

Chat with Ronnie C. With a relieving sense of self-mockery, he reveals his customary interest in Python's financial affairs, business arrangements, etc. RB looks around gloomily. 'Too many comedians here,' he says. 'Not so good for character actors.' He too is obsessed with Python's wealth. 'All millionaires now?' he asks, not wholly unseriously.

Peter Cook, who wasn't exactly invited, is more forthcoming and entertaining. He's come straight from Vic Lownes's[1] house and somehow found himself at Barry's. He's very pleased with the video version of his Derek and Clive second LP. He says it's going to be shot in 2-D. He asks me in what part of Africa *The Missionary* was shot. Turns out his father was a DC in Nigeria. Cookie, in a rare moment of sentiment, clearly felt quite an admiration for his father – 'People ask me about influences on me – the Goons, Waugh, etc, etc – but in the end the person who influenced me most was my father.'

One of the King Brothers – Michael, I think – tells of a very funny stage act he used to work with – a man who wore a German First World War helmet and threw a cartwheel in the air and caught it on it as the climax of his act. The audience loved it. Only the rest of the cast (who used to flock into the wings whenever he was on) could see the acute expression of pain on his face every time he did it.

Monday, July 26th

With the lighting already up and the Hendy hotel room piece already played through, I'm ready for my close-ups by a quarter to nine and have done the scene by 9.30. I feel looser and funnier and much more on top of the scene than last Friday and almost wish we could do the whole thing again.

But Eric is much quieter today. He apparently suffered a 24-hour 'flu yesterday, with hallucinations and temperature. His voice is huskier than Friday and he is clearly not happy with the performance. But he improves as we go on, and cheers up too. His son Carey comes to the set, a small, bright-eyed, scrawny little lad clutching a copy of *Rolling Stone* containing an interview with his hero – Sylvester Stallone – in *Rocky III*.

Leave the studio at two. Six shooting days off – feels like a school half-term, saying goodbye to everyone. Home for a wonderfully normal, unrushed evening with family and a BBC programme on the chances of survival for Londoners in a nuclear attack.

Death from a nuclear blast would be short, sharp and sudden. Especially, the programme suggests, if you're living in Kentish Town!

To bed, very content.

---

1 Victor Lownes III was the London head of the Playboy organisation and had been the driving force behind Monty Python's first film *And Now For Something Completely Different* (1970).

Thursday, July 29th

I go up to CTS Music for the second day of *Missionary* music recording. I've never seen film music recorded before, so to enter this spacious modern studio, with its control room like a mighty ship's bridge, from which the eye is drawn downwards to a 60-strong orchestra, and beyond them to a screen high on the wall on which my antics appear, is stirring and a little frightening.

Everyone seems so competent and capable, from John [Richards] the mixer at his 36-track desk, to Mike Moran with his enormous score sheets, to Harry Rabinowitz (old acquaintance from *Frost on Sundays*!) looking not a day older, with headphones on and baton raised, to the orchestra of session men, who are probably from the London Symphony or the Philharmonic, but today are in jeans and T-shirts and reading newspapers in between cues. It's an epic undertaking and, when the Scottish themes thunder from the speakers to fill the control room, it's very moving.

RL and I have been discussing for the last few days an alternative photo idea for the print-ads – of Fortescue under a lamppost in the street, where normally only whores would stand. The contrast would be funny, there are three or four whores in the background to add any of the titillatory element Columbia might want. So it's resolved that there is no other way but for me to go to Denis this evening and heave some more money out of him.

Surprisingly, he accepts my point that we could do a better job here, and he likes the idea of the lamppost and the prostitutes. He will ring Columbia and tell them we want to shoot an alternative. The onus is now all on us to come up, in quite a rush, with something that lives up to our confident stand.

Tuesday, August 3rd

See assembly of 'Mr Creosote' at lunchtime (instead of lunch). Evidently 9,000 gallons of vomit were made for the sketch, which took four days to film. It's been edited rather loosely at a poor pace and dwelling too much on TJ's actual vomiting, but the costume is marvellous in its enormous surreal bulk, and Mr C's explosion is quite awful and splendid.

Wednesday, August 4th

The sticky heat continues. Oppressive, sluggish, still heaviness.

I feel quite tense from fatigue today and find myself at midday facing a long close-up take with my heart suddenly thudding, my voice thickening and my head swirling. Not a good sign of my condition, I feel. I just want to get away from films, film people and the whole process. But I am firmly stuck in it for the next few months.

As if to underline this, no sooner have I finished at Elstree than I have to go down to the Tower Hotel to prepare for an evening's shoot on the new poster. Peter Hannan comes along to help supervise the lighting of the street, we have four prostitutes and Angus Forbes is the photographer.

It's warm and still in Shad Thames where we're shooting, which helps to keep everybody happy and patient as the clock moves on to midnight, when we finish and drive back over Tower Bridge to the hotel to change. Find myself, dressed as a vicar, with Tricia George dressed as a most comely whore, in the lift with two American tourists. As they disembark at the ninth floor I gently remind them that 'London still swings'. 'Right!' was their nervous parting shot!

I'm home at 1.15.

Thursday, August 5th

Collected at 8.30 by Brian. I have a one-hour make-up as Debbie Katzenburg. Feel testy and rather low. For some reason the continuing news of the Israeli bombardment of West Beirut sickens me and I can't read the paper.

Eric, TJ and myself in drag, Cleese the Reaper, Chapman and TG the men. One of the few sketches involving all the Pythons.

The afternoon's work is slow – things like JC's beckoning bony finger taking up a lot of time, as special effects, animals and children always do.

TJ suggests we eat out together. Neither of us notice the irony that, although we've spent the whole day on a sketch in which a dinner party is poisoned by salmon mousse, I start with a delicious salmon mousse.

Friday, August 6th

A long morning around the table in a hot studio in drag. Simon Jones is playing the sixth member of the dinner party. He's a very good man with a quiet wit, well able to stand up for himself. In one morning he learnt the Python lesson in survival – over-act in your close-up, it's your only chance. Actually he did his piece modestly and very well.

Long afternoon as we have to dress in cottage walls every time we move round to do close-ups. GC and I are the last to be done. Then more special effects as we die. Eric and I blow out the candles then collapse, motionless on the table for 40 seconds. Cynthia Cleese hiccups during one of these long silences and sets us all off.

The day stretches on into evening and we sit and play games. JC hears that EI is dining out with David Bailey and, when EI has gone, expresses great incredulity that anyone should want to have dinner with David Bailey. Then he suggests we play a game – 'Not Michael, because he's far too nice about people' – to list our worst-ever dinner party.

After JC has been hauled back for yet another close-up of the Grim Reaper, Eric asides to me that it can't be much fun having dinner with John Cleese.

Saturday, August 7th

Tonight at six and eight are the first two public showings of *The Missionary* in America. Keep remembering this at odd times during the day. Moments of pleasurable anticipation.

Wolf a croissant, then up to Elstree for a tiger-skin fitting, only to find that my other half of the skin is in a pink suit doing the 'Galaxy Song' on Stage 3. Yet another breakdown in communication. Round to Stage 4 where mighty office buildings are being erected for TG's £100,000 'Accountancy/Pirate' epic.

Tucked in a corner is a tiny Yorkshire '30's cottage, filled with children who are rehearsing 'Every Sperm' for Monday. Little Arlene Phillips, with her bright, open face and pink and maroon matching hair and tracksuit, is taking the kids through the number. We work out some movements for me to do, and then I read the build-up lines – all about 'little rubber things on the end of me cock' – some kids snigger, the younger ones smile up at me innocently.

Home – and a relaxing evening in, broken only at one point by a huge series of explosions to the north. It's not the Israelis bombing possible PLO meeting houses in Kentish Town, or the IRA – the huge cracks and flashes lighting up this stodgy August evening are for the 1812 Overture, being played at Kenwood [open-air concert].

To bed after watching (and staying awake for) Hitchcock's *Notorious*. Superb performance by Ingrid Bergman. Very sexy. Put the phone right beside me in case I should get word from LA ...

Sunday, August 8th

Richard L rings about half past two. The news is not good. He says he's confused and disappointed and just wishes I'd been at the viewings with him. He felt the audience was unsuitable – general age between 16 and 23, predominantly male – the *Stripes* and *Porky's* sort of audience. All subtitles and understated scenes went by in silence. Howls of appreciation and whoops when Maggie (or rather, Maggie's stand-in) goes down on me under the bed-clothes and the whores hop into bed.

But the figures – considering the nature of the audience – are not as discouraging when I think about them: 2% excellent, 30% very good, would recommend to friends, 40% average, quite enjoyed it, 19% only fair, and 9% thought it the worst movie they'd ever seen.

RL rings later in the evening. Says he's spoken with Denis O'B, who was, so I hear, not downhearted. They have come up with a list of proposed cuts which they want to make next week and show at a sneak preview in NYC on Saturday the 14th. Could I come? Concorde both ways. I have to say no, as Python is away on location in Scotland and Yorkshire.

Tuesday, August 10th

Arrive at Elstree 9.15. Wide shots first, with all the kids in. Mothers in attendance.

TJ is worried that there may be a walk-out if we say either my line – 'Little rubber thing on the end of my cock' – or one of the kids' lines – 'Couldn't you have your balls cut off?' – so we plan a subterfuge. I will say 'sock' instead of 'cock' (taking care not to over-emphasise the initial letter) and then the dastardly substitution will take place in the dubbing theatre. The boy's interruption will be of a quite harmless variety – 'Couldn't you sell Mother for scrap?' – when everyone is present, but we'll record the real line separately when everyone's gone.

The afternoon is very hard work. I have to go through the opening speeches, song and routine over and over and the room is warming up, and the kids, though well-behaved, have to be continually instructed and calmed down, which gets tiring. They all call me Dad, off the set.

Finish with the children (as we have to by law) at 5.30 and for a moment Ray Corbett [first assistant director], Hannan, Terry, Dewi[1] and myself slump onto chairs in the little room amongst the discarded toys – like shattered parents at the end of a two-day children's party. Nobody has the strength to say anything for a while. Then, with a supreme effort, we gird our loins and complete my tight close-ups. I end the day wild-tracking the phrase 'Little rubber thing on the end of my cock' ... 'over the end of my cock', and so on.

Thursday, August 12th: Glasgow

Leave the hotel at 8.30. Drive half an hour out to the north of the city, past more flattened slums, rows of shops with boards and metal frames over the windows. Then through wooded, pleasant suburbs to Strath-blane, where we are quartered.

Some hanging around, talking to local press, crossword-puzzling and finally making up with mutton-chop whiskers and moustache, and squeezing into custom-made leather boots and the rather handsome navy blue uniform of a major in the Warwickshires of 1879.

Then we're driven a mile to the location – a five-minute walk up a hillside, where a British encampment has been constructed beneath a bare rock cliff, which I later gather is known in the area as Jennie's Lump.

Sudden drenching squalls of rain and cold wind cause us to abandon the planned shots and spend the day on weather-cover, with scenes inside the tent originally planned for Elstree. But it isn't only the unsettled weather which is forcing us to use weather-cover. Rumour reaches us during the morning that nearly 100 of our carefully selected and measured Glaswegian extras have walked out after a misunderstanding over costume in the local village hall.

A small group of very vocal Africans became angry when they were shown how to tie loin cloths by Jim Acheson (on the stage).[2] They had

1 Dewi Humphreys, camera operator, went on to become a successful TV director (*Vicar of Dibley, Absolutely Fabulous* and many more).
2 Acheson later won three Oscars for Costume Design: *The Last Emperor* (1987), *Dangerous Liaisons* (1988) and *Restoration* (1995).

been misled, they shouted. They thought they would be wearing suits. Poor Jim and his excellent wardrobe team faced a 1982 Zulu Uprising, as a group of two or three blacks shouted about being degraded, tricked ... dishonoured, etc, etc ... And 100 of them were taken back in buses to Glasgow.

We went on shooting – oblivious to all this – and completed most of the tent interiors by six o'clock. Back to the Albany. Bathe and change, looking out of my eighth-floor window across the wet streets to the grand, two-storey classical facade of Currie and Co, Building Trade Merchants. A fine, confident, assertive building, now in disrepair and white with bird shit. It looks as out of place amongst the new Glasgow horrors as a piece of Chippendale in a Wimpy Bar.

Dine with John Cleese and Simon Jones in the Albany restaurant. TJ restless at a nearby table with a dour Danish journalist. Simon Jones is relaxed, talkative and amusing. It turns out that he, like me, can't roll his 'r's.

Friday, August 13th: Glasgow

Cleesey very unwell this morning. We think it was the crayfish last night. At the hotel in Strathblane he looks awfully wan and up on the mountainside, as we prepare for the first Zulu attack, he is farting and belching, and at one stage actually throwing up against the barricades.

We have had to recruit white Glaswegians and brown them up as Zulus. I must say they are very patient and charge at the encampment ten times. It's a long day, heavy on extras and blood and smoke, and light on lines for the officers.

Newspapers – local and national – carry the story of the Zulus yesterday. Some very funny reports, especially in the *Glasgow Herald*. The nationals such as *The Times*, which refers to today's cast as predominantly 'unemployed youths' – note the use of the word 'youth', always pejorative – are less accurate. Still, all excellent publicity.

Try to contact Richard in New York, eventually get a rather fraught line from Strathblane to the Algonquin. Shout my instructions to some American receptionist and feel very abstracted from it all until I leave my name and the receptionist quickly returns 'As in *Ripping Yarns* ... ?' The Atlantic shrinks suddenly. But I never get to talk to Richard.

Back to the Albany. The bar is jostling with film technicians demanding of the hard-pressed barladies things like 'Two vodka tonics, two Guinness, two dry martinis, a soda water and take your knickers off.' An extra day's shooting tomorrow.

Sunday, August 15th: Bradford

To Bradford, where we eventually find the Norfolk Gardens Hotel – part of the atrocities which replaced a lot of Bradford's sturdy stone town centre with stained pre-stressed concrete. 110 of the 118 rooms are taken by our crew.

To bed 11.30. Walls wafer thin and I can hear every word from a TV blaring next door. Read half a page of Nabokov then drop off.

Woken at 2.30 by a call from RL to say that the New York preview went very well indeed with over 80% of the cards putting the film in the top three categories.

Monday, August 16th: Bradford and Malham, Yorkshire

Sixth week of Python filming – 17th week of filming since the end of March – begins with the pips from my calculator alarm slicing gently into my semi-consciousness at 6.45 a.m. It looks wet and uninviting outside.

Drive out to the location with Simon Jones, who points out to me the theatre in Bradford where Henry Irving [the great actor] collapsed, and the Midland Hotel, in whose foyer he died shortly afterwards, neglected by the hall porter who thought him a passing drunk. Sad end.

An hour and a half's drive into fine, rugged scenery up on Malham Moors.

Eric, Simon Jones and I wrap ourselves in blankets and wait in an upper room at the hostel. It's an old hunting lodge, which is now a centre for school sixth forms to come for field studies. A lot of walkers tramping around downstairs. They irritate me for some reason. Maybe it's their smug, self-satisfied preparation for all weathers.

Eric and I get into our make-up base for our Cocktail Party Ladies; outside the wind howls and the rain lashes at the windows. God knows what it must be like for Cleese, out on the moors as the Grim Reaper. Amazingly enough, in the midst of the tempest, we find that the TV set gives an excellently clear picture of a tranquil scene at Lord's, where England are fighting to save the Second Test Match v Pakistan.

JC arrives back at midday, absolutely soaked through, but in surprisingly high spirits. He takes great heart from the fact that TJ thought the shot they'd just done was second only to a day of seasickness in the Newhaven lifeboat as the most uncomfortable filming of his life.

Our appearance on the moor is put off well into the afternoon. I organise a subversive but, I feel, necessary trip to the pub in Malham at lunchtime. As I buy pints of Theakston's, I feel I have to explain to the lady at the bar why I'm in false eyelashes and full ladies' make-up. I tell her I'm in a film. She says apologetically, 'Oh, I never see films, I'm afraid. If anyone comes in here hoping to be recognised I'm afraid I can't help.' Eric, Tania [Eric's wife], Simon J and Graham C (with young friend) laugh a lot at this.

At a quarter to six I'm officially wrapped for the day, and England lose the Test Match by ten wickets. Back down to Malham Tarn Centre to frighten (or excite) the first batch of hearty walkers who've just filled the hallway after a 17-mile hike.

Thursday, August 19th: London–Bradford

At Twickenham I at last see the cut of *The Missionary* which they viewed in New York last weekend. It looks very beautiful. The relationship between Maggie and myself seems to come over well and is just as much what the film is about as the comedy.

Arrive at 8.55 at Leeds/Bradford Airport after leaving Twickenham at 7.15. Eat in my room and settle down to a long phone call with Denis O'B in Fisher's Island.

DO'B says Columbia are rapidly losing confidence in the movie, mainly because there weren't enough 'excellents' on the movie cards. He says they wanted to put it off till January and release it only in a couple of cities even then. He says he has pulled them back from this, what he considers suicidal, course, and reminded them that they are legally obligated to open the picture on the 22nd of October. But they've reduced the print now to between 400 and 600.

At last I feel we have some genuine response from Columbia – even if it is panic. My adrenaline is already flowing and I'm ready to fight for the film – to prove to Columbia not just what a good thing they've got, but why it's a good thing (because it's *different from*, not the *same as Porky's* and *Stripes* and *Arthur*), and to prove to Denis that I know better than he what works in a comedy film. It's difficult to do all this from a hotel room in Bradford, but I suddenly feel determined. This next week is crucial.

Friday, August 20th: Bradford

I'm driven out to Skipton at 7.30. A cold wind, occasional rain.

Terry has to ask some householders with strange, lop-sided faces if he could throw mud on the walls of their house. 'So long as you don't come *in*side,' they reply fiercely.

My shots are completed by midday. Buy a superb pork pie – North of England pies are a much underrated local delicacy. Am driven back to the Norfolk Gardens Hotel in Bradford, where I consume the pie with the remains of last night's bottle of Mercurey, then turn my room overlooking the bus station into an office for the afternoon.

Ring Marvin Antonowsky at Columbia – decide to put my head in the lion's mouth. He's brisk but amiable. Wants to have dinner with me in London on September 5th, will test our poster alongside their own and, in response to my queries about his reactions to the film, he says whilst not being 'ecstatic' about the results of the viewing, they are still behind the film nationwide on October 22nd. How many prints, I ask? 300–400, says Antonowsky. Going down!

Wednesday, August 25th

Because of poor weather this week, the 'Tiger Skin' scene has been postponed and we are doing the 'Hospital' today. Nice to see little Valerie Whittington and Judy Loe again. Valerie has all day with her legs apart as the Mother, Judy is the Nurse. I'm the Hospital Administrator. Suddenly occurs to me as I see them there that I've been to bed with both of them, on screen.[1]

A tedious day as I have a part which is not involved in the whole scene, but just important enough to keep me there all day.

I don't finish doing very little until after six and only just get down to the Preview One viewing theatre in time for the seven o'clock *Missionary* viewing.

DO'B has been on the whole quite long-suffering on *The Missionary* – has supplied the money when it's really come to the crunch and not interfered too much with the script. Tonight he sounds defensive and says things like 'Even if it's not commercial, I'm glad I've done it.'

[1] With Valerie Whittington in *The Missionary* and Judy Loe in the *Ripping Yarn* 'Curse of the Claw'.

Taxi home – back by midnight. Cab driven by a 'Silly Walks' fan. He calls it 'Crazy Walks'. Very weary.

Friday, August 27th

We attempt the 'Jungle' scene, so I have two parts to play – Pakenham-Walsh and the Rear End of the Tiger.

JC complains about performing against bright lights – quite rightly. It does reduce facial mobility by about fifty percent. JC mutters bitterly, and not for the first time, about pretty pictures at the expense of performances.

TG, who desperately wants to get this over with, so he can get back to his 'Pirate/Business' epic on Stage 4, is laboriously encased in a complete latex mould of a Zulu. Then the sun goes in, and does not reappear, except for a brief glimpse, when we try the shot. But TG, who's been inside the costume for an hour, has sweated so much that one side of the Zulu sticks to him.

The 'Tiger' is eventually abandoned and instead we shoot the tracking shot of the approach through the forest. Endless takes. Constant calls over the walkie-talkie for the Test Match score.

Saturday, August 28th

Today is perhaps the most crucial in the whole history of *The Missionary* so far. We will have two showings of 60 people each – one a general audience, the other my friends and sternest critics. There can be no excuses. If the response tonight is half-hearted there really isn't much we can do.

TJ and Simon are both there and I take them round to the Ship to talk about it. Both of them thought it had worked very well, but equally both felt that the reason for my journey to Scotland was not well enough explained. After a quick Pils, I'm back to Film House.

Cleese and Gilliam and Chapman have all come along. A full house. JC asks me to sit next to him and Barbara.

Good response to the painting-out of the name pre-title sequence (which DO'B would prefer to cut) and plenty of laughter from then on. Feel more comfortable with larger numbers and there are fewer embarrassing moments. Applause at the end. Close friends all seem to have enjoyed it. John Goldstone especially happy. Cleese, surprisingly, liked it a lot.

Go to eat at Bianchi's with John and Barbara, Terry G, Helen and Ray Cooper. Over the meal JC surprisingly candid about things. He says he regards *Yellowbeard* as 'a dreadful script', but is doing it mainly because GC came to him 'and actually used the word "plead"' to try and persuade JC to come in.

JC repeats what he once told Humphrey Barclay[1] about his writing relationship with GC. 'Some days I write as much as 75%. But most days it's 95%.'

Barbara very nice. She reckons *The Missionary* could have more success in the US than *Privates on Parade* as it's a more general, less specifically British theme and it's optimistic and leaves a warm feeling in the audience.

No-one, however, felt it would be a blockbuster. A nice, likeable, gentle film.

Wednesday, September 1st

Fakenham Press Ltd, who, to my pleasure, were responsible for *Small Harry*, have been closed down by their parent company. Three hundred out of work. Very sad. Fakenham being Father's childhood home, it seemed neat and appropriate that my first children's book should be made there.

Friday, September 3rd

The joy of not having to get up and go filming soon evaporated by the awareness that the last days of *The Missionary* are running out. It must be in final form by the end of the weekend.

Spend a couple of hours this morning agonising over how to alter the narration to accommodate various people's criticisms of plot and story confusion. Sort out the end quite satisfactorily, but it's in the middle of the last half, where TJ – backed up by Simon Albury – was vehement about making it clear that 'some inexplicable force' drew Fortescue to Scotland, that I have the trouble. Cleese, normally a great hunter and destroyer of woolly plots, had no trouble following the story or understanding why he went to Scotland as he did. Lynsey de Paul[2] went further and asked if those who couldn't follow the plot were mentally deficient.

---

1 TV producer and colleague of JC's from Cambridge Footlights.
2 Lynsey, singer and songwriter, was, for some time, a neighbour of ours.

Saturday, September 4th

See from *Variety* that *Monsignor*, a film starring Chris Reeve as a priest, is opening on the same day as *Missionary* in the US. Seeing the advertising reminds me painfully of the area we haven't yet sorted out – posters, etc. The image of *The Missionary*.

Take Willy and his friend Nicky to the Valley to see Sheffield Wednesday's second game of the season – against Charlton. Perfect afternoon for football. Sun, not a breath of wind and the pitch verdant and springy. Wednesday have a glorious and unequivocally deserved 3–0 victory.

Usual police presence outside – motorcycles, Alsatian dogs at the ready. The ever-present tension not relieved by their presence.

Up the main road, off which our car is parked, a crowd suddenly starts to run. There are shouts, ugly faces contorted with rage, bricks and bottles thrown. The police seem to do nothing.

I see a bottle tossed at the window of a house, another hurled from a van full of supporters, which lands and smashes beside a baby in a pram at a corner shop. Quite why the cruelty and hate behind the fighting can be so easily fanned, I don't know. And the urge to destroy and damage is strong. It's almost entirely the work of boys from 13–18, with one or two sinister older ones stirring it up.

Wednesday, September 8th

To Elstree at lunchtime to be Debbie yet again.

Jonathan Benson is the new first assistant and keeps us all cheered with his special Bensonian brand of dry wit, which comes out, just as does the dry ice, at the beginning of each take.

We are eventually free soon after 7.15. A quick transformation from Debbie to a freshly-scrubbed actor, then home and into a suit to become Michael Palin for the *Brimstone and Treacle* opening at the Classic, Haymarket.

Afterwards to a party given by Naim Attallah, described today in *Private Eye* as 'The Palestinian Millionaire'. He had red shoes, that's all I remember.

Not a bad party. Pursued Selina Scott, the lovely newsreader, and was about to introduce her to Sting as Selina Sutcliffe, realising only just in time that I was getting muddled up with the Yorkshire Ripper's wife.

Saturday, September 11th

With almost indecent haste, the day has arrived when I complete my second major feature in five and a half months. People tell me I look inordinately well – I blame the sunshine of April and May – and, apart from waking up some nights in cold sweats, or not even sleeping, I have just remained sane and I think I've given some good work. I do feel tired, but have been carried along on the energy of elation – occasionally dented by a poor day's work, or an average viewing. On the whole, I must say, I feel wonderful.

Today all the Pythons are together to be fish and, as this is probably the last time we shall be gathered in one place until February next, there is an added note of almost hysterical urgency around. Iain Johnstone's[1] BBC crew are filming the ABC '20–20' film crew filming us trying on our fish harnesses. I'm a goldfish, Graham a grayling, the two Terries perches and John is a carp.

It's a very weird and effective make-up, making us all look like John Tenniel's *Alice* pictures – semi-anthropomorphised.

'Shit, it's Mr Creosote' are the memorable last words of the day, nine weeks after John and I had begun the film in the chapel of the Royal Masonic School.

As if to bring everything full circle, RL rushes into the dressing room as lashings of solvent are being applied to my hair to remove the glue, with Polaroids of the day's poster session.

On the way home in the car TG and I discuss it and TG feels it's too solemn and stylish and too busy. He feels that we should be looking for a much simpler, more direct approach. Even something as corny as lipstick on a dog-collar, he says.

Sunday, September 12th

As I lie awake, some time around nine o'clock, I feel with great certainty that Richard's second attempt to produce an alternative to the Columbia poster is still not right. It lacks a sharp and clear indication that *The Missionary* is comedy – it's fun, something to be enjoyed.

1 Iain was a producer and presenter of BBC's *Film Night*. He was also an author and later worked with John Cleese on the book of *A Fish Called Wanda* and the screenplay of *Fierce Creatures*.

TG's aside about a dog-collar with lipstick on comes into my mind. It's clear, neat and simple. As soon as she's conscious I tell H about it and she enthuses.

Tuesday, September 14th

Run in the morning. The Heath is filling up again as if summer had returned unexpectedly. Pass a group of ladies with easels in a line and five straw hats and five cotton skirts all painting next to each other.

Sit out after my run and soak up the sun – read on with Nabokov, write some letters, then collect my *Missionary* outfit from Bermans for another and final attempt to crack the poster.

Drive down – roof open, a balmy evening – to W8, to yet another photographer's studio.

As it gets dark I clamber once again into my *Missionary* robes, Sandra [Exelby – make-up] plants a thick, rich red kiss on the dog-collar – we try various angles of kiss – then I'm out in the street, where one should be on such a warm and beckoning evening, trying the silly expressions.

About nine o'clock I'm called in to take a very urgent message from Helen. She had heard from Mark Vere Nicoll, who had in turn just been rung by Antonowsky with the alarmingly sudden news that if *The Missionary* is not delivered to Columbia by this Friday they will pull out of the deal.

I call Antonowsky to try and find an explanation. He's out at lunch. Could I call back in 45 minutes?

Finally get through to Antonowsky. I ask him what's going on over the delivery dates. MA goes straight into some story about Richard Pryor involving Columbia in a damaging lawsuit because the final, fully edited version had not been shown to the blind bidding states. MA cannot let this happen over *Missionary*. 'It's us who have to pay, not you,' he garbles on. The movie must be ready to be shown within a week of this Friday or they're stuck.

'Can we deliver it by Monday?' I ask – any delay will help us.

'I'm only the middle man,' Marvin, President of Marketing and Distribution, pleads.

Tom McCarthy is the man to talk to about delivery.

At 12.30 a.m. I get through to DO'B at the Carlyle Hotel. He is in a fighting mood. MA had called him this morning and said that the movie was off, there was no deal. DO'B had argued with him for an hour and left MA in no doubt that if he pulled out he would have a major lawsuit on his hands. Anyway, DO'B has now declared war on the man who [he] said only a week ago was decent and straight. Any communications with Columbia must be noted down word for word and any agreements struck must be passed on to Denis so vital evidence is in writing.

I sense that Columbia still have some hope for the picture, but Denis firmly believes that they are now trying desperately to extract themselves. But then this is probably de rigueur in Hollywood, I comfort myself as I drive back home.

Wednesday, September 15th

Good news is that Columbia have not renewed attempts to cancel the film. Tom McCarthy is being helpful and we hang on by the skin of our teeth. But it was Richard who suddenly brought me down to earth by reminding me that the movie opens in the States five weeks from tomorrow. No wonder they are desperate for delivery.

Thursday, September 16th

Indian summer continues. Balmy, sultry sunshine – more like the South of France than South of England. Work at desk in the morning, lunch with Kathy Sykes [producer's assistant], a treat for all her hard work. Eccentric restaurant in Richmond called the Refectory, beside the church, run by a rather fine-looking man with a weathered, baggy-eyed face.

I have to let myself dwell for a moment on the vagaries of chance which end up with my sitting at lunch with Eric Sykes's daughter nearly 30 years after Graham and I sat and watched his programmes on the telly in Sheffield and dreamed of nothing finer to do than be Eric Sykes. Now I find Kathy telling me that Eric wants a part in my next film.

Saturday, September 18th

The roads of London are so empty at 5.15 on a Saturday morning that any other vehicle glimpsed in the rear-view mirror appears as a threat.

Pick up Loncraine, who groans unhappily as we head out onto the A40. Still pitch dark when we reach Rank Labs at Denham, and their long, low modern buildings and general Hollywood aspect only increase the dreamlike quality of the experience.

To the viewing theatre to see a checkprint taken from the interpositive that leaves for the States this very day. Although there are only a handful of people watching, most of whom have seen the movie endlessly, I feel tight-stomached at the lack of reaction, until someone else enters and starts to laugh most encouragingly.

The laughing man turns out to be Mike Levy – one of the top men at Rank. 'Lovely movie,' he says and then starts to take his own lab apart for not projecting the print with the correct light intensity. Once that is corrected we can see, to our relief, that there is nothing wrong with the print itself. Peter Hannan is very unhappy about the grading in two or three places and will be going out to the States on Wednesday to make the changes in LA. This is our last line of hope.

A sour-looking man brings any further discussion to an end by pointing out that he has to take the film to the States today. So I leave Denham at eight o'clock with the sun already hot and my film being loaded into the back of a Cortina Estate.

RL and I have breakfast with Hannan at a South Ken café. We are preoccupied with what's wrong with the film, rather than what's right. What a long way we've come from the euphoria of the early rushes, five and a half months ago.

Wednesday, September 22nd

Drive down to Knightsbridge for lunch with David Puttnam. Large numbers of police are about, closing off roads in preparation for the TUC Day of Action march. Down an almost empty Pall Mall with policemen lining my route. Can't help thinking how many police witnesses I would have if there were an accident. Probably two or three hundred.

Puttnam is already at a table in Mr Chow's – eager, voluble, enthusiastic, but a listener as well as a talker. He's been at a government-run committee this morning and is off to give a speech to Channel 4 this afternoon. *Local Hero* is coming along wonderfully and he thinks it may have as big an impact as *Chariots of Fire*. He has projects involving Rowan Atkinson, he's bought the rights to *Another Country*, he's produced a Channel 4 series, *First Love*, and has a new movie which starts shooting in Dallas in October.

We moan together about lack of time to read, be with the family (he's 41 and has a 20-year-old daughter). He asks me how I manage. I say it's quite simple, I just act as my own safety-valve. I don't have a secretary and an office set-up as he has; I take on as much as I can myself cope with, which is generally too much, but not half as much as the indefatigable Puttnam.

I hardly remember what we ate. I drank Perrier, he a bloody Mary. He told me of plans for filming the complete works of Dickens. He'd come up with the idea on holiday when, it seems, he'd read several of the books and a biography of Dickens himself. He's costed it at £50 million and is keen to find out whether Shepperton has the space for a brand new Dickensian back lot. If the project happened on the scale Puttnam was talking of today it would be a rich prize for any studio.

He's very pleased to know that I'm proposing an across-the-board percentage share-out for the crew on *Missionary*, as he did on *Chariots* and *Local Hero*. He gives me some useful advice on how to set it up. He estimates that on *Chariots* the crew will each get £1,500! His secretary, who is on something like half a percentage point, will get £75,000!

He doesn't seem anxious to get away and we chatter on for a couple of hours – about a mill he's bought in Malmesbury, where the mill-race will be used to generate electricity, about Jacqueline du Pré, in a wheelchair at a nearby table – and about the possibility of working together. He wants me to write one of the *First Love* films.

Return call to Ken Blancato in LA. They 'love the concept' of our latest poster and will be testing it at the weekend, but definitely using it for some of their smaller ads.

Friday, September 24th

Spend the afternoon reading the six children's books I have to review for the *Ham and High*. Very English all of them – and all printed in Italy. Alternate between moods of determination to criticise quite severely and general easy-going bonhomie. Hardest thing to write is the opening paragraph – my attitude to children's books. Am stuck on this when the time comes for us to brave a prolonged downpour and drive down to the Aldwych to see some Indian classical dancing from our ex-babysitter Asha Tanha.

Asha dances her Arangetram – a solo display of various classical South Indian dances. She's on stage for an hour and a half – and to see quiet, slight, soft, retiring little Asha dancing, miming and holding an audience of 150 for that long is a real eye-opener. She dances very gracefully and it's a difficult combination of rhythm, balance, expressions and story-telling. Very beautifully done.

I feel the frenetic pressures of London life very satisfactorily loosening and, although the music is not easy for the Western ear, I felt very much better when we left at ten than when I came in at half past seven, rushing out of the rain and the lines of stopped traffic on the approach to Waterloo Bridge.

Saturday, September 25th

Changeable, tempestuous weather. Helen collects a kitten, which we call Denis.

Sunday, September 26th

I scribble a few notes for a speech at today's cast and crew viewing of 'The Mish'.

Conventional, but not over-enthusiastic applause. I suppose many of them have seen it before, or are looking at their own work. I can't see why I should have expected this to be the best audience so far.

But almost before the 'HandMade' title has faded, Denholm is leaning over my seat, enthusing rapturously. He thinks it's 'marvellous, a little classic', and both he and his wife go on for some time in this encouraging vein. Helen still loves it and Tom, who was there with his friend Jasper, is very pleased with it too. No rush of hand-shaking fans, but a solid majority of those who think it successful.

Stay talking until five o'clock, then home. Have not eaten and feel very lumpen with the wine. Tom and Jasper are thumping out jazz improvisations on the piano, Rachel and Willy are encouraging our new cat, Denis, to hurl his little body round the kitchen, so I take to bed for a half-hour, then sit rather sleepily and read the papers.

Down to LBC for a ten o'clock programme on which I am to be the Mystery Guest. Evidently one caller susses me out within two minutes, but they don't put him through until 10.30. Meanwhile, I've been guessed as Danny La Rue, Larry Grayson, Melvyn Hayes and Kenneth Williams.

Watch *Roseland*,[1] and enjoy Denis going crazy. So nice to have another Denis in my life.

---

1 1977 movie about the Roseland Ballroom in New York City. Not a commercial hit but very touching.

Wednesday, September 29th

Columbia are postponing the opening of *Missionary* to November 6th. Reason given is that there are now four other 'major' movies opening on October 22nd.

Linda Barker from Columbia calls, presuming I'm coming out for the three weeks to October 22nd anyway. What's the point of doing promotion which climaxes two weeks prior to the film opening? She reacts like she'd never thought of this one before and promises to talk to her bosses.

Conference call around ten from Antonowsky and Roginski. MA starts by saying that all my TV appearances can be taped and used later – when I protest that I'm not going to work my ass off on a publicity tour which doesn't include the last two weeks before the movie opens. Compromise suggested – I do the college circuit as planned, starting next Monday, then return to the UK for two weeks and then come back for one week LA, one week NYC.

To bed a little grumpily with the TG/Stoppard script of *Brazil* to read.

Thursday, September 30th

Driven to Elstree. Work on some last-minute rewrites of the 'Middle of the Film'. Then into a wonderful, off-the-shoulder, 1950's style costume, supplied at the last minute by Vanessa Hopkins, which brings back all those images of my sister and *Heiress* magazine and her first smart grown-up posed photograph.

Work very solidly in a concentrated spell from eleven until two, without, I think, even leaving my armchair. As I give my final speech, I really do feel that at last it's over.

Saturday, October 2nd

TG comes round and we talk about *Brazil*. I feel that the story of Jill and Lowry takes forever to get off the ground and there is more observation of the tatty world of the future than plot development. Some repetition of good ideas, too. TG feels that Stoppard has softened it a bit, and I think he may be right. The characters talk without any edge. Their behaviour is observed with amused detachment rather than commitment. And the scale of *Brazil* is such that it cannot just be a gentle story like *The Missionary*. TG films for much higher stakes. Still, many good moments, effects, surreal dream sequences, which will work.

Sunday, October 3rd: London–Washington DC

Gather together my things for the first week of *Missionary* promotion, including sketches, bits of old speeches – anything that may help. Remember that Graham Chapman used to begin his US college appearances by asking the audience to shout abuse at him.

Landed in Washington in early evening. Dulles Airport, set in mellowing, wooded Virginia countryside, was unexpectedly quiet. I was paged at customs and given VIP treatment, rushed through and out into a waiting limousine by a girl called Sherry.

As we drove into Washington she showed me some of the 'merchandising'. T-shirts with 'The Missionary University Tour' unexceptionally written on them. A polo-neck with 'The Missionary' and the words 'Give Your Body To Save My Soul' on.

At eight o'clock – one o'clock a.m. my time – I go into a press conference for college students. There are about 20 people there and Marvin Antonowsky sits in as well. Many of them have seen the movie and I'm told they laughed a lot at the showing, but one black student I spoke to didn't think it would mean much to a black college audience.

Marvin seems well pleased, though, and likes what he calls 'all the additions'. Over dinner – soft-shell crabs – he fishes for what I'm doing next. Suggests a re-make of *Kind Hearts and Coronets*. Confirmed that he didn't like *Privates on Parade*. Says he finds Nichols' work too black and cynical. But we have another of our easy, friendly, convivial meals. We never seem to be at a loss for things to chat about.

Monday, October 4th: Washington DC–Toronto

An idea occurred to me for the start of my proposed University of Maryland speech. Owing perhaps a little to memories of Edna Everage's showmanship, it was that I should compose some lines of rather bad poetry in honour of the University of Maryland.

At 9.30 Sherry arrives to take me downstairs to talk to a reporter from a month-old daily newspaper *USA Today*. We have breakfast in Les Beaux Champs – 'A French restaurant self-assured enough to serve American wines'. Grapefruit, scrambled eggs and bacon, ignore the 'Bakehouse Basket'.

The reporter saw the movie at the Washington showing last Friday. He himself liked it but did not enthuse, and he *was* worried by the big launch, multi-print treatment. He felt that Columbia will drop it like a hot potato if it doesn't perform commercially.

To the campus of Maryland University.

The students take me round back passages and up fire escapes to a theatre where I am billed to speak. 'Meet Michael Palin. Free.' say the posters.

Inside the theatre are TV crews, photographers, a stage, a dais and a full house of 750 students (with some turned away, I hear). Seeing a brown paper bag I grab it, empty out its contents and enter the auditorium with it over my head. Two besuited young students say nice things in introduction and I'm given a scroll for making the world laugh and then a floppy, big soft toy turtle.

Wednesday, October 6th: Chicago

To Northwestern University, north of Chicago on the lakeside.

A picturesque, leafy campus looking out over Lake Michigan. I am to talk to a class on ... 'Acting Problems in Style-Comedy' at the Theater and Interpretation Center. It sounds pretentious, but the people involved, particularly the professor – Bud Beyer – are very warm and friendly. All nervous and sweating in the 80° humidity. Many good words about my film and the 'Great Railway Journey', which has already been shown on PBS here more times than on the Beeb in England.

The University Chaplain makes a very funny and complimentary speech about myself and the '*Mish*' and presents me with a stuffed wildcat. I read my poem and say goodbye.

To Columbia Pictures headquarters in a faceless office building in a half-completed plaza beside O'Hare Airport. I'm photographed with the girls and do my Prince Charles bit, shaking hands with everybody. I learn that they are very pleased with the exhibitor's reaction in Chicago, Minneapolis and Milwaukee. '*Mish*' will open in 14 theatres in the Chicago area – including two prime sites. Everyone seems very keen and hopeful.

Thursday, October 7th: Dallas

Alarm call at 7.15, but I've been awake since seven, trying out lines for today's poem. Southern Methodist University is not easy to rhyme.

A crowd of maybe 200 kids are gathered in the open air around a makeshift stage. I'm presented with a plaque for being 'A Missionary for British Humor in the US'. Poor PA is a curse, but my poem in response goes down well. I feel like an old-style politician at the hustings – talking off the back of a truck. The audience is receptive and appreciative and after I have finished there follows a custard pie throwing contest, which I am to judge. Taken quite seriously by beefy male students (no women contestants), including one who delivers a custard pie on a motorbike, à la mediaeval tournament.

Friday, October 8th: San Francisco

My first appointment of the day – a live interview at Station KQAK, the Quake. As I entered the limousine, Melanie [my publicity lady] chilled me to the marrow with the news that 'Really crazy things are happening down there. Robin Williams has been there since six o'clock with some other improv comics and it's just really crazy!'

Oh, God . . . Dear God, do I have to?

There was a bustle of excitement, then I was shown into the studio itself, which was densely packed with fans. They had nowhere to sit and clearly no provision had been made for their presence at all, but there they all were, like the crowd at one of Jesus's miracles, squashed into this hot and airless room, gazing at their heroes – in this case Alex Bennett, a gentle, bespectacled DJ, Robin Williams, red-faced and driven with comic improvisation like a man exorcising some spirits, and a local comic, who had a neat moustache and was also working hard, though no match for Robin.

I was cheered on entry and shown to a place midway between these high-pressure comics and two microphones. 'This is worse than the Queen's bedroom,' quipped I, helplessly . . . looking round at the sea of faces. Suddenly everyone, I realised, was staring at me, waiting for me to be witty, marvellous and funny. It was a nightmare come true – like some massive overdose of shyness aversion therapy.

Robin Williams was in his element, switching with incredible speed and dexterity into an ad-libbed playlet. Never at a loss for words, and remarkably consistent. He held the show together. Jeremy, with the moustache, and myself, shared a microphone – there was no point in my sharing Robin's. The humour was West Coast – brittle, topical, cruel, mocking, black, but with some wonderful flashes of fantasy. RW took the new film *Road Warrior* and turned it into 'Rhodes Warrior', the tale of a rogue Rhodes Scholar left alive on earth after the holocaust – 'Tough, educated, he read his way through trouble'.

The worst moment was when I was asked to describe *The Missionary*. It sounded so leaden and mundane in the midst of all this sharp, hip humour – as if it were coming from another world. I was left helplessly asserting, in the silence that followed my dull little description, 'It *is* funny . . .'

But the biggest test of the day is yet to come. My visit to the campus of San Francisco State, where Columbia, I'm later to learn, have been working very hard on my behalf.

To everyone's relief, there is a crowd – estimated at over 1,000 – clustered in the bright sunshine around a makeshift stage. It's San Francisco, though, and my 'award' this time is not to be presented by a nervous student or a well-meaning chaplain, but by – what else in SF – a comic.

My 'introducer' is Jane Dornacker, a big, busty lady, who wears her 'Give Your Body To Save My Soul' T-shirt quite spectacularly. But she does like to talk. It's a fierce, competitive world, the world of improv, and once you're up there and it's going well, you stay. She is getting quite raunchy by now, with jokes about haemorrhoids being a pain in the ass and masturbation in San Quentin. I can see the organisers are getting twitchy because there are innumerable TV crews covering the event and there is precious little material they'll be able to use. In fact one has given up altogether. Eventually Dornacker draws to a close and has to give me my award for 'moral virtue'.

Read my poem, heavy on royal family jokes, which they love out here. Thank God for Michael Fagan.[1]

Monday, October 18th

J Goldstone had rung to tell me of a private screening of *My Favourite Year* – the Peter O'Toole film comedy which has received such good

---

1 Fagan, an Irishman, had twice broken into Buckingham Palace. In July 1982 he got as far as the Queen's bedroom and talked to her for ten minutes before being apprehended.

reviews in the US. I went along to the EMI Theatre in Wardour Street where, a few weeks ago, I was biting my fingernails showing *Missionary* to my friends.

Before I left I spoke to Sue Barton in New York, who cheered me no end with the news that *Cosmopolitan* had written a very good review of *The Missionary*. So it's two against one so far. (*Newsweek* good, *Time* not so good.) Not a bad start.

My Favourite Year was a lovely little film. A light piece of nostalgia for the 1950's, based on Mel Brooks's experience as a writer for Sid Caesar. For anyone who's hosted *Saturday Night Live*, it had extra significance, being shot at NBC in 30 Rockefeller Plaza and being all about the problems of star guests on live shows.

It felt much the same weight as *The Missionary*. Gentle humour, laced with slapstick, enjoyment of characters as much as plot, and shot through with moments of pathos (beautifully handled by Peter O'Toole). Seeing it, and bearing in mind its early success in the high-energy world of US comedy, gave me as much hope for *The Missionary* as the news about *Cosmopolitan*. I left the cinema with the feeling that I hope people will have after *The Missionary*.

Tuesday, October 19th: Southwold

Up to Suffolk. Ma meets me in the new Metro. She doesn't use first gear, as it's rather difficult, and at the moment mistrusts most of the gearbox, but seems a lot safer than in the ageing 1100.

It's warm and dry enough to sit out in the garden before lunch, and in the afternoon take Ma for a walk, in a friendly wind, out onto the cliffs beyond Covehithe.

Saturday, October 23rd

Columbia call and ask if I could find out from Maggie S if she will come to the States at any time. Not really my job, but Maggie has a way of making things difficult for anyone to get decisions out of her.

Ring Maggie. She won't say 'yes', but she does know that it helps the movie to appear in person and I think that for me she will do a couple of days in New York.

Home to start packing when TG arrives. He wants to talk about '*MOL*'. He saw it at an excellent showing (he says) on Tuesday. He felt weak points were 'Hendys' (too long, but liked) and the tiger skin exchanges and Eric's Waiter and Arthur Jarrett. But his real worry is his own piece. It will be 15 minutes at least and he wants to know my feelings about its inclusion or not in the main body of the film.

All this in our bedroom, with me in underpants checking how many pairs of socks I might need and Helen in curlers about to change.

We go off to see 'A Star is Torn' – a one-woman show by an Aussie lady called Robyn Archer, which is playing to packed houses at the Wyndhams. She sweeps briskly through a repertoire of impersonations of great popular lady singers of the twentieth century, many of whose qualification for inclusion in her act seem to be that they died of drug abuse round about the age of 40. I'm sure this cheers up my 40-year-old wife no end.

Sunday, October 24th: London–Seattle

A strange feeling of unreality as I go back to *The Missionary* and its American opening. I'm sure I shall fall into the swim of things, but at the moment I just feel a deadening sense of weariness.

My scalp itches and I've forgotten to pack any toothpaste. My little kitchen and my family come to mind in sharp contrast to the world I shall inhabit for two weeks, and I know that I am coming near the end of my ability to lift up, inspire, charm, enthuse and everything else that has had to take me away from home so much this year.

Our 747 dips below Mount Rainier, tallest peak in the 'contiguous' USA, impressive and Paramount-like out of the southern windows, and we are on the ground in Seattle nearly an hour and a half late at about 3.30. The reward is a smooth, efficient, clean, empty terminal and the quickest entry ever into the US.

Monday, October 25th: Seattle–Los Angeles

At 8.30 we leave for my first appointment – an appearance on a local morning TV show – *Northwest AM*.

Back to the hotel to talk to a Jewish girl from New Jersey. Her quick, nervous speech and voluble hand gestures are definitely un-Seattlian. Talk for a half-hour over coffee, then I'm led downstairs to a group of six, mostly young and studentish scribblers, waiting for a brunch interview.

We take off an hour late and run into a heavy concentration of rain clouds.

Wonderful dialogue behind. A fat woman with a dog in a basket.

'Oh, my ears feel funny,' she exclaims as we descend into LA.

'Hold your nose and blow,' suggests a helpful neighbour.

'Blow what?' she cries, mystified.

We are bundled off briskly in LA. Almost a couple of hours late, but through the airport, or rather the half-rebuilt shell of it, in about 20 minutes. Outside a shambles of pick-up vehicles, including my enormous length of grey limousine, which is accompanied by a dapper little matching grey driver, who takes me direct to the Academy of Film and TV Arts.

At the Academy I meet Ed Roginski and Marvin, and other Columbia folk, as cocktails are being served before the showing to what seems to be a large and impressive audience, full of critics and film folk.

Grit my teeth over the sound in the pre-title sequence – how I want that hymn sound to crescendo! – and the grubby darkness of the boat sequence (one of the less successful in the movie), but the audience respond well and pick up most of the possible laugh moments, applauding occasionally. Marvin, next to me, disconcertingly keeps checking his watch.

The Longleat sequence is clearly going to become a classic, with Hordern's performance beyond criticism.

Marvin takes myself and Linda Barker, head of talent relations (!), to a meal at Trumps – all white walls and very chic. I think I ate some bass. Best news is that we have picked up another good review in *New York Magazine*.

Tuesday, October 26th: Los Angeles

A brief meeting with Marvin A and Randy Wicks to show me two alternatives for the newspaper ads – one has 'Michael Palin', the other 'Monty Python's Michael Palin'. I am against the 'Monty Python' mention and Marvin gives in to me, though he would rather use it. The small print ads are using the lipstick on the collar picture – so all that extra work was worth it.

Four interviews in my quite small suite fill the afternoon, then off to *The Merv Griffin Show*. These are the appearances I look forward to least. The movie is sacrificed to the ego and image of the host – which is what these shows are all about. Merv just makes money and grins egregiously. He has not seen the movie.

I wait in a green room, with no sign of a decent drink, together with two 'nutritionists' whose book *Life Extension* is a national best-seller in this land of instant cures. They remind me of the old quacks of the Wild West selling patent medicines. They are an extraordinary pair. He talks incessantly, she, small and wiry, shows me her arm muscles.

As I'm leaving the studio Jack Lemmon passes, with a crowd of guests. A publicist asks me if I want to meet Lemmon and before I know it I'm shaking hands with the great man, who turns out to be a Python fan – as are all his family, he says.

I tell him that he and Peter Sellers are my favourite comic actors of all time. As if he's been on chat shows so often, Lemmon quickly cues into an anecdote about Sellers writing a whole set of false reviews of a Lemmon film which completely fooled him. But he looked baggy-eyed and unfit, and a slight slurring of the words and blurring of the gaze suggested he'd been at the old liquor. But at least I'd told him how wonderful I thought he was.

I've survived the day pretty well on adrenaline, but as I relax over a meal with Polier and Knopf and their wives at the Mandarin in Beverly Hills, I begin to wilt.

I glean from them that Columbia are confident enough in *The Missionary* to have increased the prints to 500, that Polier and Knopf reckon three million dollars for the first weekend would be what they would hope for, and that they share my view that outside the big cities the film could be slow.

Thursday, October 28th: Los Angeles–New York

Alarm call at 6.30. Down to the limousine at seven. The sun is still not up as we start towards the airport. Tom, the driver, is a Romanian, and this accounts for his strange, very correct English. He works for a firm whose boss was once Elvis Presley's bodyguard and who specially asked him to tell me what a total fan of Monty Python Elvis was!

I'm at LA Airport and checked in by 7.45. 'Vicky' is our stewardess for the flight. As she goes through the ritual of checking our names, she comes to the seat next to me – a rather overweight, middle-aged American announces his name is Boyer. 'Oh, that's pretty,' she returns automatically.

Delivered about six to the Sherry Netherland. Two windows look straight down 5th Avenue into the forest of skyscrapers and the others look the length of Central Park South and out to the Hudson and the New Jersey shoreline.

Monday, November 1st: New York–Boston

Collect magazines, as this is the first day of public reviews.

Anson of *Newsweek*, we already know, liked it. *Time*, we suspected, didn't, and mercifully their totally dismissive review is short – though top of a column in which three movies are contemptuously tossed aside under the heading 'Rushes'. I find myself in company with Sean Connery and Fred Zimmerman's *Three Days Last Summer*, and the almost universally mocked *Monsignor*, with Reeve and co, as victims of Richard Schickel's contempt.

But *New York Magazine*'s David Denby runs it as his major movie story of the week, with a photo and the subhead '*The Missionary* is a satirical and naughty film – an aesthetically pleasing object that's also very funny.' Columbia's rep is very pleased and now feels we have enough to launch the movie on Friday *with* reviews.

At three Stuart from Columbia arrives with a middle-aged reporter from the *New York Post*. The trend of the *Post*'s questions reflects the newspaper. Why do we always go for religion? Do I expect shocked reactions? Surely the sight of a priest in bed with three women at *once* is going to cause some problems? (Smacking of reporter's lips.) When I point out that I am never seen in bed with three women he seems genuinely perplexed and shakes his head in disbelief. 'Well I'm *sure* I saw you in bed with three women.'

Into the traffic on what has become a hot and sultry evening, as I head out to La Guardia and catch the Eastern shuttle to Boston.

I'm no sooner there than a local TV station is clipping mikes to my shirt and sitting me down in the foyer beside the popcorn with a light glaring in my face and an earnest lady reporter who hasn't seen the movie. She asks me questions like 'Do you believe in God?' and 'Your children are very important to you, right? How are you structuring *their* future?' She actually runs out of tape on the question 'What do you believe in?'

After the session, at which I'm encouraged by this predominantly young audience's applause when I mention the names of Maggie Smith and Trevor Howard, I'm taken out to eat with Michael Bodin, the critic of the *Boston Globe*.

He thought *The Missionary* was a good film, but could have been a great one. Interestingly enough, he used the Magna Carta line in Africa as an example of the promise of greatness which he felt the first five minutes of the movie held out. This line was inserted at the very last minute of the very last dub.

We talked about movies until the waiters began to put chairs on tables at a quarter past twelve. (He it was who told me of the latest piece of linguistic butchery at the hands of the anti-sexists – in nearby Cambridge, Mass, the term 'waitress' is out, replaced by 'waitrons'.)

Tuesday, November 2nd: New York

I'm beginning to develop a phobia about American make-up artists. With very little grace they just slap on layer after layer of base and powder until I resemble Michael Palin about as much as the Madame Tussaud's waxworks resemble real people. Today a large black lady in a curiously confusing blonde wig works me over. 'I saw you on *Good Morning America* ... you looked awful ... all white ... what was the trouble?'

'Make-up,' I replied with pleasure.

Wednesday, November 3rd: New York

As the release day comes nearer, I feel myself wanting the pace to accelerate.

Variety calls the movie 'congenial but commercially uncertain'. It's a mixed review, complimenting me on my acting, liking the film, finding some 'wonderful moments' and 'exquisite photography', but managing to sound quite negative in conclusion. The script could have gone into more detail on three of the sub-plots, it said.

The doubts sown by *Variety* are encouragingly countered by *Hollywood Reporter*, which thinks the film an artistic and box-office winner for Columbia. This is the only review so far to suggest we might make money, and coming out of such a hard-nosed journal as the *Reporter* makes it doubly welcome.

Thursday, November 4th: New York

I go on to *The Letterman Show* in the last half-hour. I bring a grubby cellophane bag of things to present to Letterman but refuse to open up. He never tries to get into the act much and just lets me go on. I overact and fool about shamelessly. But he shows a clip and reaffirms that the reviews have been good and I get some laughs and applause and at 6.30 another show is over.

Back to the hotel, wash, change, then drive downtown, collecting Richard Loncraine on the way, to talk to a film class. Disconcertingly, they take a straw poll (before I've been revealed to be there) in which 40% of his audience say they didn't like the film. One woman who did like it, says 'I hate Michael Palin, but I loved this movie.' Richard nearly died at this.

We drive in search of tomorrow's *New York Times*. The excitement mounts as we find ourselves a half-hour early at the newsstands, so we head for the steamy rear of the *New York Times* building.

We wait in the car as Stu [Zakin, from Columbia] disappears into the night. He races back. Our pulses race with him. 'It's there!' he cries. 'It's there!'

'Well bring it, for God's sake . . .'

'I need *change*,' Stu shouts, in a rare show of excitement. We have a rushed whip-round and he disappears again.

At about 10.10 he reappears with two copies of tomorrow's *Times*. I read one. Richard and Stu the other. I start from the top. Stu, much more practised, flips through to the end. He is the first to discover it's a good review. We have the most important critic in New York, and another daily paper to boot. That's two out of three, whatever else happens. Relief and joy.

Back on my own in the Sherry Netherland at 1.15. I spread out the *New York Times* lovingly. Better than Canby's review is the big ad for *The Missionary* which contains quotes from four good reviews, including one from *US Magazine*'s Steven Schaefer, which I didn't even know we had. 'Don't Miss The Missionary – a delight from beginning to its marvellous end.' 'Hilarious – Michael Palin is smashing' – *Cosmopolitan*. 'Michael Palin has finally left his mark' – even *Newsweek*'s backhanded compliment looks stirringly impressive in big print.

How on earth can I sleep? Who can I ring? They won't be up in England, so I try and sleep and will ring early.

There can have been few better moments when I've laid my head on the pillow than at the Sherry Netherland Hotel, New York City, as the rain finally breaks the late heatwave.

Friday, November 5th: New York

And the news continues to be optimistic. Rex Reed has given us a glowing review, which makes a clean sweep of all three New York daily papers.

Over to WCBS and Independent News Network to meet Jeff Lyons. At the end of the radio interview he asks if I will put my voice on tape for his home answering machine. Apparently he asks everyone he interviews to do this and now has an unrivalled collection of phone answerers, including David Niven, Peter Ustinov and Max von Sydow.

Then round to the crowded, noisy, dark security of the Oak Room at the Plaza for a drink with Nancy and Bruce Williamson – the *Playboy* film critic. Bruce is very good company, a droll but not pushy teller of stories and a lover of trains to boot.

During the afternoon the gilt has been slightly skimmed off the top of the critical gingerbread. I picked up a copy of the *Washington Post*, to find myself judged very harshly by one Gary Arnold, who seems to have felt the film was an unmitigated disaster for which I was almost entirely to blame.

Saturday, November 6th: New York–London

Helen and I have been apart for nearly four months this year, and when I called her yesterday, full of excitement at the news from NYC, she sounded so glum that I changed plans to leave on Sunday and decided to go back as soon as possible. I've been sustained over the past few weeks by interviews and the anticipation of reaction. Now the first wave of reaction has come and gone I want to get away from limousines and hotel rooms and do things for myself again.

On to Concorde, which leaves on time at 9.30. Only famous face I recognise is Rupert Murdoch, spectacles low down on his nose, looking like a don putting finishing touches to a thesis.

We cross the Atlantic in three hours and 15 minutes and I'm home at Julia Street six hours after leaving the Sherry Netherland. Lovely to see them all again.

I ring Neville, Maggie Smith, Norman Garwood [our art director] and Peter Hannan in a mood of great elation. Thank God it's over.

Sunday, November 7th

Denis rings from Dallas in mid-afternoon. We have apparently done well in New York and Los Angeles, but not well outside the major cities. He gives me some fairly wretched figures: 800 dollars for the first night in Boulder, Colorado; equally unimpressive in Las Vegas – just over 1,000 dollars; Phoenix 1,500 for the first night.

Denis saw a rave review in Dallas last night, but it isn't doing any business in the south as a whole. Denis's projection for the first weekend is 1.8 million dollars – a long way from Knopf and Polier's estimate given to me as we sauntered down Rodeo Drive, licking ice-creams, ten days ago.

Monday, November 8th

I decide to call Polier and Knopf in LA direct. The weekend has been by no means the failure Denis suggested. Whilst not looking like a block-buster, the figures for three days are 'highly respectable' (Dan's quote). They are likely to reach 1.86 million for the weekend, not 1.3. But isn't this considerably short of the three million estimate? 'Oh, no, our three million forecast was for the *week.*'

'This is no hit and run picture,' is how Dan put it. Still awaiting Columbia's verdict. They won't be ecstatic, says David, but there's a fair chance they'll get behind it.

Tuesday, November 9th

A fine, clear morning. Helen says I should stay in bed, but I do enjoy breakfast time with the family. I like to wake up with them.

Cleese rings mid-morning. He asks me if I will write a letter to the Press Council supporting him in his case against the *Sun*, which published an account of the Zulus in Glasgow story quoting JC as saying to the black extras 'Which one of you bastards did a rain dance?' JC is very cross at the total inaccuracy and will not let the matter rest. The *Sun* have not been helpful. He wants TJ, myself and Ray Corbett [the first assistant director] to help out as witnesses.

Thursday, November 11th

Spent the early part of the morning writing a thank you letter to Antonowsky – something he probably doesn't receive very often, but I *do* feel that Columbia ran the campaign very competently.

Then drive down to the South Bank for the first film of the London Film Festival – *Scrubbers*.

Scrubbers turns out to be a well-made film with superb and convincing performances from the girls. Mai Zetterling has succeeded in giving flesh and blood to characters who are normally regarded as 'beyond society'.

The only problem I had is that the depiction of prison life has been done so often and so well recently in a series of documentaries. So, in *Scrubbers* there were many moments when I felt myself caught up in cliché – the stock psychiatrist, the hard governor, the keys in locks, the clang of doors. But the girls were Mai Zetterling originals, and were the heart and soul of the bleak, gloomy, violent picture.

Friday, November 12th

RL has rung to say that Warren Beatty had called from Hollywood to say how much he had enjoyed the movie (these are the little unexpected bonuses which are as much a part of the satisfaction of making a movie as any grosses).

Out for dinner to Judy Greenwood's[1] in Fulham Road. She lives in a comfortable, homely clutter above her own antique shop with a dog, a daughter and a builder husband called Eddie who has an earring and had just broken his toe. Judy is forthright, easy company – with striking Palin looks.

I defend comprehensive education and the NHS rather limply to Eddie, who has no scruples about buying a better education or buying himself out of pain ... And why not? I wonder gloomily – arguing out of form more than conviction.

Saturday, November 13th

Write to Al Levinson after reading his short story 'Nobody's Fool' – a piece of real-life drama thinly fictionalised and very revealing and moving. Al

1 Judy is my cousin. Youngest daughter of my father's sister Katherine.

is so near to being a good writer, but just fails, sometimes – as in 'Millwork' – by the very tip of his fingernails. So I write back encouragingly, but cannot offer more concrete support – like an unqualified rave or an offer to publish. I still have most of *Travelogs* unsold.

Denis rings at six o'clock. As soon as I hear 'unfortunately', I know that *Missionary* has not made a solid commercial showing across the States. New York he hasn't heard from, but Chicago, even after the TV ads extolling its virtues through the reviews, is 33% down. San Francisco 27% down, Denver 31%. Even Los Angeles – where Denis says all word is that *The Missionary* is a resounding success – is 10% down.

The final overall figures will continue to be 'mediocre' and 'so-so' until Columbia pull out from 'between the mountains'. If we had opened only in NYC and LA *The Missionary* would have been hailed as a triumph. *That's* what irks me tonight.

Sunday, November 14th

A day for sitting at home with the Sunday papers and a lot of wine at lunchtime.

But I have agreed to go to the Oxford Children's Book Fair, and at half past eleven I leave, with somewhat sinking spirits, to drive out along the splashy A40.

At Oxford it's bitterly cold. I park by the new Law Library. An elderly man in a blue overcoat passes me; on his left breast a string of medals, tinkling softly. Of course, it's Remembrance Sunday – poppies and war veterans, with the added immediacy of the Falklands War this year.

Nearly all the grimy façades of my day have been cleaned, resurfaced and repointed. Oxford seems generally more opulent. The Randolph Hotel, where the Book Fair is taking place, full of well-heeled diners.

Up to the Ballroom. My presence is announced over a forbidding PA system and I'm given a chair, a table and a pile of books to sit beside. By four o'clock I've sold about ten copies of the book [*Small Harry and the Toothache Pills*]. David Ross [from Methuen] and the organiser from Blackwell's Children's Shop seem very pleased, though my presence seemed to me something of a waste of time.

Nice, silly evening at home, all of us playing a game after supper and being noisy. Then, after the children go to bed mercifully early, H and I sit by the first fire of the winter.

Monday, November 15th

Called Polier and Knopf at one o'clock and their news rather took the stuffing out of this gentle, easy day. *Missionary* is down 25–30% everywhere, including the NY and LA areas, in its second weekend. The take for the weekend was 1.4 million, as opposed to 1.86 the first weekend.

The 'good news', as Knopf puts it, is that Columbia are still supporting the movie with TV (in NYC) and press in the big cities. It's doing well in Toronto and Vancouver. Not holding up on Broadway/Times Square, where they have now sussed that it's not a sex movie! All the quality areas of cities are still reporting good figures – but David says rather ominously that the picture 'may not be long for this world'.

Thursday, November 18th

S Albury rings. He would like to do an Eric Olthwaite series for Granada, with someone like Charles Sturridge directing and himself producing. Everything about the idea, apart from being Eric Olthwaite for a year, appeals to me.

Friday, November 19th

Twelve years ago, when William was born, I was in the middle of shooting my first film *And Now For Something Completely Different*. Today my seventh film, *The Missionary*, is at No. 2 in the list of Top Grossing Films in the US.

The appearance of *The Missionary* above *ET* and the rest (for one glorious week!) was the high point of this crowded day.

Went down to the Python office and signed things and saw Lena, Steve's Swedish book-keeper, celebrate her last day at the office. Apparently she's always leaving packets of tampons around, so they presented her with a smart little case with a special plaque on it engraved with her name and the word 'Tampons' in very large letters.

Then, via shops, home to prepare for William's ambitious disco party, which is to be held tonight at No. 2.

The party runs from seven until half past ten. About 18 invited. The boys arrive earlier than the girls, but the girls, when they do appear, virtually take over the music and dancing. Some of them, in black berets with short skirts and black fishnet stockings, look about 23. The boys look younger, less self-assured, and spend most of the early party throwing and squirting things up the far end of the room. My heart sinks for a while. The girls talk, all at once and at the top of their voices, about clothes.

But gradually everyone thaws out. By the end I actually have a few boys dancing with the girls (they've been scared stiff of them for most of the evening). We have a joke-telling competition which is quite successful, and at 10.15 most of them seem unhappy to leave. Several of the girls give me a kiss for working the disco as they disappear into the night. Nobody smoked and nobody drank (probably their last year of innocence).

Tuesday, November 23rd

Halfway through the evening David Knopf returns my call. The third weekend is much as expected. Sadly no miracles have been performed. *The Missionary* has slipped 32%, below a million dollars for the weekend, and may lose up to 100 prints, which Knopf is not too unhappy about, though he is trying to persuade Columbia to keep as many prints working over the big Thanksgiving holiday weekend as possible.

'What do they feel about *The Missionary*?' I ask David, full of innocent curiosity. 'They've forgotten it,' returns David with admirable bluntness.

Wednesday, November 24th

Writing a speech for tonight's Young Publishers' meeting. Meeting takes place at the Cora Hotel in Tavistock Place, a stone's throw from Gandhi's statue. Not that anyone would want to throw stones at Gandhi's statue.

A full room – maybe 70 or 80 present. Behind the table are, left to right, Geoffrey Strachan, Sue Townsend, whose *Secret Life of Adrian Mole* has made her Methuen's newest best-seller, a very nice girl from the SPCK who is chairing the meeting, myself and Nigel Rees.

Tonight's theme is Humorous Publishing. Geoffrey is serious and efficiently informative. Sue Townsend is endearingly and honestly confused. 'I can't talk, that's why I write,' was the way she began her speech. Nigel Rees was smooth and seemingly nerveless, as befits a BBC radio personality.

I spoke last and the speech made people laugh very well for the first five minutes, then slightly less so as I warmed to the theme of 'Geoffrey Strachan – The Man Whose Life Was Changed by Humorous Publishing'.

A productive hour of question and answer. One lady who asked the quite reasonable question as to whether or not men preferred Python was told very sharply by another woman in the audience that the question was quite irrelevant! At the Spaghetti House in Sicilian Avenue I sat next to Sue Townsend, who I thought would be the most fun. She lives in Leicester and is quite happy about it. Especially as she is within stone-throwing distance of the house in which Joe Orton was born. Not that anyone ... (That's enough – ed.).

Thursday, November 25th

To Cambridge Gate for a financial discussion with Steve and Anne. For over an hour they briefed me on the appalling problems of trying to give some of my money away – in this case five percentage points of my *Missionary* royalties to be divided amongst the crew. Because I was not the company which hired the crew in the first place I'm almost totally unable to make any agreement to reward them in a way in which I shall not be severely fiscally penalised. Infuriating and frustrating.

Saturday, November 27th

Up, earlier than I would have wished, to take Willy to William Ellis to play rugby. He says he's doing it to be the first Palin to actually play in a W Ellis school match (Tom was often selected but always avoided playing). As I left him outside the school gates on Highgate Hill at a quarter to nine on this very cold, foggy morning, I could only feel sorry for him.

Drove down to Old Compton Street. Snatched a quick look at *Variety* before driving off and saw, to my surprise and pleasure, that *Missionary* is No. 3 in the US in its second week and holding quite respectably at over 6,000 dollars per screen.

Time Bandits is No. 4 on re-issue, so yours truly is the proud author of two films out of the American top four. If only I could feel that it meant something.

Sunday, November 28th

Missionary showing at the London Film Festival. The performance is sold out. I'm taking both grannies, as well as Angela, Veryan, Camilla and friend Deirdre from Strathblane (scene of Python's 'Zulu' episode) and Marcus.

A good feeling to see everyone hurrying out of the cold night into the QEH to see my film. 1,250 people inside and throughout there is regular laughter and prolonged applause at the end. Fulsome praise from Geoffrey Strachan and family and Barry Took and family and others who I don't know. Mother bears up really well, revelling in the pleasure of not just meeting Barry Took, but hearing such praise of her son from him.

Neville had reservations, when we all went for a meal afterwards, of the production-value-swamps-the-comedy nature. He felt I could have made it funnier and more robust if I'd been let off the hook. Terry J, who loves much of it, had similar reservations and told me to stop playing such dull characters!

Tuesday, November 30th: Southwold and London

The weather has settled over the weekend into a stable coolness. Last night it was two degrees below freezing. Leave home at 9.45 with Granny and reach Croft Cottage two and a half hours later. Suffolk is beautiful today in the bright, crystal-clear sunlight. Walk up the road past the sugar-beet collectors at work in the fields.

Cheered up by news from David Knopf that *The Missionary* take was up 15% at Thanksgiving weekend. The picture has now gathered in six and a half million dollars, but the best news of all is that Columbia now consider it 'playable'. (Paul Mazursky's *The Tempest* was evidently *not* playable.)

Dinner at Odin's with Marvin Antonowsky. Marvin still thinks a select-ive release would have worked better, but he admits that you can prove almost anything with hindsight.

He says emphatically that it has established me as a performer and advises me to get an agent for the US. I told him that my primary interest was in writing a movie – 'That's fine,' chomps Marvin, drooling walnut and lettuce salad. 'Next time write it present day and not too British.'

He will play *The Missionary* until Christmas then take it off and re-play it again in February, with press, in selected markets. 'The one thing *The Missionary* has done,' affirms Marvin, 'is established your creditability outside of the group ... I shouldn't say this to you, but you are now established as a *very* good light comedy actor!'

I buy Marvin the meal and we part, with a bear hug, in Devonshire Street, soon after eleven.

Thursday, December 2nd

Largely spent assembling speech for the Society of Bookmen tonight.

Leave for the Savile Club at six o'clock. Walk across Christmas-crowded Oxford Street and arrive by 6.30. The dark-panelled lobby of the unexceptional house in Brook Street is no preparation for the prettiness of the upstairs rooms in which the Society are holding their Christmas dinner. Beautiful walls and ceilings, the dining room picked out in eggshell blue and evidently based on a room in the Nymphenburg Palace at Munich (a nice link with Python!)[1] and the anterior room equally delicate, but in autumnal colours.

No-one recognises me at first and they all look frightfully impressive, reminding me of university dons – not exactly smart and well groomed, but rather academic and a few very distinguished manes of white hair.

I've based the first part of my speech on the fact that Sir Hugh Walpole, the founder of the Society, is not mentioned in the *Oxford Dictionary of Quotations*. But very few of the assembled gathering seem to know or care much about their founder – so the first minute or so is received politely. Realise that they are going to be a difficult audience. Clearly they aren't going to laugh uproariously. Nothing so uncontrolled. But I persevere and adapt my pace and the level of delivery and salvage some respectable applause.

Then some questions. One particularly granite-faced old man asked me who my three favourite humorous writers were. Why three, particularly, I don't know. 'Nabokov,' I began. He clearly didn't regard this as serious, so to annoy him further I followed it up with Spike Milligan. 'Oh, he's a bore!' says this most interesting of men.

Then a squarely-built, rather rabbinical-looking figure rose momentously and I felt I was about to be publicly denounced. But instead he suggested that, as my speech had been probably the best he'd ever heard at the Savile, the restrictions on reporting be lifted, allowing the *Bookseller* to reproduce my magnificent words in full. Only a few people supported this particular line, however, and I was left with the curious sensation of

1 We filmed there for Python's German show in 1971.

having simultaneously delivered an excellent speech to half the room and a dreadful one to the rest.

The man who had so fulsomely praised me turned out to be one Tom Rosenthal, Chairman of Secker and Warburg and Heinemann. He later asked me, most respectfully, to sign his menu.

Friday, December 3rd

Collected *Variety* and saw that *The Missionary* was still in touch with the leaders in its third week – at No. 6. New York seems to be saving *The Missionary* almost single-handed.

As I draw up outside the shop in Old Compton Street to buy the paper, I hear on a newsflash that Marty Feldman has died after finishing *Yellowbeard* in Mexico [he was 47]. The *Mail* rings later for some quotes. My best memory of Marty is that he was the first person to talk to me at my first ever *Frost Report* meeting back in 1966.

Take Helen and her friend Kathryn Evans to the Lyric Theatre to see Spike Milligan's one-man show, which opened last night. Only half full, I would estimate. Rather tattily put together, with a lot of lighting and sound botch-ups.

He obviously knew I was in because he kept shouting for me ... 'Is Michael Palin here, and has he paid?' Then in the second half he read a poem for me.

Monday, December 6th

In the evening we go out to dinner at David Puttnam's mews 'empire' in Queen's Gate, Kensington. Beautifully furnished and full of fine things, but also a lovely mixture of irregular spaces, large kitchen and small bedrooms off passageways, and a spacious upstairs sitting room with an unlikely roaring wood fire. A country farmhouse on three floors.

He's off to the States on Thursday to show the first cut of *Local Hero* to Warners. Compared to Columbia, his approach to marketing *Local Hero* in the States is very sophisticated – involving the enlistment of ecology groups and other special interest groups that can be identified and given preview showings, etc.

Puttnam confesses to loving working out grosses – sitting up long into the night with his calculator.

The Oscar for *Chariots of Fire* – Best Film 1981 – is almost casually standing on an open bookshelf. A heavy, solid, rather satisfying object. Has a Hollywood star ever been clubbed to death with an Oscar? It feels in the hand like an ideal offensive weapon.

Wednesday, December 8th

Richard has received a letter from Denis O' B, thanking him again for his work on '*The Mish*' and offering him five more percentage points on the film. 'Now I know it's officially a flop,' was RL's reaction.

Thursday, December 9th

A drunk in charge of a Volvo banged into me in Camden High Street. I tried to borrow a pen from passers-by, but they were all drunk too. It was like a dream.

James Ferman, the film censor, had seen '*Mish*' today, given it an 'AA' and said he thought it marvellous, one of the best comedies he's seen. Now why can't we put that on the poster instead of 'AA'?

Saturday, December 11th

Up through Covent Garden to Leicester Square to see *ET*.

The theatre is, of course, packed solid, and the lady next to me starts crying quite early on. It *is* a magical film, affecting and fresh and surprising and delightful despite all the prolonged build-up. I would think it almost impossible not to enjoy it if you have any sense of magic and imagination. It's pitched perfectly and, though many of the moments and situations are on the verge of being at least clichéd, at worst corny and sentimental, the picture succeeds all along with its supremely confident story-telling. Rachel is the only one of our party who comes out in tears, though I have been brought, pleasurably, to the brink on half a dozen occasions.

Later that evening Spike Milligan, in conversation on BBC2, names me as one of the few people (Norman Gunstone and Tommy Cooper are two others) who make him laugh.

Tuesday, December 14th

Set off, in a mad rush caused by a rash of ringing telephones, to meet my fellow dignitaries by Kentish Town Station.

We gather beneath a brightly painted canopy, salvaged with great imagination by a couple of local architects, BR and Camden Council from the remains of Elstree Station. Camden School for Girls sing carols behind the red ribbon, and a member of Camden's planning department struggles to make himself heard over the dual roar of Kentish Town traffic above and British Rail's trains beneath whilst being totally upstaged by an eccentric-looking old lady, with what appears to be a laundry bag, on the dais behind him.

My celebratory ode goes down extremely well and as soon as I've finished there is an instant demand for copies. I'm posed for silly photos and asked by one passer-by if I do this sort of thing professionally.

To Nigel G's[1] gallery, where I meet him and Glen Baxter, a cartoonist with Python-like tendencies, whom I greatly admire. Baxter has a thick tweed overcoat and a podgy, easily smiling face below a knitted tall hat. He looks like a sort of Yorkshire Rastafarian.

We talk over how best Nigel and Glen B could get a film about Baxter together. He's avoiding doing too many more of his *Impending Gleam*-type pictures as he feels he's almost saturated his own market. It's not just that there are a spate of bad Baxter imitations, but what hurts him more is that some people think the worst of them are done by him.

Call David Knopf. The bottom seems to have completely fallen out of *The Missionary* on its sixth weekend. A meagre 248,000 dollars. Knopf again strongly recommends collaboration on a film with John Cleese. 'Comedy team of the '80's,' says he.

Sunday, December 26th: Abbotsley–London

Early lunch and, at 1.30, a rather hasty and precipitous departure for London, as I have to be at a Python film viewing at three o'clock. Only an hour from Abbotsley to Gospel Oak. Roads very empty until we get into London. Lots of people taking Boxing Day constitutionals on the Heath. Drop the family off, unpack the car, then down to Wardour Street.

The Bijou is packed and hot and smoky. All sorts of familiar faces there – Arlene Phillips (who's just been turned down as choreographer for the new Travolta film, she tells me), Jim Acheson (still full of

1 My cousin Nigel Greenwood, elder brother of Judy, was much respected in the art world as a dealer and gallery owner. He spotted Gilbert and George early and Glen Baxter too. He died in April 2004.

excitement about the New York Marathon – he says I *must* go next year) and old acquaintances rarely seen these days like John Sims [the photographer] and C Alverson [writer and collaborator with Terry Gilliam on *Jabberwocky*]. Eric I conspicuously absent.

The film seems to go very quiet about a third of the way through, but ends very well, with 'Creosote' the high point. Afterwards I find that most people felt the first half worked very satisfactorily and if there *were* any longueurs they were either in the 'Pirate/Accountant' sequence or towards the end. But most people seemed to be quite bowled over by it.

This time five out of six Pythons have seen the film. There are no drastic differences of opinion. Everyone feels that TG's 'Pirate/Accountant' section should be in the film, not as a separate little feature on its own. And everyone feels it should be quite heavily pruned. I suggest it should be ten minutes at the most, Terry J about eight, Graham, quite firmly, seven. GC gets a round of applause from the meeting for his performance as Mr Blackitt, and TG for his 'Death' animation.

Thom Mount from Universal, who has come over to discuss release dates, etc, breaks in to announce that he thinks the film is wonderful and he would hardly change a single moment. As he's quite liked and respected by us all, this does visibly change the mood of the discussion.

Universal want some previews in the US as soon as possible to test reaction. They want to attempt a first ad campaign too.

All of which puts considerable pressure on my Indian travelling companion Mr Gilliam, who must cut his 'Pirate' piece, complete his animation and discuss ads, all before he meets me in Delhi on the 23rd of January.

1983

I was about to take on a mini world tour. A combination of a family holiday in Kenya (organised by Monty Ruben, who had sorted out our Missionary *shoot in Africa), publicity for* The Missionary *in Australia and a long-awaited tourist visit to India, where I was to meet up with Terry Gilliam. The quickest way from Kenya to Australia was via South Africa, where apartheid was still in place.*

Sunday, January 9th: Nairobi–Johannesburg

Aware, as I write the heading, of the ludicrous ease of world travel today. Here I am imagining myself in the steps of Marco Polos and Vasco da Gamas and Livingstones and Stanleys – or any one of a dozen Victorian lady missionaries – and yet between 9.30 and 12.30 this morning I passed Mount Kilimanjaro and the Ngorongoro Crater, crossed the Zambezi in flood, flew over the Limpopo and reached the Transvaal – and all this with no greater discomfort than waiting for the next Buck's Fizz to arrive.

Land 20 minutes early at Jan Smuts Airport in Johannesburg. The ambivalence of the world's attitude to South Africa is apparent straight away. Here is a smart, expensive, efficient international airport and yet there are not enough airliners using it to justify the installation of jetties.

Most conspicuous absence of course is the American airlines. And one can understand it – America, for all her faults, has confronted all the problems of an open, free, multiracial society and taken its share of riots, marches and protests. South Africa has tried to avoid the issue.

My driver is a black and, as we drive in through neat and tidy suburbs, past white congregations filing out of church, it all looks so peaceful and contented and comfortable that I'm forced to ask him a few journalist's questions. His replies are not voluble, or emotional, but it's clear that he does not see things with quite such rose-tinted spectacles. 'In England it is better, I think.'

He doesn't say much for a while, but just as we are turning towards the hotel he says 'I have dignity ... just like anyone else ... This is what they won't let you have here ... dignity.'

My hotel turns out to be a characterless Holiday Inn amongst a lot of equally characterless buildings that comprise the characterless centre of Jo'burg. There is a station which is about 100 years old, red brick and vaults and marble columns and elephant's head motifs and a frieze depicting, I presume, the Great Trek.

In the middle of all this I find the Blue Room Restaurant. Tables set out with solid Sheffield stainless steel, plates bearing the emblem of South African Railways on substantial wooden tables set beside polished marble pillars. Whatever the food, I have to have my lunch in the middle of this faded splendour. The meal is one of faded splendour too. I choose an Afrikaans dish, Kabeljou, which turns out to be a rather chewy piece of battered fish, which reminds one how far Johannesburg is from the sea.

Afterwards I walk into the station beneath a 'Whites Only' sign. Make my way down to the platform and, like a good trainspotter, walk up to the sunlit end where the big locomotives wait.

As I return I find myself, for convenience sake, taking the nearest stairwell, and the fact that there's a long line of blacks going up it too doesn't occur to me as at all odd until I come out at the top of the stairwell into a completely different Johannesburg from anything I've seen so far. Broken cans, discarded bottles, dirt, blowing paper, and, though it's full of people, none of them is white.

I realise, with a momentary mixture of fear and embarrassment, that I am indeed in a 'Blacks Only' world. There is no hostility, though – the blacks are just busy talking, meeting, napping, lolling – they're in their own world. What I object to most of all is that I should have been made to feel some guilt about being amongst these people.

It's this feeling of a shadow nation of blacks, which just isn't acknowledged, which is the most disturbing impression of SA.

Monday, January 10th: Johannesburg–Perth

In the First Class cabin is a family who are emigrating from SA to Australia. The father is a solicitor and avocado farmer – parents English, he was born and bred in SA. But now he's taking his family out. He points to them. 'There's no way I shall let them die fighting for an indefensible cause.'

He talks bitterly of the arrogance and inflexibility of the Afrikaans National Party. The English are treated almost as badly as the blacks by them, he said. Although he had a prosperous farm, he had no clout in politics at all. The Afrikaners are a small, self-perpetuating elite –

repressive, intolerant and dogmatic – and it's they who have driven him away.

Arrive at Perth at 2.30 a.m. Met by Doug O'Brien of GUO Film Distributors, a big, friendly, gentle man, to whom I take an immediate liking. Into Perth to the Hilton Parmelia – a big, new hotel, one class up from the President Holiday Inn, Jo'burg. Now I'm a film star and I have a suite on the eighth floor. All I can see outside are swirling freeways and lights on hills.

I've never been further from home.

Tuesday, January 11th: Perth, Western Australia

To lunch at a restaurant with a fine, indeed stunning, view over the waterfront. Arthur, the owner of an 18-cinema chain in Perth and area, and Norman, GUO's theatre owner in the city, were dining with us.

Arthur has a fine line in Aussie swearing, specially effective because the phrases come out quite naturally and without affectation from this fairly elderly gentleman. Describing a local millionaire called Bond – 'Of course, he stuck his cock in a cash register' (i.e. he married into money). A Sydney Indian restaurant is recommended with the warning that it used to be known as 'The Blazing Arsehole'.

Back to the hotel afterwards. Not welcome in the restaurant as I have no jacket. The receptionist immediately takes the side of the restaurant. 'One of the waiters had a heart attack tonight, so they may be a little tense in there' – pure Fawlty.

Friday, January 14th: Adelaide and Sydney

To ABC Adelaide for two very pleasant and easy BBC-style chats with programme hosts who were both very complimentary about 'The Mish'. Another station at which a man called Carl phones in and goes into a swingeing attack on me for being sacrilegious, etc. At one point he throws in Pamela Stephenson's name, blaming me even for her – and calling her a 'wicked Jezebel'.

At Sydney we are met by John Hartman, Managing Director of GUO.

To my room at the Regent – a 30-storey brand new hotel, from one of whose 19th-floor rooms I have a breathtakingly impressive panoramic view of the harbour, the bridge, the Opera House and the shores of North Sydney.

A surprise phone call from Basil Pao, who is in Sydney after three years' 'exile' in Hong Kong. He says he has just received a call from John Goldstone asking if he will design a *Meaning of Life* poster.

No sooner have I put the phone down than Goldstone himself rings to confirm a rumour I heard that Universal want the *Meaning of Life* to open in America at Easter.

Saturday, January 15th: Sydney

Meet Basil in North Bondi. He's at the home of a small, pretty, quite tough lady called Lydia, who is the agent of Jim Sherman [a playwright] and Philip Noyce, the director of *Newsfront*.

We drink champagne looking out over North Bondi Beach, and the scene reminds me, again with great poignancy, of my holidays at Southwold – brown, barefoot people coming home to little bungalows for supper, the toilets and bus shelters at the edge of the cliff, the sun and salt-tarnished paintwork and, above all, the feeling of lazy days. Quite, quite different from Africa *and* America. It's all so terribly … terribly English.

We eat at a nearby restaurant – really good food, not posh or pretentious, just very well cooked. Meet Bruce Chatwin there – he is rather sneery about things in a slightly aggressive, camp way which I don't awfully take to. There's almost an edge of cruelty somewhere there. Anyway, we bravely persevere in eating out in a force 5 gale, whilst being visited every now and then by drunken naval officers who recognise me and bring us complimentary glasses of port.

Then into the Rocks area again, where we go to see a group Basil knows. As they finish playing the room empties, leaving a lot of men without women and a crush of empty Fosters cans just dropped on the floor. 'This is the fall of Australian heterosexuality,' says Lydia.

Sunday, January 16th: Sydney

Wake about 10.30 with a cracking headache. Am extremely delicate for the rest of the morning. Bathe gingerly. Walk up to the corner of George Street to meet John Hartman, who is taking me for a drive up the coast to – I hardly dare contemplate the word – lunch.

It's a hot day – about 25 Celsius – and I'm picked up in the white Mercedes by a chauffeur complete with grey suit and peaked cap. I'm driven north along suburban roads that eventually blend into a déjà-vu Essex. I have to avoid sharp movements of the head, so when John Hartman in the back faithfully points out the (very few) objects of interest, I move like a man in an invisible neck brace.

I must be acting the interested passenger quite convincingly, as he appears determined to show me the local beaches. We stop at one and Vince, the chauffeur, parks our white Merc right up by the sand dunes and we have to pile out and walk around like a brace of property developers. How much I would rather be just lying out in the sun like everyone else. 'You've got a lot of clothes on for the beach,' comments a passing girl bather.

I'm mistaken for Eric Idle – only this time by someone who met Eric only last week, an Englishman who manages four of the England cricket team, who are now losing one-day games with the same consistency that they lost the Test Matches. He says they'll be in Sydney on Wednesday, so I promise I'll arrange seats for them at Wednesday's '*Mish*' preview.

Sunday, January 23rd: Delhi

Very quickly through the airport. I'm in the queue behind a Yorkshireman from Keighley who's just come in from Taiwan. I push my luggage trolley up a short, drab, ill-lit passageway and out – into India.

Huddled shapes spring towards me out of the darkness – men with scarves tied round their heads, as used in comic strips to denote sufferers from toothache. 'Taxi, sir?' I look vainly round for some sort of 'authorised' sign, determined to avoid falling into the clutches of the unlicensed, but I have made the fatal mistake – momentary hesitation – and within seconds my cases have been wrested from me and bundled into the back of a taxi.

There are six Indians already in the cab. The owner turns them out with much arguing and shouting and ushers me into the back. We start the engine, we stop, we argue, the boot is opened, more shadows appear from the dark, and suddenly my cabbie is gone, replaced in the driving seat by a young, unshaven desperado with an oily cloth tied bandanna-fashion round his head. He is joined in the passenger seat by another wild and mad-eyed individual. They look like archetypally dangerous men, but they drive off and out of the airport and strangely I feel quite safe and reasonably confident.

Eventually (though they miss the entrance once) we find the Imperial

Hotel in Janpath. Not impressive, but at least familiar – there are even American Express signs about. A message from TG in my cubby-hole, welcoming me to India. My bags are carried up to my room.

A succession of Indians in white cotton uniforms appear, elaborately bowing and scraping, turning the bed back, turning lights on and generally doing lots of things I don't really want them to do. Then the chief bed-turner waits and asks me if there is anything I want. Because he is there, I ask for a beer, and he arrives many minutes later with a bottle of something by the name of Jasmine Parrot, which tastes sweet and is quite undrinkable.

At eight I am in the breakfast room, which is full of waiters, but not of guests. TG arrives about five minutes later. The rendezvous has worked. It had seemed quite unlikely when we parted four weeks ago, agreeing to 'See you for breakfast in Delhi'.

TG and I take an auto-rickshaw and our lives into our hands, and head towards Old Delhi.

We are dropped near the entrance to the Old City. The street is full of people, animals and every kind of activity – men being shaved on little wooden platforms, dogs with awful sores lying peacefully beneath huge cauldrons of some steaming dal, children, cows, cyclists, an old man turning a makeshift Ferris wheel made of biscuit tins or petrol cans. It's Gilliam's world completely – just what he tried to recreate in *Jabberwocky*.

We visit a Jain temple. Off with our shoes and socks. Rich smell of incense mingled with sweaty feet. The strict Jains believe that all life is sacred, even bugs and flies. On our way to the temple we passed an elderly, quite chubby, entirely naked man being led through the streets. In any other country, I suppose, the little group around him would probably be police ushering him into the nearest paddy-wagon. Here in India he's a holy man.

Continually seeing things which nothing, except fiction, has ever prepared me for. For instance, outside the Red Fort is a man selling false beards – and TG has a picture to prove it.

Monday, January 24th: Delhi and Agra

Alarm goes at six. Pack in the sepulchral gloom of my room and set off with TG into the mist of a slowly-emerging Delhi dawn. A shadowy world of hooded, cloaked shapes.

Onto the Taj Express bound for Agra. We are in First Class Air-Conditioned.

We pull out on time, through this strange, atmospheric, blanketing morning mist which gradually clears to reveal the much read-about sight of Indians crouching in waste ground by the railway line and donating their night-soil. Little botties catching the morning light.

We are offered breakfast by a waiter in white cotton denims – stained and dirty. We order omelette. It arrives, accompanied by a banana, two pieces of toast and a battered Thermos of tea. The omelette is cold, thin and pinched.

For me one of the great beauties of the Taj Mahal is its setting. Not so much the well-known line of fountains which approaches from the front, but the Jumna river which flows along the back of the Taj. I sit out on the marble terrace with the shimmering iceberg-like bulk of the Taj Mahal on one side, and look out over the wide river bed, mostly dry, with its two or three bridges and, in the haze a mile away, the impressive long line of the battlements of the Agra Fort.

At the Mughal Room Restaurant. Not very good curry served whilst an impassive Indian quartet played 'My Way'.

Tuesday, January 25th: Agra–Jaipur

Refreshed and ready for the fray again. Book a taxi to Fatehpur Sikri and back.

Our taxi driver leaves us at the gates to the great palace, built during our Elizabethan period by the Emperor Akbar as the capital of the Moghul Empire, and then for some reason abandoned in favour of Agra. Towers and cupolas and columns all please the eye and lead from one to the other both literally and visually. And it's on a ridge, so there are views from the pretty turrets across the quiet landscape of green fields.

TG and I cannot believe that tourist groups are given one hour only to visit this wonderful complex. We even found a complete 'bath-house wing' which no-one else was being shown. Cool vaulted chambers, a hypocaust and several rooms all linked – presumably for the various temperatures.

We are taken then to Agra Fort Station. No 'Air-Conditioned Firsts' for us this time. We are in Hard Plastic First. An Indian gentleman, whom we come to know as our guardian angel, warns us, before he alights at the first stop, to bolt the door after him or else 'the students will try to get in'. He doesn't elaborate on this, but we follow his advice.

After a few minutes of pleasant rattling along through the outskirts of Agra the door handle rattles, then the door is banged, then the handle is wrenched more persistently. It is 'the students'.

At the next stop faces appear outside the window. 'Why will you not open the door?' TG holds them at bay through the bars, trying to explain the First Class ticket system. 'You are not right-thinking!' they shout back. Then the train starts off again and they resort to more heavy banging, laughter and jeers and then, rather more disconcertingly, leaning out of the window next to our compartment and staring in. It all helps to pass the time and after an hour or so they get bored.

We arrive in Jaipur at a quarter to eleven. Outside the station the rush of rickshaw and auto-rickshaw drivers is broken up and dispersed by bearded men with batons and sticks. There seem to be 30 or 40 auto-rickshaws lined up and no trade, so TG has little trouble in beating some poor local down from ten to four Rupees (about 75p to 20p). Our driver hurtles us through the streets of Jaipur like a man demented, his cloak billowing out in the cool night breeze.

We are staying at our first Palace hotel – Maharajahs' homes so enormous that they have been recycled as hotels. This one is called the Rambagh Palace. A long drive approach and impressively sizeable floodlit walls. TG is very rude about it and blames me for wanting such First Class travel!

To bring us even more rudely back to civilisation, there is a film crew here. They're shooting *The Far Pavilions* and have just had a party on the front lawn of the hotel. TG is recognised by the props man, who worked on *Time Bandits* with him.

Wednesday, January 26th: Jaipur

Breakfast in a cavernous dining room of immense size, furnished in a sort of European hybrid manner – a cross between Disneyland and Versailles, as my travelling companion describes it.

About nine we leave for the town. Outside the hotel Omar Sharif is learning his lines beside a row of parked cars.

We walk through the back streets of Jaipur. The Indians, unlike the Africans, don't seem to mind a bit having their photographs taken – in fact they arrange themselves in rather decorative poses and leave their names and addresses with you afterwards if it's been a particularly good one.

We return to the Rambagh Palace, who confirm that we have no rooms for the night. Indian Airlines' flights to Udaipur are booked and there is no chance of us getting on the overnight train because it comes from Delhi and is bound to be full.

We are recognised. The [*Far Pavilions*] director turns out to be Peter Duffel. He's a softer Lindsay Anderson lookalike. Amy Irving, his leading lady, asks to be introduced, though it turns out I'd met her briefly at Lee Studios when she was filming *Yentl*. She hears of TG's and my plight and offers one of the spare beds in her room for the night should we be desperate!

Then Vishnu comes into our lives. Vishnu is older and looks a little wiser than the average run of motor-rickshaw drivers and he it is who takes us to the bus station to try and book on the overnight 'de-luxe' bus.

After watching their heads shake negatively for ten minutes I begin to give up, but eventually Vishnu is summoned into a dark corner and within minutes he's back, trying to restrain a proud little smile. Money exchanges hands and we are on the de-luxe bus to Udaipur.

When we see the de-luxe bus, we are somewhat taken aback. Our seats are right at the front with a partition little more than two foot six inches in front of us. The seats don't recline and the journey time is nine hours.

Thursday, January 27th: Udaipur

Stop at 3.30. Realise, as we pile out into the clear and pleasant night air, that I'm rather enjoying the journey – it's not an ordeal at all. There's something very calming about being in India. They don't fight and fluster and bite their nails and moan and complain and it makes for a very unstressful atmosphere. No toilets at this stop – so just a pee in the darkness and a cup of sweet tea. Enjoy the understated feeling of camaraderie amongst the passengers, of which we are the only two whites.

It's a clear, bright day and after breakfast TG and I are off up to the City Palace. Another enormous labyrinth of rooms, stairs and temples. It was lived in not long ago and has a rather sad museum with old Rolls Royces, mangy stuffed bears, many beautiful paintings of tiger and elephant hunts and life-sized cardboard cut-outs of the Maharajahs, which are quite a shock.

Sit in my room with a Herbert's lager and watch the light fading on the shore and feel very peaceful. TG and I eat at the hotel, then have a

last drink out beside the pool in the courtyard which is all lit up. We're
the only ones to use it.

Friday, January 28th: Udaipur–Delhi

I'm at the airport even before the staff . . . they're just unlocking the doors.
So I'm first at the check-in counter. A small, rotund, self-important little
man eventually surveys my ticket and pushes it aside. 'Only OK passengers
now, please.' My jaw must have dropped visibly, for he continues 'You are
only wait-listed, please wait until the aircraft comes in.'

Suddenly I feel how far Udaipur is from anywhere else. Times, figures,
estimates click round in my head, but no comforting alternative presents
itself. But hope brightens as the plane is obviously emptier than I've
expected and at last, with as little emotion as he'd turned me away, he
takes my ticket, scribbles across it, and hands me a boarding card.

Arrive at the Imperial, to find a telegram giving the first weekend's
Missionary figures. Sydney outstanding, Melbourne disappointing and
Adelaide very good! Late lunch at the Imperial. For the sake of *Ripping
Yarns* and *The Missionary*, in which characters were always eating it,
I choose a plate of kedgeree, which is superb, and a bottle of Golden Eagle
beer.

Tuesday, February 1st

Up at 8.15. The children rush upstairs to tell us, as we are dressing briskly
in freezing bedroom, that John Cleese is on TV in his pyjamas. It's true.
He's the star showbiz guest on this, the first programme of TV-AM –
another new TV company started by David Frost and the second supplier
of breakfast programmes to have started this year.

TJ rings. He's just back from a lightning Concorde trip to the US for
Meaning of Life previews. Two showings in Yonkers went so badly that TJ
and JG didn't even bother to look at the cards. An audience of young
(15–22) cinema-goers predominantly. Eighty walk-outs.

TJ's spirits restored by a showing in Manhattan which was very well
received. As often happens under pressure, some sensible cuts have been
made quite quickly – 'Luther' is gone and much of the 'Hendys' too. The
film sounds trimmer. Universal, as a result of these last showings, are
definitely going ahead on March 25th, but with a limited release –
probably even less than *The Missionary*.

At 12.30 call John Hartman in Sydney – *The Missionary* is evidently No. 3 in the country. The good news is that attendances were up everywhere in the second week.

Friday, February 4th: Southwold

On the way to Ipswich I complete the last few pages of '*Anna K*' – the book that has been my friend and guardian throughout Kenya, South Africa, Australia and India. Find the last few chapters – Levin discovers The Meaning of Life – rather comforting. I resolve to live my life better and not get angry with people any more.

Tuesday, February 8th

Very cold still – getting up is not fun. But I sleep on this morning very easily, feeling that only now have I readjusted and caught up on my sleep after the World Tour. The builders arrive and start digging foundations for the extension to No. 2.

As Cleese is coming to dinner tonight, I feel I must see *Privates on Parade*, my HandMade stablemate. It's on at the Classic Hampstead, so I go to the 3.35 showing. The 'conversion' of the Classic to a three-screen complex has been so brutal that the Screen One has been set on a new level halfway up the old auditorium. Even the old wall decorations have been left, severed, as a reminder of the modest but homely theatre it once was. A long, flat, empty space extends between audience, who number 15 this afternoon, and screen. But it's in focus and the sound is clear, so I have to be thankful for that.

The concert party numbers are well done and, as they were at the core of the stage success, are performed with panache and attractive skill by Denis Quilley and S Jones and others. Cleese and Michael Elphick are impressive at first, but gradually the film is dragged down. Relationships are hinted at, briefly consummated, then dropped just as they might have been getting interesting and Cleesey becomes saddled with the unenviable task of providing comedy as a palliative for all the floundering 'serious' realities of war at the end.

He ends up with a desperate silly walk in the closing credits – as if finally confirming that the film is supposed to be a comedy, despite the balls being shot off, etc, etc.

Thursday, February 10th

To Duke's Hotel to meet Mike Ewin – HandMade's distribution man
since December. Short, stocky, homely figure with a respectable suit. He
does come up with one or two classic remarks for a film distributor,
particularly his cheerful admission that he hasn't seen the film ... 'But,
you know, Michael, I don't think it's really necessary to see a film to know
what sort of film it is.'

Walk through St James's Square and into the Haymarket to look at our
launch theatre and meet the manager.

The manager, Brian Rami, is quite a character. Youngish, aggressive,
Greek Cypriot I should imagine. He is a theatre success story – taking
tickets in Hackney two or three years ago, he's won Classic's Manager of
the Year award. He briskly goes into the attack with Ray [Cooper] and
myself, asking where our posters are and where the trailer and photo
displays are, as he could have been playing them for the last week. 'Good
man,' I say, in response to his enthusiasm. 'Don't "good man" me,' he
replies sharply, '... just give me the goods.'

Snow is beginning to fall quite thickly as Ray and I enter the scarlet
and black world of The Hutton Company, but, as the *Sun* might say, we
were soon seeing red of a different kind. The complications with the
poster's artwork, combined with the time it will take London Transport
to hang them, make it now likely that the posters will not appear until
the 1st of March, two days before the film opens.

I am quite unable to control my anger and frustration. Colin
MacGregor [who's in charge of our campaign], in his languid public-
school manner, tries his best to calm things down, but I'm afraid there's
no stopping me. Silence and heads hung everywhere.

Friday, February 11th

Today Colin MacGregor informs me that London Transport have agreed
to start displaying posters on Underground and buses from February
18th – two weeks earlier than yesterday's date – and that with a bit of luck
they can arrange to have poster artwork completed by the weekend. I hate
to say it, but violence does seem to work – even if it's only the violence of
my opinion.

Monday, February 14th

To Mel Calman's gallery at 12.30. We talk of ads, posters and the lack of good design. More positively we talk over the idea of opening a cinema in Covent Garden. It's something I've heard mentioned elsewhere, but somehow, this being a Monday lunchtime and the start of a week, Mel imbues me with great enthusiasm for the idea and, as I walk back to the car, I feel all the elation of one who has just acquired a cinema in Covent Garden.

To Bertorelli's, where a researcher for the Time Rice (Freudian slip), Tim Rice Show on Wednesday is taking me to lunch. Pre-interview interviews seem to be all the rage now. It's a very bad habit imported from America. So I talk for an hour or so to this keen, rather aggressive Scots girl, who asks me dreadful questions like 'Does comedy have a comic significance?' 'Is comedy a moral force on the world stage?' I get very twitchy about three o'clock, when she still has ten questions left to ask.

Sunday, February 20th

I drive over to Lime Grove at seven o'clock for an appearance on *Sunday Night*. Into the quaintly termed 'hospitality room', where I'm offered some wine from a bottle they keep on the window sill outside.

We record about a quarter to eight. Eric Robson, who did one of the 'Great Railway Journeys', is the presenter – a solid, dependable, likeable man. As the credits roll and the contents of the show reveal filmed reports on how Christianity is coping in the poverty-stricken conditions of South America, *The Missionary* seems embarrassingly frivolous.

The Dean of St Paul's, another interviewee, smiles a little uncertainly at me, as the story of the film is being explained by their resident reviewer – himself a clergyman. His review of the film is not awfully good. He thinks it 'a 50-minute television programme blown up to 90 minutes', 'not very serious', 'an adolescent fantasy', etc, etc. 'My fantasies are much more grown-up,' he ends. They do drop themselves in it, these people.

The trouble is, as this is a religious programme, *The Missionary* is treated, out of perspective I think, as a carefully thought-out comment on the church. When he accuses the satire of being rather limp and safe, I counter by saying that the church gets the satire it deserves. Feel a few frissons cross the studio as I say this and hope the Dean of St Paul's doesn't mind.

Monday, February 21st

Bad news comes in early evening when Ray rings to say that the trailer has hit fresh, and quite unexpected, snags in the shape of the film censor, who has refused to grant our trailers anything less than an 'X' unless we remove mention of the word 'prostitutes' and cut a sequence in which I say 'I was just telling Emmeline how relatively unimportant sex is', despite the fact that he has given both these lines clearance for any audience over 15. The ridiculous thing is that he will allow us to replace 'prostitutes' with 'fallen women'. The mind boggles.

Thursday, February 24th

Good news of the day is that Maggie Smith has agreed to come to the press screening and may even appear on *Terry Wogan*.

But the day's excitements are not over. At home, as Helen is getting ready for another evening's badminton and the spaghetti's boiling away on the hob, Mel Calman calls to tell me that à propos our St Valentine's Day enthusiasms for a cinema in Covent Garden, he has heard of a building for sale in Neal's Yard! It's No. 2, has a salad bar on the ground floor, room for a gallery and coffee bar on the first, an acupuncturist on the second and a self-contained flat on the top. Cost £275,000. I'm very keen. Keen to buy in such a special spot as Neal's Yard and keen to help Mel C and the Workshop. Watch this space!

Stay up until 1.15 to watch the Bermondsey by-election, the culmination of a particularly vicious and intolerant campaign against Peter Tatchell. The Alliance Party are crowing. Labour *do* seem to be in quite serious trouble.

Saturday, February 26th

Arrive at TV-AM's still-unfinished studios in Camden Town. Bright, light, high-tech building decorated in the Very Silly Style, with representations of pagodas and African jungles. It's like one huge Breakfast TV set.

I'm on talking about *The Missionary*. Parky likes it. Calls it 'an important film', too, and shows a clip. They give a number on which viewers can call me with any questions. Over 200 questions come in, and they're all very excited at TV-AM as it's the largest number of phone calls for anyone they've ever had. I wish George Harrison 'Happy Birthday' on air – even though he's incommunicado in Hawaii. But I am wearing the Missoni sweater he gave me and at least ten of the calls are about this.

William and I stay for breakfast with Parky and Mrs Parky – a nice Yorkshire couple – in a rather narrow and cramped canteen which Parkinson complains about. He seems to be quite brisk with his working colleagues. I shouldn't think he suffers fools gladly.

Monday, February 28th

Off to the Classic Haymarket. The press show has run for about 75 minutes. Brian Rami is very enthusiastic about the whole thing. There is applause at the end (very rare in critics' screenings), but only he and I know that it was Rami who started it!

Walk down across Pall Mall to the Turf Club. At least it's a dry, quite pleasant day. Upstairs at the Turf, in two elegant, high-ceilinged rooms, there is a good crowd of pressmen, plus one or two of the Fallen Women and Phoebe.

Maggie S herself arrives about half past twelve. She still hasn't seen the film and I feel that she will probably continue to avoid it, as is her habit. But she looks very bright and attractive and sparkles for the press she dreads so much.

Mr Chandler, the rather icily elegant major-domo, is all smiles and very obliging today. 'All the gentlemen of the press seemed to have enjoyed the film ...'

As I'm about to go, Mr Chandler appears up the stairs once more ... 'Do you know Medwin?' And sure enough, Michael Medwin, looking very perky in what looks like an oleander-pink scarf, comes bounding up behind him and I find myself drinking a further couple of glasses of champagne with him at the bar downstairs.

Mr Chandler keeps saying 'He'll have to become a member, you know,' in a generous fashion. And Medwin promises to propose me and says that 'Chalky' White[1] and Albert Finney will second me. We talk over the

1 Our colloquial name for Michael White, the celebrated producer and major investor in *Holy Grail.*

film industry. He seems quite sanguine about 'going into the city' and getting money and most hurt that *Memoirs of a Survivor*[1] (much praised) did not receive the commercial attention it deserved.

Tuesday, March 1st

To the City University to be the 'guinea pig' at one of Bob Jones's press conferences at the Department of Journalism. After an hour of this, drink with some of the tutors there. I'm listened to with far too much respect these days. I suppose it must have changed me somehow. I no longer have to look for an audience. They gather around me – even quite intelligent people – and wait for the oracle to utter.

Home to anonymity and abuse from children.

Thursday, March 3rd

Missionary opening day.

An equivocal review in the very influential *Time Out*, specifically criticising my role as being inadequate to support the film, is followed by a short, but very negative piece in *City Limits*. In the *Guardian*, Derek Malcolm has me casting the paper aside in disgust and sitting head in hands in that deep, sudden desolation that only a bad crit can bring. But when I read him again, I realise it's quite a praiseworthy review, but rather obscurely written.

Terry J rings and suggests squash and lunch, which I eagerly accept. TJ has been at Technicolor labs doing last-minute work on the *Meaning of Life* print. It's now a time panic as bad as anything that happened on *The Missionary*.

I'd forgotten about the *Standard*. Have a quick scan through Alexander Walker and it is very good – for me and the film. A big photo, lead story, headline 'Mission Accomplished', phrases like 'The *Missionary* is very, very funny' and a comprehensive relishing of the finer points of the movie which almost makes the piece look like an extension of our own advertising. This puts a new spring in my step and a quite different complexion on the day.

Drive into the West End to the Classic Haymarket. The acting manager,

1 1981 film written & directed by David Gladwell from a Doris Lessing book. It starred Julie Christie. Michael Medwin was the producer.

Ken Peacock, is in the bar. He's very pleased and reckons it could take £2,000 at the end of the day. The best Thursday for ages, he says.

Up to the projection room to say hello. My handiwork slowly unwinds from the longest spool I've ever seen. Rather exciting seeing it all through the small windows.

Friday, March 4th

A rave review of *Missionary* in the *Mirror* and the *Daily Mail* and the *Daily Express*. I only come down to earth a little with *The Times* – but even that headlines its film column 'Great Comic Acting' and only attacks the script for not being better.

Helen returns with the *Financial Times*, which also says many positive things, but in the end wanted 'a bit less caution, a little more anarchy', whereas Coleman in the *New Statesman* called *The Missionary* 'unfashionably well-written', which I don't understand but like very much.

Then after lunch there is quite suddenly a great anti-climax. The film is out and running. The radio and television shows will be looking for new celebrities and different shows next week.

At this very moment I have nothing to do – no problem to solve, no crisis to defuse, no-one to hustle . . . just a grey, wet day coming to an end and some writing which I can't settle down to. This evening Helen and three of her badminton chums are going to see my film. I shall stay at home.

Have supper with the boys and, feeling very weary, go to bed early.

Sunday, March 6th

A marvellous *Sunday Times* piece by David Hughes ending 'Here is a serious humorist trying his comedy for size. Not yet finding a visionary focus. Lacking edge. But your bones tell you that he will soon make a real beauty of a film, as exciting in achievement as this lark is in promise.'

The *Telegraph*, the *Mail on Sunday*, the *Express* and the *News of the World* are all highly complimentary. Castell in the *Sunday Telegraph* concludes 'Beautifully tailored and consistently funny, *The Missionary* is bound to convert you.'

We should publicise these reviews as quickly as possible. No time for faint hearts. We have stolen a week's march on *Local Hero*, which will be shouting about its success very soon, but it will be a similar sort of critical response and I want as many people as possible to know that *The Missionary* was there first.

Take Helen and the children to La Cirque Imaginaire, a lovely, gentle, funny circus-style entertainment performed by Victoria Chaplin, her husband and their two children. A real family circus with no animals more dangerous than a rabbit, a toucan and two ducks.

Wednesday, March 9th

To L'Escargot to meet Mike Fentiman and Robin Denselow's girlfriend Jadzia to discuss my making a half-hour documentary in their *Comic Roots* series. I liked him and they warmed to my ideas and it looks like we have ourselves a show. In June, probably.

I aim to start work on a new screenplay in April and May, break in June for *Comic Roots*, and complete at quite a leisurely pace during July and August. Rewrites in September and October, by which time ready either to begin setting up filming or to write something with TJ.

Drive down to the Classic. Traffic at a standstill in St Martin's Lane as the teachers and students are marching in protest against education cuts. Eventually reach the bottom of the Haymarket. My silly vicar looks quite striking above the marquee.

Thursday, March 10th

Nikki [from HandMade] calls to tell me that Cannon Classic will be taking an ad in *Screen International* to announce that *Missionary* has broken the house record! And a projectionist at the Barking Odeon has been arrested by the police for taking a print of *The Missionary* home with him in the boot of his car – with intent to tape it!

Tuesday, March 15th

To the Odeon Haymarket to see *Local Hero*. Apart from reservations over the Houston interiors – where both design and direction seemed less sure and the jokes, about American psychiatrists, more familiar – the film quite captivates me. Forsyth is remarkable in his ability to recreate on screen the accidental quality of humour – the way things that make you happy happen so quickly, spontaneously, that try as you can you never quite remember afterwards.

Princess Margaret is coming to see *The Missionary* at the Classic Haymarket tonight. Brian Rami is in an advanced state of excitement. 'She is one of your greatest fans,' Brian relays to me, and urges me to come down if I can.

I speed down to the West End, arriving with about five minutes to spare. Brian R is, of course, immaculate, and looks my faded jeans and windcheater up and down with alarm. In the end Princess Margaret arrives with such speedy precision that I don't have a chance to see her as she moves quickly, but hastelessly, up the stairs behind a phalanx of very tall people. She *does* want to meet me, Brian confirms, so could I come back at a quarter to nine.

At a quarter to nine I stand clutching my signed copy of the '*Mish*' – should I have written to '*Your* Royal Highness Princess Margaret' in it? – waiting for the performance to end. Martin, the projectionist tonight, is very excited, as are the predominantly Asian and African sales staff.

Down the stairs comes the little lady, almost gnomic in the relative size of head to body, and clad in black. She shakes my hand easily and talks without formality. I can't remember much apart from apologising that I should be there at all at the end of the film – waylaying cinemagoers! But she says she thoroughly enjoyed it and asks about the Scottish location, so I am able to tell her that it [Ardverikie House] was nearly the Royal Residence once. We chat quite easily and she introduces me to her very tall friends and they all laugh and endorse her opinion. Then she is taken out and past the queue – clutching my signed book.

Brian R and I drink a coffee afterwards. This film has already given him much pleasure, but tonight surpassed anything.

Tuesday, March 22nd

The telephone goes. It's Richard L. Richard has left home.

'Where shall I go? What should I do?' As if I know. Nothing in my experience quite prepares me for this. The enormity of the split he's now admitted clearly frightens him. I tell him if he needs help, or a bed, or company, that I shall be here.

Write letters and prepare stew for supper. Then, just as I've served, Richard arrives. His normal behaviour is so near to hysteria that it's difficult to tell how abnormal he is at the moment.

He eats the stew (later, when I'm trying to explain to Rachel that Richard's behaviour is because he's very, very unhappy, she philosophises 'Well, at least you got rid of the stew'). When I come downstairs from reading *The Secret Garden* to Rachel, he's asleep on our sofa.

There's not much more I can do and, feeling quite weary myself, I go to bed and to sleep at eleven.

Sunday, March 27th

A wet, dull Sunday. Helen [back from skiing in Austria] unpacks and very gradually begins to readjust to life at sea-level.

Potter around at home, unburying No. 2 from the builders' dust and debris of the last six weeks. It's quite exciting – like a new house emerging from hibernation. Tom P will move in here after Easter.

Watch and delight in *Betjeman* – the final episode. Full of gems – he's such a warm, kindly, generous but cheeky presence. On top of a cliff in Cornwall he's wheeled into shot clad in a black bomber jacket with a 'Guinness' tag inexplicably obvious over the left breast. His mouth senile and droopy from the effects of Parkinson's (that I know so well), but his eyes alive, alert and mischievous.

He's asked if there's anything in his life he really regrets ... He considers a moment, the Cornish clifftop wind untidying his hair and making him look such a little, isolated, vulnerable figure ... 'Yes ... I didn't have enough sex ...'

Monday, March 28th

We have used up most of our £80,000 launch budget, but Denis has agreed to about £5,000 extra to continue support over the upcoming Easter weekend. I hear from Ray that Stanley Kubrick wrote to Denis congratulating him on the *Missionary* campaign, which he had noticed, admired and envied. For an apparent recluse he keeps in touch, it seems.

To lunch at L'Escargot. Colin Webb of Pavilion Books is at another table. He tells me that the *Time* critic, Richard Schickel, who has given '*MOL*' such a good (and important) review, really *did* like *The Missionary*, despite his dismissive piece. He had been in a 'very depressed state' when he wrote it and has since seen it again and thinks it 'a gem of its kind'.

Home about six. The phone rings instantly. It's Tim Brooke-Taylor conveying to me an offer to direct a new Gounod opera at the Buxton

Festival. We have quite a long chat and he tries his best to persuade me to do something that both of us agree is tantalisingly out of the ordinary. But I end up turning it down and inviting Tim and Christine to dinner.

Terry Gilliam appears. He looks rather careworn. America was awful, he says. He was unable to sell *Brazil* to Paramount or Universal and is extremely bitter about Hollywood studios all over again.

Tuesday, March 29th: London–New York

Exactly one year since I began filming *The Missionary* I leave the house to catch the 10.30 Concorde to New York. The flight (all £1,190 of it) to New York is being paid for by Universal Pictures for my work on behalf of the second film I made last year – *The Meaning of Life*.

A limousine takes me into New York, past the burnt-out tenements of Harlem to the discreetly comfortable Westbury Hotel at 69th and Madison. It's a fine, clear, cool day – the buildings stand out sharp against piercing blue skies.

Visit Al and Claudie on my way to the first interview. They have been through a bad four weeks – awful journey back from Paris and Claudie recently very ill and worried at one point that her bronchitis was cancer. Also a new property company have taken the block and want to make Al an offer to sell his lease, so they may contemplate a complete move to Sag Harbor in the early summer. Their little daughter Gwenola delightful, smiling, full of beans.

Drive back uptown to a bar/restaurant in the theatre district for a drink with Richard Schickel, his wife and daughter. He officially rescinds his review of *The Missionary*, saying quite sportingly that he shouldn't have dismissed it and anyway his wife had disagreed with his views right from the start. So that made me feel better and we now have quite a good relationship.

Off to Broadway Video, at Lorne's invitation. It's all looking very smart now. In a basement studio in the Brill Building Simon and Garfunkel are working on a new album, which has taken one and a half years already. They're listening to a drummer, Eddie Gatt, doing over-dubs.

Paul greets me effusively (or as effusively as Paul ever could be), then goes back to careful concentration on the track. Art Garfunkel sits behind him and nods his great beaky head every now and then – '*That's* good' – but Simon is really in control. Art passes some coke on the end of a penknife. I decline, much to Lorne's comic disapproval.

Friday, April 1st: New York–London

Down to another ABC studio to record an interview with a man whose extravagant name – Regis Philbin – denies his very regular appearance. We do ten very successful minutes. The producer of this new show is Bob Shanks – the man who six years ago was responsible for the butchering of the six Python TV shows which took us to court and eventually won us custody of the shows. He looks older and more unkempt. Quite shockingly different from the trim, smooth executive with nary a hair out of place whom we fought at the Federal Court House.

He jokes about it as we shake hands. 'We met in court … '. Really he's done us a lot of good in the end and it's a curious coincidence that less than 12 hours before meeting Shanks again, I heard from Ron Devillier that we have sold the Python TV shows to PBS for a fee of at least a million dollars for two years.

Sunday, April 3rd: Easter Sunday

Helen has not slept much and is groaning in pain at eight o'clock on this Easter morning.

Throughout the morning she is in great pain and discomfort. Cheerful Doctor Rea arrives at midday, quips about my appearance on the back of buses, examines Helen and takes a sample. He has no bottles, so I have to run downstairs and fetch one of Helen's marmalade jars.

The doctor takes a quick look at Helen's specimen, holds it up to the light for all Oak Village to see and pronounces it like 'a rich Madeira'. He says Helen has all the symptoms of pyelitis – an infection of the tubes leading from the kidneys to the urinary tract. He prescribes some pills, which I rush out to Belsize Park to fetch from a Welsh chemist, who's also seen me on the back of the buses.

Sunday, April 10th

Collect the Sunday papers and try to put off further rehearsal for the Stop Sizewell 'B' concert as long as possible.[1] I feel an enormous disinclination to appear on stage tonight. A wave of weariness which I feel sure is mental

1 Sizewell 'B' was a nuclear power plant planned for the Suffolk coast. It was built between 1988 and 1995.

more than physical. I have been so much in the public eye over the last year or so – and each day, with very few exceptions, I've been required to smile brightly, chat optimistically and generally project constantly, when all I really want to do is to disappear from sight for a while.

Dinner at Mary's is a welcome break – very jolly, with Granny G declaring that she has grown cannabis in her garden ... 'And I'm growing more this year' – but I have to leave after an hour and drive down to the Apollo Victoria for the call at 3.30. The theatre is huge and it takes me half an hour to work out a way through the labyrinth of tunnels to our dressing room, which TJ and I are sharing with Neil Innes and Pete Capaldi (one of the stars of *Local Hero*).

At four o'clock the cast is summonsed to the foyer to hear the running order. Various bands – Darts, UB40, Madness – and a strong selection of comedy groups – Rik Mayall and the Young Ones, National Theatre of Brent, as well as Neil and Julie Covington and Pamela Stephenson. TJ is told that they couldn't do an explosion, so he decided to cut 'Never Be Rude to an Arab'.

Then a long, long wait whilst UB40 monopolise the stage, which is filled with a vast and forbidding array of speakers, amps, wires, leads, plugs and sockets which make Sizewell 'B' look as dangerous as the Faraway Tree. Backstage is a no-man's land of bewilderment and confusion.

Jeanette Charles – the Queen's lookalike – arrives in our dressing room about seven to add yet another bizarre element to an already lunatic situation.

The curtain doesn't go up at 7.30 as the bands are still rehearsing. Jeanette C, now totally transformed physically and mentally into the Royal Person, protests vigorously at the delay – 'I have to go to a Bar-Mitzvah ... ' she announces imperiously to some desperate and confused dis-organiser. 'When quarter to eight comes I must go like a bat out of hell to Chigwell.' Very Joe Orton.

Monday, April 18th

Begin writing new screenplay. Rather than spend days or weeks on elaborate research or agonising over a subject, I decide to ride straight in on the 'Explorers' idea which came to me about four months ago.

To dinner with Graham and David. Was supposed to be with TJ as well, but he rang this morning, having had Creosotic eruptions during the night, to cancel. Take GC to Langan's Brasserie. He's half an hour late. Still, I enjoy sipping a malt whisky at the bar and watching caricatures of rich people entering. Feel like I'm watching a parade of the people George Grosz used to draw.

GC looks a bit drawn and haggard and, as always, has the slightly distracted air of, as TJ put it, 'someone who wants to be somewhere else'. Great praise for Peter Cook for keeping everyone happy in Mexico and Eric for being 'divine' (according to David). GC goes back to the US for *Yellowbeard* sneak previews this week. He has reached the stage of not knowing whether anything is working any more.

Friday, April 22nd

To the BBC to discuss further my *Comic Roots* piece with Tony Laryea, my director.

The headquarters of *Open Door* is, ironically, almost impossible to find. I drive past it several times and in the end have to ask directions at Lime Grove.

Talk to Tony in an office full of clutter and overflowing out-trays. Very John le Carré. I tell him my thoughts about the structure of the piece. He is a little taken aback when I suggest David Frost as someone to interview. But he was seminal to the Palin career. It's taking further shape and looks like being a very rich programme. At least an hour's worth at the moment.

Talk to a Dutch journalist for an hour. He has 38 questions.

John Goldstone makes one further attempt to persuade me to go to Cannes – using a free ticket for Helen as bait. I can't, I'm going to Newcastle. Suggest Helen goes with one of the others!

Sunday, April 24th

I embark on mass picture-hanging and clearing up in the garden until Gilliam arrives and we talk about the state of the world for an hour and a half. He *is* going to Cannes, but isn't going to wear a dinner jacket for the special evening showing. Says he'll only go if the dinner jacket very obviously has vomit all over it.

He says that he misses working in the flexible Python way and that Tom Stoppard is much more of a professional writer, wanting to be sure he's being paid before doing rewrites ... and 'Stoppard's stuff is so hard to rewrite'. But they are at the casting and location-hunting stage.

Monday, April 25th

J Cleese rings to ask us to dinner. He says he's writing his own thing and would I play a man with a stutter?

At 2.15 two young men, Edward Whitley and another whose name I forget, come to interview me for a book on Oxford. They were meant to come last Friday, but their car had broken down. They're quite pleasant, rather plummy-voiced Oxfordians. I expect from the more comfortably-off classes.

But their interviewing is less comfortable. They are aggressive and rather impatient (nothing new with students), but with an added and more sinister tone – it is as if they have made their mind up about Oxford and what it was like in my time, and nothing I say would really change what they want to think. Whitley, especially, is a clumsy, gauche questioner.

In short, what I had hoped would be a pleasant chance to recall what Oxford was to me, turns into an inquisition. I pour them coffee and try to cope with all their questions, but there is such a humourless, sour feeling emanating from Whitley that it isn't easy.

I know I have another one-hour interview to go to at 3.15, as do they, and when, at 3.20, they turn their probing eye on to *The Missionary* and begin, in rather measured, well-rounded tones, to pull it to pieces, I quite simply run out of patience with their hostile cleverness and leave the house.

On to a Python '*MOL*' meeting with the two Terrys and John G and Anne. TJ and I put together a nice little 40-second radio ad and it's quite a jolly session. Goldstone says '*MOL*' is over 10 million gross in the US, but we need 40 million gross to start making money.

Tuesday, April 26th: London–Oslo

Out to Heathrow about one o'clock. Time for a coffee, then onto a Super One-Eleven to Oslo. At three o'clock UK time, four o'clock Norwegian, we're over the mainland of Norway and flying across a chill and desolate snowscape of forests and frozen lakes and finally into Oslo itself.

A man comes out to welcome the flight on a bicycle. We leave the plane and down to the terminal through holes in the tarmac. John Jacobsen,[1]

---

1 John Jacobsen, a writer and general fixer, was Norway's greatest Python fan.

thin, bearded, with his odd, ironic gaze, meets me and drives me into the centre of town and the Continental Hotel. Pleasant, local feel to it and a large room overlooking the main street of the town.

Don my suit and tie and am taken at eight o'clock to the Continental Hotel dining room (the best restaurant in Oslo, I'm told). Here I meet my hosts for tonight, the two who run all the cinemas of Oslo – for, like alcohol retailing, cinema exhibition is here a municipal monopoly. The dark lady with a sad, Munch-like face is Ingeborg. The middle-aged, friendly, unassuming man is Eivind. 'You are not so high ... ' begins the dark and Garbo-esque Ingeborg, 'as on the screen.'

Wednesday, April 27th: Oslo

To a restaurant overlooking the city for a late lunch with Jahn Teigen, the Norwegian comedian/singer/composer, who became even more of a national hero when he returned from the Eurovision Song Contest two years ago without a single point.

He's a tremendous Python fan, but a very intelligent one too and I like him enormously. Having a lunch together is a real relaxation from the usual round of slightly forced politenesses which these trips are all about. He's making a film about King Olaf, the tenth-century Norwegian hero. His concerts sell out all over the country and he's clearly the biggest fish in this quite lucrative pond.

Thursday, May 5th

Forty years old. Feel tempted to write some pertinent remarks about The Meaning Of It All – a mid-life, half-term report on Michael P. But there isn't much to say except I feel I'm still going – and going very hard and quite fast – and the pace of life and experience doesn't seem to show any sign of flagging.

I feel that I've entered, and am now firmly embarked on, a third 18-year 'section'. The first 18 were my childhood, the next 18 my preparation and apprenticeship and now, for better or worse, I *am* established. If I died tomorrow I would have an obituary and all those things.

The very fact that Rachel should creep round the door of our room at eight o'clock, full of excitement, to tell me that my birthday was announced, over my picture, on BBC Breakfast TV, shows what status I have had thrust upon me. I have the feeling that, as far as the public is concerned, I am now their Michael Palin and they are quite happy for me to remain their Michael Palin for the rest of my (and their) life.

So here I am. Healthy and wealthy and quite wise, but I can stay and sit comfortably or I can move on and undertake more risks as a writer and performer. Of course I *shall* go on, but, as another day of writing my 'new film' recedes and disappears, I realise that it won't be easy. And I should perhaps stop expecting it to be.

Friday, May 6th

Running on the Heath this morning, pounding away the effects of a poor, anxious night's sleep, my mind clears as my body relaxes and I resolve to extricate myself from some of the many commitments in which I have become entangled over the years.

This morning Clive Landa rang from Shepperton. Clive tells me that Lee Brothers have made a £2 million offer for the studio and two property companies are also anxious to buy it (and knock it down, of course). I feel that all my efforts over the years have counted for very little – and, to be honest, I haven't been asked to contribute a great deal of time and effort anyway. So I think I shall proffer my resignation as soon as possible.[1]

The crucial problem over the next months is whether or not I shall have time to write a screenplay by August. It's clear that *Comic Roots* will take up at least four weeks and the ever-increasing demands of publicity will devour much of the rest. Unthinkable though it might seem, I feel strongly that I must extract myself from *Comic Roots*. I shouldn't be spending four weeks on my past, when I'd rather be spending it on my future.

Saturday, May 7th

I open the Camden Institute Playgroup Fete.

I spend three-quarters of an hour 'being a celebrity' and trying to avoid a persistent mad camerawoman who wants me to do something 'goofy' for the *Camden Journal*. And all the time I'm doing this public smiling I'm inwardly trying to prepare myself for my next confrontation – with Tony Laryea over *Comic Roots*.

---

1 Clive Landa was Managing Director of Shepperton Studios. In view of the amount of work I was doing elsewhere I sent in my letter of resignation on June 2nd after nearly seven years as a director.

We talk upstairs in my workroom. I put to him, unequivocally, all the problems I foresee and ask if there is any way I can get out of doing the programme. Tony uses no moral blackmail, nor emotional entreaties either; he says that if we don't do it now we will never do it and, although there was theoretically time to find a replacement for me, he obviously doesn't want to. He is understanding of my problem and we end up going through the schedule cutting my time spent to its finest.

Sunday, May 8th: Cannes

Am met at Nice Côte d'Azur Airport by Duncan Clark, CIC's head of publicity. I feel in good shape and the Mediterranean sunshine only improves things. As we drive through the neat and tidy streets of the outskirts of Nice and on to the road to Cannes and Monaco, I begin to feel a distinct whiff of the Scott Fitzgeralds. Terry J arrived yesterday and has already taken all his clothes off and run into the sea for a TV crew.

Our car draws up outside the Carlton, where I'm staying. One or two confused photographers put their cameras up, but it's hardly a star arrival and I notice one of them still has the lens cap on.

Meet up with the others on the terrace at the Carlton at half past eight after a bath. Graham and John T, John G and the two Terrys and wives. With them is Henry Jaglom (whose *Sitting Ducks* I enjoyed so much), so we have time for a short exchange of compliments over a beer. His new film is being shown out of competition on Wednesday evening – the same time as *The Missionary*.

Monday, May 9th: Cannes

This is Python day at Cannes. We are officially announced – each one introduced – and our answers instantly translated into French. Neither the questions nor the instant translation process make for an easy exchange of information and certainly they don't help our jokes. One woman claims to have been physically ill during 'Creosote'.

I am asked about Sheffield and I end up telling the world's press that Sheffield girls have bigger breasts because they walk up a lot of hills.

Then we are taken up on to the roof and given a photo-grilling of Charles and Di-like proportions, with cameramen fighting each other to get dull pictures of us. I've never, ever been the subject of such concentrated Nikon-ic attention. It's all very silly and years ago we would all have been persuaded to be much more outrageous.

Then, suddenly, we're free. The Terrys, Graham and Eric go back to the hotel to prepare for the splendours of the Gala Presentation of '*MOL*' tonight, and me to return to England en route for Dublin. But as long as we are here we're good publicity fodder and, as GC and I walk along the Croisette, some keen young photographer asks earnestly that we come to be photographed with Jerry Hall – 'She's on the beach, just there . . . ' he pleads.

After Missionary *promotion in Dublin and Newcastle, I took a short film-writing break in Canonbie, north of Carlisle.*

Friday, May 13th: The Riverside Inn, Canonbie

Awake at eight. On the radio the news is all of pre-election sparring. Margaret Thatcher's transformation into Winston Churchill becomes increasingly evident as she singles out defence (i.e. wars and the Falklands) as the main issue of the election.

Down to the wondrous Riverside Inn breakfast. I'm offered a duck's egg. Very large and tasty and rather nice as I can see the duck that laid it from my window as I write. It's white. Called Persil, they tell me.

Short walk, then up to my room, with its disconcertingly sloping floor, to wrestle with the problems of a nymphomaniac drug addict accused of the ritual murder of a well-known Scottish footballer. The rain comes down gently and steadily, with sudden enormous surges – unlike my writing. I cannot reconcile myself to the 'Explorers' tale completely. There isn't enough that is new, original, different and exciting about the characters and I feel that the Polar icecap will look great for five minutes, then lose its grip on your average audience hungry for laughs.

Saturday, May 14th

TG comes round. He came back from Cannes last night. He now has his money for *Brazil* – a Universal deal for US, and Fox worldwide. Very pleased. Asks me if I'm available to play Jack Lint. I say no, of course not, but he knows I am.

Monday, May 16th

Tackle backlog of desk-work from last week. Talk to Mike Ewin who tells me that we are actually *up* by £120 in our eleventh week at the Classic H. He's also pleased with good, but not sensational, provincial figures thus far. 'The trade is pleasantly surprised,' as he puts it. And we have a second week at Weston-super-Mare, which he considers a considerable triumph!

Less good news from David Knopf, whom I phone in LA. The re-release of the '*Mish*' ran only three weeks in LA and has just opened at the Sutton in New York to little enthusiasm, leading him to rate the chances of a complete national re-issue unlikely.

And Python's '*MOL*' is fading. It did well in each area for about three weeks and that was that. It now looks as if it will take less in the US than *Brian* (nine million as against eleven).

Wednesday, May 18th

Feel rather dejected this morning. Even the news that Buckingham Palace has requested a 35 mill print of *The Missionary* to be taken aboard the Royal Yacht can't lift me from a very black gloom. Anger at everyone around, myself most of all. Feel frustrated by lack of time to write and not even sure if I want to write what I'm writing.

Watch Chas McKeown's prog on TV,[1] his first series for BBC TV. Some good jokes, nice lines, spoilt by heavy LE mugging. There ought to be something that you could put in the tea at the Beeb canteen to stop quite reasonable actors going at comedy like a bull at a gate.

Thursday, May 19th

John Goldstone phones at 8 a.m. to tell me that *Meaning of Life* has won second prize at Cannes – the Special Jury Prize.

Write up and type out my *Comic Roots* basic script. My writing time for the 'Explorers' first draft is now narrowed to six weeks, but I try hard not to think about this.

I collect the boys from the William Ellis swimming gala at Swiss Cottage. Tom has come second in two of his races and both he and

---

1 It was called *Pinkerton's Progress*. Set in a school, it was written by Charles and directed by Gareth Gwenlan.

William have been members of successful relay teams, so they're both in very good spirits.

Sunday, May 22nd

Read all the papers in the hope of some blinding revelation as to who to support at the election. Cannot stomach Thatcher and feel that her faceless, obedient Tebbits and Parkinsons are about to inherit the party. Labour is the only likely alternative, but they are hamstrung with doctrinaire stuff about quitting the EEC and abolishing the House of Lords and far too vulnerable to the boring constituency committee people and the intolerant, grumpy unions. I suppose I shall vote Labour in the hope of giving Thatcher as big a shock as possible.

Monday, May 23rd

I take a taxi down to Piccadilly – to the Royal Academy Dinner at Burlington House. The great mystery of the evening – which is why I was unable to turn down the invite – is why I am there. Who is my friend amongst the luminaries of the Royal Academy? After all, I haven't set foot in there for over a year.

Inside my coat is checked and I ascend the staircase between lofty marble pillars towards a circular chamber from which come the pleasant, rich strains of a small orchestra.

I am announced by a man in a scarlet jacket and received by Sir Hugh Casson, a diminutive, rather cheeky-looking man resembling a perky cockatoo. He is very charming, considering he doesn't know me from Adam, and he in turn introduces me to a pair of be-medalled, beaming buffers.

Then I am in amongst the central rooms of the Academy, offered what I think is champagne, but which turns out to be rather ordinary Spanish sparkling. I look at all the pictures – all ready for the Summer Exhibition – and I look at all the worthy academicians who are gathering and I suddenly think – suppose I meet no-one all evening who knows me.

I am sat next to a lady called Meg Buckenham. She has a direct, unaffected good nature which makes me glad of my luck. She made up even for the presence of Kasmin, the gallery owner, on my other side. Small, tanned and noisy. He regales everyone who will listen with stories of himself and seems very sure that he is the most desirable sexual object in the room.

Across from me is Ruskin Spear – a man who looks exactly like Father Christmas. He speaks in a deep, richly-textured, gravelly voice and seems to be gently mocking everything around him. He calls me 'Palin' in an amused schoolmasterly tone. 'I'm bored, Palin . . . ' he will suddenly say.

We have speeches from Princess Alexandra. Beautifully poised, regal and smiling winningly, but it doesn't make up for a terrible line in royally-delivered cliché. Sir Hugh Casson, sprite-like, is up and down between each speaker, jollying everyone along. It's his 73rd birthday and he's presented with a huge cake in the shape of the leaves of an opened book.

Lord Gowrie speaks for the government. He's in the Northern Ireland office. He has a thick head of hair and looks fashionably attractive in the Yves St Laurent mould, but again his looks belie his speech-making capabilities and he turns in a smooth, but vapid performance.

Sir Hugh is up again eagerly and he hands over to Lord Goodman, who replies to Sir Hugh's toast on behalf of the guests. I've never seen the notorious Lord Goodman in the flesh – only in *Private Eye* caricatures, where he is portrayed always as some vast lump topped with an elephant-like head. Although Goodman isn't quite as gargantuan as they make out, he is an extraordinary-looking creature and the prominent ears, with their dark, hairy inner recesses, are riveting. But he has the gift of the gab and scuttles through a quite unprepared speech very mellifluously. I warm to him. He is not malicious, nor cheap. He speaks intelligently and quite wittily.

Sir Hugh makes the final speech – one last attempt to butter us all up. Apparently I am present at 'one of the great banquets of the year'.

After all these toasts and some belligerent shouts of 'Rot! Absolute rot!' from Kasmin beside me, we are free to leave and mingle and take brandy from the trays carried through.

By this time several of the RA's are becoming tired and emotional and the limping figure of Ian Dury and the academician Peter Blake have joined our little group, and I'm being asked by Peter Blake to accompany him over to the Caprice for a 'nightcap'. Say farewell to Sir Hugh on the stairs. He gives Meg B a long hug. I feel like the errant young suitor in the presence of a father-in-law.

Across to the Caprice, walking slowly so Dury can keep up. He's very jokey and good value and keeps calling me Eric. At the Caprice a rather drunk young blond cruises round the tables and ends up in deep discussion with him. This is Jasper Conran. As usual on these occasions nobody really knows why anyone else is there, and it's very bad form to ask.

Sunday, May 29th

Helen packs in preparation for Newcastle trip with the children. Play snooker and try my hand at capitals of the world on the new BBC computer. I really can't wait for everyone to be gone, so I can set to work on 'Explorers' (I have a tantalisingly clear week ahead).

Another hour of halting progress brought to a rude conclusion by the appearance of TG. He's just back from working with Charles McKeown – the two of them are rewriting Tom Stoppard's script for *Brazil*. He's already setting up *Baron Munchausen* as his next film, in case *Brazil* really doesn't work! American majors have forked out 12 million dollars for rights to distribute – only thing they don't like about *Brazil* is the title.

Home to bed, in silent, empty house, by midnight.

Monday, May 30th

I make a clear start on opening scenes. But still the whole project seems arbitrary. My heart is just not in it. Staying here whilst the family is away to avoid distractions, I find myself waiting quite eagerly for distractions.

Tuesday, May 31st

Michael White's office ring – the Turf Club is still pursuing my membership and wants details of birthdate, place of education, interests. Think of lying and putting down 'horse-racing' (Alison D suggests 'horse-spotting', which I like), but settle for the dignified restraint of 'writing and travel'.

Monday, June 6th

With not very worthy feelings of guilt, reluctance and resentment, I acknowledge the fact that I could and probably should have spent more time on the '*MOL*' radio commercials which we're recording this morning.

Drive into town at 9.15, new Phil Everly tape blaring, roof open. André's just back from two weeks in California looking more successful every time I see him. JC arrives, GC doesn't.

John looks very hairy with beard and long black hair. He is in quite a skittish mood and wants to do lots of silly voices. He does an excellent Kierkegaard. He's just finished work on a book with his psychiatrist – 'Seven or eight weeks solid . . . I just haven't had a moment.' Fall to talking about autobiographies. John wants to call his '24 Hours From Normal'. And for a Python biog we both like the title 'Where's Graham?'

Friday, June 10th: Southwold

After breakfast accompany Ma into Southwold. 'This is my son Michael – you've probably seen him on the television.' And if that doesn't work, it's followed by the blatant – 'He's in Monty Python, you know . . . !'

Saturday, June 11th

Up at eight. Preoccupied with the NBC piece [for a new show called *The News Is The News*], and the problems of learning three and a half minutes of straight-to-camera material by half past ten. A very lordly Daimler arrives to collect me at ten. The driver wears thin and expensive-looking leather gloves.

By the time we reach Whitehall I have almost learnt the piece, though haven't been able to go right through without a fluff. The Queen is Trooping the Colour in the Mall and there are crowds everywhere. With the boldness of the blissfully ignorant, my Daimler turns into Downing Street at half past ten – third or fourth in a line of similar limousines, except that they all carry ambassadors or diplomats on their way to fawn to the recently re-elected Leaderene.

Of course I'm turned back, having been given no clearance by NBC, and my driver dumps me unceremoniously in busy Whitehall.

A guardsman on duty asks me to sign the inside of his peaked cap. ('It's all I've got,' he says apologetically.) A rather attractive lady PC grins at me.

Producer and cameraman appear.

We retire to the pub opposite to kill the half-hour before the No. 10 Press Officer arrives. At midday it's decided that valour is the better part of discretion and all three of us march up to the police barrier. The particular constable on duty this time recognises me as no threat to the

PM and we're in and walking up the narrow street – one of the most famous, if not *the* most famous, narrow streets in the world.

The camera is set up, alongside a permanent display of three or four video cameras and a group of pressmen drinking cans of Harp lager and not looking at all respectful of the hallowed ground they're on. Behind me the rather dull façade of No. 10. I notice all the net curtains are dirty.

With little fuss and bother we start shooting. After a while the press hacks stop talking to each other and come to listen (this in itself is very disconcerting). Some of them I can see falling about with laughter and this encourages me through to the end of an almost perfect take.

And not a moment too soon. A very senior PC looms up and looks very cross. The photographers seem delighted and snap away at him telling us off. We're asked to leave. As we do so, reporters cluster around asking if I'm the new Home Secretary, etc, etc.

Thursday, June 16th

Pick up Ray Cooper and he and I set off for a day at Henley.

George is waiting for us before the recently scrubbed walls of Friar Park. He wears a shaggy old sports jacket which he claims has been threaded through with dental floss.

Transfer from Ray's hired black Range Rover to George's black Porsche. George drives us to Marlow as if he is at Silverstone. We dine at The Compleat Angler. It's superbly sited beside the broad weir at Marlow, looking out over a view which is the very epitome of nature tamed.

George, as usual in such places, is extremely ill at ease to start with. He resents the 'posh' service and feels that, considering he can afford to buy the restaurant several times over, the staff are unnecessarily snotty. But he loosens up over a bottle of champagne. Some excellent smoked salmon, and trout, and a second bottle – this time of Aloxe Corton '69.

We laugh a lot and talk about films and not being able to write them. I think George thinks that I've come to see him to ask for money, and offers it eagerly and generously. But when he finds out that all I have to tell him is that I can't write a film by August he sympathises and loosens up. 'I've been trying to retire for half my life,' he mourns.

Back at Friar Park, George runs through whole scenes of *The Producers* word for word – acting the parts out extremely well. Olivia has some American girlfriends who have 'dropped in' whilst touring Europe. When they've gone, Ray opens some pink Dom Perignon, which is very rare and must have cost the earth, and we sit in the little kitchen and talk about Python and things in an easy, effortlessly friendly way.

George gives me a souvenir as I leave – a baton belonging to the Chief Constable of Liverpool, which GH took off him at the Liverpool premiere of *A Hard Day's Night*!

Saturday, June 18th

The general ease and pleasure of the day added to by the fact that we only have to walk ten yards or so for our dinner tonight. To the Brazilians who are renting No. 24. Elias, who is the husband, a psychoanalyst, cooks. He is an intellectual in the Continental sense of the word – critical, left-wing, multi-lingual, serious, a little intimidating. She is voluble, full of laughter, from a massively populous peasant family.

They are not a grumbling pair, but do criticise the English reserve – the long faces of neighbours.

He has come to study because the best of the German Jewish psychoanalysts came here before the war and it is, as a result, the best country in the world for the study of psychoanalysis. But the British immigration people are very difficult and always give him a hard time when he returns to the country. They're never violent, they never confront you with any direct accusations, he says, they just make you feel bad.

Tuesday, June 21st

Leave for Ealing at one [for *Comic Roots* filming]. The set, to represent No. 26 Whitworth Road [my birthplace in Sheffield], is at Tony Laryea's brother's house and looks quite effective.

At 2.15 Spike M arrives. As usual with him there is a brittle air of tension and unpredictability, but he and I sit down and natter for a half-hour about the Goons – the coining of words like 'sponned' [as in 'I been sponned!']. He raves about 'Eric Olthwaite'. I rave about Eccles.[1] By the time the second camera is up and ready to shoot he seems to have relaxed.

An aeroplane thunders low overhead as soon as we start. His answers to my questions about the Goons are almost identical to the answers I always give when asked about the Pythons – we did it to make ourselves

---

1 At one point in the interview I told Spike how I'd only seen Peter Sellers once. 'I passed him in the corridor at Wembley Studios.' To which Spike replied crisply, 'Very painful.'

laugh, to laugh at authority, we always had a love/hate relationship with the BBC, etc. Even the name 'The Goon Show' was their own and only reluctantly accepted by the BBC, who wanted 'The Crazy People Show'.

Then Spike has to leave and my mother arrives. She is very nervous, as one would expect of someone making their TV debut at the age of 79, but soon gets over it as we sit together on the couch and in the end she is utterly professional and quite unflapped. She tells her stories smoothly and says delightfully disarming things such as (of *The Meaning of Life*) '... Of course it's very rude ... but I like that.'

Friday, June 24th

Rush away at midday to Gerry Donovan to have the temporary dental bridge he put in four years ago checked. He reminds me that 'It usually comes out about this time of year.' Last year when I ate a call-sheet on the way back from '*Mish*' filming in Liverpool and the year before in some pleasant Cretan village as I tucked into freshly spit-roasted lamb. But this year, touch wood, it remains.

Monday, July 11th

Out in the evening to a screening of *Bullshot* at the Fox Theatre. George H is there and Ray and Norman Garwood and David Wimbury [the associate producer] and various others. Twenty or thirty in all. Find the first ten minutes very ordinary, and the overplayed style rather off-putting, but the film gradually wins me over, by its sheer panache and good nature.

George opts to drive with me from Soho Square to Knightsbridge, but when I can't find where I've left my car, I feel he wishes he hadn't. A bit like an animal caught in a searchlight is our George when out on the streets and I can see him getting a little twitchy as he and I – a Beatle and a Python – parade up and down before the diners on the pavements of Charlotte Street, looking for my car.

Of course no-one notices and eventually I get George into the Mini and across London. He gives me a breakdown of one or two of the Indian cults currently in this country – Rajneesh I should be especially careful about. No inner discipline required – just fuck as many people as you can. Sounds interesting.

Our Chinese meal gets quite boisterous owing to the presence of a dark, slightly tubby Jewish girl who does 'improv' at the Comic Strip. I find these American 'improv' people the most difficult of companions. Most of them are perfectly nice, decent, reasonable company until they start performing – which is about every ten minutes – and you are expected to join in some whacky improv.

But we outstay most other people in the restaurant and become very noisy and jolly and all drink out of one huge glass and muck around with the straws and end up on the quiet streets of Knightsbridge being appallingly loud at a quarter to one.

Thursday, July 14th

Have been offered the part of Mother Goose in the Shaw Theatre panto and also the lead in a new Howard Brenton play – rehearsing in August. Torn on this one, it sounds the sort of heavy, non-comedic role that might be quite exciting and unusual for me. But August is hols and September/October is writing with Terry J.

Spend the afternoon being photographed by Terry O'Neill for *TV Cable Week*. Terry is a Londoner with an insatiable curiosity about everything that's going on – the Test Match, jazz (when he finds out that Tom is learning the saxophone), films (he's directing his first picture in the autumn – *Duet for One* – Faye Dunaway, his wife, in the lead). Very much one of the lads – I can remember playing football with him ten years ago. He was a good winger. He's down-to-earth and unpretentious and probably keen to be the best at everything he does.

Photos everywhere – with railway, at desk and with family. All self-conscious to some degree, except Rachel, who loves being photographed!

Sunday, July 17th

At seven, after cooking baked beans and toast for the children's supper and leaving Thomas in charge again, we drive out to Olivia's party at Friar Park.

Arrive there about 8.25 and cannot make contact through the intercom on the locked gates, so we drive round to the back gate and press more buttons. A passing horsewoman suggests we try again – 'Probably got the music on rather loud,' she explains.

When we do gain admittance, there is a very restrained group of people standing politely sipping champagne, and listening to nothing louder than a harp, in a tent at the end of the lawn. Friar Park, pristine and floodlit, looks like the venue for a *son et lumière*, up on the rise behind us.

Joe Brown arrives. Calling everyone 'gal' or 'old gal', he proceeds to rave about 'Golden Gordon', repeating all the moments – but unlike Spike getting them word for word right. He has been able to get over here because the promoter of his concert was hit by a sock filled with billiard balls and is temporarily out of business.

The champagne flows liberally and people wander about the house. In his studio George demonstrates a machine which will make any sound into music electronically.

We meet Nelson Piquet, the Brazilian driver who came second at Silverstone yesterday, and John Watson is here too.[1] Piquet a little, perky, pleasantly ambitious Brazilian. He loves his work. No doubts, no fears, from what he says.

The evening cools and the setting is quite perfect. Derek [Taylor] tells me the code used to avoid mentioning drugs specifically. 'I've got all the Charles Aznavour albums to play tonight' means an evening of the naughtiest, most illicit substances, whilst a Charles Aznavour EP may just be some cocaine ...

And so, on this high note, we drive out of this dreamland, down the M4 back to reality.

Wednesday, July 20th: Southwold

Catch the train at Gospel Oak. Breakfast on the 8.30 from Liverpool Street. Mum collects me and drives me in her blue Metro back to Croft Cottage.

Have to do some PR with her new neighbours. At one point he takes my arm and leads me to one side ... He apologises, hopes he's not speaking 'out of turn', but my mother is ... 'well ... no longer a young woman', so have I 'any contingency plans'?

---

1 Piquet was the Formula One champion that year, as he was in 1981 and 1987. John Watson, from Northern Ireland, had won the British Grand Prix in 1981.

Thursday, July 21st: Southwold

A restorative nine-hour sleep. Outside the best of English summer days –
a clear sunlight sharply delineating the trees and cornfields. Sparrows
already at dustbaths in the garden below.

Sort out some of Daddy's old papers – finally commit to the Lothing-
land Sanitary Department many of the school bills, school insurance
bills, etc, which he had painstakingly kept. Learn from the family record
that my grandfather – a Norfolk doctor – was also a very keen photographer and had exhibited in London. He was a gardener of repute
and a Freemason. He and his wife sound a fiercely competent couple.
Founding the local Red Cross, etc.

Home for lateish ham supper. Helen tells me about her BUPA medical
screening today and of the dashing doctor Ballantine who picked her leg
up and waggled it about!

The evening almost spent (and both of us weary) when Alan Bennett
rings and, with much umming and aahing, asks if I would like to read a
part in a new screenplay he's written. It's about a chiropodist, he says . . .
oh, and pigs as well. Of course I fall eagerly on the chance and a neat man
called Malcolm Mowbray – fashionably turned out – brings the script
around.

Read it there and then – such is my curiosity. Slightly disappointed
that the part of Gilbert Chilvers is not a) bigger, b) more difficult or
different from things I've done. But he does have his moments and it's a
very funny and well-observed period piece (set in 1947).

Decide to sleep on it.

Saturday, July 23rd

To the seven o'clock performance of *King of Comedy* at the Screen on the
Hill. Very enjoyable – one of the less dark of Scorsese's modern parables,
with much wit and many laughs and another extraordinary and skilful
and concentrated and successful performance by De Niro. Jerry Lewis
(one of my childhood heroes) excellent too.

Come home and, over a cold plateful and glasses of wine, think about
the Bennett play. Decide that it is not a difficult or special enough part to
drop either my writing with TJ, Belfast Festival commitments or semi-
commitment to TG. Ring Alan in Yorkshire, but cannot get him.

Sunday, July 24th

Up to Abbotsley – driving through heavy, but very localised storms and arriving in time for a tennis knock-up before lunch. The air is heavy and damp and the sunshine breaks through only occasionally.

Hang the hammock and play more tennis – pursuits that mark the summer and for which I have literally had no time for two years. A lovely afternoon.

Alan Bennett is up in North Yorkshire and he says the lights have all just gone out. I tell him of my liking for the *Private Function* script, but of my problem with commitments until the end of the year. 'Oh, it won't be till May at least,' counters Alan. 'That's the earliest Maggie's available.' [He wants Maggie Smith to play my wife.] So there seems no point in saying I've decided over the weekend not to do it.

Sunday, August 7th

Rave preview by Jennifer Selway of the *Observer* for Friday's *Comic Roots* – Michael Palin's 'brilliant' half-hour. I can't remember this adjective ever being applied to my work *before* it's been seen – only on rare occasions many years after when affection has distorted the memory.

Sunday dinner together – watch a Scottish/Canadian writer [Robertson Davies] on the excellent series *Writers and Places*. Feel a great appetite for all things written and described. Maybe it's the relaxing break of ten days in France which has finally cleared my immediate work problems away and let other aspects of life come to the front of my mind and imagination.

Thursday, August 11th

Tom and his friend Paul Forbes leave at seven to cycle to Brighton. Helen says she can't help being worried about them.

Drop the Mini at the garage to be serviced, then Helen drops me at Alan Bennett's house on the corner of Gloucester Crescent. A camper van with what looks like carpet covering it is parked in front of the front door. Alan opens it – a little hesitant, a touch of awkwardness and an instant warmth as he shows me in to the crepuscular gloom of a sitting room which seems to have been very carefully protected against daylight. Mark Shivas and Malcolm Mowbray are on a couch against the far wall. Alan offers me a comfortable old chair and disappears to make coffee.

I long to have a good look round, but am aware of Shivas and Mowbray wanting to talk and set us all at ease. My overriding impression of the place is of elegant dusty clutter – rather like the set for Aubrey's *Brief Lives*.

Alan reappears. We talk politely of France ... holidays ... then Shivas asks me about my availability. Well, I can't go back on what I'd said to Alan ... I *do* like the piece and well ... they are all watching me ... yes, I'd love to do it.

From then on we discuss finance generally and I realise that Shivas wants someone to bankroll the entire project and so far has no definite bites. In answer to his questions about HandMade I cannot but recommend he try them – though it somewhat complicates my position, as the Bennett film will be taking away time from my own project for HandMade.

After an hour there doesn't seem much more to say. Slight feeling of reserve, which does not emanate from Alan, but more likely from Shivas. I suddenly miss Richard. Everything's a little too polite and circumspect. Walk home.

Tom rings from Brighton at 11.30. He got there in four hours. They're coming back by train.

Spend the rest of the morning writing my obit tribute to Luis Buñuel for *Rolling Stone*.

Saturday, August 13th

In the *Telegraph*, a *Comic Roots* review under the nice heading 'Chortling beamish boy', I learn 'there is something roundly Victorian about Michael Palin's face, a durable cheerfulness not to be found among other members of Monty Python's Flying Circus ... alone of the Python team he can deflate cant without venom', but cautions 'John Cleese's angry logic is missing from his humour'.

At five o'clock Felice[1] and Richard cycle up here. RL has a film to direct now, and is into top gear, with that bristling, bubbling, provocative self-confidence which he adopts to paper over the doubts beneath.

---

1 Felice Fallon, an American writer, became Richard Loncraine's second wife in September 1985.

Sunday, August 14th

To Angela and Veryan's 'Jubilation Party' at Chilton. It's to celebrate, or mark the occasion of, Angela's 50th birthday, V & A's 25th wedding anniversary, Jeremy's 22nd and his top 2nd in Politics at York. It's all been organised by the family as the caterers went bust a week ago.

So we are parked in a field by Marcus and a nice, bright-eyed girlfriend of Camilla's from Oxford, with whom she is going to Mexico and the Yucatán this holiday. I'm green with envy.

As the early cloud clears a perfect day develops. Not unpleasantly hot, but hot enough to make the ample shade from the big copper beech and lime trees on the lawn seem very welcome.

The moat is filled, now the bridge has been repaired, and is covered in a solid green veneer of duck-weed. New-born ducks skid around as on the surface of a billiard table.

Lots of Herbert relatives, and the slightly disturbing presence of Sir Dingle Foot's widow, Lady Dorothy. She used to be engaged to Daddy, and he called it off when she wouldn't agree to drop her political affiliations with the Liberals. Now I feel she regards Angela and me as the children she never had. 'Can't go too near people – I fall over so easily,' she warns. She invites Helen and me to one of her parties ... 'I do enjoy a good party.'

Angela in a '50's-looking dress which could have been one of the earliest she wore. And that's meant as a compliment. Can she really be 50?

Monday, August 22nd: Glasgow

To the ABC cinema complex at Sauchiehall Street. Met by the manager – neat moustachioed war veteran with Royal Signals tie. Up to one of their many 'lounges' where a 'spread' is laid out for the hungry and thirsty press at present sitting watching my film.

So I move into fifth gear and smile a lot and am completely helpful and co-operative and remember names and show a polite and hopefully completely straight face, even when a little old lady from the *Jewish Echo* asks me why I called the film *The Missionary*. Actually it is not as daft a question as it sounds, her point being that the title might put people off, which is something I've heard before, and which troubles me because I'm sure it's true.

Then en-taxi to the Woodside Health Centre, where it has been arranged for me to have the second part of a typhoid vaccination. The Health Centre is set amongst a jumble of modern blocks of flats, which have largely replaced the solidly stone-built red sandstone tenements which look rather good wherever they've been renovated.

The doctor writes on my form '*The* Michael Palin', and sends me off to the Treatment Room. Can't help reflecting on the glamour of showbiz as I sit in this little roomful of the ill amongst modern tower blocks with litter blowing all around. Eventually I'm seen by a stout, warm, friendly nurse and jabbed.

Tuesday, August 23rd: Edinburgh

At breakfast in the rather appealingly dilapidated, unmodernised, Scots-Gothic country house that is the Braid Hills, the ceiling starts to leak and champagne buckets and washing-up bowls are requisitioned with great good humour by the staff.

At midday I take a taxi to the Dominion Theatre, where *The Missionary* will open on Tuesday. It's an independent cinema in the smart Morningside area of the city, run by the genial Derek Cameron with an attentiveness which befits one whose father built the place (in 1938). The bar and restaurant are run and designed as places to linger and they have a busy clientele of all ages, who come here, some of them, just to eat and meet.

Local Hero is in its 17th week and *Gregory's Girl* for a third year. Bill Forsyth's favourite cinema? I ask Derek C. Oh yes, he says, when he comes here he just raises his hands to heaven ...

I cannot think of a pleasanter place for *The Missionary* to have its Scottish premiere.

Saturday, September 3rd

After breakfast TG drops in. I haven't even finished reading his *Brazil* and was hoping I'd have this morning to complete it, so can't give any very knowledgeable criticisms. But I like the part of Jack Lint and TG says he has kept it away from De Niro – just for me! So it's agreed that I'll do it. Filming probably some time in December.

Later in the morning Terry takes me up to the Old Hall in Highgate – his new £300,000 acquisition. Horrible things have been done to it inside, but its garden bordering on Highgate cemetery and the panorama of

London from its plentiful windows are almost priceless. Of course it's enormous and rambling, but still just a town house, not a country manor. And TG needs the challenge of the space like a drug. I find the damp old smell of the wretched conversions make the house depressing, but TG says it has quite the opposite effect on him because he knows what he can do with it.

Read *Water*, the latest DO'B project from Dick Clement and Ian La Frenais, who are his latest blue-eyed boys. DO'B would like me to play the part of Baxter. First 16 pages are wonderfully funny, but it all falls apart and there isn't a laugh after that. No characters are developed, new characters are thrust in instead and the jokes become stretched and laboured.

Sunday, September 4th

Dick Clement rings re *Water*. I'm honest about my feelings and, indeed, it's refreshing to talk to someone like Dick who is intelligent and tactful and is, after all, a TV writer with an impressive record – *Likely Lads*, etc. We can understand each other's language. He professes his liking for naturalistic comedy, and yet sees *Water* as an international film. I tell him that I think 'international' comedy a very dangerous concept.

I find Dick's choice of Billy Connolly to play the black revolutionary a real commercial cop-out ... 'Well, he'll be sort of brown,' Dick reassures.

Monday, September 5th

Hear to my great disappointment that the '*Mish*' has not opened well in Scotland. And despite my great welcome by Derek Cameron at the Dominion, and his great hopes for the picture, I hear from Mike Ewin that he's pulling it off after three weeks to put in *Tootsie* – again.

Python, on the other hand, had its best provincial figures anywhere in the UK at Edinburgh. Nearly £10,000 taken in the first week of the Festival. And '*MOL*' continues strong in the West End, where it's out-performed *Superman III* easily.

Tuesday, September 6th

Today Tom and William start the new school year. This is for Tom the start of serious work – the run-up to 'O' Levels.

Helen says Tom is just like her at school, scatty, easily distracted and not really happy being taught maths and French and things. But neither of us should draw too much satisfaction from seeing neat parallels between our children's efforts and our own. They are not us, after all, they're them.

I go on down to TJ's and we read each other our starts. Both quite respectable, both start in space. Jim Henson rings, anxious for TJ to commit to directing a piece called 'Labyrinth'.

Tuesday, September 20th

I am tempted by a phone call from Ray Cooper to attend the first of a two-night concert in aid of Multiple Sclerosis, in which many great rock stars of the '60's, all friends of Ronnie Lane who has MS, will be appearing, including Ray C.

As if starved of live performance for so long, Ray tucks into the opportunity with gusto. I've never seen him live before, only heard the legendary tales. And he is a revelation. Impeccable timing and precise movements combined with a sense of high theatrical style which just avoids being camp or purely exhibitionist, is wondrous to behold.

But even Ray is upstaged by the extraordinary appearance of Jimmy Page, who weaves his way around the stage like a man who has been frozen in the last stages of drunkenness, before actually falling over. He sways, reels, totters, bends, but still manages to play superbly. The others look on anxiously and Ray tells me at the end that Page isn't well . . . 'And he lives in Aleister Crowley's house.'

But the coup of the evening is the appearance of Ronnie Lane himself. Led, painfully slowly, onto the stage by Ray (who is everywhere) and Harvey Goldsmith, he is strong enough to sing two numbers. Very moving.

And Ray, going at his gong like the demented anti-hero of some nineteenth-century Russian drama, hits it so hard that it breaks and falls clean out of its frame.

Thursday, September 22nd

Another good morning's work on 'The Man Who Was Loved'.[1] Really

---

1 Like a number of other film-writing ideas around this time, this was a Jones/Palin screenplay that remained on the drawing board.

solid writing, not stop and start stuff, and few interruptions. Let letters pile up and just get on with it.

Terry comes up at two and we have a read-through. He has opened out the Viking saga (with a good song) and he likes what I've done on the modern, slightly more serious story. It does look as though we could have two films! Some discussion, then we swap scripts again and work on until after five o'clock. A good and productive working day – like old times.

Then TJ goes off to sign copies of *Erik the Viking* at the Royal Festival Hall and Helen and I go down to the Methuen Authors Party at Apothecaries Hall in Blackfriars.

As we go in, Frank Muir is on the way out. Some hail and farewell chat. I remember *The Complete and Utter Histories* – and his courage in putting them on. He remembers our piece about the waves of invaders in ninth- and tenth-century England being controlled by a man with a megaphone.

Only later in the evening do I find out that Frank's latest book for Methuen is called *The Complete and Utter My Word Collection*!

David Nobbs is anxious that I should read his latest novel because it's set in Sheffield. I'm afraid it's on a pile with dozens of things people have sent me to read. Even just acknowledging that they've sent them cuts my reading time down to about a book a month at the moment. This is another area of my life I must sort out.

Friday, September 23rd

Alison rings with the latest offers. BBC Bristol are doing a heritage series about Britain – would I write the one on transport? *Omnibus* want me on a programme about taste. Yet another video magazine seems to have begun, just to annoy me. Interview about *Missionary* and *Ripping Yarns*? And at last, at the grand old age of 40, the first offer to play Hamlet – at the Crucible, Sheffield.

In the evening we go down to Terry's for a meal with Ron Devillier. TJ cooks marvellous Soupe Bonne Femme, herring and roast pork, with lots of salads and bits and pieces.

TJ plays his accordion and the dog, Mitch, sings. However, Mitch will shut up instantly if anyone laughs.

Wednesday, September 28th

I read perceptive E M Forster remarks about his own fame. He says it made him idle. People were just happy for him to be who he was – to be what he had done, and there was no need for him to sully an already impeccable reputation by doing anything new.

To Shaftesbury Avenue to see *Yellowbeard*. On the plus side are likeable performances from Eric and Nigel Planer and Marty and Peter Boyle and a neat, classy cameo from Cleese, good costumes and some fine Caribbean scenery and excellent music. Against this a very disjointed piece of direction – no-one seems to know what they are doing or why – some dreadful hamming by the likes of James Mason and Cheech and Chong[1] which kills the few good lines stone dead.

Thursday, September 29th

Nancy L rings and after weeks of dithering I say yes to the *Saturday Night Live* date for January 21st. I don't really want to do the show again, but it does make a good focal point for my mother's trip to America.

Monday, October 3rd

Am offered the lead in 'Cinders' at the Fortune Theatre when Denis Lawson leaves in January. Turn it down on grounds of incompetence – I can't sing very well and certainly can't dance.

At 12.30 Helen and I leave for Kew Gardens, to attend a launching party for Bill Stotesbury's Tarot-designed book on structural engineering. Turns out to be a marvellous relief from the traditional wine and gossip launches. For a start we go by train, round the backs of North London. Pleasant walk to the gardens at Kew, except for the deafening noise of incoming aircraft – which means all conversations have to have Nixonian gaps in them. Helen insists on filling my pockets with conkers.

We are shown coffee and bananas (which used to be sent straight to the Queen, but aren't any longer) and a palm dating from 1775 and propped up like John Silver on long steel crutches. And trees that are now extinct, called cycads, which dinosaurs used to feed on.

---

1 Richard 'Cheech' Marin and Tommy Chong were an American stand-up comedy duo. Their material drew on hippies, free-love and the drug culture generally.

Tuesday, October 4th

A very dull day. I sit in front of the Viking saga all morning with hardly more than a page filled. The trouble is not that I can't think of anything to write, but that I can't think of anything *new* to write. The historical setting with the contemporary characters has been so well explored in *Grail* and *Brian*, and when I start to write on with TJ's adventures in boats I'm into *Time Bandits* territory. The law of diminishing returns.

Wednesday, October 5th

Into black-tie for the BFI 50th Anniversary Banquet at the Guildhall. Find I'm the only Python invited – though, among the 700 guests there are many whose contribution to British films is far less obvious than TJ or TG or any of the rest of the team.

As at the Royal Academy Banquet, I am next to a lady who is excellent company – in this case Christine Oestreicher, who made a short called *A Shocking Accident*. She is funny and quite good to have a giggle with at all the pomp and circumstance around.

'Trust you to have a girl next to you,' says John Howard Davies.[1] He is rather cross, having read somewhere that there were to be no more *Ripping Yarns* because the BBC couldn't afford them. I say I thought it was the main reason and he rather curtly agrees with me, but mumbles about there being others.

There are speeches and presentations of gold medals to Marcel Carné, Orson Welles, Powell and Pressburger[2] and David Lean.

Prince Charles makes a neat, effortless speech. Surveying the gathering he says it resembled an extraordinary general meeting of Equity. Harold Wilson has to go to the lavatory during the royal speech. Orson Welles re-tells stories about John Gielgud and gets massive applause, then we all 'retire to the library' for drinks.

Barry Took is very agitated about *The Meaning of Life*. He hated it, his

1 John, a child actor who played the lead in David Lean's 1948 film of Oliver Twist, directed many top BBC shows including the first series of *Fawlty Towers* and the first four shows of *Monty Python's Flying Circus*. He was Head of Comedy at the BBC in the late 1970's, when the last of the *Ripping Yarns* were made.
2 Michael Powell and Emeric Pressburger produced, wrote and directed some of the most stylish and inventive British films, including *A Matter of Life and Death* (1946) and *Red Shoes* (1948).

daughter hated it – 'she even preferred *Yellowbeard*' – and 'the daughter of one of the richest men in Hong Kong hated it'. His attack is rambling but persistent. He won't leave the thing alone. Badly shot, disgustingly unfunny – back to 'the urine-drinking' aspect of Python, he thundered. All in all, from an old friend, a strange and manic performance. But then Barry is strange, and there are more chips on his shoulder than you'd find on a Saturday night at Harry Ramsden's.

Sir Dickie Att and Tony Smith are working overtime, shovelling celebrities in front of Prince Charles, who is still here, wandering around. As I am telling Ray of the vehemence of Barry T's outburst, Prince Charles catches my eye. A moment later he steps across to me . . .

'I loved your film,' are the first words of the heir to the throne to me. Not a bad start. He was speaking of *The Missionary* . . . he loved the locations, especially Longleat. I ask him where he saw the film – 'Balmoral,' he admits, lowering his voice. Princess Margaret had recommended it, evidently.

Attenborough is a little concerned that the Prince's unscheduled chat with me is going on rather a long time. He begins to move him away. The Prince calls to me . . . 'I hope you'll make another one.' 'Yes, I will . . . if you've got any ideas.' At this the Prince returns . . . 'As a matter of fact I have got an idea.' Attenborough's face, already red with effort, goes puce and his eyes dart from side to side.

So Prince Charles tells me his idea, which is from a press cutting he'd seen about a home on the South Coast for people suffering from phobias. Every sort of phobia was catered for. He says he told Spike Milligan and he loved the idea. 'I'll write it and you can be in it,' is my parting shot. To which he responds well. A nice man, and easy to talk to.

I go to say goodbye to Sir Dickie, as most people seem to be drifting away, and he clutches my arm emotionally – 'Have you seen Orson?' I haven't seen Orson. 'You must see Orson . . .'. He finds a lackey . . . 'Take him to see Orson.' I'm not really desperate, but Sir Dickie insists. 'He's in a little room, outside on the left.'

And sure enough the Great Man (in every sense of the word) is sitting at a table in this very small, plain side-room, which looks like an interview room in a police station.

Orson comes to the end of a story, at which the adoring group of four or five young and glamorous guests laugh keenly. Then I am brought forward. 'Michael Palin from the Monty Python team.' Orson rises, massively, like the sun in India, and grasps my hand. He is clearly confused, but smiles politely. His head is very beautiful and he has a fine, full head of hair. I congratulate him on his speech.

His eyes flick to one side as another visitor is ushered into his presence, one of the Samuelsons,[1] who is telling Orson of the wonderful collection of film memorabilia he has. Orson is responding with polite interest again.

Sunday, October 9th

Take the Levinsons, who are staying with us, to the zoo. I enjoy the visit, especially seeing the delight in Gwenola's (21-month-old) eyes as she watches the prowling tigers and calls out 'Charlie!' – the name of the cat next door in Sag Harbor.

From the zoo down to Covent Garden. Take them into St Paul's – the actors' church. There on the wall of the church is an elegantly simple plaque to Noël Coward – and this the day after I read in his diaries his version of the Bible story – 'A monumental balls-up.'

We watch *Comic Roots*. Then, over Calvados, talk about the state of the world – and the soggy, comfortable, stifling affluence of the late '70's and '80's, as a contrast from the '60's, when it was exciting to write and new things *were* being said. Tell Al that I no longer feel the burning urge to write another film. I want to go to Rangoon.

Friday, October 14th

Ring Anne and express my total lack of interest in a proposal from a BBC producer to do a series called 'Monty's Boys'. Documentaries all about 'the greatest comedy group ... etc, etc ...' We really must avoid being embalmed by the media. If the BBC think we are so wonderful, marvellous, legendary, etc, why did they only repeat 13 shows in nine years?

To a fitting for *Brazil* at Morris Angel's with Jim Acheson and Gilly Hebden. Jim a bit jolly after a lunch with Robert De Niro who has agreed to do the part of Tuttle. Feel quite tangible sensation of excitement and pride at the prospect of sharing the billing with such a hero of mine. Jim says that all the talk of *Brazil* being awash with money is quite misleading. Says he hasn't much more than for *Bullshot*.

1 Sydney (later Sir Sydney) Samuelson started one of the most successful film service companies in the UK. He also was one of the leading lights behind the founding of BAFTA.

Saturday, October 15th

Tom off to play rugby at Edgware. A wild day outside – the barograph plummets and as I write up in my room there are gale-force gusts which threaten to take the whole room away. And it pours. A great day to be at the work desk, but I have to leave at 12.30 to have lunch with Denis and Ray.

We talk of the 'Pig' film, as DO'B calls the Alan Bennett piece. I feel DO'B is unhappy about the Bennett/Mowbray/Shivas group. He senses that there could be another *Privates on Parade*, whose demise he now largely ascribes to arrogance on the part of Simon Relph [the producer] and Blakemore. Again I mistrust DO'B's view of history – surely he wasn't forced into doing *Privates*, it was his scheme. Also I sense that DO'B doesn't have a great sympathy for what I really like in the script – the sense of location, period detail and atmosphere.

Home and begin reading TG's latest *Brazil* script. Nod off. TG drops by. My fee demand is the big talking point. It came as quite a shock to them.

Monday, October 17th: Southwold

DO'B calls. He has had a very good meeting with Mark Shivas and is all set to go ahead in April on the 'Pig' film!

Thursday, October 20th

Anne J rings to report *Brazil*'s 'final' offer in reply to my/her request for £85,000 for my services. They've offered £33,000 and reduced the time by a day. Anne is not at all pleased. I abhor such negotiations. It's all silly money, but I find their attitude typical. Lots of bragging about the money available, then suddenly a complete tightening of the belt as reality strikes. And in a film like *Brazil* the priority is clearly being given to the sets, props and special effects. But we play the game a little – if only to establish our resentment at the treatment. So for today I'm not doing it for a penny less than £50,000!

After dinner Anne rings with the result of the day's progress on *Brazil*. They have not shifted on the £33,000, but have agreed to a percentage.

Saturday, October 22nd

To Belfast. The British Airways shuttle has improved its service no end, as a result of serious competition from British Midland, and the flight, though full, is on time and well run.

Past the roadblocks, but apart from a couple of green flak-jacketed UDR men patrolling, no overt signs of the troubles. Lunch at BBC Broadcasting House. Double security on the doors.

On the programme with me is a Belfast boxer called Barry McGuigan. He's fighting for the European middle-weight title in four weeks' time and goes to Bangor Sands to train. No sex for four weeks, he tells me. He's a completely unaffected, straightforward man. He pronounces 'guy' as 'gay', which makes for interesting complications, and refers to God as 'the Big Man'.

He and I face a panel of Belfast teenagers, some of whom look quite terrifying with either Mohican hairstyles or completely shaved heads. But the questions come easily. The best one they ask me is 'Now you've made all this money, do you still want to make people laugh?' The questioner perhaps doesn't realise what a raw nerve he's touched.

Wednesday, October 26th

To the Turf Club at lunchtime. Peter Chandler introduces me to Jimmy and Brian the barman and Edward on the door. Have a glass of champagne in the snooker room and a toasted sandwich. Rather like being back at Oxford – notice-boards and people older than me calling me 'sir'. Ask Chandler about the horse-racing connections.

The club has many owners and trainers, but, he continues without a trace of unpleasantness, 'isn't open to jockeys'.

After supper go to see a Michael Powell film, *The Small Back Room*. A war story, set in spring 1943, full of psychological insights, shadows and claustrophobia, as well as much comedy and a bomb disposal thriller ending. The theatre is disappointingly empty, but three rows in front of me are Harold Pinter and Lady Antonia.

Thursday, October 27th

At 6.30 I go to Rail House at Euston to the launch of a book on Britain's railway heritage.

Cornered by two reps from Michael Joseph. Talk turns to the US invasion of Grenada. One of them feels we shouldn't let ourselves be pushed around all the time.

I get rather irritated with his mindless jingoism and say quite bluntly that I thought us wrong to go to war over the Falklands. He reels backwards with a strangled cry and our relationship isn't the same afterwards.

Monday, October 31st

Cleese rings. Brief tirade against *Private Eye*, who call him Sir Jonathan Lymeswold – he thinks that Ingrams is motivated largely by envy, in that he wanted to be an actor at one time. Ask JC how his time off to read books is going. Nothing has changed. JC isn't reading books all day long but deeply involved as ever with Video Arts – which swells with success daily, engulfing John's free time like a great unstoppable creature. But I ask him to lunch at the Turf next week – a chat for old times' sake – and he's pleased about that.

Wednesday, November 2nd

My writing progress reflects the weather conditions. Dull and Soggy. But as I run at lunchtime an idea breaks through the mists.

The Heath is eerily atmospheric. Closed in, the mist adding a touch of menace, making the front of Kenwood look shadowy and insubstantial. The solution to the predicament of the businessman who is lost on his way to work is that he has died. He is in Hell. Hell as the basis for the film – very strong. A clear image and one which you could describe in one sentence, but not one which in any way restricts our flights of fancy.

Ring TJ when I get back. He's enthusiastic. I feel wonderfully encouraged by this breakthrough and the more I think about it, the more levels it can work on. But no time to pursue it now, as I have to do domestic business such as buying fireworks for Saturday's party.

Then in the evening meet Michael Barnes for a chat. We meet at the Turf, but aren't able to eat there as there is some stag night. Hoyle, the night porter, is very nice to us as we are ejected ... 'We *do* have an arrangement with the Institute of Directors, sir, I'm sure they'd be pleased to see you.' I wish I had his confidence.

Friday, November 4th

Nick Lander of L'Escargot confirms that he will do my Ma's 80th birthday party lunch – even though it means opening the restaurant specially.

Have cleared a number of calls, etc, by eleven and start to elaborate on the 'Hell' idea. Become very bogged down. It could go in so many directions – can't decide which, so write very little.

Ma rings, because she's just seen the news and wanted cheering up after seeing the bucket in which Dennis Nilsen boiled boys' heads.

Monday, November 7th

To Crimpers in Hampstead for my *Brazil* hair cut – a strange-looking affair which makes me look like Alexander Walker.

Out into milky afternoon sunshine and near 60's temperatures, feeling conspicuous in my new head, to Alan Bennett's for a chat with him and Mowbray over 'The Pig Film'. They haven't a final [Pork Royale was still in the running] title yet. Make some suggestions about seeing Gilbert and Joyce arrive at the town at the beginning and one or two other comments which Alan writes down. My strongest crit with a much-improved script is the way Gilbert fades away at the end.

As we leave I notice that there is someone living in the Dormobile parked tight in his front garden. 'She's watching television,' whispers Alan ... 'She?' 'Oh ... I'll tell you all about it next time,' he promises ... And I leave Malcolm, Alan and the old lady watching TV in his garden.

Thursday, November 10th

Lie in bed casting anxious thoughts about *Brazil* out of my mind. Like seeing James Fox on TV last night and realising what a finely-controlled actor he is. Why wasn't he Jack Lint? Like worrying that I should be worrying so much about something I know I can do.

At nine o'clock Jonathan [Pryce] and Terry G arrive for our read-through. Jonathan is low-key, halting and rather unconfident about the lines. Old actors' ploy – on the day he will be firing on all cylinders and I shall have to work hard to stay on the screen. Terry G would like me to smoke a pipe. I ask him to get me one, so I can practise in Ireland.

At twelve we go our separate ways – Jonathan to Hampstead to have yet more hair off, and me to lunch with John C at Duke's Hotel.

JC is delighted with Duke's and views with amused admiration this 'new side' of my life – as he calls my recently-developed St James's/Turf Club axis. We have an effortlessly pleasant wander around various subjects near and dear to our hearts.

JC shows off with a few names of the more esoteric Spanish painters. Professes an enjoyment of art galleries and a desire to go on a journey with me somewhere.

We both enjoy our lunch so much we decide to make it a regular feature. Or this is the last shouted intention as we part company in the still warm, but declining November sunshine in St James's.

Saturday, November 12th

Help Helen prepare a meal for Elias and Elizabeth – the Brazilian psychiatrists from next door. Helen makes a wonderful meal – tomato and tarragon soup, followed by gravadlax and chicken in a creamy sauce, apple pie, cheeses – Beaume de Venise.

Elias gives me a short, revealing history lesson about Brazil. A totally exploited country (by Britain and Portugal) until the late nineteenth century. Books forbidden there until 1832. No university until 1932. Didn't realise that Brazil's independent history was so short.

Elizabeth is great fun, but both are hopeless Francophiles – France is beyond criticism as far as they're concerned. To go to France or Italy, they say, after England is to go into the outside world! They think the English press are the worst in the world when it comes to analysis of foreign news.

I returned to Belfast for a second stint at the Festival. This time my one-man show was more ambitious and played for four nights at the Arts Theatre. With my debut in Brazil *imminent, it probably wasn't the wisest thing to have done.*

Sunday, November 20th: Belfast–London

A very cultured shuttle flight back, with musicians, singers and actors all anxious to be on the first plane to Heathrow. I sit next to Lizzie Spender, a publicist and part-time actress who's well connected. She is to play my wife in *Brazil* and we meet quite by coincidence.

Home by a quarter to one. Feel a desperate need for air and space before *Brazil* envelops me, so I take a Sunday run (usually something

I avoid as the Heath gets busy). Feel well-stretched, but cannot run easily as have pulled a muscle in my side in last night's record-breaking round the auditorium bid. (10.07 seconds!)

Set off, with Terry G, to Wembley for a run-through on the set of our Big Scene tomorrow. The studio is bitterly cold inside, but the set's very exciting. Jonathan arrives. I always feel he is rather taut – as though something inside is finely tuned, wound up with precision to be released at just the right moments – when he's acting.

We work through the scene and I try the various props such as electronic temple-massagers – American barbershops, 1950's. We're there for about three hours, then gratefully home again for a Sunday dinner – only the second meal I've had at home in ten days.

Monday, November 21st

On the set there is the well-behaved unfamiliarity of the first day on a new picture – and a big new picture, scheduled for 25 weeks. But there are many *Missionary* faces, and my progress to the set is constantly interrupted with handshakes and reintroductions. I feel it must be making Jonathan rather fed up. It helps me, though, and the early part of the day is as agreeable and jolly filming as I can remember. TG on good form, and the camera and sound crew are excellent company.

But the character of Jack Lint is still vague in my mind and after lunch, when I'm into the three or four fast speeches of jargon, I fluff more than once.

I realise that I should have spent much more care and thought in preparing for the part – thinking more about the character, spending more time with Jonathan and more time learning difficult lines, and not going to bed so late in Belfast. But we get through it, and I'm not sure how the effect of my uneasiness will show. At the end of the day TG says he has never seen me as nervous before.

Tuesday, November 22nd

Collected at 7.15. A very cold, crisp morning. Ice on the car windows.

We start shooting in Jack's office a couple of hours later. Take the scene through to the end on my close-ups. Then we work back through it on Jonathan. We have completed the scene – eight pages of close-packed dialogue – by four o'clock.

By then the race is on to complete two other short scenes, scheduled for the day before. One involves me packing a case, fitting my bullet-proof vest, taking my jacket and leaving the office whilst talking rapidly to Jonathan. Two or three times I come completely unstuck on the lines – 'sabotaged adjacent central service systems, as a matter of fact in your block'. We complete the scene, but it's a jolt to my pride and confidence that I was not more in control.

Home to prepare supper for the children, as Helen is in UCH Private Patients' Wing, having the growth on the end of her finger removed under general anaesthetic. I have a day off tomorrow and can look forward, at last, to a night's sleep without anxiety about filming.

Friday, November 25th

I suppose I should have smelt a rat when my call was set for ten. Far too generous a call for anyone who is going to be used during the day. But I take some work in.

In between whiles walk up to the set, which is dominated by a massive 30-foot-high piece of totalitarian architecture. The lobby of the Ministry of Information. Very impressive and rich in bits of comic detail. Nuns looking with approval at little displays of military weapons.

TG has hit upon a very striking style by mixing the gadgetry of *Star Wars* with a 1940's world. He's avoided the space suit, high-tech look which everyone has done to death and replaced it with the infinitely more sinister effect of modern TV surveillance techniques being used amongst McCarthyite, G-Man figures and costumes.

Highly apologetic second and third assistants inform me that I shall not be needed for the second day running – which is a pity as I've two or three times felt just like doing it.

Saturday, November 26th

Helen, Oak Village police snoop, rang her 'Crime Prevention Officer' today to report a shady man at old Miss Clutton's house and was told, after a long delay, 'I'm sorry, your Crime Prevention Officer doesn't work weekends.'

Denis O'B calls. He's trying again with *Water*. But having re-read the script I know it's going to be only a slightly more exciting version of *Yellowbeard* and *Bullshot*.

At the same time I reassert my inclination to do Bennett's film. He sounds as though he has not yet decided on this. Was he waiting to see if I bit on *Water*? They have John Cleese already, he says. Why has John said yes? It's another ordinary, mediocre part which he will be able to do with his eyes shut ... But he's old enough to decide for himself. Or has he said 'I'll do it if Mike will do it'? I have always said no to *Water* and have said 'no' again today. It's not my thing.

Tuesday, November 29th

Collected by [my unit driver] Roy on a cold, dark morning at 7.10.

No waiting around today. A concentrated morning's work on the first encounter between Sam and Jack. I start tense – projecting and acting. But, gaining confidence from repeated successful takes, I'm able to deliver a genuine, easy-going Jack – not the college boy pin-up that TG perhaps had in mind, but an unforced, easy naturalness that I never had last week.

TG looks battered. Unshaven, dark-rimmed eyes, one of which is bloodshot. But he's clearly in seventh heaven – doing exactly what he enjoys best.

Wednesday, November 30th

Back to the TJ/MP script today after a three-week lay-off.

TJ sounds unusually relaxed about it ... he admits he no longer feels the desperate pressure to make a film as soon as possible. Our reputation is such that we must maintain a very high standard – and if this takes a while, then we are lucky to have the time to spend getting it right.

Back home, see Julian Hough[1] wandering about in Oak Village. A strange, slightly disconcerting presence. He himself admits he's spent four sessions 'inside' (a mental hospital) in the last few years, and is now putting together a one-man show, having left Patrick Barlow and the National Theatre of Brent. He has a cup of tea and, having talked of his plans, he leaves, ambling off in an amused, unrushed gangle down Oak Village.

Nancy [Lewis] rings to ask if I will speak at the wedding, as her father can't be there. I'm honoured.

---

1 Julian Hough was a strange, tormented and talented actor who appeared in one of the *Ripping Yarns* and who had hugely impressed Terry Jones and myself when he appeared with Patrick Barlow in the *Messiah*, the first production of the eccentric and funny National Theatre of Brent.

Friday, December 2nd

Car picks me up at eight. To the studio where, to my amazement, I am finished and done with by eleven o'clock. The scene in which I leave the office, take the lift and leave Info Retrieval, talking to Jonathan the while, is at last complete and the bulk of my work on *Brazil* is over.

Saturday, December 3rd

To St Paul's, Covent Garden, for Nancy and Simon's wedding.

A heavily bearded Eric Idle slips into the row next to me. What an extraordinary place for a Python reunion. A year after making our second 'blasphemous' comedy, we're in a church singing 'Love Divine All Loves Excelling'.

Cleese, alone, is two rows in front. He keeps making Dick Vosburgh laugh by singing with great emphasis words like 'next', long after everyone else has stopped. Gilliam, with family, is in the front. Terry has his duvet-like coat and, with his new, short haircut, Eric says he looks like an 'inflated monk'. Jones, also with family, has a Mac that makes him look like Jones of the Yard and, entirely suitably, Graham is late!

Someone has alerted the press and there is a barrage of photographers, who try to get all the Pythons to link arms with the bride and groom. John and Graham totally ignore them. But eventually, after persuasive lines like 'Two minutes and we'll leave you alone', we are snapped and can go back to reacquainting ourselves with those we haven't seen for far too long.

Then Helen and I take a taxi down to Glaziers Hall, beneath London Bridge. A man in a red coat is announcing. We give our names as 'Mr and Mrs Figgis'. The sight of Nancy in white looking like an 18-year-old in her first dress already brought tears to the eyes at St Paul's. Simon looks ineffable and timeless, but Nancy does seem to have leapt back 20 years.

Simon's best man, Philip, small, with a short beard, has asked if he can break the rules and speak before me, as he is the only non-professional to speak. Turns out he's a barrister and in fact the *only* professional to speak. A very clever, witty, slightly long speech, with hardly a glance at his notes.

I have my usual copious sheaves of longhand, but, despite sherry and champagne, I manage to read them quite spiritedly and everyone seems